D1314028

THE

IN-DEPTH,

I N S I D E

STORY BEHIND

WINDOWS™ 95 —

THE PHILOSOPHY,

DESIGN,

AND ARCHITECTURE

OF THE

NEXT GENERATION

OF MICROSOFT® WINDOWS

FOREWORD BY STEVE BALLMER,
EXECUTIVE VICE PRESIDENT, MICROSOFT CORPORATION

EPILOGUE INTERVIEW WITH MICROSOFT SENIOR VICE PRESIDENT PAUL MARITZ
AND MICROSOFT VICE PRESIDENT BRAD SILVERBERG

INSIDE

WINDOWS 95™

ADRIAN KING

Microsoft PRESS

PUBLISHED BY
Microsoft Press
A Division of Microsoft Corporation
One Microsoft Way
Redmond, Washington 98052-6399

Library of Congress Cataloging-in-Publication Data
King, Adrian, 1953-
    Inside Windows 95 / Adrian King.
        p.   cm.
    Includes index.
    ISBN 1-55615-626-X
    1. Windows (Computer programs)   2. Microsoft Windows (Computer
file)   I. Title.
QA76.76.W56K56   1994
005.4'469--dc20   93-48485
                                                               CIP

Printed and bound in the United States of America.

1 2 3 4 5 6 7 8 9   QMQM   9 8 7 6 5 4

Distributed to the book trade in Canada by Macmillan of Canada, a division of Canada Publishing
Corporation.

A CIP catalogue record for this book is available from the British Library.

Microsoft Press books are available through booksellers and distributors worldwide. For further information
about international editions, contact your local Microsoft Corporation office. Or contact Microsoft Press
International directly at fax (206) 936-7329.

Acquisitions Editor: Mike Halvorson
Project Editor: Erin O'Connor
Technical Editors: Seth McEvoy and Dail Magee, Jr.

CONTENTS SUMMARY

TABLE OF CONTENTS

CHAPTER TWO

INTEL PROCESSOR ARCHITECTURE **33**

CHAPTER THREE

A TOUR OF CHICAGO **63**

CHAPTER FIVE

THE USER INTERFACE AND THE SHELL **157**

CHAPTER SIX

APPLICATIONS AND DEVICES **223**

CHAPTER SEVEN

THE FILESYSTEM **275**

CHAPTER EIGHT

PLUG AND PLAY **309**

CHAPTER NINE

NETWORKING **341**

CHAPTER TEN

MOBILE COMPUTING **381**

EPILOGUE

LEAVING CHICAGO **407**

FOREWORD

I first met Adrian King in 1981, on the floor of a trade show in Amsterdam. I was new to Microsoft—a small company of 75 people with $7.5 million in revenues—and I was on my first trip to Europe to meet customers and distribution partners. The trade show turned out to be a flop—more exhibitors than customers. Adrian and I by ourselves might have outnumbered the customers.

We had a lot of time to talk to each other, and I found out that Adrian had graduated from the University of Liverpool with a master's degree in computer science and had joined Logica, a big European consulting outfit, straight out of school. It was clear right off that he understood technology and a lot else besides.

We tried to figure out why the aisles were so empty, and that got us into talking about the future for software. I remember thinking that Adrian was an impressive guy and reflecting that with more people like Adrian involved, the software business might really take off. But even in our freewheeling exchange of ideas, we didn't come close to envisioning today's incredible market for software.

A little later, Adrian managed to convince Logica to branch out from their consulting business into software products—no small feat at the time—and they became Microsoft's European XENIX partner. Through the early 1980s, Adrian and I worked together to develop the European XENIX business. Then, in April of 1984, we met to review XENIX support issues. That's how it started out, anyway. During the first half of the meeting, Adrian did his best to convince me that Microsoft had to do a number of different things to improve our XENIX product support. During the second half, I did my best to convince Adrian that he really ought to become our XENIX product manager and take care of those things himself. With a little help from Bill Gates, I was able to persuade Adrian to do just that.

Adrian did a great job, and before long we gave him even more to do. He eventually became our director of operating systems products, picking up responsibilities for MS-DOS and Microsoft OS/2 as well as

XENIX. At the same time I was focusing on Windows, which had become a big priority for the company. We had come to believe that using a mouse with a graphical user interface was a natural, intuitive way to use a computer. Adrian worked on the early Windows projects, and in November of 1985 I put him in charge of Windows/386.

The effort we put in on the early versions of Windows was a foundation for the blockbuster success of Windows 3.0 and Windows 3.1. The work that Adrian and the rest of the team did on the Windows/386 project formed the basis for much of Microsoft's MS-DOS support in Windows 3.1 and even in Windows NT, for example. And many of the people from that Windows/386 team are still involved in our Windows development today.

Adrian went on to other important projects at Microsoft, and then in 1991 he left to pursue his interest in peer-to-peer networking at a smaller company. I'm sure that if Adrian were still at Microsoft he'd be deeply involved in the development of Windows 95. But at least he's back in the Microsoft orbit—this time as a chronicler, the author of *Inside Windows 95*.

Microsoft's goals for Windows 95 are the same goals we've had for every release of Windows. We want to make computing even easier. We want to increase end user productivity. We want to provide a development platform for the desktop. We want to provide a high-volume, low-cost operating system that will spur industry growth and innovation. We believe that Windows 95 will accomplish these goals and that Windows 95 will be even more important to the PC world than Windows 3.1, which now has over 60 million users.

The list of great new features for Windows 95, a true 32-bit operating system, is amazingly long. Windows 95 will offer a vastly improved user interface, true multitasking, a freshly designed filesystem, better connectivity, better support for notebook PCs, easier installation and configuration—all with performance at least as good as Windows 3.1 performance.

I'm very excited that Adrian has written this book about our most important Windows operating system ever. We're lucky that Adrian turned out to be a good writer too because he has a perspective that only someone from the old days could bring to bear on the history and the accomplishments of the "Chicago" Windows project. Everyone will want to read *Inside Windows 95*—the interested power user, solution providers, developers, and administrators. I heartily recommend this book to anyone who will want to take full advantage of the technological innovations in Windows 95. Adrian does an excellent job of explaining the major architectural components of the system and provides a lot of insight into the thinking behind the design and implementation of Windows 95. I've greatly enjoyed reading his account of the project and the product in this book, and I think you will too.

Steve Ballmer
Executive Vice President, Microsoft
Redmond, Washington
August 1994

PREFACE

Writing a book about a yet to be released software product and publishing it before the product even ships has to be asking for trouble. Throw in other factors such as the fact that the product in question is one that literally thousands of people will examine and critique in minute detail, and you can easily build a case for declining the writing opportunity. So, of course, I accepted. *Inside Windows 95* is the result.

When I started working for Microsoft in 1984, I'd already known the company as a customer and development partner for a few years. One thing I'd learned very quickly about Bill Gates and Steve Ballmer is that they never, ever give up on something they believe in. In 1984 and 1985, even with massive delays in its initial planned shipment, Windows was the something they weren't giving up on. My first office at Microsoft was next to Steve Ballmer's. One day, after more bad news about Windows shipment dates, he and his assistant packed everything up and moved downstairs to occupy new offices in the midst of the Windows development team (a group maybe ten strong at the time). Steve was now the Windows project manager, and he wasn't about to give up.

Windows 1.0 eventually shipped in late 1985. Describing the market's reaction as lukewarm is akin to describing Bill Gates as well off. I remember installing the first Windows Software Development Kit on an IBM PC XT and being at different moments impressed by its features and bewildered by its complexity. Looking back on it now, I can see that it was of course sheer madness for Microsoft to believe that Windows could succeed on the limited hardware available at the time.

But Microsoft wasn't about to give up. Through successive versions, Windows gradually got better and the hardware got faster and more capacious. In 1987 and 1988 I managed the project that produced Windows/386 and launched it on the first 386-based PC: the Compaq Deskpro. It was my favorite time at Microsoft, and the entire project team—all fifteen of us—were rather proud of Windows/386. In comparison to MS-DOS it still didn't sell worth a darn. Even Steve Ballmer was beginning to think that OS/2 might be the right strategy.

But Microsoft didn't give up, and on May 22, 1990, Bill Gates introduced the latest and greatest release of Windows—version 3.0—to a rapt audience in New York City. Things were different this time. It was obvious to me in the theater that day that Windows was about to become a seven-year-old overnight success. And it did. Bill and Steve would probably try to convince you it was planned that way. Don't believe it. Whether the galaxies were finally in correct alignment, or a confluence of market factors finally came about, or sheer determination finally carried the day is no longer relevant—Windows was finally a hit.

I was involved only a little in the development of Windows 3.0 and not at all in the development of Windows 3.1. Shortly before I left Microsoft in 1991, I began working on what was eventually to become part of the base operating system for Windows 95. Clearly I was not destined to escape the project entirely, and the opportunity to write this book on Windows 95 for Microsoft Press is one I've enjoyed a lot. Watching a Windows release once again is fascinating. The scope of the work that goes into a major new release of Windows these days is staggering, with hundreds of people involved rather than only a few dozen.

Of course, I'm only writing about what many have built and others have yet to go out and sell. Although the Windows team at Microsoft is considerably bigger these days, it still includes a few people from back when Steve Ballmer was the project manager. And Steve's current role at Microsoft as Executive Vice President of Sales and Support means that he is now in charge of the worldwide sales campaign for Windows 95. Windows 95 will enter the market under some competitive pressure. Proponents of UNIX, OS/2, and NetWare certainly haven't relaxed their attempts to improve their own products and their market shares. But Windows 95 is definitely the product to beat. I'm quite sure Steve won't give up on this challenge either—which means that nothing has really changed since 1985 except the location of Steve's office and the size of his marketing budget.

Special thanks go to Erin O'Connor and her team at Microsoft Press for overcoming my English and several other obstacles in the preparation of this book. Claudette Moore and Mike Halvorson got the project started, and several people at Microsoft gave time and assistance to the project, for which I'm grateful. George Moore and Joe Belfiore in particular were always willing to answer my questions. It has been more than a year since I began work on this book, and, as I write, I know there's still a lot of work left to finish Chicago. That effort is but a tiny part of the total still needed to ship Chicago and make it a success. The industry magazines have already published their first reviews of the Chicago Beta-1 release. IBM has launched its anti-Chicago advertising campaign. The pundits and self-styled experts have begun their critique of a product that won't be in the stores for months yet. Windows 95 has a long way to go before it will be a runaway success. But I'm sure that will happen. Microsoft won't give up before it does.

If you'd like to talk to me about this book or about Windows 95 in general, I'm readily available on the Internet as *adriank@gravity.wa.com*. I hope you find at least some of the book useful and enjoyable. Thanks for taking the time to read it.

Adrian King
July 12, 1994

Publisher's Note

As we went to press, some aspects of Windows 95 were still under a general nondisclosure agreement, but Microsoft had made public a great deal of information about Windows 95. This book offers an interpretation of that information, and the author's conclusions are based on his exploration of Beta-1. The "Chicago" story continues to unfold, and the product will continue to be refined. For up-to-the-minute changes in information on Windows 95, we recommend that you periodically visit the WIN_NEWS forum, which you can find at the following locations:

On CompuServe: *GO WINNEWS*
On the Internet: *ftp://ftp.microsoft.com/PerOpSys/Win_News/Chicago*
http://www.microsoft.com
On AOL: keyword *WINNEWS*
On Prodigy: jumpword *WINNEWS*
On Genie: *WINNEWS* file area on Windows RTC

You can also subscribe to Microsoft's electronic newsletter *WinNews*. To subscribe, send Internet e-mail to *enews@microsoft.nwnet.com* and put the words *SUBSCRIBE WINNEWS* in the text of the e-mail.

When Windows 95 is released, be sure to head to your bookstore for complete accounts of developing for and using Windows 95.

Microsoft Press
September 16, 1994

INTRODUCTION

To describe this book as an account of everything you could possibly want to know about Windows 95, or indeed as an account of everything in Windows 95, would be to mislead. The sheer scope of the Windows 95 development project makes it impossible to write the only book about the product you'll ever need to buy. If you're an avid student of Windows, I'm sure your sagging bookshelf will have to bear further strain in the months ahead. If you're a regular user, you'll find a whole host of new and exciting features to explore in Windows 95.

First a warning. Even as I write, Windows 95 is still in development and scheduled for release a few months into the future. Microsoft made the first external release of the product in August 1993. After installation, one of the first icons you were tempted to double-click on produced this unsettling screen:

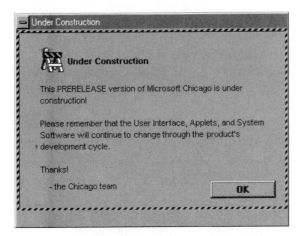

In many other places in the product you could find similar warnings: *subject to change, not yet implemented,* and so on. It seems appropriate to use the Under Construction screen at the front of this book. My warnings won't be as dire, though, since this book does describe features you really can expect to find when Windows 95 hits the streets late this year. This book is current as of the Chicago Beta-1 release that

Microsoft shipped in June 1994. By and large the product was feature complete at the time of that beta release. However (and here's that warning), since the book has to go to the printer before the product ships, there will undoubtedly be some changes of detail in the final release of the product. And the incompatible goals of exploring every last feature of Windows 95 and still producing this book in advance of the product means that some features won't be examined in much detail and some features will be left out altogether.[1]

The intention of the book is to provide a technical introduction to the Windows 95 system, including enough detail to satisfy any Windows user and most system administrators and Windows programmers. The book is also "Inside Windows 95," meaning that the emphasis is on what the system can do, how it does it, and why its features were designed and implemented in particular ways. If you're looking for a book that teaches you how to use the Windows 95 interface, how to customize Windows 95, or how to write Windows 95 applications, this book isn't it. But this book does give you a thorough analysis of the system architecture and explores every important new feature of Windows 95.

Windows 95 is a major product release for Microsoft. It incorporates significant new features for exploitation by developers, and major advances in the user interface and in system usability that should benefit the end user. Since Microsoft Windows has become such an immensely successful product, new releases bear a burden of backward compatibility. Windows 95 has to carry forward the MS-DOS legacy. And Windows 95 isn't Microsoft's only Windows family operating system. Windows 95 must take its place alongside Windows NT and the forthcoming Cairo system. Chapter One explores the goals of the Windows 95 project, the constraints on the development team, the market for the product, and the role of Windows 95 in Microsoft's overall systems software strategy.

When I began work on this book, Microsoft's internal planning had Windows 95 shipping at the end of the year—the year 1993. Windows 95 would have been truly unique among operating systems if it had shipped on the originally planned date. As I write, the testing status of Windows 95 suggests that there's a reasonable chance that it will indeed ship at the end of the year—the year 1994.

---

1. One major "change" that did make it into this book is the Windows 95 name. Everyone had been assuming that Chicago's real name would be Windows 4.0. In July 1994 Microsoft decided on the Windows 95 name to align the operating system with a planned company-wide revision of product names. Fortunately, they made the decision just before the book went to press.

One aspect of the product that I can't cover in this book is exactly how Windows 95 will be packaged and priced. Microsoft executives are characteristically vague about these issues when responding to direct questions. To some degree, that's a competitive response; the final packaging and pricing decisions are rarely made until quite late in a project's life cycle. It will probably work the way most other similar decisions at Microsoft do: at some point Steve Ballmer will simply tell everyone what the different boxes should contain and how much they'll sell for.

One difficult question I confronted as I developed this book was how much introduction to the underlying hardware (the Intel 386 processor) and software (Windows itself) to provide. Some authors expect you to read other tomes as prerequisites to their own. Still others try to teach you hexadecimal arithmetic before presenting the intimate details of fault-tolerant system design. In the end I decided to support this book's mission by including the information I would need to refer to while talking about the more advanced details of Windows 95. Chapters Two and Three therefore provide a basic description of the Intel 386 processor architecture and the Windows system architecture. If you know these subjects intimately, you can skim quickly through those two chapters. If you never knew much about those subjects, the two chapters should equip you to deal with the new information about Windows 95 in the rest of the book. If you're like me and can't always remember exactly how the 386 paging mechanism works, or precisely what a Windows task *really* is, Chapters Two and Three can serve as a close at hand reference to Intel and Windows architecture.

Windows 95 is built on an operating system base that adds major new capabilities to the system. Some of these new features, such as the new filesystem, have already appeared in other Microsoft operating system products, notably Windows NT and Windows for Workgroups. Windows 95 integrates these new features and other features to provide a full 32-bit protected mode environment for Windows applications. And although MS-DOS compatibility is retained, there really isn't a collection of files in Windows 95 that you can point to and label as MS-DOS. Windows 95 really is a complete operating system for the very first time in the history of this product line. In Chapter Four we'll explore the inner workings of the Windows 95 operating system base.

Every user of Windows will see a dramatic revision in the on-screen appearance of the operating system. In addition to revising the appearance of Windows, Microsoft has changed many of the interactive procedures and added a unified system control application. In Chapter Five we'll analyze the user interface and the new system shell. That chapter contains a lot of screen shots illustrating various aspects of the shell, and I'm quite sure that some of the details of these screens will change in the final product. I already know that the visuals for the Start menu are a little different, and the "now it's there, now it's gone" game continues with the shell's trashcan: post–Beta-1, the trashcan was back in the product.

Windows 95 introduces some significant changes in both the Windows graphical subsystem and the Windows implementation of device support. For the first time a Microsoft Windows system takes on the challenge of device-independent color—a feature that has become critical to many graphical applications. A major improvement in the architecture for display drivers is also a highlight of the new system-level features you'll see in Windows 95. In Chapter Six we'll take a look at all of these changes.

The architecture for supporting disk devices and their associated filesystems has also changed considerably in Windows 95. A layered device architecture derived from the Windows NT design provides full protected mode support for hard and floppy disks and CD ROM devices. And integrating support for new disk devices into the system becomes comparatively trivial in Windows 95. Although Windows 95 continues to use the MS-DOS FAT filesystem as its default storage scheme, the design of the new installable filesystem manager opens the door for improved filesystem support in the future. Right now, the most visible enhancement in the Windows 95 filesystem is its support for long filenames—finally relieving us of the tiresome 8.3 filenaming convention that has dogged us since 1981. In Chapter Seven we'll inspect the new filesystem design.

Although not limited to operation in the Windows environment, Microsoft's Plug and Play technology makes its system debut with Windows 95. Fully implemented, Plug and Play makes the task of configuring and managing a complex PC a trivial one. Apple Computer won't be able to run those Windows commercials any longer. In Chapter Eight we'll explore the need for Plug and Play and its implementation under Windows 95. Plug and Play capable systems have a life outside Windows 95, and I fully expect Plug and Play systems to be a highlight of this year's COMDEX/Fall trade show. The Plug and Play technology really does work, and if you spend a lot of time messing around with computers, you'll find the benefits of Plug and Play to be compelling—

so much so, that I'd recommend your waiting to buy a Plug and Play system as your next.

Windows 95 integrates its support for network systems into the new filesystem architecture. Windows 95 will support several simultaneously active networks—each with multiple connections—and provide consistent interfaces to any underlying network for applications. Some of these features were seen for the first time with the release of Microsoft Windows for Workgroups version 3.11 in the fall of 1993. In Chapter Nine we'll examine network support in Windows 95. The sudden surge of popular interest in the Internet prompted Microsoft to include Internet access utilities in Windows 95 quite late in the development project. It seems likely that the "Internet readiness" of Windows 95 will be a focus of at least some of the early marketing for the product.

Microsoft intends Windows 95 to play a significant role in the growing mobile computing market. Windows 95 features related to that market range from integrated support for pen-based computers to an enormously improved remote network access capability and support for the use of laptop docking systems. In Chapter Ten we'll consider these features together under the general topic of mobile computing. Windows 95 will include support for pen input devices and the associated "inking" operations. Unfortunately, that topic didn't make it into this book—publishing deadlines are a little more rigid than software development deadlines.

Apart from the pen computing capabilities, the only other major feature of Windows 95 that is not a topic of this book is multimedia support. It will be there in the product, but even as late as the spring of 1994 its precise architecture and features were still rather vague. Microsoft seemed to think it was pretty significant that there is a version of the popular Doom game running under Windows using the newly announced WinG graphics library. Game products are really the final bastion of MS-DOS–specific software. Whether Windows 95 multimedia support will be good enough to conquer the games market remains to be seen.

There are components of Windows 95 that will have been in development for well over three years by the time you can go out and buy the product in a store. The first order of business is to look at what Microsoft has been trying to achieve in all that time.

CHAPTER ONE

THE ROAD TO CHICAGO

Throughout its design and development, Microsoft Windows 95 had the codename "Chicago," and the introductory slide for early product presentations depicted a map of the USA entitled "Driving Towards Chicago...." Windows 95 was not designed and developed in a vacuum—there were a lot of stops on the way to Chicago. Beginning with the first release of Windows in November 1985 and continuing through the spectacularly successful introduction of Windows 3.0 in May 1990 and beyond, Microsoft's total investment in Windows has been enormous. Until version 3.0, the commercial returns hardly merited the investment. But no one has ever accused Microsoft of giving up easily, and Windows slowly and steadily improved in both capabilities and sales. The introduction of Windows 3.0 was a watershed event. It was as if the world had suddenly discovered the benefits of Windows, and versions 3.0 and 3.1 sold in great numbers.

In truth, a number of factors contributed to the seemingly sudden success of Windows 3.0. Personal computers using the Intel 386 chip were then becoming affordable. By the time Windows 3.1 was released, 386 systems were commonplace and cheap. The 386 systems provided good performance and the best platform for Windows to run on. Equally as important, the amount of system memory and the quality and performance of video hardware finally matched the requirements set by Windows. Given the now adequate level of system performance, the real benefits of the graphical user interface became apparent to large numbers of users.

Microsoft had long extolled the benefits of Windows, but only a limited number of high-quality Windows-based applications were available before version 3.0. Virtually every demonstration of Windows included Microsoft Excel, Aldus PageMaker, and very little else. There ← were occasions when Microsoft's own applications development group questioned the wisdom of pinning all their hopes on Windows, and there were many internal debates, both formal and informal, over the relative priorities of MS-DOS, Windows, UNIX, and OS/2 as application platforms. Windows 3.0 changed every company's perspective significantly, and within several months of its release, the level of application support for Windows had grown dramatically. Software developers were no longer faced with the question of whether it was worthwhile to develop a Windows version of their application—it was simply a question of how fast they could get the Windows version to market.

Even industry journals that had relegated Windows to the also-ran category changed their view. As the numbers of users converting to Windows rose, so did the level of press coverage. Within two years, reviews and discussion of MS-DOS–based products had become the minor news items, and new journals concerning themselves only with Windows had begun to take up a significant amount of magazine rack space.

It was on this stage that Windows 95 would be introduced. Before version 3.0, new releases of Windows had received some polite (and a lot of impolite) interest and had earned the product a few new customers. After all, those were the days when OS/2 had been designated "the next big thing." In that context, Windows version 3.0 was an overachiever, surprising everyone with its improved features and popular success. Microsoft released version 3.1 primarily to solve the problems that widespread use of the 3.0 product had exposed.[1] The product team knew that the stage would be different for the introduction of Windows 95. Expectations were high. Every feature and nuance of the product was certain to be exhaustively examined, discussed, and criticized.[2] Windows 95 had to be the best version of Windows ever, and the goals the team set for the product had to address the need to incorporate dramatic and worthwhile improvements. With sales of the current version of Windows topping a million copies a month by mid-1993, any new release of the product also needed to be totally reliable.

---

1. Foremost among these problems was the infamous UAE—the Unrecoverable Application Error. Although UAEs were most often caused by bugs in application programs, everyone blamed Windows for UAEs. Eliminating UAEs was the driving motive behind the development of Windows 3.1.

2. One illustration of this high degree of interest: within two weeks of Microsoft's first, limited, external release of the beta, someone had (illegally) provided a copy to *PC Week*. They promptly published a review of the beta—almost a year in advance of the product's planned release date.

Thus, the general goals for Windows 95 were set: build a great new product that includes compelling new features and that is totally reliable—and, of course, develop it quickly. If you've ever worked on a software development project, you probably recognize those grand goals. And you know that every project team has to reduce those nebulous aims to specific targets. With Windows 95, it was no different.

The Mission for Windows 95

Although the goal is expressed in different ways and set in different contexts, one phrase summarizes the mission of the Windows 95 development team: make it easy. The mission to make every aspect of the PC running Windows 95 easier for users, support staff, hardware manufacturers, and software developers consistently reasserts itself. The project mantra often added a qualifying phrase: make it easy, not just easier. Throughout the design and development cycle, each aspect of Windows 95 had to undergo scrutiny within the "make it easy" context.

Help for the End User

Ease of use is an overused phrase in the computer industry. Not that many people find computers easy to use. Most people find Windows easier to use than MS-DOS, but the Windows 95 team recognized that on an absolute scale there was a lot left to do before using Windows would become "easy." These are some of the problems the team recognized:

- Many users remain intimidated by computers. Many potential customers won't buy a PC for the same reason.

- Common tasks, such as setting up a printer, are still far too arduous and error-prone for many users.

- Carrying out a complex operation, such as remote data access, is difficult for sophisticated users and close to impossible for most other people.

The scope for the team's mission also needed broadening. It would be no good making Windows easy to use if the systems on which it ran remained difficult to set up and configure. And Windows 95 itself had to be easy to install and support. To make things easy for the end user at the expense of the MIS department would be self-defeating.

3

Hardware Platforms

The basic architecture of today's average PC is that of an IBM PC AT–compatible machine, circa 1984. Despite many innovations in components, the overall system design has remained largely unimproved. Beyond encouraging manufacturers to ship PCs with at least a 386SX processor, 4 MB of RAM, and good video boards, Microsoft had done very little in the way of systematically persuading hardware companies to innovate.

Microsoft saw Windows 95 as an opportunity to change the status quo to the benefit of both the end user and the system manufacturer. Central to this effort was the development of the hardware Plug and Play specification, prepared jointly by Microsoft, Intel, Phoenix Technologies (the BIOS suppliers), and Compaq, among others. Plug and Play aimed to eliminate most of the problems associated with setting up and configuring PC hardware. No longer would the user need to know, for instance, what an IRQ or an I/O port address was. The users, their support staffs, and the system suppliers would all benefit from the improved ease of system setup.

Microsoft's other major step to encourage renewed hardware innovation was the decision to finally remove Windows reliance on MS-DOS as its underlying operating system. Successive releases of Windows had incorporated more and more operating system functions, and MS-DOS gradually came to be used as little more than a rather inefficient disk filing system. This trend culminates in Windows 95—a complete operating system implementation that incorporates all the features required of a fully protected 32-bit multitasking operating system. The user needs only to install Windows 95 on the machine; MS-DOS doesn't have to be present on the system at all. Windows 95 continues to support MS-DOS applications using a compatibility feature that has its roots in Microsoft Windows/386, Microsoft OS/2, and Windows NT.[3]

Windows 95 offers the system manufacturer the opportunity to produce improved hardware that doesn't have to conform strictly to the old IBM PC AT design. Such improvements include the incorporation of an improved BIOS and plug-in cards that cooperate with the operating system during system setup. Since device driver software always controls access to any hardware within a Windows 95 system, the user can add any new device provided it has a Windows device driver.

---

3. Although no code is repeated, members of the Windows 95 team had accumulated a significant amount of expertise when they had implemented similar compatibility features for these other operating systems.

The need for older-style BIOS compatibility no longer exists unless the device must also support MS-DOS operations.

For the Developer—32 Bits at Last

Although the mission statement for Windows 95 emphasized making it easy for users, support staff, and manufacturers, the lifeblood of Windows is still application programs. Early on in life, Windows gathered support from application developers slowly. After the introduction of Windows 3.0, that trickle of support grew into a veritable torrent of new applications. But developing a Windows application was never an easy task, although the quality and variety of development tools and training material have improved by leaps and bounds over those of a few years before. Windows 95 support for 32-bit programs helps the developer significantly:

- Developing 32-bit programs is just plain easier than developing for the 16-bit segmented model required by earlier versions of Windows.

- The Windows 95 32-bit API is compatible with the API supported by Microsoft Windows NT. Developers who want to produce products for both operating systems have an easier time developing and supporting their applications.

- Windows 95 itself uses a 32-bit memory model, and many of the limits of earlier versions of Windows disappear as a result. Valuable system resources, such as file handles, are plentiful. Application developers no longer have to come up with clever schemes to minimize their demands upon the system.

Naturally, the availability and quality of applications for the new release will help determine the success of Windows 95. At the same time that Microsoft worked on Windows 95, they expended even more effort on the development of Windows NT and associated products such as the Advanced Server version of Windows NT. Further mystifying the choice of platforms available to the application developer was word of yet another Microsoft operating system—code-named Cairo— which began to circulate in late 1992.[4] Today the success of each of

---

4. Chicago's project codename was originally "Tripoli"—a city "very close to Cairo." Humorists on the Windows team then asserted that the name ought to be "Spokane"— a place not very far from Microsoft's headquarters in Redmond. Eventually, "Chicago" was chosen—more because that was the site of the Windows 3.1 introduction than for any other geographic significance.

these operating systems remains undetermined, but before going further along the road to Chicago, we'll look at how Microsoft sees the role of each product over the next few years.

Shall We Go to Chicago or Cairo?

Over the last few years, every one of us has had several opportunities to change PC operating systems. The sheer size of the installed base of MS-DOS systems and application software creates enormous inertia, and with no compelling reason to change, people simply don't. This hasn't stopped a variety of vendors from trying to replace MS-DOS with a better mousetrap. UNIX, for example, in all its versions, has been around even longer than MS-DOS, and each year brings a renewed pledge of unity and coherence from the UNIX vendors. Usually the vendor infighting reasserts itself about six months later, and UNIX returns to its status of technical overachiever and commercial also-ran.

Microsoft, in partnership with IBM, tried to replace MS-DOS with OS/2. After a few years and tens of millions of dollars spent in development and promotion, OS/2 was nowhere in the market. Microsoft abandoned its OS/2 efforts shortly after the introduction of Windows version 3.0, when it became clear that Windows would be very successful and OS/2 would never be a good enough product to justify a switch from MS-DOS. Microsoft did press on with the development of another advanced operating system, however—Windows NT. Why? Hadn't enough money been wasted on trying to replace MS-DOS? Wouldn't it have been better just to improve MS-DOS itself?

Technically speaking, MS-DOS is a severely limited operating system. Its inability to support proper multitasking, memory protection, and large address spaces makes it a poor base for environments where the user wants to run several complex applications while connected to a network. Fixing these problems involves much more than making modifications to MS-DOS—it really does take a new operating system. To a degree, Microsoft was able to incorporate some necessary improvements to MS-DOS into successive versions of Windows. Multitasking, limited 32-bit application support, memory protection, and other features are now all functions of the current release of Windows. This way of evolving an operating system also passes the test for commercial rationality. Since Windows required MS-DOS to be on the system already, it was easy for users to upgrade, and Microsoft could add new functions without having to change MS-DOS itself. In fact, by the time Windows version 3.1 appeared, Windows used MS-DOS for not much more than loading programs and managing the disk filesystem.

First Stop—Chicago

Windows 95 is a major step in an evolutionary process. On a system running Windows 95, there is no longer any need for a separate product called MS-DOS. Windows 95 takes over all the operating system functions. You install a single product, and when you boot the system, you go directly into the Windows environment. You'll no longer see the familiar C:> prompt at which you typed the *win* command. Naturally, Windows 95 retains MS-DOS compatibility so that you can still run all of your existing TSR programs and any other MS-DOS applications you use. But the basic architecture of Windows 95 is Windows with MS-DOS compatibility. It is not MS-DOS running a Windows subsystem.

There are a lot of technical reasons for implementing Windows 95 this way. Relying at all on MS-DOS as the basic operating system would have reduced the capability and performance of the overall system. Now Windows truly supports the functions needed for advanced applications and networked systems.

This evolutionary progression in the architecture was also feasible from a marketing perspective. When Windows wasn't very popular, it would have been impossible to persuade people to give up MS-DOS and move to an alternative. This conversion is exactly what the OS/2 campaign failed to pull off. Now Windows is popular, and users spend much more time running Windows applications than they do MS-DOS applications. Thus, Windows 95 is a great upgrade to Windows 3.1, and yes, you can still run those aging MS-DOS applications.[5]

At this point, you might be wondering whether Microsoft is once again predicting the imminent demise of MS-DOS. Probably not. There is an active MS-DOS development group at Microsoft, and MS-DOS versions 5.0, 6.0, and now 6.22 attest to their efforts. The possibility of the protected mode operating system components of Windows 95 forming the basis of an MS-DOS 7.0 release was the subject of much questioning and speculation during 1993. Microsoft would not confirm the speculation, at least not by July 1994, but it's impossible to ignore the commercial success of the retail upgrade packages for MS-DOS 5.0 and 6.0. An MS-DOS 7.0 upgrade release could provide both significant user benefit and plenty of revenue dollars.

---

5. Demonstrating their personal bias quite succinctly, Microsoft executives referred to the release of WordPerfect 6.0 for MS-DOS as "the last great DOS application."

Clients and Servers

Apart from the move to Windows, the other major trend over the last few years has been the widespread adoption of high-speed local area networks. Sometimes these LANs have been installed where there were no computers before, and now they are often installed to replace mainframe- and minicomputer-based systems. Each machine on the network usually operates in one of two roles: as a client (typically the system that's on your desk running your applications) or as a server (where the systemwide databases and other shared resources, such as printers, are found).

For a client system, you need a high level of usability, great graphical display performance, and an easy to manage network connection. Some newer machines, such as the smallest portable systems, probably spend a lot of their time not connected to anything. At some point, though, even they have to become true clients, perhaps to print a file or to connect to an electronic mail network.

For a server, you need performance, performance, performance, and, of course, performance. Actually, the modern PC network server needs to offer a lot of complex features:

- Performance. The server operating system must be very efficient at transferring data across the network. To meet the performance demand, the operating system must also support machines using multiple processors, very high speed, high capacity disk drives, and high-performance network hardware.

- Robustness. This word means that the system doesn't crash and that if it does, it doesn't destroy data in the process. This requirement extends to the operating system's ability to protect different programs from each other's weaknesses. If your wide area communications server falls over in a heap, for example, you'd certainly prefer that it didn't take the database server down with it.

- Security. Securing data has always been a concern for any computer system that many people can access, whether the access be by virtue of proximity or through incoming telephone lines. Research efforts in the last few years have formalized many aspects of data security, and modern operating systems are expected to meet some specific requirements. Most governments insist that computer systems meet demonstrated, and certified, security standards, and many corporations have adopted a corresponding policy.

■ Network management. If you have a large network that is geographically dispersed, you need the software tools that allow you to manage it effectively. Activities might range from simple tasks, such as adding and removing network printers, to finding and updating every copy of a particular application program throughout the network. *software distribution*

■ Transparent distribution of data and processing power. Ideally, a network system should allow the user to retrieve data and access other resources without having to know the network locations of the objects in question. Although your client desktop system participates in locating and using resources, it's the server that has to figure out where a resource is and how to give you the most efficient access to it.

Of course, you'd like all these server features on your client machine as well. Unfortunately, implementing these advanced capabilities takes a lot of software, and that translates into the need for more memory, more disk space, and more processor speed. Someday we'll all have 500-MHz processors with gigabytes of memory in our laptop machines and we'll install the most powerful version of everything. Of course, by then, we'll have figured out some new feature that we simply must have and for which we still won't have enough hardware capacity. Until then, the configuration of most desktop and portable machines is likely to be a lot smaller and cheaper than a server configuration. Operating system vendors generally target a particular product toward either the client-type machine or the server machine.

Microsoft's operating system development efforts acknowledge the differences between these two basic system types. For the high-volume client-type machine, Windows 95 is the product Microsoft wants you to use. As we'll see when we look at the features of Windows 95, there is a very close mapping between its features and user requirements within the client market segment.[6]

The lowest-power machine configuration the Windows 95 team had in mind was an Intel 386SX–based system with 4 MB of memory, a VGA display, and 80 MB of disk space. In 1994, that's a pretty simple and cheap configuration. But Windows 95 had to run at least as well as Windows 3.1 on such a system. The Windows 95 team didn't try to implement the complex security features or multiprocessor support offered

---

6. Another early Windows 95 marketing slogan—every Microsoft product accumulates many before the final tagline is chosen—was "the ideal client system."

by Windows NT.[7] Such features would have added a lot to the operating system's hardware requirements, and most users simply don't need or want such features. Certainly for the portable computer market, which represents a large share of potential Windows 95 sales, such features are neither applicable nor even desirable.

For the server market, Microsoft says choose Windows NT. With Windows NT, you'll get virtually unlimited capacity and the features that meet all of the server requirements we've just looked at. Many users will have computing requirements that demand the capabilities of a Windows NT machine right there on the desktop. Their work will also justify the use of a machine with the power of an Intel 486, 16 MB of memory, and 256 MB of disk space. Today that's still a pretty impressive configuration for a desktop machine, but for a network server it's not much more than an entry-level configuration. Of course, the incredible pace of improvement in personal computer hardware will make that 486 configuration a low-end system within a couple of years, and users will be able to choose to move up to Windows NT functionality with no loss of performance.[8]

And On to Cairo

The first thing to note about Cairo is that its new features don't make up a complete operating system. Cairo will actually appear as Microsoft Windows NT version something point something. Windows NT will continue as the base operating system, performing all the memory management, task management, device handling, printing, and so on. In some ways, this arrangement is similar to the way in which successive releases of Windows before Windows 95 added new capabilities to the MS-DOS operating system. For Cairo, however, the underlying operating system is an immensely powerful one. Microsoft freely acknowledges that in the first release of Windows NT it sacrificed advances in usability to designing and building an operating system with a sophisticated and long-lived architecture. Cairo seeks to augment the native capabilities of Windows NT rather than add features that should be in the operating system proper.

---

7. Windows NT also runs on processors other than the Intel 80386/486/Pentium family. This portability was never a goal for Windows 95. The enormous difficulty of maintaining full MS-DOS and Windows compatibility, let alone the implementation effort that would be needed, made this idea a non-starter.

8. Remember that it was only early 1988 when the very first 16-MHz 386 machines with 4 MB of memory were considered to be high-end systems.

If you plan to use Windows 95, then, in a sense you'll use the first incarnation of Cairo. In particular, the new look of the Windows 95 interface and of the system shell will appear in Cairo too.[9] There will be a lot more to Cairo than the new look, of course, but as far as appearance is concerned, you'll be immediately familiar with the product. Cairo will be a completely object-oriented system, allowing you to query networkwide for a data object and examine it as you choose. Cairo will make it easy for you to query the network for all the memos authored by people in your department, for example. You won't need to know anything about filenames, filename extensions, what servers might contain the document files, and so forth. If your network administrator increases capacity by adding a new network server and splitting the data between the old and new servers, Cairo will keep track of what happened. You'll formulate your next query and get the results oblivious to the fact that a configuration change has occurred.

No doubt you're wondering how much hardware power will be necessary to run Cairo effectively. No doubt a lot. No doubt you'll need a machine that today would be considered only for duty as a network server. But by the time Cairo comes up for adoption as the mainstream operating system, that amount of computing power will be available in a reasonably priced desktop machine. Someday microprocessor engineers may reach an absolute physical limit, but that seems likely to be a day that you and I won't much care about.

So what of Windows 95 in this networked world? Microsoft plans to extend the Windows role as the perfect client-side operating system and to ensure its continued suitability for less powerful hardware, portable machines, and pen-based systems—few of which will run Cairo. Through an update to Windows 95, Microsoft will make available the tools that client systems will need to access Cairo systems effectively. You'll use your Windows machine to formulate queries, for example, but it will be the Cairo systems that take care of searching the network and retrieving the information. Application programs designed for the Cairo environment will exist as distributed applications. Part of the software will run on the Windows machine and communicate with a server-side application running somewhere else on the network.

---

9. A lot of the original design for the new user interface was actually done by people on the Cairo team. It was up to the Windows 95 group to implement the interface and bring it to market, but there was an ongoing effort to ensure consistency with the evolving Cairo design.

Summary

During 1993 Microsoft began the usual seeding process that precedes all of their major product releases. The company repeated its intention to build Windows into a family of compatible operating systems that would cover market requirements from mission-critical corporate computing to consumer devices. The executives who gave the public presentations used the slide shown in Figure 1-1 to illustrate their view of the evolution of the Windows family.[10]

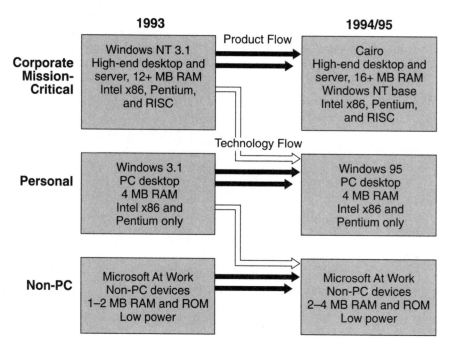

Figure 1-1.
Evolution of the Windows operating system family.

As you can see, a coherent story underlies all the different products. The products evolve in capability, and features can migrate to other operating systems as microcomputer technology allows. Microsoft itself is a firm believer in the continuing growth of microprocessor capability. This increase in horsepower is largely what allows the advanced features of, say, Windows NT version 3.1 to appear in other operating systems.

---

10. The form of this slide changed over time, but the basic message remained the same.

Whether Cairo will be successful is a question that can't be answered for a few years yet, since its story will be played out much further into the future than the Windows 95 story. Let's get back to our main subject and take a detailed look at what the Windows 95 team set out to do.

Project Goals

Let's review the market context for Windows 95:

- Windows 95 would be the next release of an immensely popular product, Windows 3.1.

- A huge amount of installed software, both for MS-DOS and for Windows, placed some stringent compatibility requirements on Windows 95.

- There was a real desire on Microsoft's part to make Windows 95 easier to set up, use, and administer.

- There was a need, principally for the benefit of Windows application developers, to dramatically improve the fundamental capabilities of the system. More resource and memory capacity, better performance, and support for more complex programs appeared at the top of most petitioners' lists.

- Windows 3.1 appeared in mid-1992. Obviously the next version of Windows had to make it to market in a reasonable amount of time after that—meaning that 1997 wouldn't cut it.

- Other operating system development projects were proceeding in parallel at Microsoft. Care had to be taken to ensure compatibility with both Windows NT and the Cairo efforts and with the release of Windows for Workgroups 3.11 in November 1993.

From the very early discussions about what the Windows 95 product should be, there emerged a specification that translated these loose market requirements into a more precise statement of goals for the project. Each section of the more detailed specification addressed these ten issues almost as ten commandments and described how each particular feature met the basic project goals.[11] The specification grouped

---

11. By the time work on this book began in earnest in April 1993, the *Chicago Feature Specification* was approaching its eighth substantial revision and stretched to over 200 densely printed pages. Who said software was all about writing tight code?

the ten issues as "The Four Requirements" and "The Six Areas for Improvement." By and large, these ten goals remained unchanged during the development project.[12] Here's how the feature specification summarized them (verbatim):

The four requirements:

- Compatibility

- Performance equal to or better than Windows 3.1 performance on a 4-MB system

- Robustness

- Product availability in mid-1994

The six areas for improvement:

- Great setup and easy configuration (Plug and Play)

- New shell and user interface visuals

- Integrated and complete protect mode operating system

- Great network client, peer server, and workgroup functionality

- Great mobile computing environment

- Windows 32-bit application support

A lot of this book is a detailed examination of the major new features of Windows 95. Before launching into the detail, it's worth taking a brief look at what these project goals really mean.

Compatibility

Compatibility is both the dream and the nightmare of everyone who develops products for the PC market. The basic PC architecture was defined by IBM's very first product introduction in August 1981. Once the clone (later "industry standard") manufacturers were established and software developers had figured out what compatibility meant for them, the industry grew spectacularly. Compatibility means that you and I can walk into a computer store, buy any PC product there, install

---

12. The original requirements specified "great 4-megabyte system" and "product availability in the first half of 1994." As you can see, the performance goal became more precise and the availability goal extended beyond its upper bound.

it, and expect it to work. Great news for us. Unfortunately for the developers of PC hardware and software, compatibility means that you and I can walk into a computer store, buy any PC product there, install it, and expect it to work. Any developer has to do a certain amount of compatibility testing before releasing a product. For a straightforward application program, the developer's testing problem is a finite one that might only involve testing on popular networks and with popular printers. For a more complex product, such as a memory resident communications program that runs in the background, the testing matrix becomes much larger. The development effort could involve testing for compatibility with different networks, different modems, and different versions of MS-DOS, PC-DOS, DR-DOS, and Windows, with other memory resident programs, ad infinitum. This testing burden represents a substantial part of the product's development cost.

Now consider Windows 95. For the product to be successful, it simply had to be compatible with everything that had gone before—not only Windows applications software, but MS-DOS applications, device driver software, and network software, to name the principal foes. If the product were truly compatible, the reasoning went, the new features alone would persuade every user to upgrade without a second thought.[13] And the absence of a "real" MS-DOS in the Windows 95 architecture was a radical revision that seemed guaranteed to produce some difficult to solve compatibility issues. Clearly, Windows 95 needed a massive compatibility test effort, and that's what the Windows 95 team set about organizing.

The Compatibility Fallback

Microsoft also decided that Windows 95 needed an ultimate compatibility fallback. Everyone was sure that the fallback would be invoked only in the event the user wanted to run some ancient, obscure game software. But the fallback did represent a good insurance policy against any case in which Windows 95 broke the compatibility regime.

The fallback solution is to allow the user to exit completely from Windows and run an actual real mode MS-DOS. While the system runs in this mode, a small software loader stays resident in memory. That's the only component of Windows 95 still memory resident while the system is in MS-DOS real mode. Once the user finishes off the Klingon empire, the software loader traps the application program's exit call and reloads Windows from disk, returning the system to its normal state.

What about NetWare DOS commands

---

13. Referred to in Microsoft vernacular as a "no brainer upgrade."

Performance

The earlier versions of Windows garnered a healthy measure of criticism on several fronts. Poor performance was an oft-repeated complaint. Looking back at the hardware configurations then available for Windows, it seems amazing that the product was even usable. In 1985, Windows was able to run on a 286-based system with a poor display adapter (the CGA), a single megabyte of memory, and a fairly slow hard disk. Any popular laptop system today has a comparatively much improved display and better disk hardware, four times as much memory, and a processor probably 25 or 30 times faster than the first 286. Naturally, Windows has obeyed one of the unwritten laws of computer science and expanded to consume all the available hardware resources.

It's hard to measure the performance of a Windows system in absolute terms. Does a benchmark reading of 15 million Winmarks mean that you'll see your desktop publishing package run at lightning speed? Generally, users will judge a product's performance from its response time. Snappy screen redrawing, fast file opening and closing, and quick scrolling operations always make a good impression. Less easy to observe but equally important to the overall system performance are operations like network data transfers and program swapping. The operating system vendor thus has to invest in two parallel performance measuring activities: checking individual operations, such as how fast a program can read a file, and observing the whole system as it runs a mixture of applications and data transfer operations.

Microsoft's development teams have always focused on performance issues. They tune individual software components for improved speed and reduced memory consumption as well as raise overall system performance by removing undesirable interactions among different components. Within Windows 95 itself, new features such as the 32-bit protected mode filesystem and dynamically loadable device drivers were aimed at improving system performance. Would the end user like to see the system run even faster? Of course, but the recent performance of Windows 3.1 on the base configuration 386SX with 4 MB of memory is generally considered as reasonable.

For Windows 95, the development group set itself the goal of running as well as or better than Windows 3.1 on the same base hardware configuration. Not very ambitious, you might say. However, this goal took into account that the system had to include the new capabilities such as the Plug and Play subsystem with its dynamic reconfiguration facility at the same time that it ran the application mix. Adding significant functionality while maintaining the same level of performance is ambitious. By simple extension, a Windows 95 system doing exactly what the Windows 3.1 system did, on the same hardware, ought to run faster. Measuring different application mixes, modeling end user activities, and playing with the variables have been staple ingredients of Windows 95 performance analysis.

The key, repeated phrase in Microsoft's later Windows 95 presentations was "as well as Windows 3.1." The recurrence of this phrase emphasized the fact that Windows 3.1 on a 4-MB system running Microsoft Office and using OLE performs dreadfully. The Windows 95 team didn't try to address this problem. In fairness, they couldn't. An application mix of this complexity demands more memory—at least 8 MB and probably more. Fortunately, early 1994 saw 8 MB becoming the default configuration for many machines, so, to some degree, the problem would be solved by the time Windows 95 was released.

In early 1994, performance tuning began in earnest, and all of the project status reports for Windows 95 dwelt on performance tuning issues for some months. By the time of the Beta-1 release, Windows 95 performance was already as good as or better than Windows 3.1 performance in almost every respect.

Robustness—Adieu UAE?

A robust system is a system that doesn't crash—whatever the user or application programs do to it. If one program goes awry, the user can halt it without affecting the operation of any other programs or losing any data. If a program makes erroneous requests for operating system services, the system protects itself by terminating the offending program with no effect on other programs.

Windows 3.0 was roundly criticized for system crashes. The infamous unrecoverable application error (UAE) was a widely publicized, and poorly understood, problem. Windows 3.0 reported a UAE whenever it determined that the system itself had reached an inconsistent state. An application used a file handle to access a file that had been deleted, for example. For most of the UAEs, the error was actually in the application program and not in Windows itself. However, Windows 3.0 did a poor job of validating system requests generated by application programs. Thus, an application could make an invalid request that Windows happily accepted and tried to process. By the time the error was discovered, there would be nothing left to do but crash the system as a rather primitive last line of defense. Fixing this problem was a focus of the work to produce Windows 3.1, which carefully validated almost every system request before processing it. As a result, many application vendors had to release updates of their products to fix software bugs that had never been discovered before. The experience was a painful one for all concerned, and the Windows 95 team was in no rush to repeat it.

The development team wanted Windows 95 to be extremely robust, with almost no possibility of a system crash caused by an application program or other external factor. How do you go about ensuring this? A lot of the answer goes back to the basic design of the system: incorporating careful validation of application requests, protecting system data regions, and isolating individual software components. In particular, the new 32-bit application programming model allowed the Windows 95 team to implement full memory protection for individual 32-bit programs. Not only are 32-bit programs protected from each other, but the system is also fully protected from these programs. (Some improvements were also made for 16-bit programs, but the options were limited because of compatibility constraints.) Once all of this is done, you test and test and test some more.

Timely Product Availability

The eternal battle between the sales and marketing group and the development group within any software project comes down to deciding when the product is ready for release. Microsoft always sets an estimated release date for a product way ahead of detailed planning. Then the development team either cuts features or extends the planned release date to allow completion of all the development work. Factors that influence the release date include when the previous version was released, the overall scope of the work for the new version, and how competitive the market is. The decision to bless a particular version of the software as the "golden master"[14] involves many people from the product group, senior managers within the development division, product support personnel, and often Bill Gates himself. If the product is simply not ready for release because of performance inadequacies or major bugs, there's no debate—you slip the date, and the development team continues its work. But there finally comes a point when the software is in good shape, all the introduction materials are ready, the support personnel are trained, and the printed documentation is waiting in the warehouse.

---

14. In Microsoft parlance, the development group prepares a succession of "release candidates" before shipment. When everyone is satisfied with the quality of the software, the final release candidate becomes the golden master from which the manufacturing group prepares the production version.

There are still some bugs that could be fixed if you were to wake up the development team and get them to put in yet another day or another week of effort. Do you ship the software or do you wait? In any complex software product, from any company, bugs always remain in the shipping version. Experience and judgment dictate when those bugs are sufficiently unobtrusive that the software really is ready for shipment.

Windows 95 has been no different in this respect. By the middle of 1993, Microsoft had come up with the product's original, and rather vague, shipment goal of "the first half of 1994." This date would be about two years after the release of Windows version 3.1, and that was one major factor in choosing the planned ship date for Windows 95. Once the scope of the work was better understood, the development team pinned the release date down more firmly to "mid-1994." Plans were also made for a succession of limited releases to software developers, beta test sites, and others before the final general release. This cycle of controlled releases began in August 1993, almost a year before the planned general release date. The fact that a pretty complete and functional version of Windows 95 was available that early on says a lot about the extent of the testing and improvement effort Microsoft planned for the product before it would release the final version.

Well, guess what? The team completely blew the mid-1994 date. In fact, the Beta-1 release barely made it before the end of June. Once again, it proved to be beyond human ability to accurately forecast the completion date for a complex software project. This difficulty is not unique to Microsoft's release date predictions. Virtually no one is able to forecast with any accuracy, but Microsoft's plans are often very public. The most public statement of the release goal was Bill Gates's speech at the 1994 COMDEX/Spring show, when he demonstrated Windows 95 and committed to a release date of "before the end of the year."

How well "before the end of 1994" will be met remains to be seen. But rest assured that many long workdays and sleepless nights have yet to be invested in Windows 95.

Easy Setup and Configuration

Setting up and configuring a Windows system has never been a trivial task. Each new release has improved the process, but even the setup for Windows 3.0 and 3.1 (considered to have made quantum leaps in this area) has continued to baffle a lot of users. The "make it easy" directive governed much of the effort invested in improvements to the system setup and configuration procedures. The Windows 95 team decided to concentrate on these areas for major improvement:

- Hardware configuration. The Plug and Play initiative was intended to dramatically ease the process of configuring PCs, and Windows 95 would be the first operating system product to support the Plug and Play standard that Microsoft, Intel, Phoenix Technologies, and others were preparing.

- Installing and configuring Windows 95 on an existing Windows 3.1 system. The team felt that this process ought to require no user involvement beyond swapping diskettes at the right time. After all, if a system ran Windows 3.1, someone must have solved any setup or configuration problems already. Windows 95 ought to be able to use the earlier effort to ease its own installation process.

- System administration and reconfiguration procedures. Every aspect of the existing system was carefully analyzed to improve ease of use. For example, the team felt that any user ought to be able to set up a new printer without a problem. With Windows 3.1, that had not always been the case.

The Plug and Play Initiative

The Plug and Play standard was an effort with a much broader scope than simply Windows 95. Intended by its sponsors to be independent of any particular operating system, Plug and Play defines extensions to the existing PC hardware architecture, together with new BIOS and device driver capabilities that aim to shield the user from hardware setup and configuration issues. Apart from the physical process of plugging a system or a device in and turning it on, Plug and Play takes over the problems of identifying a device, assigning the device the correct hardware configuration resources (such as an interrupt request level), and configuring the appropriate device driver software.

Plug and Play is also independent of any particular bus architecture. It will use ISA, EISA, Micro Channel, PCMCIA, or any other bus architecture that has some market share. In the case of the ISA bus, in which there is really no hardware support for Plug and Play operations, the specification defines a new adapter card interface. For a small additional hardware cost (perhaps 25 or 50 cents) and with some new software, an ISA adapter card can become Plug and Play compliant. For even non-Plug and Play systems, a large amount of effort went into developing device recognition and configuration capabilities. We'll take a detailed look at the whole Plug and Play architecture in Chapter 8.

Configuring Windows

Configuring Windows itself has become something of a black art. Lengthy articles, and even whole books, devote considerable attention to every one of the often obscure lines in the Windows WIN.INI and SYSTEM.INI files. Coupling the contents of these two files with the contents of the basic CONFIG.SYS and AUTOEXEC.BAT files means that the user trying to modify or improve the operation of Windows faces a daunting task. The Windows 95 team decided to subject every single entry in the configuration files to detailed scrutiny. If an entry really wasn't needed, why was it there? Furthermore, why were there so many special case entries? Could better default selections avoid the need for additional entries? Did Plug and Play make some entries redundant? The more settings that could be eliminated, the easier the system would be to understand.

Apart from the files that control Windows operations, many applications use private initialization files or add parameter information to the WIN.INI file. Rationalizing this whole configuration mess was long overdue, and the Windows 95 team adopted the solution designed by the Windows NT group. Windows NT uses a special file called the *registry* to contain all the information relating to hardware, operating system, and application configuration. Entries in the registry are available to application programs through defined application programming interfaces. Applications can add to and retrieve their private configuration settings using registry access APIs. No longer can the user edit the text in a configuration file and introduce inconsistencies or other errors. Windows 95 uses the registry concept in an identical way, and as developers update application programs for Windows 95, the jumble of configuration files will disappear.

User-Level Operations

Many basic system management operations, such as setting up printers or modifying the layout of the Windows desktop, ought to be available to every user. Yes, they're there, but some of them are awkward to use and difficult to comprehend. Windows 95 addresses this problem by consolidating and simplifying many of the day-to-day operations that all users must perform on their own systems.

New Shell and User Interface

The most immediately striking aspect of Windows 95 is the new look of the screen display. Microsoft uses visual designers on all of its projects these days, and the attention to details of the Windows 95 appearance is remarkable. No longer does a programmer spend a mere hour designing a new icon for a control panel function. The process now involves a visual designer who carefully considers the intent, appearance, and overall consistency of the new visual element. At first glance, there's no obvious difference between individual screen elements of Windows 3.1 and those of Windows 95—no immediately apparent changes in an icon, for example. But if you look closely, you can see the subtle alterations to the shading and the shadow illusion around the icons in the Windows 95 version. As you can imagine, a lot of debate and painstaking effort went into the revision of the appearance of Windows 95. Later in the book, we'll examine these changes in detail.

The New Shell

Much more than just a pretty new face, the Windows 95 shell is a major functional step forward. Asking a Windows 3.1 user to identify "the shell" elicits some interesting responses. Some people have no idea what the shell is. Those who do have an idea will often identify the Program Manager as the shell component. Further questioning about how the File Manager, Print Manager, Task Manager, and Control Panel fit in with "the shell" will usually leave even the most expert Windows user confused.

This confusion is not because the user doesn't understand the system: Windows actually is rather confusing. For example, why do you configure printers using the Control Panel, alter print characteristics using the Print Setup option on the application's File menu, and then control print spooling using the Print Manager? Most proficient Windows users become accustomed to these procedures and forget about the awkwardness, but trying to introduce a naive user to the system and justifying, or even explaining, this scattered approach is difficult.

Fortunately, Microsoft itself recognized the problem a long time ago, and the Windows 95 release represents a serious effort to unify and improve the collection of system functions that form the shell. Of course, there are some major new features beyond that:

- OLE 2 is the first step in Microsoft's initiative to move toward a document-centric application architecture. The Windows 95 shell supports OLE 2 functions and consistent drag and drop capabilities.

- Electronic mail is almost a given in a networked environment. The shell supports an electronic mail interface directly.

- Long filenames—at last you can name a file *My chicken chili recipe* and not have to use CHCHRECP.DOC, ensuring that a month later you won't have the vaguest idea what the file contains.

- File viewers have become popular for allowing a user to examine a formatted file without having to access the application that created the file. Windows 95 incorporates a set of viewers.

- Pen gestures that were originally defined for Microsoft Pen Windows have been revised and incorporated directly into Windows 95. As the base of pen systems expands, Windows 95 will support pen systems without having to add new operating system components.

- MS-DOS applications will most likely live forever. Although Windows 95 appears to hasten their demise by providing a better Windows environment, the support for MS-DOS applications is also improved in Windows 95. MS-DOS window sizing, copy and paste operations, and the use of TrueType fonts within an MS-DOS application are among the improvements.

Complete Protected Mode Operating System

Later on in the book, we'll look at exactly what protected mode is and at what it means to Windows. Suffice it to say at this point that use of the protected mode removes memory limitations—that is, the 640K barrier disappears—and provides a solid basis for ensuring system robustness. The greater part of Windows 3.1 is a protected mode system. MS-DOS itself, however, remains a real mode system. Consequently, a system running Windows 3.1 continually switches back and forth between protected mode and real mode.[15] The switching overhead detracts from system performance.

The decision to implement Windows 95 as a complete system, no longer reliant on MS-DOS, opened the door to dispensing with all the remaining real mode components. In particular, the filesystem (handled by MS-DOS when you run Windows 3.1) and the mouse driver could

---

15. Actually, virtual 8086 mode—it's not quite as bad as real mode.

now be rewritten as protected mode software. Given the protected mode base and its enhanced capabilities, other improvements were obvious. For example, the print spooler could become a true preemptively scheduled background program. And some of the limitations of the Windows device driver model (the so called VxDs) could be removed, allowing VxDs to be dynamically loaded and unloaded rather than reside permanently in memory as in Windows 3.1.

The other aspect of completeness that the development team planned to tackle was filling in the gaps still present in Windows utility functions. Windows 3.1 has no equivalent to the MS-DOS Chkdsk program, for example. If you want to run the Chkdsk utility, you have to exit Windows to do it. Getting rid of such inconveniences was all part of the goal to provide a complete operating system.

Also on the list of operating system improvements was the removal of redundant and conflicting functions. Windows 3.1 introduced a very successful printing model that incorporated a single major module supplemented by small, simple device-specific printer drivers. This model had a number of positive effects, including the elimination of a lot of duplicate code in the different printer drivers and the promotion of the quick development of new drivers with fewer errors. Windows NT made use of a similar concept to standardize disk device support. Windows 95 would continue along the same path by using a similar model for its hard disk, SCSI device, display, and communications driver support.

32-Bit Application Support

Along with the growth in complexity of modern operating systems and computer networks has come a growth in the depth and breadth of single application programs. No longer does a word processor simply allow you to put words on paper. Customers expect spelling and grammar checking functions, a thesaurus, page layout facilities, and a host of other features. The sheer scope of today's application programs calls for the consumption of large amounts of memory, disk space, and processor cycles. Despite the fact that Intel's first true 32-bit chip began to appear in PCs in 1988, MS-DOS and Windows have never fully supported 32-bit application programs. Rather inadequate solutions, such as the DPMI standard incorporated into Windows 3.0, have been little more than stopgaps to the developers who desperately needed 32 bits' worth of memory addressing.

Windows NT was Microsoft's first operating system in the Windows family to offer full 32-bit support. Windows 95 will join Windows NT in supporting Microsoft's Win32 32-bit application programming interface. From the application developer's point of view, 32-bit support provides three major benefits:

■ Access to essentially unlimited amounts of memory. A single Win32 application program can access up to 2 GB of memory. ✓

■ A much easier to program memory model. Writing software for a so called "flat," or linear, 32-bit address space provides relief from the vagaries of the Intel processor family's segmented architecture. A programmer can design data structures without having to worry about the boundaries and limitations imposed by a 16-bit memory model. ✓

■ A consistent application programming interface. The Windows API contains hundreds of functions that together involve thousands of parameters. In Windows 3.1, some of the parameters are 16 bits and some are 32 bits. It is a rare programmer who can remember which is which and never make mistakes while writing code that calls these APIs. Win32 functions consistently use 32-bit parameters with a consequent reduction in programming errors. ✓

Before the development of Windows 95, Microsoft defined a subset API termed *Win32s*. Included within the Win32s definition were all the APIs that, if strictly adhered to, would allow an application developer to produce software that would run on both 16-bit Windows 3.1 and 32-bit Windows NT. Win32s was in fact a true subset of the Windows NT API and was made available on Windows 3.1 through the use of a library that converted the Win32s 32-bit API calls to the native 16-bit API calls of Windows 3.1.

The Windows 95 team needed to improve on the original Win32s API set and originally defined a *Win32c* API set that took Win32s as its base and added a number of APIs specific to Windows 95. For example, device-independent color capabilities (important in most desktop publishing and drawing programs) will appear for the first time in Windows 95. The term Win32c became quite confusing, quite quickly, and many questions about the relationships among Win32, Win32s, and Win32c convinced Microsoft that they needed a simpler story.[16] After an interval, the Win32c term was dropped altogether, and the Windows 95 Win32 API set became simply a subset of the full Win32 API, defined (at that time) by Windows NT and slated for expansion in the Cairo era.

The exact definition of the Win32 API set and the individual levels of support in each operating system for the Win32 API can be found only by consulting the appropriate documentation. Microsoft's intention is to allow an application program conforming to the Win32s API to run on any Windows operating system (from Windows 3.1 onward). Applications that use more advanced capabilities cannot necessarily be supported on every version of Windows. For example, applications using the advanced security features available in the Win32 API will run only on Windows NT and its direct successors.

The Jump to 32 Bits

Moving to the 32-bit API under Windows 95 introduces an interesting discontinuity, and for once, discontinuity provides a useful break with the fully compatible past. Since developers who decide to use Win32 must modify their application code, Microsoft reasoned that they could impose a rule on developers requiring that every API in an application be a Win32 API. Thus, not only do you modify your code to incorporate the new 32-bit device-independent color APIs, but you also modify all the other Windows API calls to conform to the Win32 interface. This includes the basic APIs that deal with issues such as file management and memory allocation.[17]

Given this new application model, and its associated rules, the Windows 95 team could incorporate some significant new capabilities into Windows 95. Since the system would know that it was dealing only with applications that conform to the Win32 rules, it would know how to manage the applications a lot more effectively than it could the existing 16-bit applications. Under Windows 95, the benefits realized by an application that bases itself on Win32 extend far beyond simply having 32 bits' worth of memory—notably:

■ Preemption. A Win32 application is fully preemptible, meaning that the operating system can suspend its execution at any moment in order to switch to a higher-priority task. In

---

16. The first interesting marketing sleight of hand simply modified the interpretation of the *c* in Win32c to say that it was for Win32 common, rather than Win32 Chicago. This didn't go far enough, however.

17. To their credit, Microsoft supplied a program analyzer that simplified a lot of the grunt work needed to complete this type of conversion.

general, this means smoother response (an hourglass displayed by one application no longer means that you can't switch to another to do something useful), better system throughput, and avoidance of the data loss that can come from an application's having to wait too long for control of the processor.

√ ■ Separate address space. A Win32 application runs within its own protected memory region. No other application can scramble its code or data.

√ ■ Thread support. Often a single application would like to do two things at once—perhaps writing a backup copy of the current document to disk while still allowing the user to edit the on-screen text. Under Windows 3.1, multitasking within a simple application is an awkward and error-prone feature to implement. An application's ability under Win32 to utilize multiple threads of execution provides a structured way to perform multitasking.

Networking and Mobile Computing

Microsoft originally introduced its peer-to-peer local area networking extension for Windows in the fall of 1992. Windows 95 essentially incorporates the Windows for Workgroups local area network functionality and thus mirrors the model that Windows NT established. Microsoft has long espoused the belief that networking capability is a fundamental part of the operating system. Separating networking and operating system products into different categories, or using special purpose operating systems for network servers, really isn't the way to go. However, Windows 95 enters a world in which Novell servers make up the major part of the installed base. For Windows 95 to become popular in a Novell-dominated network environment, it needs to offer much more than its own brand of local area network support.[18] Thus, Windows 95 includes software that ensures its host system will be fully equipped as a NetWare client machine.

Beyond its support of local area network facilities, Windows 95 has many other features that involve communications. From simple telephone line dial-up facilities to support for the latest generation of

---

18. Whether peer networking will literally be given away in the Windows 95 box is a packaging issue that probably won't be decided until shortly before Windows 95 ships. It may be packaged as a separately priced add-on.

mobile, handheld devices, Windows 95 aims to be about as good a client machine operating system as it can be, including

- Client support for all popular networks: Novell's, Banyan's, Microsoft's, and others.

- Multiple client support, allowing a client machine to connect simultaneously to different networks—perhaps to a Novell local area network and to a TCP/IP-based wide area network.

- A peer server capability that matches the original capability provided by the Windows for Workgroups product. Workgroups or smaller businesses can thus avoid the need to dedicate a machine to server functions.

- Electronic mail support based on the message application programming interface (MAPI) and extending to facsimile devices as well as popular electronic mail networks.

- Remote connectivity and administration features that provide efficient access to and management of a local area network over a low-bandwidth connection. Windows 95 acknowledges the "traveling PC" phenomenon in its support for file synchronization capabilities and effective data transfer over a low-speed connection. Thus, you can dial back to home base and download a copy of a document at a decent speed. When you revise the document and take it back to the office, Windows 95 helps you figure out how to synchronize your hotel room edits with the local master copy.

- Pen support. The pen-based computer revolution was predicted, and then it never really happened. Even so, there is a steady growth in the use of pen computing devices. Windows 95 incorporates support for pen-based machines. As and when the revolution occurs, your Windows 95 software will be ready.

Bringing Windows 95 to Market

Describing what the Windows 95 development team set out to accomplish begs the question of whether the product will be successful. The mission of making a Microsoft product a success involves many other Microsoft groups. Some of these groups, such as the product support division, aren't fully engaged in seeing to the success of the product until it ships to customers. Everyone involved faces a considerable challenge. Success for Windows 95 means selling tens of millions of copies. Sales of only a few million copies (usually an indication of a runaway software bestseller) will be a commercial disaster.

Outside Microsoft, the most important group influencing the success of Windows 95 will be the independent software vendors (ISVs) courted by the company's developer relations group (DRG). If the ISVs devote their resources to writing applications for Windows 95, competing operating systems such as IBM OS/2 and Novell NetWare will suffer by comparison. Windows 95 presents an unusual selling job for Microsoft in that they must persuade the application developers to take presumably perfectly fine Windows applications and modify them. The DRG spent much of 1993 evangelizing for Microsoft's OLE technology and the 32-bit API of Windows NT that would appear in Windows 95 in 1994. Whether the benefits of OLE and the 32-bit capabilities of these operating systems are compelling enough to warrant major investment by the ISVs remains to be seen.

Microsoft provided the ISVs with a lot of early information about Windows 95 in a series of design reviews held in Redmond during the summer and fall of 1993. The audience for these events was usually fairly small (the largest made up of perhaps 100 people), and Microsoft always prefaced such an event with a warning that many product features were expected to change. The participants also had an opportunity to influence the Windows 95 design team. The team often asked for comments on possible solutions to issues that had not been entirely decided. Early on, the possibilities for change were quite numerous, but as the planned shipment date drew closer, these opportunities to influence the Windows 95 team naturally diminished.

As Windows 95 gathered marketing momentum, the product team's goals were translated into the market message behind the product. Customers are most influenced by the perceived benefits of any product, and Microsoft used the Windows 95 project goals as the basis for their initial customer presentations. In the early fall of 1993, Microsoft's first closed door product briefings identified three main benefits of Windows 95:

- Easy to use—based on the Plug and Play capability, the new shell, and the extensive use of Microsoft's OLE 2 technology.

- Powerful 32-bit multitasking system—based on the new operating system kernel, the new filesystem, and the improvements in device support.

■ Great connectivity—based on the new networking components and the mobile computing enhancements.

The first of the more public product briefings was given to a group of industry journalists on May 12 and 13, 1994, in Redmond. The press rollout was scheduled to take place shortly before the Beta-1 release, which was actually supposed to be ready to hand out at the briefing and to coincide with the launch of the marketing campaign that precedes every Microsoft operating system product release.

At that rollout, the product goals were restated in short form—"easy," "more powerful," and "more connected." The marketing message has retained a degree of consistency throughout the project.

Whether these benefits are enough to sell Windows 95 to the end user is a subject for the future and for a different forum. Certainly Microsoft has every chance of success with the product. Their early 1994 estimates indicated that about 50 million copies of Windows would be in use by mid-1994, with perhaps 60 to 70 percent of all new machines shipping with Windows already installed. The principal target market for upgrading existing Windows 3.1 users will be about 60 percent of the installed base.[19]

For Microsoft—The Bottom Line

Altruism is rarely a consideration in Microsoft's business thinking. Yes, some product characteristics, such as compatibility and ease of use, are deeply ingrained in the thinking of every person in the product development groups. The Windows 95 team tried as hard as anyone to meet the ease-of-use goal, and indeed, their motivation did extend far beyond the simple desire for commercial success. However, the team also wanted to sell one heck of a lot of software. Work out the numbers and you'll see that selling a Windows 95 upgrade to every existing Windows user would translate into a billion dollars of revenue. The team knew that if Windows 95 really could achieve the "make it easy" goal, the door to more new users and more software sales would be unlocked. Building a great product was definitely the number one goal. Selling lots of copies came in a close second.

---

19. Microsoft classifies these users as "active" users; that is, they are people who periodically upgrade some part of their computer systems, be it hardware or software. The rest simply don't upgrade anything (and probably drive a 10-year-old car quite happily as well).

Conclusion

In this chapter, we've looked at the underlying goals and philosophy behind the Windows 95 development project and at a synopsis of the major new features. Entering a mature market, the product has to meet some stringent compatibility and performance goals as well as introduce new features that will motivate Windows users to upgrade and will attract new users to the Windows platform. Windows 95 is also an important component in Microsoft's systems software plans. Married to the strengths of Windows NT, it becomes part of an enterprise-wide computing system and introduces some of the Cairo product concepts for the first time. As our review of the development team's self-imposed ten commandments suggests, Windows 95 is also an ambitious project. How Microsoft plans to meet the target it has set for itself is what most of the rest of this book is about.

Windows 95 is an Intel processor–based operating system. The Intel family of processors has had a significant influence on both MS-DOS and Windows over their lifetimes. In return, Windows has influenced Intel's processor designs. In the next chapter, we'll look at the Intel processors and highlight the features that have an impact on the design and operation of Windows itself.

CHAPTER TWO

INTEL PROCESSOR ARCHITECTURE

Inside every fine operating system beats the heart of a good processor. In our case, it's very definitely Intel inside. Windows 95 has been designed and developed for Intel processor–based systems only. Microsoft's high-end operating system, Windows NT, broke with the Intel tradition in order to allow vendors to choose from a variety of processor types as the base for a system, and Microsoft and its development partners have introduced versions of Windows NT for the MIPS R4000, the DEC Alpha, the PowerPC, and other advanced processors. None of these chips is compatible with the Intel processor family, so the only way to get existing applications for Windows or MS-DOS to run on one of these processors is to include some form of Intel processor emulation with the Windows NT version for the processor. For a Windows NT user, the performance overhead of the emulator isn't a real problem. After all, that user bought Windows NT principally to use on a network server or to run a new native 32-bit application. Any slowdown in such a user's occasional use of an existing 16-bit Windows application isn't really an issue. There are also some thorny problems associated with running MS-DOS applications on Windows NT. The preservation of the Windows NT security model prevents a lot of older MS-DOS applications from running, for example. But running MS-DOS programs just isn't the role a Windows NT machine is meant to fill, so Microsoft decided that putting restrictions on Windows NT's 16-bit application environment was acceptable.

For a Windows 95 user, Microsoft felt that any similar restrictions or performance overhead for running 16-bit applications would be completely unacceptable. After all, most Windows 95 users would already be using Windows on their desktop or laptop machines. Their main initial reason for installing Windows 95 would probably be to have their existing applications run faster or better. Any compatibility or performance problems for 16-bit applications would be a major barrier to the mass acceptance of Windows 95.

Thus, the Windows 95 team had to provide 100 percent compatibility and zero performance overhead to the Windows 3.1 user. Tough goals. Fortunately, Microsoft's experience with early versions of Windows, OS/2, and Windows NT had equipped them with the expertise they needed to meet these goals. Microsoft's experience also told them that the compatibility and performance goals could not be met for Windows 95 running on a non-Intel processor. Any dreams of a portable version of Windows were laid aside early on. Windows 95, and any direct successors, will forever run on Intel processor systems only.

Intel Inside

One could write a book devoted to the low-level details of Windows 95 and its interaction with the Intel processor and the system that contains it, but that is not the purpose of this chapter. We'll look at some aspects of the hardware that have to be understood in order to make sense of some of the Windows 95 features we'll look at in detail in later chapters—particularly Windows 95 memory management, its support for MS-DOS applications, and the new Plug and Play services. However, this chapter is certainly not intended to be an exhaustive treatment of the subject.[1] Most of the information in this chapter will relate to the 80386, 80486, and Pentium processors that Windows 95 runs on. A lot of the less relevant details have been left out or simplified. You may already know more about the Intel processor family than you care to remember. If you do, I suggest that you go straight to the next chapter. If you don't care to know a lot about the Intel processor family, don't worry: the rest of the chapter deals only with the details of the hardware you need to know about. We'll get back to the Windows 95 software very soon.

---

1. Of the many books that do provide an exhaustive treatment of hardware issues, a good one is Ross Nelson's *Microsoft's 80386/80486 Programming Guide* (Microsoft Press, 1991).

Here's what we'll look at in this chapter:

- The Intel processor family—the continuing influence of the original 16-bit Intel processor, the 8086, on all versions of Windows because of the MS-DOS software compatibility requirement

- Processor architecture and modes—the basic design of the Intel chip family and how the processor can be made to run the different application types (MS-DOS, 16-bit Windows, 32-bit Windows)

- Memory management—the different methods for handling memory allocation on the Intel 80386 processor

- Protection—how the 80386 processor allows the operating system to protect itself and to protect applications and devices from one another

The Intel Processor Family

Intel introduced its first 16-bit microprocessor, the 8086, in 1978. IBM ensured the role of Intel processors in subsequent computing history by adopting the Intel 8088 (a slightly slower version of the 8086) for the IBM Personal Computer in 1981. Microsoft (figuratively, at least) took its place on the podium with MS-DOS, the operating system it implemented for the IBM PC. Successive models of the PC, from IBM and its competitors, have continued to use Intel processor chips and copies of MS-DOS in vast numbers. Somewhere, someone is buying a PC right now. It probably has an Intel processor inside, and it probably comes with a copy of MS-DOS. This buying process is repeated tens of millions of times a year, and many fortunes, Intel's and Microsoft's included, have been made as a result.

From the software point of view, the Intel processor family has gone through two major architectural changes since 1978. These changes appeared with the 80286 and 80386 processors. From the hardware designer's point of view, there have been other major design changes, such as the integration of the processor and floating point processor capabilities on the single 80486 chip. These hardware changes, together with many other feature and performance improvements, are often denoted by product name suffixes such as SX and SL. Each change almost always meant more speed and rarely required any major modification on the part of the operating system software designer. That was not true in the case of the major architectural revisions introduced with the 80286 and 80386 processors. At the risk of offending some hardware designers, we'll look primarily at the processor design revisions that enabled significant new software capabilities.

Backward Compatibility

The single most important aspect of the Intel processor design has been the backward software compatibility of the different chips. And successive versions of MS-DOS have ensured that this compatibility feature has been readily available to both programmers and users. Every MS-DOS program ever written for an Intel 8086 will run unchanged on a Pentium processor. This compatibility has allowed users to buy newer and better hardware with every change in processor generation and carry with them the applications they know and use every day. I'd be willing to bet that many copies of version 1.0 of Lotus 1-2-3 are still in use. Amazingly, the very first release of Microsoft Windows (1985) would actually run on a floppy disk–based PC with an 8088 processor (1981). That same software will still run on a Pentium-based system today.

Software compatibility has been the key to the success of the Intel processor family and, to a large extent, the key to the success of the whole personal computer industry. When Intel released the 80286 processor in 1982, the announcement lauded, in addition to compatibility, its higher speed and new "protected mode." Unfortunately, the protected mode wasn't compatible with the 8086. In 1984, IBM introduced its first 286-based system, the IBM PC AT. Microsoft didn't try to exploit the protected mode with the MS-DOS release (version 3.0) for the PC AT. MS-DOS used the 286 simply as a faster 8086. However, Microsoft did release XENIX, its UNIX-derivative operating system, for the PC AT. XENIX was the first operating system that tried to exploit the 286's protected mode of operation. But XENIX didn't try to provide MS-DOS software compatibility. A few years later, the designers of OS/2 made valiant attempts to exploit the 286's protected mode while retaining that all-important property, MS-DOS software compatibility. There were many shortcomings.

If all of this sounds confused, it was. In truth, Intel's implementation of 8086 compatibility alongside the 286 protected mode feature was poorly designed. For example, once an operating system had switched the processor into protected mode operation, there was no way of switching back to real mode other than by simulating a complete reboot of the machine! This and other deficiencies meant that the 286 processor was rarely used as anything other than a faster 8086. However, the mistakes with the 286 design and the early experience from operating system projects such as OS/2 ensured that the next processor in the family—the 80386—came out right. The 386 offered 8086 compatibility, 286 compatibility (which ultimately might not have been worth the microcode), a new 32-bit mode (*386 native mode*), and an unusual new mode of operation called *virtual 8086 mode.* This last feature enabled the implementation of an operating system that could run not just one, but many MS-DOS programs compatibly *and* simultaneously. Microsoft helped Intel design virtual 8086 mode and harnessed that mode initially with the release of Windows/386 in 1987. Other operating systems—Quarterdeck's DESQview, IBM's OS/2 version 2.0, and many versions of UNIX—also used the virtual 8086 feature to good effect. The successor processors in the Intel family, the 80486 and the Pentium, preserved the virtual 8086 mode feature, and today most operating systems, including Windows 95, continue to exploit it.

The most recent releases of Windows have been designed only for the 80386, the 80486, and recently, the Pentium processors. Essentially, Windows has treated each of these processor types as a 386. A number of low-level processor features have to be managed differently, but none of this low-level management is visible to an application program or indeed to most of the Windows operating system itself. Thus, we won't get into the intricate details of, for example, how Windows 95 manages floating point operations on the different processor types. In the rest of this book, you'll see references to only the 386 processor. Read this to mean "386, 486, or Pentium." The keys to understanding how Windows exploits the Intel 386 processor architecture are in its management of memory, its processor modes, and its protection scheme. That's what we'll look at next.

Processor Architecture

The Intel 8086 introduced a microprocessor memory architecture referred to as *segmented addressing.* Similar schemes had appeared in the design of other, generally much larger, computers, but the 8086 was the first major microprocessor to employ the technique. Since all MS-DOS programs throughout the 1980s were written for compatibility with the 8086 (and Windows 95 still has to be able to run those programs), it's important to understand the 8086 memory architecture.

The 8080 and 8086 Processors

The 8-bit predecessor of the 8086—the Intel 8080—allowed a program to address a total of 64 kilobytes. Each addressing register of the 8080 was 16 bits. Sixteen bits gave you 65,536 total addresses and thus 64K of address space. Intel tried pretty hard to make the 8086 compatible with the 8080 and did preserve the 16-bit address registers. Intel's goals for the 8086 were much loftier, however, and they added four *segment registers* to the 8086, allowing a program to address up to 1 megabyte of memory. Essentially, a segment register points directly to the first byte of a memory segment. A segment can begin at any 16-byte chunk of memory (what Intel called a *paragraph*). Adding 1 to a segment address points you to a memory address 16 bytes higher in memory. Using this segment address as a base address (that is, as address zero for this segment), the programmer can then use another processor register to reference any byte within the subsequent 64K. The processor simply combines the contents of the segment register and an address register to form a unique 20-bit address. Twenty bits gives you 1,048,576 total addresses and thus 1 MB of address space. Figure 2-1 shows how the 8086 performs the address arithmetic. Note that the operation of combining the contents of the segment register and the address register to obtain the final memory address is carried out by the processor itself. No direct action is required on the part of the programmer.

The segment registers on the 8086 have to be manipulated by the programmer. When the operating system loads an application, it initializes the segment registers before running the application. After that, the application code manipulates the segment registers as it needs to. Most early MS-DOS programmers and compiler writers learned many tricks for efficiently using the 8086 segment registers.

This segmented memory architecture has been both a boon and a pain for software writers. On the plus side, the segmentation allowed the use of techniques such as expanded memory—with a combination of software and hardware tricks, segments of 8086 memory could be temporarily replaced, effectively increasing the total memory available to a program. On the minus side, segment management was a chore for anyone developing large (that is, larger than two 64K segments) applications.[2] Scanning through a 100,000-element array of 2-byte integers,

---

2. During the development of the first version of Windows, signs proclaiming *SS != DS* were popular in many programmers' offices. The signs were intended to be a constant reminder to the developers. They hoped the signs would lead to fewer bugs.

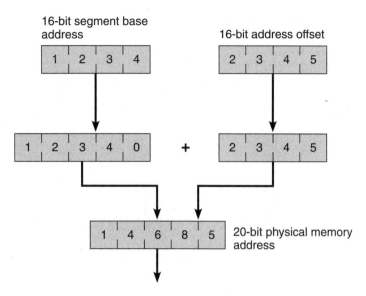

Figure 2-1.
Intel 8086 address calculation.

for example, meant reloading the appropriate segment register at least three times during the scan. Programmers used to larger machines, or to microprocessors such as Motorola's 68000, were more accustomed to a *linear address* scheme. With a linear addressing architecture, the programmer would simply increment a single (usually 24- or 32-bit) address in order to scan the entire physical memory present on the system.

The 640K Barrier

The 1-megabyte memory limit of the 8086 architecture never received wide public attention. Instead, the infamous 640K limit in DOS was the popular target for much ire and ill-informed criticism. So where did the 640K limit come from? The designers of the original IBM PC decided to reserve 384K of the 8086's enormous 1-megabyte address space (remember, this was 1981) for hardware and system software purposes. The remaining 640K was free for use by DOS and application programs. Within the upper 384K were the BIOS code, screen memory, and other system elements. Figure 2-2 on the next page is a reproduction of the first published memory layout of the original IBM PC.[3]

---

3. *IBM Technical Reference #6025005.* The first edition was published in August 1981.

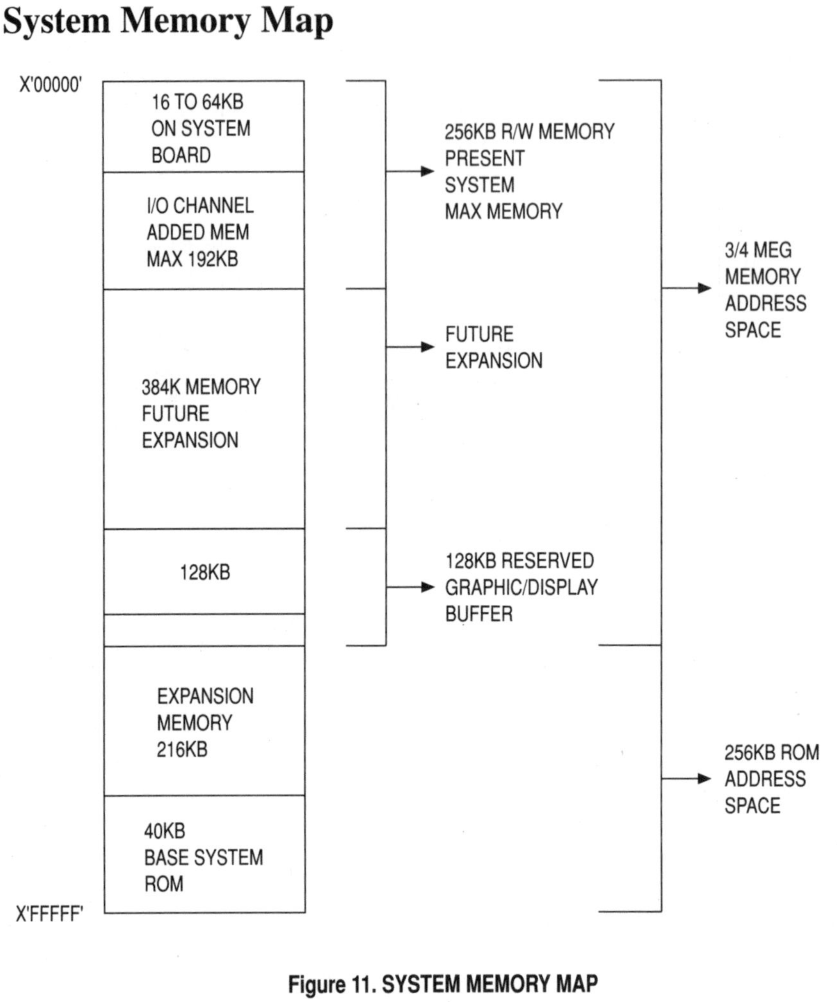

System Memory Map

Figure 11. SYSTEM MEMORY MAP

Figure 2-2.
The first published memory map for the original IBM PC.

DOS really had little part in determining the 640K limit, and the layout for the first megabyte of memory on a PC still has an impact on the design of operating systems today. If you want to build an operating system that runs MS-DOS programs, many of which expect to find certain resources at the specific addresses chosen in 1981, you have to develop some method for supporting this memory layout.

The 80286 Processor

Enter the 80286 and protected mode operation. Once again, software compatibility was a key goal in the design of the processor, so the 286 designers retained the basic instruction set and addressing method of the 8086. Indeed, at power on, the 286 operates in *real mode* (a term coined at that time to designate operation in 8086 mode) and behaves for all intents and purposes just as an 8086 does. But Intel added the new *protected mode* of operation to significantly increase the processor's capabilities. An operating system can programmatically switch the 286 from real to protected mode, and in protected mode, the processor's segment registers are used very differently.

In protected mode, the processor uses the contents of a segment register to access an 8-byte area of memory called a *descriptor*. Within the descriptor is the information that determines the actual physical address of the memory location the program is trying to reference. Figure 2-3 on the next page shows how the 286 combines the segment register, descriptor information, and address register to produce a 24-bit physical memory address. It's like having a key to a numbered safety deposit box that contains the real address of the location for a rendez-vous. The segment register actually contains an index into a table of descriptors. Each descriptor can be set up to address a different area of physical memory. (Note that in descriptions of protected mode operations, the term *selector* is customary for describing the contents of the segment register. Since the value in the register isn't actually a memory address, there is some justification for yet another term.)

A descriptor contains a lot more information, related primarily to memory protection issues. The operating system sets up all the descriptors for a particular program within a contiguous area of memory called a *local descriptor table,* or *LDT*. Each program running on the 286 has its own LDT. The operating system also sets up a *global descriptor table,* or *GDT*. The operating system uses the GDT to allocate memory for itself and, for example, to allow several programs to access the same area of physical memory. The operating system can place the GDT and each application's LDT anywhere in memory. Two special hardware registers, the GDTR and the LDTR, are set up to contain the base addresses of the tables for the currently executing program. When the operating system switches tasks, it will typically change the base address in the LDTR. Usually, the GDTR remains unchanged while the system is running. Reloading the GDTR and LDTR registers is a privileged operation performed only by the operating system. The system does not allow application programs to modify the contents of these registers.

41

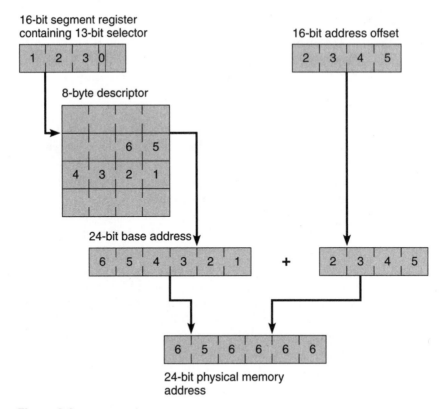

Figure 2-3.
Memory access on the 80286 processor in protected mode.

Two aspects of the new protected mode architecture are important to note.

- Protected mode introduced the notion of memory protection. Unless a program's LDT contains a descriptor for a particular area of memory, there is no way for the program to access that part of memory. Thus, an operating system can set up an environment in which several programs run concurrently, each in its own protected memory area. The 286 actually has protection capabilities beyond this, and we'll look at all the details when we examine the 80386 processor. Typically, the OS uses the GDT descriptors to allow different programs to access the same area of physical memory.

- The architecture's provision for indirect access to memory via the LDT or GDT allows the operating system to use any suitable area of physical memory as a segment. The segments of one program need not be contiguous and can even be different sizes. As far as the program is concerned, it has access to all the memory described by its LDT. The program doesn't know, or care, exactly where in physical memory the segments exist. Figure 2-4 shows how such an allocation of memory might appear within a system running two programs that share access to one particular memory segment.

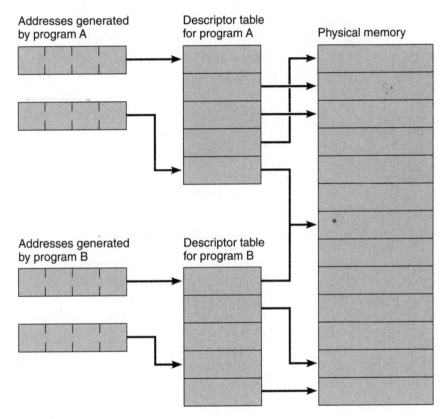

Figure 2-4.
Hypothetical memory allocation for two programs running on an
80286 processor in protected mode.

The 80386 Processor

Note that the 80286 retained the 8086's awkward segmented address-ing scheme. A programmer, or a compiler and linker, still had to be sure to set up segment registers with the correct selector, and the code that could scan through that ubiquitous 100,000-integer array still was not pretty.[4] This deficiency alone made Motorola's 32-bit microprocessor family the almost unanimous choice for manufacturers designing UNIX workstations. Intel had to respond to this market pressure, and they did, introducing the 32-bit 80386 processor in 1987.

Microsoft worked closely with Intel during the 80386 design phase and strongly influenced the capabilities of the new *virtual 8086 mode* supported by the 386.[5] Microsoft's interest in the project was to make sure that the 386 included all the capabilities necessary to allow new operating systems to run existing MS-DOS programs. Microsoft had a lot of battlefield experience from meeting this requirement over the course of several operating systems and versions of operating systems, and the work they'd put into OS/2, MS-DOS 95, and Windows, all for the 286 processor, had persuaded them that there had to be an easier way. Sometimes silicon chips don't turn out quite the way the designers intended, but in the case of the 80386, Intel got it right. The new 32-bit capabilities and the virtual 8086 mode feature worked well from the time of the first production samples of the 386, and apart from changes to internal details, those features remain the same in the 80486 and Pentium processors.

Windows 95 is a 386 operating system, so we need to take a close look at the features of the 386 (and by extension of the 486 and the Pentium) that are important to Windows 95's operation. Software compatibility for the now enormous installed base of MS-DOS software remained an overriding consideration, so PC manufacturers[6] first released systems that used the 386 as a yet faster 8086—turn on the power and the 386 runs in real mode, precisely emulating the 8086. However, the 386 evolved from the 286 in a number of distinct ways, all of which called for a new operating system to make the new features of the 386 available to application programs:

- Internally, everything grew from 16 bits to 32 bits—all the registers, the memory addresses, and so on.

---

4. If you're interested in the more amusing aspects of microprocessor history, you might like to revisit Intel's 286 sales campaign of the time. Their explanation of why a segmented architecture beats a linear architecture is a triumph of marketing over science.

5. In fact, the I/O permission bitmap, so important to virtual mode operation, was present in the 386 largely because of Microsoft's lobbying.

6. Compaq was the first company to introduce a PC that used a 386 processor, and this was the first time that one of the so-called "clone" manufacturers broke ranks. Compaq's low-risk bet helped push IBM out of its industry leadership position.

■ Although the 386 preserved the notion of segments, a single segment could now be 4 gigabytes in size as opposed to a mere 1 megabyte. For all intents and purposes, the programmer could now treat the 386 as though it had a linear address space. Intel finally had a real 32-bit microprocessor.

■ The 386 improved the memory protection scheme further. An operating system designer could now implement a full *virtual memory* scheme on the 386. (Note that virtual memory and virtual 8086 mode really aren't related, terminology notwithstanding.)

■ An operating system could switch the 386 processor at will among its different operating modes. The properly equipped 386 system could run 8086, 286, and new 32-bit 386 programs simultaneously.

■ The virtual 8086 mode and the associated *I/O permission bitmap* allowed the implementation of complete MS-DOS software compatibility within a protected multitasking system.

80386 Memory Addressing

The 80386's software compatibility features ensure that in real mode it operates just as an 8086 does. Address construction is the same as for the 8086, and all extraneous information (notably the high-order 16 bits of each register) is simply ignored during execution. In protected mode, the operating system that controls program loading and execution must set up a program's descriptor table in such a way that the processor knows how to interpret the memory address information. The protected mode process for calculating a physical address on the 386 is similar to that of the 286: the processor uses the contents of a segment register as an index into a descriptor table, and the descriptor table entry contains nearly all the remaining necessary information—"nearly" all because the 386 allows an operating system to implement a complete paged virtual memory scheme. When the operating system enables paging, the address information extracted from the descriptor table must go through a further level of interpretation before it is used as an actual memory address.

80386 Descriptor Format

Figure 2-5 on the next page illustrates the layout of a single descriptor table entry on the 386. Let's look at each field in a little more detail.

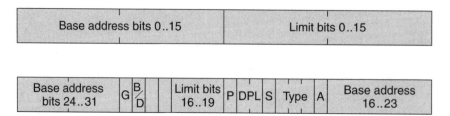

Figure 2-5.
80386 descriptor table entry format.

Base Address   The processor forms a 32-bit address from the four base address fields. Once assembled, the address specifies the first memory location of the memory segment the program wants to reference. Adding the 32-bit offset address generated by the program completes the address of the memory reference. For a 286 program, byte 7 of the descriptor (bits 24 through 31 of the base address) is always 0, since the 286 can deal only with 24-bit base addresses.

This arrangement is the basis of the addressing mechanism for 32-bit programs. Each program has to deal only with a consistent 32-bit linear address. The operating system sets up the base register to point to the first byte of the program's code or data segment, and no further segment manipulation is necessary. Since a 32-bit quantity provides such an enormous address space, only a tiny number of programs will ever need to indulge in segment register trickery.

This absence of the need for segment register manipulation is an important performance benefit. On the 286 running in protected mode, every time the contents of a segment register change, the processor must check to see that the new selector is a valid one—that is, that the new segment register contents address a memory segment allocated to the program. If the selector is not valid, the processor generates a *general protection,* or *GP, fault.* This selector validation process consumes many processor cycles, and when segment registers are frequently changed, as they must be on the 286 running in protected mode, overall program performance degrades. On the 386, most programs will never reload the segment registers and consequently never suffer the performance hit.

Limit   Two fields form the 20-bit *limit* quantity, which specifies the upper limit of the memory segment addressed by the descriptor. Twenty bits, as a byte address, is only 1 megabyte. But didn't we just say that segments could be 4 GB in size, rather than just 1 MB? Read on.

G Bit The single *granularity* bit specifies whether the processor inter-prets the limit field value as *byte granular* or *page granular*. Byte granular-ity means that the processor interprets the limit value in terms of bytes. This setting (0) assists in running 286 programs correctly. Page granu-larity means that the processor interprets the limit value in terms of pages. Memory pages on the 386 are 4K in size, and 20 bits' worth of 4K pages equals, lo and behold, 4 GB of memory.

D or B Bit This bit is the D bit if the memory segment contains pro-gram code. The value 1 means that the segment contains native, that is, 386, instructions. The value 0 means that the segment contains 286 code. This bit is the B bit if the segment contains data. In this case, the value 1 means that the segment is larger than 64K.

P Bit The *present* bit denotes whether the memory segment is present in physical memory. This information is an important aspect of the vir-tual memory scheme implemented by Windows 95 since it allows the operating system to differentiate between an invalid memory refer-ence—one in which the program tries to access memory it doesn't own—and a reference to a memory segment that has been temporarily swapped out to the hard disk.

DPL The 2-bit *descriptor privilege level* field specifies the privilege level for the segment—zero through three. The contents of the DPL field, together with the privilege level of the currently running program, play an important role in the Windows 95 protection system. Code running at ring zero, as the terminology goes, has the privilege of executing cer-tain instructions that ring three code does not. Code at ring three, for example, can't turn interrupts on and off. Windows uses only two privi-lege levels—zero and three—despite the fact that the processor also supports privilege levels one and two. Someday there may be a good reason to use the extra privilege levels, but it hasn't come along yet.

S Bit The *segment* bit is always set to 1 for a memory segment. The value 0 means that the descriptor references something other than memory. The "something other" can be one of several special data structures used by a 386 operating system to control aspects of device interrupt handling and memory protection.

Type Field The 3-bit *type* field specifies the memory segment type—for example, an execute-only code segment or a read-only data segment. The

47

contents of the type field help the operating system maintain memory protection. An attempt to modify the contents of a read-only data segment would obviously be an error, for example.

A Bit   The *accessed* bit indicates whether any program has referenced the memory segment. Any reference to the segment causes the accessed bit to be set to 1. The Windows 95 memory manager uses the accessed bit in its virtual memory scheme. If a memory segment has never been accessed while in physical memory, the physical memory it occupies becomes an excellent candidate for the operating system to reclaim it and allocate it to another program when the need comes up. And if there has been no access to the segment, it obviously has never been modified, so Windows can reclaim the memory for another use without having to write the segment out to disk.

The Descriptor in Summary

As you can see, the layout of a 386 memory descriptor is hardly the most elegant data structure ever devised. The layout is really an artifact of the earlier processors with which the 386 has to remain compatible. However, the descriptor does contain the information necessary to implement a fully protected multitasking system with virtual memory support. Windows 95 implements exactly that, and apart from the first hardware initialization sequence after power on, Windows 95 always runs in 32-bit protected mode with virtual memory enabled.

Virtual Memory

Simply put, virtual memory is a method for allowing several concurrently running programs to share the physical memory of the computer. (Note again that *virtual memory* and *virtual mode,* or *virtual 8086 mode,* are very different. The phrase *virtual mode* refers to the operation of the 386 processor in virtual 8086 mode. The context will determine the meaning of any other use of the word *virtual.*) The techniques for implementing and managing virtual memory date from many years before the introduction of the 386.[7] In fact, the early research on virtual memory was so good that the most effective techniques for handling virtual memory have changed very little since its earliest implementations. The

---

7. Over the years, many manufacturers and research institutes have laid claim to the "first" distinction. The earliest implementation of virtual memory was probably the one by the Atlas research group at the University of Manchester, England, during the late 1950s and early 1960s.

management of virtual memory is entirely under the control of the operating system. As far as any individual program is aware, it has access to all the memory it needs all the time. A simple example should illustrate how Windows 95 manages virtual memory.

Let's say that we have a Windows 95 system with 4 MB of memory and a hard disk with plenty of free space. Windows 95 itself, with the Shell, the Print Manager, and so on, might take up a megabyte of the available memory. On the disk is a word processing program we decide to run. Once loaded, this program occupies 2 megabytes, and we load in a large document that includes several different fonts. Altogether, this document consumes 400K of the remaining megabyte of memory. Now we decide that we need to incorporate a table of numbers in the document. The numbers reside in a spreadsheet, so we have to run the spreadsheet application to cut and paste a copy into our document. Windows 95 obligingly loads the spreadsheet application and its data into the remaining 624K of memory. Well, maybe—if we still used VisiCalc it could. Obviously, this software and data won't all fit into memory at the same time. But from our user point of view, things do work exactly as described. The system and both applications are running, so to us it seems that everything must be in memory. Everything is actually held, not in the available 4 MB of physical memory, but in virtual memory.

Virtual Memory Management

The system's virtual memory is made up of the RAM in the computer and the Windows swap file on the hard disk. The operating system manages this total available memory by swapping program and data segments back and forth between RAM and the swap file. For example, if the instructions in a particular code segment are to be executed, the segment must be loaded into RAM. Other code segments can stay on disk in the swap file until they're needed. A disk data buffer area within a data segment has to be in RAM if the disk transfer is to succeed. Whenever a segment is not held in RAM, the operating system can mark its absence by clearing the present bit in the appropriate segment descriptor. Then, if an access to that segment is attempted, the 386 will generate a *not present interrupt* that notifies the operating system of the problem. The system will arrange to load the missing segment into an available area of RAM and then restart the program that caused the interrupt. All of this swapping and notification is transparent to the application program. It's up to the operating system to carry out these housekeeping activities.

Good Virtual Memory Management

Of course, the art of designing a good virtual memory system revolves around issues such as how much of a program to keep in RAM at any one time and which segments to move from RAM to disk when RAM is full and the system needs space for a new segment. A poor virtual memory manager can slow the system down considerably. Since copying from the disk and copying to the disk are relatively slow operations, the goal of good virtual memory management is to minimize the total number of swap operations. After all, if the operating system is busy swapping, programs aren't running and no useful work is getting done.

The 386 helps things a lot by allowing the implementation of a *paged* virtual memory scheme that allows the operating system to carry out all memory allocation, de-allocation, and swapping operations in units of pages. On the 386, a memory page is 4K and each memory segment is made up of one or more 4K pages. (Small page sizes are generally more efficient because many programs exhibit a trait called *locality of reference*. For example, a program might repeatedly execute only a few instructions to scan through a text file searching for a particular string of characters. Allocating a single page for the program's code and a single page for a data buffer could satisfy this program's memory requirements for several seconds, even though the program is, in total, much larger.) Windows 95 implements such a paged virtual memory system. You'll often run across the words *paging, page file*, and *page fault* in descriptions of memory management operations. These terms are essentially identical to the *swapping, swap file*, and *not present interrupt* terms used in the earlier description of virtual memory management.

As you can see if you study the 386 segment descriptor format in Figure 2-5, there appears to be no way to allocate memory in units as small as a 4K page without wasting a lot of the memory. The trick is in the interpretation of the address once the operating system enables paging. During initialization, the operating system will first switch the processor into protected mode and then enable paging operation. Once enabled, paging stays on until the system shuts down. With paging enabled, the 386 alters the interpretation of the 32-bit address first obtained by adding the base address from the descriptor to the offset generated by the program. Figure 2-6 illustrates the splitting of this 32-bit quantity into three parts. The top 10 bits (31 .. 22) are an index into a page table directory. Part of each 32-bit quantity in a page table directory points to a page table. The next 10 bits of the original address (21 .. 12) are an index into the particular page table. Part of each page table

32-bit linear address

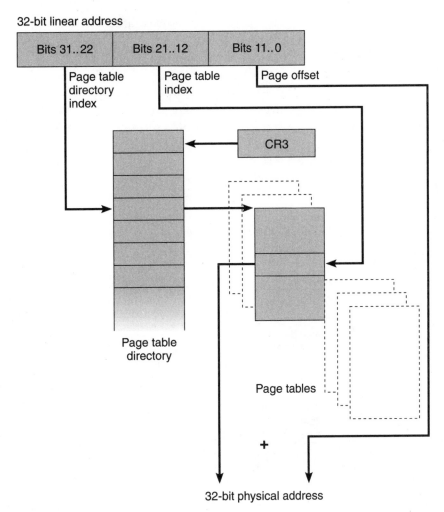

Figure 2-6.
80386 paged virtual memory address decoding.

entry points (finally) to a page of physical memory, and the remaining 12 bits of the original address (11 .. 0) make up an offset within this page of memory. The operating system anchors the entire structure by storing the address (for once, a physical address) of the page table directory for the current program in a special processor register called *CR3*. Each time the operating system switches tasks, it can reload *CR3* to point to the page directory for the new program. Although it sounds laborious, the whole address decoding process takes place at lightning speed within the chip itself. Memory caching techniques ensure that frequently used page table entries are available with no additional memory references.[8]

To fully support the virtual memory scheme, page table entries contain more than just the address of where to find the next link in the chain. Figure 2-7 shows the contents of a single 32-bit word in both the page table directory and page table entry structures. The page table directory and each page table consume one 4K memory page (1024 entries in each). If you care to do the math, you'll see that this allows the entire 4 GB of a program's address space to be properly addressed. However, look at the numbers: a page table directory that points to 1024 page tables could mean that the system has to use 4 MB of memory (1024 page tables, each 4K in size) simply to store the page tables. Fortunately, the flag bits in the page table directory allow the system to store the page tables themselves on disk in the paging file. Thus, if you run a very large program (for example, a 1-GB program, which will need 256 page table pages), the system will swap page tables as well as program code and data pages in and out of memory.

Page table directory entry

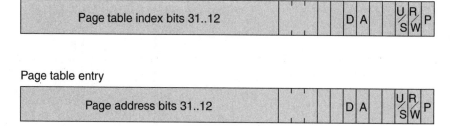

Page table entry

Figure 2-7.
80386 page table directory entry and page table entry formats.

To fully support the virtual memory operations and the 386 memory protection system, the page directory and page table entries include a number of flag bits. The processor itself modifies some of these flags directly. The operating system manages others. Let's look at a few of these fields in detail.

---

8. Intel's experiments indicate that the required page table entry is found in the cache more than 98 percent of the time.

D Bit   Whenever a program modifies the contents of a memory page, the processor sets the corresponding page table *dirty* bit. This tells the operating system that if it wants to remove the page from memory to free up space, then it must first write the page out to disk to preserve the modifications.

A Bit   Any reference—read, write, or execute—to a page causes the processor to set the *accessed* bit in the corresponding page table entry. The virtual memory manager can use this flag to figure out whether it's wise to remove a particular page from memory. A page with the access bit clear for the last 10 seconds, for example, has never been accessed. Removing that page from memory is probably a better choice than removing a page that was definitely in use during the same time period. Windows 95 uses a standard algorithm known as *least recently used (LRU)* to determine which page to remove from memory. The more recently used a page, the less likely it is to be re-allocated.

P Bit   The *present* bit is set to 1 only when the page table or memory page addressed by the table entry is actually present in memory. If a program tries to reference a page or page table that is not present, the processor generates a not-present interrupt and the operating system must arrange to load the page into memory and restart the program that needed the page.

U/S Bit   The *user/supervisor* bit is part of the 386's overall protection system. If the U/S bit is set to 0, the memory page is a supervisor page—that is, it is part of the memory of the operating system itself—and no user-level programs can access the page. Any attempted access causes an interrupt that the operating system must deal with. In Windows 95, as in earlier versions of Windows, this illegal memory reference might lead to one of the now infamous *General Protection Fault* messages. Since any such access attempt is the direct result of a bug in the application program, it's hard to know what else to do with the offending program.

R/W Bit   The *read/write* bit determines whether a program that is granted access to the corresponding memory page can modify the contents of the page. A value of 1 allows page content modification. A value of 0 prevents any program from modifying the data in the page. Normally, pages containing program code are set up as read-only pages.

Mixing 286 and 386 Programs

As we have seen, the 286 and 386 processors interpret the contents of their internal registers and the resultant memory addresses in very different ways. Nearly every Windows application program to date has been written and compiled as a 16-bit program—meaning that it uses the instructions and memory addressing operations of the 286 processor. One of the major improvements in Windows 95 is its support for 32-bit programs that use the instructions and memory addressing operations of the 386 processor. Windows 95 itself is a mixture of 16-bit and 32-bit code. Mixing the two programming models efficiently is a major development challenge.

The major problem is allowing 32-bit code to make calls to 16-bit code and vice versa. Since the memory address formats are completely different—32-bit base address and 32-bit offset vs.16-bit segment register and 16-bit offset—simply jumping between 32-bit and 16-bit code is insufficient: the memory address format must also be changed.

To mediate between the two models, Microsoft developed a technique it calls *thunking*. A *thunk* is a short sequence of instructions responsible for converting the memory addresses from one format to the other. For example, when a 32-bit application makes a call to a Windows User function, the Windows kernel accepts the call and its 32-bit parameters and then calls a thunk. The thunk translates the parameters and addresses to 16-bit equivalents and then calls the 16-bit User routine.[9]

The efficient operation of the *thunk layer,* as it's called, is critical to the performance of Windows 95. In Chapter 4, we'll look at exactly how Windows 95 uses its thunk layer.

The Protection System

Any modern operating system must offer protection capabilities: protection of the user's data, protection of one program from others running concurrently in the system, and protection of physical devices from unauthorized access. Windows 95 harnesses all of the 386's protection facilities to deliver these capabilities.

---

9. User is one of the Windows 95 components still implemented as 16-bit code. Compatibility issues coupled with the project schedule were the principal reasons that User didn't get translated to 32-bit code.

Memory Protection

We've already seen some aspects of the 386 protection mechanism that relate specifically to memory protection:

- The provision for the operating system to set up page tables that describe exactly the areas of physical memory a program can access

- The read/write page table entry flag that prevents a program from modifying the contents of a read-only page or a program code page

- The user/supervisor flag that allows the operating system to protect all of its own memory from any access by an application

Whenever an application tries to access a memory location that is not within its current memory map, the 386 processor generates an interrupt and hands the operating system a collection of information about the problem. In a couple of cases, the memory reference will actually be quite legal and the operating system must arrange to add the appropriate memory page to the application's memory map. For example, a function call within the application can push onto the program stack parameters whose requirements exceed the memory currently allocated to the application. The operating system responds by arranging to add pages to the application's stack space and then restarts the application as if nothing had happened. With applications for Windows, there are also cases in which the operating system would like to allocate more memory to an application but has simply run out.[10] Sometimes the user sees a dialog box that says system resources are too low to continue, and sometimes the application simply fails. Windows 95 reduces the likelihood of this type of problem by greatly expanding the number of available operating system resources. Essentially all system resource requests are now satisfied by the operating system's allocating memory from a 32-bit protected mode memory pool.

In still other cases, an invalid memory reference message might indicate some sort of software problem—an application's incorrectly trying to access memory past the end of one of its data structures, for instance—and the system would have no choice but to terminate the

---

10. The most common case of this, under Windows 3.0 and 3.1, is exhaustion of the 64K GDI heap space.

offending program. Those of you who have used earlier versions of Windows will, no doubt, have seen enough *Unrecoverable Application Error* and *General Protection Fault* dialogs to be familiar with the handling of such a situation.[11] Fortunately, the quality of Windows development tools and application testing has now reached a level that makes this type of error rare.

Operating System Protection

There is more to protection than memory management. There has to be a way to prevent applications from maliciously or inadvertently corrupting the operation of the system. The several special 386 instructions that deal specifically with task switching, interrupt handling, and other system management issues are cases in point. Clearly, the Windows 95 kernel has to be the only software able to perform these operations. If an application could interfere with these delicate operations, mayhem would be bound to ensue. The 386 provides for this protection requirement by maintaining as many as four processor *privilege levels*.

Software running with privilege level zero can do anything it wants to: change page tables, switch processor modes, turn paging on and off, halt the processor, and so on. The Windows 95 operating system executes with privilege levels zero and three. Applications run only with privilege level three and are subject to its several restrictions. A program with privilege level three that tries to execute any of the privileged instructions—specifically the task switching, interrupt handling, and system management instructions mentioned earlier—will cause the processor to generate an interrupt. The operating system will retrieve the interrupt information and will, most likely, terminate the offending program.

The 386 has some complex mechanisms for managing software running at any of the four privilege levels. You'll hear the phrase "running at ring three," for example, meaning that the processor privilege level is set to three for the program in question. The more privileged

---

11. In fact, most UAEs under Windows 3.0 came from an application's making Windows function calls using incorrect parameters. By the time the system would figure this out, it would have no choice but to terminate the offending program. Windows 3.1 added parameter validation. An application's passing illegal parameters to the system resulted in an immediate return of an error to the application. Some applications couldn't handle the error return and failed in strange ways.

the software is (that is, the lower its privilege level), the more it can do to affect the operation of the system or of other programs running under the system.

There has to be some controlled way for the processor to switch between privilege levels—when an application program calls an operating system service, for example, or when a hardware interrupt causes a device driver to execute. The 386 provides for this switching by means of a *gate,* a specialized descriptor table entry that allows control transfers to occur between rings. There are actually four different types of gate: *call, interrupt, task,* and *trap.* A call to the operating system, a hardware interrupt, or an error condition such as a protection fault causes an entry to ring zero code via a gate. As processing is en route to a more privileged execution level, a new instruction pointer and stack pointer come into use and some sensitive data is stored in a protected area of memory. The corresponding return to a less privileged level restores the context of the less privileged code. Since it is the operating system that sets up the gates originally, the operating system remains in control of what happens during these transitions—ensuring that system integrity isn't compromised.

Device Protection

The device protection issue revolves around correctly sharing a resource, such as the hard disk, or preventing two programs from both trying to use a nonshareable device, such as a COM port, at the same time. Windows 95 handles a lot of the device management issues itself, but the 386 also has a significant part to play.

Low-Level Device Access

At the basic hardware level, a program controls all input/output operations by manipulating the processor's *I/O ports* and *interrupt requests* (usually referred to as *IRQs*). You've probably installed in your PC adapters whose documentation refers to their use of specific I/O addresses and IRQs. Adding a third serial port (the COM3 device) to a system usually involves much frustrating effort to prevent conflicts between the third COM port and the existing COM ports. The conflicts in question are those between the I/O addresses and the IRQ. Unless you set up the third COM device with a unique I/O address and IRQ, the controlling software can't determine which device it needs to take care of when an I/O request is made.

From the inside looking out, the I/O ports appear to be similar to a memory address. There are a total of 65,536 (64K) possible I/O ports on the 386, though the majority of them are never used. Programs control devices by reading from and writing to the appropriate I/O ports by means of special instructions. In the case of a COM device, placing a byte of data in the appropriate I/O port will cause the data to be sent down the attached wire. An interrupt manifests itself as a temporary pause in the processor's current activity, coupled with the execution of a piece of software that has been specifically set up to be responsible for dealing with the interrupt. When a hardware interrupt occurs, the 386 arranges an orderly suspension of the current program and then begins execution of some other code from within the operating system. A device generally initiates an interrupt whenever it needs attention—when a data transfer has been completed, for example. The processor and associated hardware take care of generating interrupt signals and moving bytes in and out of the I/O ports. The operating system is responsible for installing and configuring the various routines that manage the data transfer process and other housekeeping activities.

High-Level Device Access

Windows 95 and most other operating systems control peripherals by means of *device drivers*. These software modules control all aspects of a device's operation—moving data to and from memory buffers, handling interrupt requests, and so on. An application requests access to a device by making a device open call to the operating system. If the call is successful, the application can then read and write data with a further series of system calls and, finally, close the device. This holds true whether the device is a single resource such as a COM port or a shared resource such as the hard disk. In the case of the hard disk, the open request is obviously for a file on the disk rather than for the disk itself. In this ordered world, device management is relatively easy and the system concerns itself most with the efficiency of the I/O operations. All these application requests are defined as part of the Windows API. The operating system validates the API calls, hands them to the appropriate device driver, and assists in error management and task scheduling.

Unfortunately, it isn't that easy when you want to run MS-DOS applications concurrently with Windows applications. In particular, many MS-DOS applications believe that they are in total control of the system. They don't try to account for other applications that might be running simultaneously with them, and they may try to access device hardware directly. For example, most terminal emulation programs will manipulate the COM port I/O addresses without making any operating system requests. This direct access leads to a number of problems on a Windows 95 system when you want to allow simultaneous execution of more than one MS-DOS application:

■ Two applications could try to access the same device at the same time. There has to be some way to prevent this conflict.

■ Typically, a 386 program that controls a device directly is running at ring zero. If Windows 95 allowed an application to do this, that application would have access to other privileged system resources. To protect other programs, such privileged execution must be avoided.

■ A program that believes it is in sole control of the system might sit forever in a loop waiting for something to happen— a key depression or a character from a COM port, for example. If no other program can run at the same time, the performance of the whole system sinks to nothing. This kind of dominance has to be prevented.

Using the 80386 Device Protection Capabilities

Windows 95 uses a whole range of tricks to avoid these device access problems while still allowing older MS-DOS programs to run without modification. And the 386 provides one hardware feature crucial to the successful implementation of this MS-DOS program support: the I/O permission bitmap, a hardware mechanism that allows Windows 95 to manage device access for every program running on the system.

Whenever Windows 95 starts a new application, it determines whether the application is a Windows application or an MS-DOS application. Windows applications all use operating system APIs to access files and devices, so each Windows application runs at ring three and has no permission to access any device directly. A Windows application will request access to all devices by means of API calls. If the Windows application does try to access a device I/O port, the 386 will signal a protection fault to the operating system and Windows 95 will terminate the offending application. Each time the user starts an MS-DOS application from the Windows 95 shell, the application will be set up to run in virtual 8086 mode in a new *virtual machine* (VM). Windows 95 must account for the possibility that the MS-DOS application might try to directly access any of the hardware devices attached to the system. To accommodate that possibility, Windows 95 sets up an I/O permission bitmap for each VM. The bitmap is an array of flags, one flag for each of the 386's I/O ports, that specifies whether the application can access the I/O port directly. If no access is granted—the normal case—the 386 signals a general protection fault whenever the application refers directly to the I/O port. For an MS-DOS application, a direct access attempt is not necessarily a program error, as it is for a Windows application. For example, a communications application will access the I/O ports for the COM device directly. For the application to run correctly, Windows 95 must allow this I/O port access to happen—assuming that some other program is not already in control of the same COM port. This whole treatment of virtual machine management and direct device control—referred to as *device virtualization*—is a key element of Windows 95. The most important aspect of device virtualization to note here is that the 386 provides the hardware facility for selectively protecting the I/O ports on an individual, program-by-program basis and informing the operating system each time a direct access occurs.

Virtual 8086 Mode

Without the virtual 8086 feature (most often called simply *virtual mode*), running MS-DOS applications under Windows 95 would be as difficult and error-prone as running them under OS/2 or Windows on the 286 processor. If you used earlier versions of either OS/2 or Windows on 286 systems, you'll remember both the errors and the major limitation: only one MS-DOS program could run at any one time. Clearly, I/O permission handling is a key requirement of the 386's virtual 8086 mode. A few other issues are important in Windows 95 running in virtual mode.

Virtual 8086 mode is an inherent part of the protected mode architecture of the 386. Programs running in virtual 8086 mode are running in protected mode. On the 286, MS-DOS programs didn't have a virtual mode (protected mode) to run under. To run an MS-DOS program on the 286, there was no choice but to run the processor in real mode. Real mode provided absolutely no memory and device protection, and what's more, the MS-DOS program had to occupy the first megabyte of the system's address space. The 386 solved all of these problems:

- Virtual 8086 mode execution remains subject to all the 386 memory and device protection rules. The operating system has control over the resources it allocates to the virtual mode program. The 386 reports to the operating system any attempted access to resources outside the allocated set.

- The operating system can load virtual mode programs anywhere in memory. The 386 translates virtual mode addresses using the 386 protected mode rules. All of the 386's paging capabilities are in play in virtual mode, so virtual mode programs running on the 386 can be swapped just as other protected mode programs can be.

- Unlike running an MS-DOS program on the 286 by means of a switch to real mode, running a virtual mode program on the 386 doesn't require a lengthy mode switch operation. Task switching between a Windows application and an MS-DOS application on the 386 is much faster than it was on the 286.

Setting up a virtual mode program on the 386 is straightforward. Once the program is loaded, the operating system simply identifies it as a virtual mode program by setting a single flag in one of the 386's control registers. The 386 then imposes the rules of 8086 program execution on the virtual mode program. Specifically, registers are 16 bits only (not 32 bits) and addresses are 20-bit values generated exactly as they would be on an 8086. Of course, this is only half the story. Emulating an 8086 processor is one thing. Emulating an entire PC, including MS-DOS, is entirely another. That problem has been passed along to Windows 95 to solve.

Conclusion

The Intel microprocessor has accumulated enormous capability since its simple beginnings with the introduction of the 8080 in 1974. In a scant twenty years, the microprocessor has matched or surpassed the capabilities of any mainframe processor costing thousands of times more. Along the way, the designers at Intel have had the good fortune to be able to learn from one failed experiment in protected mode—the 80286—and get it right the next time. The 80386 architecture, particularly its support of virtual 8086 mode within a paged virtual memory scheme, has proved to be the right platform for building today's advanced 32-bit operating systems. The successor processors, the 80486 and the Pentium, have adopted the same basic architecture without change, and it's a sure bet that successors to the Pentium will do the same.

Windows 95 takes full advantage of all of the 386's capabilities. There's a lot going on under the hood when you run applications on Windows 95. Fortunately, neither the user nor the application programmer has to pay much attention to Windows 95's system and program management activities. This is as it should be.

That was the basics of how the hardware works. Now for the software. It's time to look at Windows itself.

CHAPTER THREE

A TOUR OF CHICAGO

In this chapter, we're going to take a tour through Windows 95—looking briefly at the structure of the system and the associated terminology. You may know Windows intimately already, in which case there'll be sections of this chapter that you'll skip through quickly. Chapter Four is where the detailed examination of Windows 95 begins. The goal for this chapter is to give you a sufficient grounding in the Windows system so that you can approach the new material in Chapter Four with ease. Although a lot of the information in this chapter is common to both Windows 3.1 and Windows 95, it will be Windows 95 that we dissect. Even if you've spent the last few years disassembling the several versions of Windows, you may want to flip through this chapter to make sure that my terminology matches yours and to get a quick overview of the structure of Windows 95.

Here's what we're going to look at in this chapter:

- The structure of the Windows system, including the graphical components of Windows and the system's support for Windows applications and MS-DOS virtual machines

- The Windows multitasking model

- The elements of the Windows user interface

- Some aspects of Windows application programs

System Overview

Over the course of successive version releases, Windows has grown from its original role as a graphical extension to MS-DOS to encompass many of the functions of a full operating system. From its very first release, Windows handled program loading functions. With Windows 95, the transformation is complete. Windows is now a complete operating system with MS-DOS compatibility built in. The Windows 95 "single application mode" allows you to run MS-DOS as a fallback operating system if you want to run an application that can't function under Windows.

Figure 3-1 shows a block diagram view of the major components of Windows 95. Let's look at these components in a little more detail.

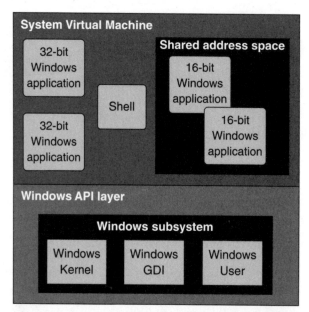

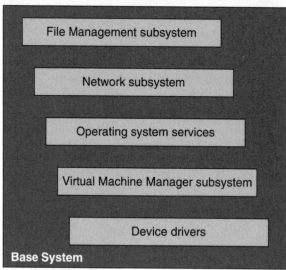

Figure 3-1.
Windows 95 system architecture.

The **System Virtual Machine** (or simply *System VM*) is the name given to the environment in Windows 95 that supports all the Windows applications and the Windows subsystem components such as the Graphics Device Interface (GDI).

32-bit Windows applications are the new Windows applications that use the 32-bit memory model of the 80386 processor and a subset of Microsoft's Win32 application programming interface (API). In Windows 95, each of these so called *Win32 applications* has a private address space that's inaccessible to other applications. 32-bit applications can be preemptively scheduled by Windows 95.

The **Shell** is a 32-bit Windows application that provides the essential user interface to the system. The Shell in Windows 95 consolidates the functions of the Windows 3.1 Program Manager, File Manager, and Task Manager utilities into a single application.

16-bit Windows applications are the "older" Windows applications, the ones you use on Windows 3.1 today. These applications use the segmented memory model of the Intel processor family—really an 80286 memory model. As in Windows 3.1, the 16-bit applications running under Windows 95 share a single address space and can't be scheduled preemptively. You'll hear Microsoft refer to these applications as *Win16 applications.*

The **application programming interface layer** in Windows 95 provides full compatibility with the existing Windows 3.1 API as well as support for the new 32-bit API accessible only to 32-bit Windows applications. The 32-bit API is a subset of Microsoft's full Win32 API first seen in Windows NT and in the Win32s add-on for Windows 3.1.

The **Windows Kernel** supports the lower-level services required by Windows applications, such as dynamic memory allocation. For Windows 95, the Kernel provides these services to both 16-bit and 32-bit applications.

GDI is the core of Windows' graphical capabilities, supporting the fonts, drawing primitives, and color management for both display and printer devices. Although GDI in Windows 95 continues to support existing 16-bit applications, it includes significant new features available only to 32-bit programs.

User is the window manager—the Windows 95 component that manages the creation and manipulation of on-screen windows, dialogs, buttons, and other elements of the Windows interface.

MS-DOS Virtual Machines support the execution of MS-DOS applications under Windows. As in Windows 3.1, the user can run multiple MS-DOS VMs concurrently. Windows 95 includes several new features designed to improve the user's management of these VMs, but the basic design for MS-DOS VM support hasn't changed a great deal.

The Base System

The remaining modules implement various aspects of the underlying operating system in Windows 95. The collection of these components is usually referred to as the *base system*.

File management has changed dramatically in Windows 95. In Windows 3.1, it's MS-DOS that controls the local hard disk filesystem. This MS-DOS control impaired the performance of Windows, and the opportunity to improve filesystem support didn't really exist while MS-DOS remained in control. Under Windows 95, the situation is entirely different. Notably, MS-DOS is no longer used for the management of files on local disks.[1] The new file management subsystem provides a series of interfaces that allows all local disk filesystems (including the CD ROM filesystem) and multiple network filesystems to coexist.

The **network subsystem** is the latest incarnation of Microsoft's peer-to-peer network first seen in the Windows for Workgroups product in 1992 and later seen in Windows NT.[2] The network subsystem uses the new file management subsystem to coordinate its access to remote files. Other network suppliers can also plug their products into the new file management services, allowing a user to simultaneously access more than one type of host network. Windows provides built-in support for SMB, Novell, and TCP/IP protocols.

---

1. As we noted in Chapter 1, there may yet be a version of MS-DOS that also includes the new filesystem capabilities. But it won't be the MS-DOS we're familiar with.

2. As of July 1994, it isn't clear how Microsoft will package the Windows 95 networking features. They might all be in the same box as Windows 95, or they might not.

Operating system services in Windows 95 include major components such as the Plug and Play hardware configuration subsystem as well as a miscellaneous collection of functions such as those that fulfill date and time of day requests.

The **Virtual Machine Manager** is the heart of the Windows 95 operating system. It includes software to implement all the basic system primitives for task scheduling, virtual memory operations, program loading and termination, and intertask communication.

Device drivers in Windows 95 can come in a number of different forms—real mode drivers and so called virtual drivers, or VxDs, among others. Some systems may still require the use of older real mode MS-DOS device drivers to support particular hardware devices, but one of the development goals for Windows 95 has been to develop protected mode drivers for as many popular devices as possible, including new protected mode drivers for the mouse, CD ROM devices, and many hard disk devices.

Virtual device drivers, or **VxDs,** take on the role of sharing a single hardware device among several applications. For example, running two MS-DOS applications in separate screen windows requires the system to create two MS-DOS VMs each of which wants access to the single physical screen. The screen driver VxD has to support this sharing requirement. "VxD" is also used as a general descriptor for other 32-bit operating system modules.[3]

Windows and Modes

You may never have run Windows on anything other than a 386-based system with a decent amount of memory—in which case, you've probably only ever used Windows in its *enhanced mode*. Operationally speaking, this meant that Windows used all the capabilities of your 386 processor, including demand paging and virtual 8086 mode. If your history with Windows goes back further, to 286- and even 8088-based systems, you will have heard the terms *real mode* and *standard mode* applied to Windows. If you knew those terms then, forget them now. Windows 95 operates only in enhanced mode. In fact, there is no longer a term "mode" for Windows.[4]

---

3. "VxD" actually stands for "Virtual anything Driver."

4. With Windows 95, support for the EGA as a display adapter also disappears. A Windows capable machine now requires at least a 386SX processor, 4 MB of memory, and a VGA.

Virtual Machines

The word "virtual" appears everywhere as a qualifier for terms in Windows 95.[5] Indeed, the provision of a virtualized environment for the execution of application programs is a key to many of the capabilities of Windows 95. The most important of the "virtual" features is undoubtedly the support for the *virtual machines* that host the running programs, so it's important to understand both the associated terminology and the technical basis for Windows virtual machines.

It's easy to get confused about virtual machines. Intel uses the term *virtual 8086 machine* to describe the use of the virtual 8086 processor mode to emulate an Intel 8086 processor on the 80386. This virtual 8086 machine includes the 1-megabyte address space, the CPU registers, and the I/O ports. A *Windows virtual machine* (usually called simply a *Windows VM*) refers to a *context* for the execution of an application program. A VM context includes the application's map of addressable memory and the contents of the hardware registers as well as the Windows resources allocated to the application. Because under Windows 3.1 every Windows VM runs at least part of the time in the hardware virtual 8086 mode (which is still a protected mode), there are abundant possibilities for misunderstanding. Many books and articles about Windows fail to distinguish among the many possibilities when they use the term "virtual." A Windows VM is not the same as an Intel virtual 8086 machine. Here's what's important about Windows VMs:

- Windows VMs are either *MS-DOS VMs,* each of which runs a single MS-DOS session, or a *System VM* that provides the execution context for all Windows applications.

- The System VM runs in protected mode all the time. Under Windows 3.1, there comes a point at which the System VM switches from protected mode to virtual 8086 mode so that MS-DOS code can run. This very rarely happens in Windows 95.

- Windows uses virtual 8086 mode to run MS-DOS applications. The system uses the processor's virtual 8086 mode to erect a controllable shield around code that would otherwise need to execute in real mode.

---

5. The marketing slogan chosen for the original introduction of Windows/386 was "Virtually Everything." It's a tagline that still seems to be appropriate.

- Windows applications on Windows 95 never use virtual 8086 mode. They execute in protected mode all the way down to the bare hardware.[6]

- An MS-DOS VM is a Windows VM running an MS-DOS application in virtual 8086 mode.

- Notwithstanding their association with virtual 8086 mode, MS-DOS VMs can run in 32-bit protected mode under Windows with the mediation of a DOS extender that conforms to the DPMI interface. When an MS-DOS VM switches to protected mode, it's no longer running in the processor's virtual 8086 mode, but Windows still considers it to be an MS-DOS VM. (This is a subtlety that's rarely recognized.)

To make things potentially more confusing, the word "virtual" is also used in talk about memory addresses. In Chapter Two, we looked at the details of how the 386 translates virtual addresses, generated by an individual program, to physical addresses that reference actual memory locations. Software running in any Windows VM always generates virtual addresses. The system itself uses virtual addresses. The only time that physical addresses come into play is when the memory management subsystem sets up the processor's page tables to provide the mapping between virtual and physical addresses.

- At least in this book, "address" and "virtual address" are synonymous. The term "physical address" will mean exactly that.

- An MS-DOS VM usually has an address space covering addresses from 0 to 1 megabyte. This is a virtual address space. The system maps this virtual address to its chosen set of physical addresses using the 386's virtual memory capabilities. The pages of the virtual address space could be widely scattered in physical memory.

- The System VM can have a much larger virtual address space than an MS-DOS VM running in virtual 8086 mode. Applications running in the System VM run in protected mode and can make use of this large virtual address space.

---

6. This isn't strictly true since Windows 95 still runs MS-DOS device drivers in virtual 8086 mode if there's no protected mode driver available. But real mode drivers are an endangered species.

Windows Virtual Machines

Regardless of whether it's an MS-DOS VM or the System VM that contains all the Windows applications, you define the capabilities and current context of a virtual machine by looking at the resources allocated to it. Each VM has to include the following:

- A memory map that defines the virtual memory accessible to the currently executing code within the virtual machine.

- An execution context, defined by the state of the VM's registers (the directly accessible CPU registers as well as other controlling factors such as the CPU privilege level).

- A set of resources accessible to the application running within the VM. Within the System VM, every Windows application accesses resources using the Windows API. In an MS-DOS VM, an application uses the MS-DOS software interrupt (INT) interface and may also try to access the hardware directly.

The virtual machine environment of Windows 95 remains heavily reliant on the underlying capabilities of the 386. The 386 dependence offers advantages:

- The virtual memory allocated to each VM is separated from the virtual memory allocated to other VMs. Each MS-DOS VM runs in a private address space, unable to interfere with applications running in other MS-DOS VMs or in the System VM.

- The memory and I/O port protection capabilities of the 386 allow every device on the system to be completely protected. Any MS-DOS application can run, convinced that it has the whole machine to itself and ignorant of the fact that it might actually be sharing the host system with other MS-DOS VMs or Windows applications.

Initialization

During initialization, the operating system sets up the System VM and prepares the *global context* for all MS-DOS VMs. Under Windows 3.1, this is essentially a snapshot of MS-DOS just at the point at which the user types the *win* command. Subsequently, whenever the system creates a new MS-DOS VM, this global context is used as the basis for the new

VM's context. The snapshot includes all TSRs, environment variables, and so on. Windows 95 is subtly different from Windows 3.1 during this initialization phase. With Windows 3.1, it's up to the user to enter the *win* command and start the initialization of the Windows system. Windows 95 immediately gains control and switches to protected mode to complete the initialization process after loading—no *win* command is needed. In either case, when Windows switches to protected mode, it pushes the real mode code aside and takes control of the machine. Windows 95 still processes the CONFIG.SYS and AUTOEXEC.BAT files if they exist, so the user can still customize the global MS-DOS context by including commands in these two files.

The System Virtual Machine

The context for the System VM is a protected mode environment in which all the Windows applications run, together with the major components of the Windows graphical subsystem. The interface between any application and Windows is by means of one of hundreds of *application programming interface (API)* functions.[7] This type of interface allows applications to request system services using named function calls rather than the numbered software interrupt scheme used in MS-DOS applications. The linkage between a Windows application and the functions in the Windows subsystem is made at program load time by means of a technique called *dynamic linking*.

Windows 95 introduces support for a new class of applications: the 32-bit applications that use the Windows 95 subset of Microsoft's Win32 API. These 32-bit applications run within the System VM context, but each has a private protected address space that prevents other applications from accessing its private memory.

Windows 3.1 relies upon cooperative multitasking as the basis for its task scheduling. Under Windows 95, cooperative multitasking is still the basis of task scheduling for the older 16-bit applications. However, the system schedules Win32 applications using a preemptive scheduling algorithm. For the user of a system that runs Win32 applications only, the preemptive scheduling means faster and smoother response when several applications run concurrently.

A Windows program relies on the system to deliver a stream of *messages* to it to inform it of new events—mouse clicks in one of the

---

7. As of early 1994, one rough count had the number of Windows 95 APIs, messages, and macros totaling well over 2000.

application's windows, new programs starting up, and so forth. Under Windows 3.1, the system uses a single queue to hold all the messages that originate within the system. As a result, it's possible for one errant application to choke the flow of messages to all the applications. Windows 95 provides for the system to put messages destined for Win32 applications into private message queues, reducing the possibility of the system's grinding to a halt when one application fails to service the message queue.

Windows 3.1 relies upon MS-DOS for filesystem access. Although this is about the only significant reliance on MS-DOS within Windows 3.1, it is a weak point of the system. This remaining dependence on MS-DOS for filing support creates a whole catalog of problems that the Windows designers have grappled with over the course of several releases. They finally fix the problems in Windows 95 by replacing the MS-DOS filesystem services with a new protected mode subsystem.

All MS-DOS filesystem services are accessed by means of the INT 21H software interrupt. Within the System VM itself, the execution of the INT 21H instruction causes a general protection fault that the operating system catches and handles. Windows 3.1 deals with this fault by arranging for the System VM to switch temporarily to virtual 8086 mode so that the MS-DOS INT 21H code can execute correctly. Once the file operation is completed, the System VM returns to protected mode and the Windows application code continues to execute.

Windows 95 catches the same fault and simply hands it to the protected mode filesystem manager for processing. No switch from protected mode to virtual 8086 mode occurs, and providing there is a protected mode device driver in use for the target device, the System VM context remains a protected mode context throughout the entire operation.

MS-DOS Virtual Machines

An MS-DOS VM is a faithful replication of a PC running MS-DOS. As far as the application is concerned, the VM has a megabyte of memory with a memory map corresponding to the hardware memory map. For example, the directly addressable video display memory is at memory address B8000H. The context for the MS-DOS VM is usually, though not always, a virtual 8086 mode environment with a copy of MS-DOS mapped into the virtual address space of the VM.

Applications in an MS-DOS VM will use the software interrupt services of MS-DOS (predominantly the INT 21H services) to make system requests. Under Windows 95, these requests ultimately pass to the protected mode code that implements the system services. In the case of filesystem requests, the INT 21H call will be passed to the new filesystem manager to be handled together with other concurrent requests from applications running in the System VM.

MS-DOS VMs are set up using a VM that you never see—unless you start poking around with a debugger—and it's a VM that never contains an application that actually runs. This is the VM that is set up with the initial state of the MS-DOS environment once system booting and the processing of CONFIG.SYS and AUTOEXEC.BAT are complete. Within this hidden VM is everything that is global to the MS-DOS environment. For example, if your AUTOEXEC.BAT runs a TSR program before it starts Windows, that TSR program will be loaded and will become part of the global MS-DOS environment. Even under Windows 95, where there's less reliance on MS-DOS, you can still use CONFIG.SYS to load device drivers and AUTOEXEC.BAT to load TSRs as parts of the global MS-DOS environment.

Once this global initialization is complete, Windows needs somewhere to save a snapshot of the MS-DOS environment. It sets up the hidden VM context to be used as the initial state of every MS-DOS VM that's subsequently started. The saved hidden VM itself never runs. Later on, when you start an MS-DOS application from within Windows, the system creates a new MS-DOS VM—meaning that it allocates some memory and the appropriate control blocks within the system—and then copies into the new VM the entire global environment from the hidden VM. This copying means that the initial state of the new MS-DOS VM is exactly the state you'd achieve if you had just turned the machine on and run through the startup procedure again. This copying from the hidden VM also explains why changes that you make in one MS-DOS VM don't affect any of the others—either those already running or new VMs that you run later. To verify this inviolability of the MS-DOS VMS, simply run a few MS-DOS VMs and change the command prompt in each—local changes won't affect the saved global VM context that governs the initial states of all the VMs.

Protected Mode MS-DOS Applications

One complexity that the Windows designers have had to deal with is the fact that MS-DOS applications are not simply real mode applications anymore—they can also run in protected mode. You can trace this wrinkle back to a few years ago when the hunt for more than 640K of memory began in earnest. Expanded memory, extended memory, high memory, and the products that exploited them—such as Quarterdeck's QEMM—became popular resources. For a while, the whole situation was a mess, with various designs jockeying for position as the standard.

One group of vendors sought order by agreeing to the VCPI (Virtual Control Programming Interface) specification. VCPI was pretty good except that it didn't fully support Windows. So after a brief face-off with Microsoft, vendors came up with the DPMI (DOS Protected Mode Interface) specification. Programs that conform to the DPMI specification can run under MS-DOS and Windows and can exploit protected mode on both 286 and 386 systems.

DPMI

The DPMI specification lays out the definition of an MS-DOS software interface that ultimately allows MS-DOS applications to exploit the 32-bit protected mode while running under Windows. DPMI actually allows low-level software components called *DOS extenders* to coexist with Windows. A DOS extender supports the execution of protected mode programs that want to call on MS-DOS for file I/O and other services. The need for the DPMI specification became apparent during the development of Windows 3.0, when Microsoft and other companies embarked on parallel efforts to provide support for 32-bit protected mode program execution. Microsoft's interest was in Windows, since Windows is itself a DOS extender. It was clear that there would be a number of DOS extenders on the market, so vendors developed DPMI as a way of allowing them to coexist. Today you can find DOS extenders in use in several kinds of popular applications that need more than 640K of MS-DOS memory: compilers, database programs, and others. The interfaces to the various DOS extenders are not standardized—the DPMI interface that allows the DOS extenders to coexist with Windows is.

The DPMI–DOS extender exploitation of protected mode is essentially the best way to allow an MS-DOS program to get at more memory and to use 32-bit addressing (as opposed to struggling on with segmented addressing). Windows 3.1 implements DPMI and DOS extender functionality within a single module, so as far as a Windows programmer is concerned, the DPMI and extender services are indivisible. This architecture does allow a user to start MS-DOS VMs that run applications that make use of alternative DOS extenders rather than Windows itself as a DOS extender. In that scenario, Windows provides only the DPMI services.

The DPMI specification defines two software components needed to provide a full implementation. The *DPMI Host,* or *DPMI Server,* is the lowest-level software component responsible for administering the DPMI services. All the DPMI functions are available by means of a call to INT 31H with a function number that identifies the particular DPMI service that's required. These services really are very low level—the allocation of descriptors within the LDT or GDT and the reading and writing of MS-DOS interrupt vectors, for example.

The *DPMI Client* is any program requesting DPMI services, usually the DOS extender. Although it's possible, the DPMI interface is not intended for direct use by application programs. It's up to the client to check for the presence of a DPMI server before any attempt to call the server is made. Most DOS extenders define a private API that allows a modified MS-DOS application to call the extender for protected mode services and to provide MS-DOS services to the application while it executes in protected mode.

Multitasking and Scheduling

One of the more complex Windows activities is its allocation of the processor to multiple programs. For a program to do anything, it has to execute instructions. Since Windows allows you to run several programs at once, there has to be a way of sharing the processor among these programs. Enter multitasking—and with it a great deal of terminology and debate.

Since so much terminology is associated with the subject of multitasking, we'll need to define a few terms in this chapter. Some of the terms are frequently used in both a generic context and a very particularized context. The word *task,* as we'll see, is a classic example. Windows is, generically speaking, a multitasking system, and a Windows 3.1 task is a very precise concept, represented by specific data structures and operational rules.

In the next chapter, we'll look at the details of the Windows 95 multitasking model. In this section, we'll give the subject a general review with a Windows bias.

Multitasking Models

The generic term *multitasking* refers simply to an operating system's ability to share the CPU among several programs. Most operating system designers refer to a program in its running state as a *task,* so you can think of a task as a program loaded into memory and actually doing something. The Windows NT and UNIX worlds both use the term *process* to mean the same thing. Windows 3.1 says *task* and, occasionally, *process*. And lo and behold, the word *process* is the term in favor for Windows 95. The term *task* has been officially removed from the Windows language. The term *process* is therefore what we'll use. Really, you can think of *task* and *process* as synonyms.[8]

As soon as you run Windows 3.1, you're multitasking since you're running the Program Manager and a number of other tasks that are actually part of the system itself rather than programs with visible windows on your screen. Windows 95 is no different in this respect. A few years ago, when observers first began to discuss multitasking operating systems for PCs, you often heard comments to the effect of "I don't need multitasking. I do only one thing at a time anyway." Unfortunately, people rarely understood that a multitasking system could offer features such as background print spooling and network connectivity even if the user only ran Lotus 1-2-3 all day. Nowadays good multitasking is considered to be essential to providing an effective environment for the PC user. Even if you only run Lotus 1-2-3/W all day long, Windows multitasking enables you to manage your network connection, the Print Manager, and your communications session at the same time.

The operating system component that manages the multitasking in both Windows 3.1 and Windows 95 is the *scheduler.* The scheduler deals principally with *time* and *events*. A Windows 95 process gets a *time slice* that determines how long it can use the CPU. At the end of the process's time slice, the scheduler decides whether to let a different process use the CPU.[9] Events influence the scheduler's decisions. To the scheduler, a mouse click is an event that may mean handing the CPU to the process that owns the window in which the mouse click occurred.

---

8. At this point you probably think this discussion is becoming very arcane. Unfortunately, *process* has a precise meaning in Windows and the lack of rigor with respect to such a term in most Windows documentation can generate considerable misunderstanding.

9. Unlike Windows NT, Windows 95 doesn't (and won't) support multiprocessor systems, in which the scheduler has more than one processor to allocate to processes.

Or the scheduler may consider the simultaneous completion of a network data transfer to be an event worthy of more attention than the mouse click. In that case, the process managing the network would get the CPU, and the other process would have to wait.

You'll hear Windows 3.1 described as a *cooperative* multitasking system and Windows NT described as a *preemptive* multitasking system. Cooperation and preemption are process scheduling techniques, and Windows 95 uses both of them, so we have to understand them. Preemptive scheduling puts the operating system in complete control over which process runs next and for how long. At any time, the scheduler can take the CPU away from the current process and hand it to another one. Typically, such a preemptive act will occur in direct response to an event that demands swift attention. The scheduler associates a *priority* with each running process. If an event occurs that is of interest to a high-priority process, the scheduler will preempt the current process and run the high-priority process. The scheduler gets control of the system either when a process surrenders the CPU (it reaches a point at which it's waiting for the user, for example) or when there's a clock interrupt. Most systems will program the clock to tick between 20 and 50 times a second, and the final tick is when the scheduler gains control and can preempt a running process.

Process priorities are recalculated frequently. For example, if the system has to choose between just two processes—one with a low priority and one with a higher priority—the low-priority process will never be able to run if the scheduler doesn't dynamically adjust the priorities. The duration of the time slice plays into the calculation of priorities as well. It makes no sense to continually give the CPU to a process and then preempt the process after it has executed only a few instructions. All that will ever get run is operating system code, not your spreadsheet or compiler.

Cooperative multitasking relies upon application programmers to help keep the system running smoothly. In the cooperative technique, the scheduler can switch processes only when the currently running process surrenders the CPU. If the current process decides to recalculate π to 5000 decimal places, there's nothing the scheduler can do about it. Good programming practice for cooperative multitasking systems dictates that applications should regularly hand the CPU back to the operating system—a technique called *yielding*. An application's yielding allows the scheduler to run a higher-priority process if one is ready. In Windows 3.1, cooperative multitasking is why no amount of mouse clicking will help you when the current application has the hourglass cursor up on screen. The system duly registers all the mouse click events and adds them to the application's message queue, but until the current process surrenders the CPU, the scheduler can't switch away from it and allow another process to handle the new events.

Windows 3.1 is as insistent as it can be about getting applications to yield control of the processor. Essentially, every time an application calls the system, asking to deal with the next event, the system suspends the process and allows the scheduler to reevaluate process priorities. The lack of preemption doesn't make this way of handling the cooperative multitasking problem foolproof, however.

The absence of preemption in Windows 3.1 does make a number of design decisions easier for both operating system developers and application programmers. Neither has to worry about the operating system code's being reentrant, for instance. The system design doesn't have to account for the possibility of process preemption while system code is executing. Suppose, for example, that you run two Windows applications, both of which occasionally use a COM port to dial out and retrieve data from an information service. If one application could be preempted in favor of the other partway through the opening of the COM port, the OS would have to protect itself from the possibility that the second application would also start an open request. With no preemption, the OS doesn't have to worry: the first open request will always run to completion before the other application can run.

Ultimately, though, the lack of preemptive scheduling leads to problems. High-priority events can't be handled rapidly because an application won't relinquish the processor in time, for example; or an application that crashes will lock up the whole system because the operating system will be unable to deliver messages to other applications. MS-DOS itself has to have a nonpreemptive scheduling environment. MS-DOS knew nothing of multiple processes when it was designed, and despite the herculean efforts of many software developers to build multitasking systems on top of MS-DOS, there have always been shortcomings in the resultant products. Windows has been no exception to this nonpreemptive rule. Preempting MS-DOS at the wrong time can lead to disaster, so over the years the Windows designers have had to put up with building most of an operating system on top of a very unsuitable foundation. Windows 95 changes that.

Critical Sections

You'll hear programmers use the term *critical section* when they talk about developing software for any preemptive multitasking system. A critical section is a sequence of instructions executed by more than one process that for one reason or another must not be preempted before it completes execution. An obvious example of a critical section occurs during memory allocation.

Windows, along with most other operating systems, uses derivatives of thirty-year-old algorithms for keeping track of blocks of available memory. (It's not that the algorithms are outdated. It's just that they're as good as they ever need to be.) One particular algorithm in question maintains available memory blocks as a linked list, with a descriptor for each block that identifies its size and location. When Windows tries to satisfy an application's request for memory, it has to unlink the block from the list of available blocks.

At some point during the unlinking procedure, the list data structure is in a mess, with invalid pointers or erroneous flag bits set. If the system were to reschedule right at that point, a different process might initiate a new memory allocation request. Since the first process would not yet be complete, the new process would eventually stumble while trying to manipulate the invalid list data structure and probably crash the whole system. To guard against such a situation, the code manipulating the list maintains a critical section between the entry and exit points of the sensitive instruction sequence. Once the process enters the critical section, the system guarantees that the process will exit the critical section before any other process can enter it. This isn't to say that the system necessarily ignores other processes while a critical section is executing. For example, ignoring hardware interrupts during the execution of a lengthy critical section would be indicative of bad system design. Critical section management does guarantee, though, that once a process has entered a critical section, the system will suspend any other process trying to enter the same section.

The technique of allowing only one process at a time to execute a critical section is sometimes referred to as *mutual exclusion,* and the undesirable situation in which several processes fight to get at a protected resource such as memory by entering the critical section is called *contention.* The Windows Virtual Machine Manager has long supported critical section management for device drivers. Preemptive scheduling means that Windows 95 has to support similar critical section management functions at the API level. The newly improved nature of multitasking and preemption in Windows 95 means that you'll hear more frequently about objects called *mutexes,* or *semaphores,* that are used to control process entry and exit of critical sections.

Processes in Windows

So, amidst a collection of virtual machines and in a system that supports cooperative multitasking, what exactly is a process in Windows 95? It is one of two objects:

- Windows considers each MS-DOS VM to be a single process. Regardless of what's going on inside that VM, to Windows it is only one process.

- Each executing Windows application is also a process. Remember that every Windows application runs within the System VM, so this view of the System VM as containing multiple processes points up another difference between the System VM and an MS-DOS VM.

Under Windows 3.1, all of these processes are described within a system data structure called the *Task Database,* or *TDB* for short. Windows 3.1 actually identifies an MS-DOS VM process by marking the appropriate TDB entry as being the WinOldAp application.[10]

Under Windows 95, the tasking model is considerably more complex. The most important change from the application developer's point of view is the addition of *threads* to the system. Under Windows 95, threads rather than processes are the objects managed by the system scheduler. A thread defines an execution path within a process, and any process can create many threads, each of which shares the memory allocated to the original process. Multiple threads allow a single application to easily manage its own background activities and to offer a highly responsive interface to the user.

Modules

In Windows, the term *module* describes a related collection of code, data, and other resources (such as bitmaps) present in memory. Typically,

---

10. WinOldAp is the name given to the entity that controls a single MS-DOS VM. You'll see the name in various Windows status displays and documentation items.

such a collection will form either a single application program or a dynamic link library. Windows maintains a data structure, known as the *module database,* that identifies all the modules currently active in the system. The module database describes an essentially static collection of objects rather than the dynamic collection referenced by the task database.

Keeping a record of currently loaded modules is important because such record is the basis for the resource sharing supported by Windows. The second time you run the WordPad (née Notepad) application, for example, Windows can see that the code segments and the bitmap that forms the icon are already in use. Rather than loading a second copy and consuming more memory, Windows simply creates additional references to the resources already in use.

During the life of the system, Windows maintains a usage count for each resource. As applications make use of a resource, the system increments the reference count. When the application terminates, the system reduces the reference count. A reference count of 0 is the indication that the resource is no longer in use and that the system can remove the resource and reclaim the memory it occupied.

API Support

The Windows 95 API coverage is, to say the least, extensive. The Windows 95 API includes a subset of Microsoft's Win32 API and provides compatibility by including support for 16-bit Windows applications and MS-DOS applications. Microsoft recommends that 16-bit Windows application development cease with the introduction of Windows 95 and, to encourage developers to make that choice, makes the new capabilities of the Windows 95 system accessible only to 32-bit applications. The mere opportunity to finally abandon the Intel architecture's segmented memory model is likely to be enough reason for most developers to switch. Add in the enhancements available to Win32 applications, and switching becomes a pretty attractive option.

Windows supports its APIs by means of three major components: Kernel, User, and GDI. Kernel incorporates the most operating-system-like functions—memory allocation, process management, and the like. The User module focuses on the window management issues that come up throughout Windows operation: window creation and movement, message handling, dialog box execution, and a myriad of related functions. GDI is the Windows graphics engine, supporting all the line drawing, font scaling, color management, and printing capabilities of the system.

Every Windows application shares the code in these three modules. In Windows 95, Kernel, User, and GDI have each a 16-bit and a 32-bit implementation resident in the system. And a lot of code is shared between, for example, the 16-bit and the 32-bit implementations of GDI. Applications don't have to take any special note of this dual existence, though. The system connects the application with the appropriately sized subsystem.

Each Windows API function is accessible by means of a name—in contrast to the MS-DOS API scheme of numbered interrupts. To get an application to call on one of the services in a Windows subsystem, the programmer simply uses the target function name in the application source code and compiles and links with the appropriate libraries, and the application is ready to run. This sounds normal so far, but if you examine the compiled program, you won't find any code that actually implements a Windows API function. If you're a C programmer, you'll have used the *printf()* function frequently. Poke through the compiled program, and sure enough, you'll find a stream of code and data that implements *printf()*, and the same is true for many other functions.

What you will find if you care to dissect a compiled Windows program is a collection of references to the Windows API functions—references that are necessary if Windows is to be able to load the application correctly. And think about that *printf()* example again—every program has its own copy of the code for *printf()* linked in, whereas the Windows program that calls *GetMessage()* calls the single copy of this function that resides in the User module. So does every other Windows program. In fact, the Kernel, User, and GDI modules are all examples of Windows *dynamic link libraries* (*DLLs* for short). Windows uses DLLs extensively, and the technique that allows an application to call a DLL is *dynamic linking*.

Dynamic Linking

Nowadays it's customary to rely upon the dynamic linking capabilities of the target operating system when preparing an application for execution. Windows and Windows NT have the capabilities, OS/2 has them, and so does UNIX. A compilation and link procedure used to involve the linker in scanning object code libraries and copying large amounts of code and data into the application's executable file. No more. In a dynamic linking environment, the traditional role of the linker is now split between the link step and the program loading step undertaken by the operating system.

The linker still scans a set of libraries. Some of the libraries include runtime support code that ends up in the executable file; others simply contain references to functions that won't be fully resolved until the operating system loads the program. In Windows, such libraries are called *import libraries,* and together they contain a defining reference for each and every Windows API function. The linker scans the import library and embeds in the executable file a target module name and a numeric entry point. If an application calls the Windows *MessageBox()* function, for example, the executable program file will include a reference to the User module entry point number 1. The application's calling the GDI *LineTo()* function will embed a reference to the GDI module entry point number 19. At program load time, it's the operating system's responsibility to replace these references with addresses that are valid for use in function calls. Any module that satisfies these references via dynamic linking is called a dynamic link library. Every DLL declares a set of entry points called *exports* that satisfies the external references.

Much of Windows itself is a collection of DLLs, and the system makes heavy use of the runtime name resolution capabilities to interconnect its various components. For example, printer device drivers support a standard set of entry points. When the GDI module calls a printer driver, it references a function that will be resolved via a runtime dynamic link. Regardless of what type of printer is involved, each printer driver supports the same set of entry points. Rather than relinking the operating system when you install a new printer, you simply replace the file containing the device driver code, and the new driver satisfies the same set of dynamic links. Figure 3-2 shows the first few entries for the dynamic links exported from the Windows 3.1 Hewlett-Packard PCL and PostScript printer drivers.

```
; "DDRV HP LaserJets and compatibles"

HPPCL . 1    DEVBITBLT
HPPCL . 2    COLORINFO
HPPCL . 3    CONTROL
HPPCL . 4    DISABLE
HPPCL . 5    ENABLE
   . . .
```

Figure 3-2.
Dynamic link entry points in printer drivers.

(continued)

Figure 3-2. *continued*

```
; "DDRV PostScript Printer:100,300,300"
;
PSCRIPT . 1          BITBLT
PSCRIPT . 2          COLORINFO
PSCRIPT . 3          CONTROL
PSCRIPT . 4          DISABLE
PSCRIPT . 5          ENABLE
   ...
```

Notice that in each printer driver the names refer to functions within the driver. They could be any valid name. The external reference uses only the module name and the numeric identifier to resolve the dynamic link.

The Windows resource sharing technique also applies to DLLs. It has to—after all, DLLs are built for sharing. Loading unique copies not only is wasteful but also defeats the whole purpose of a DLL.

Support from the Base System

Ultimately, the Windows subsystem has to call on the services of the base system. This might be an explicit request—for example, to open a file. Or it might be an implicit one—for example, there's a page fault and the base system has to set about loading the missing pages from disk. In the case of an MS-DOS VM, the assistance of the base system is needed once the MS-DOS software interrupt executes.

A transition to the operating system code in the base system involves a transition between processor privilege levels. The Windows VMs usually run at ring three; the base system—the most privileged code in Windows—runs at ring zero. Chapter Four looks at the details of the transition to the base system code. The various ways in which it happens all amount to presenting the Virtual Machine Manager with an opportunity to gain control over the transition so that order can be maintained.

The base system code comprises a number of Windows *VxDs*. Although the name *VxD* and the term *virtual device driver* are used interchangeably, a VxD need have nothing to do with any hardware device. A VxD is simply a 32-bit protected mode module running at the processor's most privileged level of execution. Some VxDs do deal with hardware devices, and others supply operating system functionality that doesn't have anything directly to do with devices. The VxD architecture was originally designed as a standardized format for 32-bit protected mode code modules. There is an API, internal to the base system, that VxDs can use.[11] Obviously, the scope of these functions is at a much lower level than the scope of the services called on directly by applications.

Memory Management

Memory management in Windows takes place at two different levels: a level seen by the application programmer and an entirely different view seen by the operating system. Over the course of different releases of Windows, the application programmer has seen little change in the available memory management APIs. Within the system, however, the memory management changes have been dramatic. Originally, Windows was severely constrained by real mode and 1 megabyte of memory. Then expanded memory provided a little breathing room, and currently the use of enhanced mode and extended memory relieves many of the original constraints. Windows 95 goes further yet and essentially removes all the remaining memory constraints.

Windows 95 continues to support all the API functions present in Windows 3.1, and you can still build and run applications that use the segmented addressing scheme of the 286 processor. However, if you look at the detailed documentation for the Windows 95 memory management API, you'll see that all of the API functions originally designed to allow careful management of a segmented address space are now marked "obsolete." The "obsolete" list includes, for example, all the functions related to selector management. The reason, of course, is the Windows 95 support for 32-bit linear memory and the planned obsolescence of the segmented memory functions—yet another unsubtle hint that the Win32 API is the API you should be using to write Windows applications.

Although use of the 32-bit flat memory model simplifies a lot of Windows programming issues, it would be misleading to say that Windows memory management has suddenly gotten easy.[12] Windows 95 actually has a number of new application-level memory management

---

11. The Windows Device Driver Kit is the best reference for detailed information on VxDs and the associated API functions.

12. The Windows 95 documentation lists 45 API functions under the heading "Memory Management." The "obsolete" list numbers 28 API functions.

capabilities. All of the functions relate to the management of memory within the application's *address space,* the private virtual memory allocated to the process. The systemwide management of memory is the responsibility of the base system, and the Windows API aims to hide many of the details of the system's lower-level functions.

Application Virtual Memory

Figure 3-3 illustrates the basic layout of a Win32 application's virtual memory. Every Win32 application has a similar memory map, and each such address space is unique. However, it is still not fully protected: the private memory allocated to one Win32 application can be addressed by another application. The Win32 application's private address space is also the region in which the system allocates memory to satisfy application requests at runtime.

The system address space is used to map the system DLLs into the application's address space. Calls to the system DLLs become calls into this region. Applications can also request the dynamic allocation of memory by means of virtual addresses mapped to the shared region. Having virtual addresses mapped to the shared address space caters to the need for controlled sharing of memory with other applications.

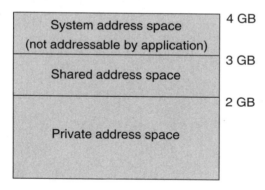

Figure 3-3.
Application virtual memory map.

Requests for memory at runtime fall into one of two categories: the application can make an explicit request for extra memory, or the system can respond to an implicit request for memory—that is, allocate memory to an application as a side effect of allocating some other resource. An implicit request occurs, for example, when an application creates a new window on screen: the system must allocate memory for the data structures used to manage the window. Windows 95 claims memory for resource allocation from a large 32-bit linear region rather than from the restrictive 64K segment used in previous versions of Windows. An ongoing problem in versions through Windows 3.1, running out of memory during resource allocation, has been largely eradicated in Windows 95.

Heap Allocation

In Windows parlance, the term *heap* describes the region of memory used to satisfy application memory allocation requests. In Windows 3.1, the system maintains both a *local heap* and a *global heap*. The local heap is a memory region within the application's address space, and the global heap is a memory region belonging to the system. As an application makes requests for local memory, its address space is adjusted to encompass the newly allocated memory. The system resolves requests for global memory from the same system memory pool used for all applications. It's possible to run out of either or both resources, although the use of a 2-GB address space makes this highly unlikely. Exhaustion of the local heap affects only a single application. Exhaustion of the global heap has systemwide repercussions.

Windows 3.1 programmers have to consider a variety of factors as they decide how to satisfy an application's runtime memory requirements. Windows 3.1 also has a range of API functions for manipulating dynamically allocated segments, and the manipulation of these shifting regions is further complicated by the underlying segmented memory model. It isn't just a chunk of memory that must be allocated. The application also needs a selector so that it can address the memory correctly. Under Windows 95, the Win32 application model does away with all these considerations. Selectors are no longer required—it's simply a 32-bit address that identifies the new memory—and the local and global heaps are merged into a single heap. The API functions that deal with selectors and the manipulation of memory regions in a segmented model all become obsolete.

Windows 95 Application Memory Management

For a Windows programmer, the Win32 API greatly simplifies the most common dynamic memory allocation chores. Furthermore, the increased capability of the underlying 32-bit architecture allowed the Windows designers to add a number of new functions for application memory management.

■ Windows 95 provides functions that support private heaps whereby an application can reserve a part of memory within its own address space. The application can create and use as many private heaps as it wishes and can direct the system to satisfy subsequent memory allocation calls from a specific private heap. An application might use the local heap functions to create several different memory pools that each contain data structures of the same type and size.

■ Windows 95 provides functions that allow an application to reserve a specific region of its own virtual address space that once reserved won't be used to satisfy any other dynamic memory allocation requests. In a multithreaded application, the 32-bit pointer to this reserved region is a simple way to provide each thread with access to the same memory.

■ Memory mapped files allow different applications to share data. An application can open a named file and map a region of the file into its virtual address space. The data in the file is then directly addressable by means of a single 32-bit memory address. Other applications can open the same file, map it into their private address spaces, and reference the same data by means of a single pointer.

System Memory Management

Regardless of changes in the details of application memory management, the Windows programming model has remained pretty consistent through the different product releases. Allocating blocks of memory at runtime, using a reference to a block to manipulate it, and ultimately returning the block to the system for re-use is the way in which Windows programmers have always dealt with dynamic memory requirements. Windows 95 is no different. What has changed, however, is the way in which the system realizes the application's requests for dynamic memory.

Starting with the Windows 3.0 enhanced mode and continuing with the Windows 95 Win32 application model, the Windows API manipulates only the application's virtual address space. This means that an application request for a block of memory will adjust the application's virtual address map but might do absolutely nothing to the system's physical memory. Remember that the 386 deals with physical memory in pages each 4K in size. This page size is reflected in the virtual address space map of every Windows application. If an application requests 100K of memory, for example, its virtual address space will have 25 pages of memory added to it. The system will also adjust the data in its own control structures to reflect the application's new memory map.

However, at the time of allocation, Windows won't do anything to the physical memory in the system. It's only when the application starts to use the memory that the underlying system memory management kicks in and allocates physical memory pages to match the virtual memory references the application makes. If the application allocates but never references a region of its virtual memory space, the system might never allocate any physical memory to match the virtual memory. The ability of the 386 to allow physical memory pages to be used at different times within different virtual address spaces is the basis for the operating system's virtual memory capabilities.

Deep within the system are a range of memory management primitives available to device drivers and other system components that sometimes deal with virtual memory and sometimes force the system to commit actual physical memory pages. But these primitives are specific to the base operating system. Neither applications nor the Windows subsystem knows or cares about physical memory. Applications can force the system to allocate physical memory only by actually using the memory: namely, by reading from and writing to locations within a page. The separation of Windows memory management into the virtual and physical levels is a key aspect of the system. Applications and the Windows subsystems deal with defined APIs and virtual address spaces. The base system deals with physical memory as well as virtual address spaces.

Although physical memory is transparent to an application, its behavior can radically affect the performance of the system. For example, scanning through a two dimensional array of data row by row using C as the programming language will cause memory to be accessed from low to high virtual addresses because C stores two dimensional array data structures in *row major order*. As the memory sweep proceeds, the system will allocate physical memory pages to match the virtual memory accesses. Byte-at-a-time access will cause the system to allocate a new physical page every 4096 references. Other languages—FORTRAN, for example—store two dimensional arrays in *column major order*. Referencing the data row by row will generate memory references to widely scattered memory locations, forcing a much higher frequency of physical page allocation and much-reduced application performance. So, although the programmer doesn't have to worry about matching virtual memory to physical memory, it is a good idea for the programmer to know something about how the underlying system primitives and hardware support the application.

Windows Device Support

The most important aspect of the Windows device driver architecture is its ability to *virtualize* devices. (Yes, it's that word again.) The greatest difference between the device drivers of Windows 95 and Windows 3.1 is the extensive use of protected mode drivers in Windows 95—in fact, it will be unusual if your system uses any real mode drivers at all after you install Windows 95. The use of protected mode for the drivers pays off in terms of both system performance and robustness. The manufacturers of disk devices can adopt a new driver architecture—borrowed from Windows NT—that almost guarantees the availability of a protected mode driver for every hard disk. In addition, new protected mode drivers for CD ROM devices, serial ports, and the mouse make the possibility of needing to support a device with a real mode driver quite remote.

Device Virtualization

The device virtualization capability allows Windows 95 to use the memory and I/O port protection capabilities of the 386 processor to share devices among the different virtual machines. Every MS-DOS VM believes it has full control over its host PC and is unaware of the fact that it might be sharing the screen with other MS-DOS VMs or with the Windows applications running in the System VM. For MS-DOS applications, the display drivers must reside in the lowest level of the operating system. Many MS-DOS applications, particularly those that use the display in a graphics mode or use serial ports, will address the hardware directly. Windows has to intercept all such direct access in order to bring order to a potentially chaotic situation. The MS-DOS application knows nothing of the need to cooperate with other applications and certainly doesn't depend on a system device driver to get the job done. With Windows applications, the system has a slightly easier task since device access is always the result of a Windows API call. Thus, the operating system has control of the entire transaction, and the system components can collaborate as necessary.

You'll sometimes hear Windows device drivers referred to as *virtual device drivers* or even *VDDs*. But most of the time, a Windows device driver is classified as a VxD along with all the other VxDs that perform low-level system functions. Device drivers are written and built just as any other VxD is—usually in assembly language and always with the freedom to access any system data structure or memory location.

Minidrivers

The Windows device driver model has undergone some changes for Windows 95. The *minidriver* architecture first used for Windows 3.1 printer drivers and more recently for Windows NT disk drivers has found its way into the display and disk driver designs for Windows 95.[13] The principal idea of the minidriver design is to provide a single hardware-independent VxD that fulfills most of the necessary driver functions. This VxD interfaces closely with a minidriver whose role is to perform the hardware-dependent functions. Each minidriver consists of a set of the hardware-dependent functions called by the controlling VxD. Windows calls the central VxD, and when necessary, the VxD calls the minidriver.

This design offers a lot of advantages. The basic design tenet is that most drivers for a particular type of device contain roughly the same code. Re-implementing the same code for every slightly different type of device doesn't make a lot of sense—despite the fact that just about every operating system has done just that for years. Reducing the implementation task for a new device to simply developing a new minidriver helps everyone. The device manufacturer doesn't have to invest in writing code that already exists. The user can look forward to much higher quality drivers that are readily available when a new device first appears. Microsoft benefits since they can justify the investment of a lot more effort in the central screen VxD, for example, rather than have the dilution of the effort among drivers for dozens of slightly different VGA devices.

---

13. In Windows NT, disk drivers are actually called *port drivers*.

In the past, a counterargument always insisted that the minidriver model would degrade performance. This argument didn't work when it was applied to printers since the nature of the device makes it very slow in comparison to the processor anyway. Even the worst printer minidriver is probably fast enough to keep a printer fully occupied. Disk device minidrivers do require more attention to performance issues. However, a disk minidriver is a simple piece of code that shouldn't have a negative impact on performance if it's correctly written. Microsoft can provide lots of good examples to device manufacturers to make sure that disk minidrivers come out right. Screen devices are quite a different issue since performance under Windows is so critical. The importance of performance makes the adoption of a minidriver model for screen drivers an interesting design choice. Microsoft's confidence in its new display driver model comes from investing a lot of very talented effort in the central VxD.[14] Of course, it's still possible for a manufacturer to ignore the minidriver architecture and implement a device driver that bypasses the minidriver architecture. The manufacturer still has this option for supporting unusual devices or squeezing the last cycle of performance out of the device.

The Windows Interface

Let's review the major elements of the Windows user interface in preparation for an introduction in Chapter Five to the rather dramatic changes to be seen in Windows 95. If you're a Windows programmer, you're already intimately familiar with the user interface terms and the various user interface components. If you use Windows extensively, you've seen and used all of the major interface elements. However, while clicking your way quite happily through a complex dialog box, you may not have thought too hard about all the different elements that make up the dialog box.

What Is a Window?

Take a look at the Windows 3.1 screen shot in Figure 3-4. It's one of the more commonly used dialog boxes in Microsoft Word for Windows. You see it every time you print a document.

---

14. "World's fastest flat frame buffer device driver" is one claim. We'll see.

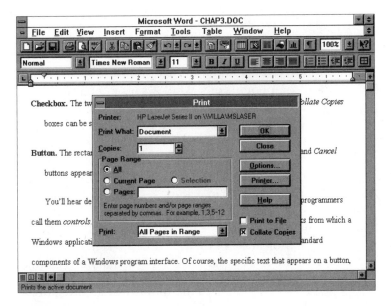

Figure 3-4.
Windows, windows, windows...

This dialog box actually contains several of the most common items used in dialog boxes—specifically:

Drop-down list box. The box to the right of *Print:*. Clicking on the arrow causes a list of items to appear from which the user can make a single choice.

Spin box. The box to the right of *Copies:*. Clicking the up and down arrows changes the numeric value in the box.

Radio buttons. The round buttons inside the *Range* box. The user can select just one of the *All, Current Page*, and *Pages* buttons. Clicking one of them causes the others to clear.

Checkbox. The two boxes at the bottom of the dialog box. The *Print to File* and *Collate Copies* boxes can be set on or off.

Button. The rectangular buttons at the right of the dialog box. The ubiquitous *OK* and *Cancel* buttons appear in almost every dialog box.

You'll hear designers refer to each of these interface items as *visual elements;* programmers call them *controls.* These and several other common elements are the building blocks from which a Windows application developer will assemble the various dialog boxes and other standard components of a Windows program interface. Of course, the specific text that appears on a button, or the size of a box (for example) will change according to the context. Windows is responsible for drawing these standard controls on the screen. The programmer simply describes the layout and dimensions of the visual elements, and Windows does the rest.[15]

The screen shot in Figure 3-4 also shows other, more sophisticated, visual elements: the scroll bars to the right and at the bottom of the document window, the toolbars containing the rows of buttons with a pictorial indication of the function of each, and the status line at the bottom of the screen. Add to these the standard menu bar and the application title bar, and you have examples of most of the visual elements in a Windows 3.1 program.

From the operating system's point of view, every single one of the interface's visual elements is a window. Not just the larger areas surrounded by the framing borders as in Figure 3-4, but virtually every visual element of the Windows interface, is a separately identified window. The operating system keeps track of all of the windows, and user actions performed in one window—for example, a mouse click on a checkbox—ultimately result in the system's sending a *message* to the application that owns the window. The message to the application takes the form of data that informs the application in which window the action took place and what happened in the window. Very often the application relies upon the system's default processing to take care of any action required in response to the message. For example, Windows itself will draw or remove the mark in a checkbox if the user clicks on the checkbox. Thus, a large amount of the code in Windows is devoted to handling all of these default actions, and individual application programs don't have to include equivalent functions. One of Microsoft's guiding principles in the design of Windows has been to include within the operating system functions that a majority of users or applications

---

15. Because Windows is responsible for drawing the controls, your Windows 3.1 applications will have the Windows 95 visual appearance when you run them under Windows 95. Since it is the system that displays the standard visual elements, a 3.1 application will take on the new look without any modifications.

will need. It's no surprise then when new visual elements such as an application toolbar—and the associated default processing—eventually appear in an operating system release. That's exactly what happens with Windows 95.[16]

The concept of window ownership is another notion central to the Windows system. Windows implements a strict hierarchy of windows. Every window must have a *parent window,* and any application may create, perhaps many, *child windows.* A child inherits many aspects of the parent, such as its default behavior. The hierarchical relationship also defines how window messages pass through the system: the youngest child window gets the first chance to process a message aimed at the window, and if it ignores the message, its immediate parent inherits the message. Ultimately the message may pass all the way to the top of the hierarchy so that the system itself can respond with the default message handlers.

The windows within our dialog box example are all child windows of the dialog box window. When the parent window disappears, so do all the child windows. When an application terminates, all of the descendant windows created by the application disappear (are "destroyed," in application programmer's parlance).

The programmer's term *control* actually refers to standard elements in the Windows interface that populate components such as dialog boxes and message boxes. Typically a control has some changeable data associated with it and will constrain what the user can do to the data. A checkbox, for example, allows only an on or an off condition, and a list box may allow the user to select only from a predetermined list of entries. The concept of a control is a little broader than this simple description indicates, but most applications use these kinds of controls. For application programmers, Windows makes the use of controls very easy by providing all the software to create, manage, and modify them and, subsequently, to determine user input.

Windows 95 User Interface Design

When contemplating changes to the appearance of Windows, the designer faces more considerations than the visual appearance of a particular element, considerations such as those itemized on the next page.

---

16. In accord with the same principle, network support and disk compression support have ultimately been incorporated into operating systems. Support for spreadsheet operations hasn't been and most likely never will be.

■ What is the default behavior for a new window? Is it similar enough to an existing window type that applications can take advantage of common processing by the system?

■ What behavior does a new window's appearance imply? A checkbox-like window that requires the user to enter a single letter or number will probably confuse most users, for instance.

■ Is the new element useful for many applications and not simply for a single special case?

■ Does the proposed new element or new appearance or behavior of an existing element actually help the user? That is, does the new or changed element provide an easier or more obvious way to do something?

Add these considerations to the more practical ones of large scale software development—how much memory is needed, how fast it will run, whether it can be finished in time—and you can see that changing the appearance of Windows 3.1 was more than just a facelift operation. The changes in the interface from Windows 3.1 to Windows 95 do aim to correct a number of flaws. But more impressive, a number of new user interface concepts make their first appearance with Windows 95. These ideas form the basis for the design of many of the new visual elements and for the design of the Windows 95 shell itself. In Chapter Five, we'll identify the problems in Windows 3.1 that Windows 95 aims to correct and look at the conceptual basis for the new appearance.

Windows Programming Basics

This book isn't about to try to teach you how to program for Windows. That subject has been explored comprehensively in hundreds of books and magazine articles over the last few years.[17] However, just to make sure that we embark on this voyage of discovery on an equal footing, let's review some basic information.

Event Driven Programming

Windows uses an *event driven* programming model that's almost more commonplace now than the procedural model everyone learned in

---

17. As ever, Charles Petzold's book *Programming Windows,* 3d ed. (Microsoft Press, 1992), remains the best introductory text.

school. First popularized by the Apple Macintosh operating system, event driven programming relies on external events to stimulate responses from an application. Mouse clicks and key depressions are the two most common external stimuli for a Windows application, although it's possible to translate any change in the application's environment into an event suitable for consumption by an application.

Windows feeds an event to an application in the form of a *message* that describes the change in the application's environment. Some messages are universal, such as those informing an application that the user has clicked on an application menu item. Other messages—for example, those indicating movement of the mouse cursor within an application window—are often of interest only to a particular type of application. Every message is associated with a specific application window, and each window has a *window procedure* associated with it. A Windows application receives messages by means of the *GetMessage()* API function, and calls Windows by means of the *DispatchMessage()* API function. Then Windows itself calls the appropriate window procedure, passing it the message to be processed. All messages are processed from within a queue that's maintained by the system and that preserves the order of the messages. If mouse click and keyboard entry messages, for example, weren't received and processed in the same order as the user entered them, the system would be out of control.

Message Handling

It used to be that every Windows application included the code fragments shown in Figure 3-5 on the next page—although you should notice one innovation in the code shown there. If you've written Windows programs, you probably have something very similar in your earlier programs. Windows applications rely upon the system to provide significant amounts of default processing. If an application isn't interested in a particular message, it simply ignores it and allows the system to apply its default response behavior to the message. Often the default processing means discarding the message altogether, and often it means that the window procedure for a particular message is simply not part of the application. For example, it is quite rare for an application to register a window procedure to handle messages sent to controls—the system's default handling of such messages is usually adequate.

```
// Start of fragment...
// Acquire and dispatch messages until a WM_QUIT message is
// received.
while (GetMessage(&msg,          // Message structure
                  NULL,          // Handle of window receiving
                                 //  the message
                  0,             // Lowest message to examine
                  0)){           // Highest message to examine
    if (!TranslateAccelerator (msg.hwnd, hAccelTable, &msg)) {
        TranslateMessage(&msg); // Translates virtual key
                                //  codes
        DispatchMessage(&msg);  // Dispatches message to
                                //  window

    }
}
// ...end of fragment

// Start of fragment...
switch (message) {
    case WM_COMMAND:  // Message: command from application
                      //  menu
        #if defined (_WIN32)
            wmId   = LOWORD(uParam);
            wmEvent = HIWORD(uParam);
        #else
            wmId    = uParam;
            wmEvent = HIWORD(lParam);
        #endif
    switch (wmId) {
        case IDM_ABOUT:
            lpProcAbout = MakeProcInstance((FARPROC)About,
                                                hInst);
            DialogBox(hInst,          // Current instance
                "AboutBox",           // Dlg resource to use
                hWnd,                 // Parent handle
                (DLGPROC)lpProcAbout); // About() instance
                                      //  address
            FreeProcInstance(lpProcAbout);
            break;
        case IDM_EXIT:
            DestroyWindow (hWnd);
            break;
```

Figure 3-5.

Fragments of the Windows message loop.

(continued)

Figure 3-5. *continued*

```
        default:
            return (DefWindowProc(hWnd, message, uParam,
                                  lParam));
            }
            break;
        case WM_DESTROY:  // Message: window being destroyed
            PostQuitMessage(0);
            break;
        default:                // Passes it on if unprocessed
            return (DefWindowProc(hWnd, message, uParam,
                                  lParam));
        }
    return (0);
    }
// ...end of fragment
```

Program Resources

Another common aspect of Windows programs is their use of identifiers called *handles* to reference every object within their environments: windows, memory blocks, files, communications devices, cursors, bitmaps, and so on. Handles are simply convenient numeric identifiers for resources that the system has allocated to a Windows program. Almost every Windows API function deals with a handle in one way or another. Sometimes a handle can be translated into a more direct reference—a memory address, for example. However, it's bad practice to do that, and under Windows 95 the unwritten rules for such translations have changed anyway.

Windows 95 Programming

Under Windows 95, the fundamentals of Windows programming haven't changed. The event driven model is still the basis for how you write a Windows program. However, there are some evolutionary changes in writing a program for Windows 95:

■ Microsoft is all but forcing developers to move to Win32 as the preferred Windows API. There are a lot of good technical reasons to go to 32-bit programs anyway, but the fact that the new capabilities of Windows 95 are accessible only to Win32 applications tends to predetermine the result.

- The programmer's access to the new capabilities of Windows 95, notably 32-bit programs and preemptive scheduling, will introduce new twists in the already complex Windows programming model. If you don't already know how to develop applications for a preemptive multitasking system, Windows 95 forces you to learn. There are also some subtle changes that the 32-bit API engenders in application code—if you looked at the code in Figure 3-5, you saw one example.

- Microsoft's Object Linking and Embedding (OLE) technology represents a massive investment in a new programming methodology that may well transform Windows programming and the nature of Windows applications. OLE has been available in advance of the Windows 95 release, but its presence as a standard component of the Windows 95 product is likely to ensure that a lot of programmers will spend a lot of time learning it.

- The programming tools now available for Windows stress more and more the object-oriented programming model evident in languages such as C++. Windows is by its nature an object-oriented environment, although purists can point to areas in which Windows deviates from a pure object-oriented model. The new tools for Windows programming tend to hide these minor deviations, and with the emphasis that Microsoft now places on OLE and the future promise of Cairo, object-oriented programming is likely to be the discipline in vogue for the next few years.

Although everything you worked hard to learn about Windows programming is still valid, there are some new aspects that Windows 95 will tend to bring into focus. OLE is not the least of these and is by some estimates as complex as the entire Windows 2.0 product ever was. However, if you're comfortable with the basic concepts of events, messages, message queues, window procedures, handles, and windows, you shouldn't find anything in the following chapters to be incomprehensible.

Conclusion

In this chapter, we took a tour through a lot of the basic terminology and some of the inner workings of Windows. If you knew most of this Windows lore already, you're ready for the new acronyms and some of the architectural changes introduced with Windows 95. If you didn't know your way around Windows, I hope you're ready for a second heavy dose.

We looked at several of the new features of Windows 95 in this chapter but ignored a lot of the detail. Chapter Four is where we're cleared for the approach to Chicago.

References

Duncan, Ray, et al. *Extending DOS.* 2d ed. Reading, Mass.: Addison-Wesley, 1991. A collection of lengthy papers about different aspects of squeezing more memory and more function from MS-DOS. The book includes a good discussion of DOS extenders and the DPMI specification.

Intel Corporation. *MS-DOS Protected Mode Interface Specification.* The definitive specification for version 0.9 of DPMI. There's also a version 1.0, but since Windows itself supports only version 0.9, this is the de facto standard. To get a free paper copy, call Intel at 1-800-548-4725.

Petzold, Charles. *Programming Windows 3.1.* 3d ed. Redmond, Wash.: Microsoft Press, 1992. A classic in its own way. The best introduction to Windows programming there is. If we're lucky, Charles is hard at work on the Windows 95 version.

CHAPTER FOUR

THE BASE SYSTEM

In this chapter and the next, we'll examine the two features of Windows 95 that most differentiate it from its predecessors. Of all the new features in Windows 95, the most prominent to the user will be the new appearance and the new system shell—the most obvious changes from Windows 3.1—and that's what we'll look at in Chapter Five. For the programmer, the support for a native 32-bit API will probably be the most closely studied new feature in Windows 95. But the 32-bit API is merely the best-documented manifestation of the changes in the underlying operating system. In Windows 95, Windows finally becomes a complete operating system. No longer is it simply a "graphical DOS extender," some critics' characterization of the earlier versions of Windows. In Windows 95, many new or revised components now make full use of the 32-bit protected mode of the 386 processor. The operating system within Windows 95 is the subject of this chapter.

Simply looking at the feature highlight list for the base operating system gives you an indication of how much is new and how much work has gone into this part of Windows 95:

- For all intents and purposes, real mode MS-DOS is gone. Finally Windows is a complete operating system with no reliance on MS-DOS and its real mode architecture and limitations.

- A new filesystem architecture and 32-bit protected mode implementation of the FAT filesystem eliminate the last major dependency of Windows on MS-DOS. The new filesystem also provides significant system performance improvements.

- Windows 95 provides full support for 32-bit applications, including a 32-bit Windows API and protected, private address spaces.

- Windows 95 provides for the preemptive scheduling of Windows applications.

- Windows 95 provides architected support for multiple simultaneous network connections.

Naturally, whatever changed in Windows 95 had nevertheless to remain compatible with Windows 3.1 and MS-DOS. The developers had the ever present specter of compatibility looking over their shoulders.

And the designers of Windows 95 had to recognize Windows NT as a preexisting operating system in much of their work. Sometimes the obligation to Windows NT helped. Windows 95 picked up components of the disk device driver architecture used in Windows NT, for example. And sometimes deference to the earlier Windows NT created quandaries: which subset of the Windows NT API set Windows 95 should fully support, for instance. As we examine the system's features, we'll draw a number of comparisons between Windows 95 and Windows NT.

What we'll concentrate on in this chapter are the underlying architecture and the major functional components of the operating system. While the project was under development, the Windows 95 team publicly referred to this collection of software as the *base system,* or simply the *base OS.*[1] Throughout the project, there was a lot of internal and external discussion and speculation about a protected mode MS-DOS version 7.0 that would provide the operating system functionality required by Windows 95. By and large, this version of MS-DOS (if it appears) will be the operating system components of Windows 95 in a different package. Since we're concerned with Windows only, we won't go into what might or might not appear in MS-DOS version 7.0.

Windows 95 Diagrammed

Software designers often discuss an operating system as if it were a living, breathing entity. Reducing such an organism to simple diagrams can't provide a complete picture of either its complexity or the subtle interactions among its different components. But given our medium,

---

1. Microsoft code-named the OS components Jaguar and Cougar. There were also dragons stalking the halls. Interesting place to work.

diagrams are what we have.[2] Figure 4-1, a variation on Figure 3-1, provides just such an inadequate view of the system's most important components.

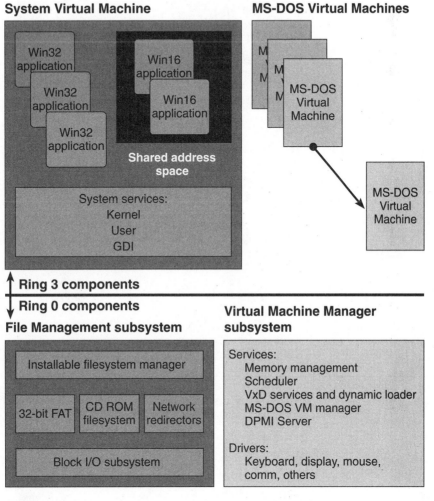

Figure 4-1.
Windows 95 system architecture.

---

2. One Microsoft designer maintains that drawing a block diagram of Windows NT gives you a neat, concise presentation showing how the system really does work. For Windows 95, a similar representation is a little more chaotic, but the diagrammatic oddities usually point to important concerns—namely, compatibility and performance.

It would be difficult to point to a single box as the base operating system since aspects of the low-level design permeate Windows 95. In this chapter, we'll concentrate on the functions provided by the Virtual Machine Manager and on some details of the System Virtual Machine architecture:

- Scheduling and memory management services
- The management of Windows-based applications within the System Virtual Machine
- The management of the MS-DOS virtual machines
- The foundation for the Windows API layer

We won't get into all of the extremely low level details of how these pieces work. We'll look at the architecture and at some of the more interesting implementation details.[3] Needless to say, you should be familiar with the material presented in Chapters Two and Three before diving into this chapter.

Windows 95 Surveyed

Let's first take another brief tour through the system and review the important components. Many aspects of the Windows 95 design are similar to aspects of the design of Windows 3.1 that you already know about. In particular:

System Virtual Machine. Windows applications all run within the context of the system VM. The 16-bit applications (the "old" Windows applications) share a single address space. The new 32-bit support provides each new application with a private address space.

MS-DOS Virtual Machines. Windows 95 supports the execution of multiple MS-DOS programs running in either virtual 8086 mode or protected mode.

Virtual Machine Manager. The VMM is the real heart of the operating system. It provides low-level memory management and scheduling services as well as services for the virtual device drivers.

---

3. No doubt there will be other books that do take on the Herculean task of looking at all of the details. The "References" section at the end of this chapter lists a few of the books that covered the details for Windows 3.1.

The major new component of Windows 95 is the File Management System. It's a completely redesigned subsystem that supports multiple concurrently accessible filesystems. Barring any old MS-DOS device drivers that might be present to support a particular device, the entire File Management System is protected mode 32-bit code. Its design supports local disks and CD ROM devices as well as one or more network interfaces by means of an *installable filesystem interface* (*IFS* for short). If you're really well connected, you can hook up and use your hard disks, your floppy disks, your CD ROM, your Bernoulli box, your Windows NT server, and your NetWare network and never leave protected mode the whole day. In Windows 3.1, it was MS-DOS that provided the filesystem support for local disks. Support for CD ROM devices and network filesystems was, at the very least, confused and confusing.[4]

The system services called upon by Windows applications—for graphics, window management, and the like—are all still there, and they retain the Kernel, User, and GDI names they had in previous versions of Windows. The major change in the system services subsystem is its support for 32-bit applications. Apart from their different memory management requirements, 32-bit applications use a full 32-bit Windows API and call upon services that are now implemented using 32-bit code. Making the mixture of 16-bit and 32-bit components cooperate effectively and with good performance was one of the major design and implementation challenges the Windows 95 team faced.

Protection Rings in Windows 95

Windows 95 exploits the Intel 386 processor's ability to support multiple privilege levels. Since the handling of these rings of protection tends to affect several aspects of system design, it's worth reviewing their use up front. Windows 95 runs the processor using privilege levels zero and three. The ring zero components are what you normally think of as the operating system proper, including, for example, the lowest levels of memory management support. Ring zero software has omnipotent power over the system: all the processor instructions are valid, and the software has access to critical data structures such as the page tables. Clearly, it behooved the system designers to ensure that the software running at ring zero would have a very good reason to be there and be completely reliable. For the most part, Windows 95 ensures these

---

4. The first release of Windows for Workgroups improved this situation some, and version 3.11 made it better yet. The protected mode FAT filesystem made its debut in the 3.11 release of Windows.

conditions. The lapse is in the facility that allows the user to install one or more new virtual device drivers to support an add-on hardware device or provide some systemwide software service. VxDs always run at ring zero, and if one of them fails, it can cripple the entire system. Unfortunately, the performance overhead that would have been incurred by putting each VxD in a private address space so that failed drivers could be isolated and halted was deemed unacceptable.[5]

Windows applications and MS-DOS applications always run at ring three, so their privileges are significantly restricted. Also running at ring three are the central components of the Windows graphical environment: Kernel, User, and GDI. The term *Kernel* has been so prevalent in descriptions of how earlier versions of Windows operate that we'll keep its sense in that context rather than adopt the more classic use of the word to describe the ring zero components of Windows 95.

Some operating systems try to use the other privilege levels offered by the Intel 386 processor. Windows 95 isn't one of them. The two-ring model (sometimes called "kernel and user modes") works pretty well for most needs. The Windows 95 designers could have come up with ways of using the other rings—running user installed VxDs at ring one to reduce the system integrity problem, for instance. But this line of thinking leads rapidly to a consideration of the various trade-offs, notably implementation effort and system performance vs. real user benefit. A ring transition on the Intel 386—a change of control from one processor privilege level to a different one—is expensive in terms of execution time.[6] A lot of processor controlled validation and register reloading occurs whenever there's an alteration in processor privilege level—that is, a jump between rings—so minimizing such transitions represents a big benefit to system performance. This is also why most of the code for the Windows graphical system runs at ring three. Incurring a ring transition for every Windows API call would likely result in system performance reminiscent of Windows 1.01 running on an IBM PC XT.

Windows 95 Memory Map

The 386 provides a 4-GB virtual address space, and Windows 95 uses it all. Within this virtual address space, the different system components

---

5. The problem did get quite a bit of attention. The Windows 95 development tools do include new VxD debugging and parameter validation capabilities.

6. A direct subroutine call to code in another segment takes 20 clock cycles on the 486. If a ring transition is involved, you need to budget 69 clock cycles. And that's one way only. The return path is expensive too.

and applications occupy regions with fixed boundaries. Figure 4-2 shows the basic memory map for the system. One duty of the Virtual Machine Manager (VMM) is to map this 4-GB virtual address space into the available physical memory.[7]

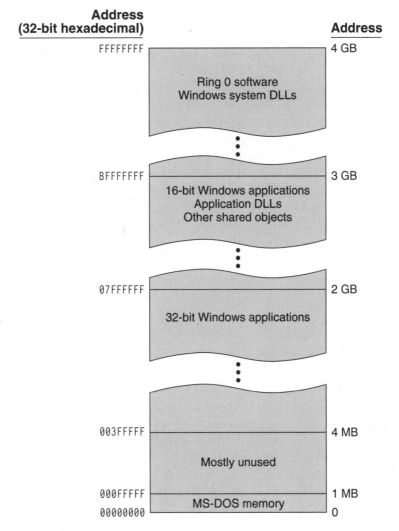

Figure 4-2.
Windows 95 system memory map.

---

7. The Windows 95 base operating system uses two selectors—28 and 30—for code and data. The base and limit for the associated descriptors are set at 0 and 4 GB, effectively providing access to the entire virtual address space.

In the system memory map, the lowest 1 MB of the virtual address space is used for the currently executing MS-DOS VM. Each VM also has a valid memory map within the 2-GB to 3-GB region.[8] This mapping allows the system itself to address the memory of a VM regardless of whether it is active. But when an MS-DOS VM runs, it's also mapped to the bottom 1 MB.

Within the virtual address space of a 32-bit Windows application, the standard development tools use 4 MB as the default load address. You can choose a lower address, but you'll incur a lot of overhead with all the fixups the system will have to carry out when it loads the application. Loading into the 4-MB to 2-GB region is immediate. The 4-MB application load address matches the address Windows NT· used for loading 32-bit applications in its first production release, so it's a sensible choice. The lowest 16K of each 32-bit application's address space (that is, virtual addresses 0 through 3FFF) is invalid. This deliberate design decision aims to trap program errors. One of the most common programming errors is the erroneous use of a null program pointer. Under Windows 95, the 0 address will generate a memory fault, an error likely to be caught by the developer and not get as far as the user.

Tasks and Processes

One significant change in Windows 95 that needs to be appreciated at the outset is the change in terminology from *task* to *process*. Windows 3.1 documentation usually used the word *task* to describe the running instance of a program. Windows 95 aligns itself with Windows NT in using the word *process* to describe the same thing. A lot of the Windows 3.1 documentation wasn't particularly rigorous in using the word *task,* so you can actually find both words used. In Windows 95, the word *process* refers, at least in the case of 16-bit Windows applications and MS-DOS applications, to the "task" you already know about.

If you study the documentation for Windows 95, you'll see that API calls such as *GetCurrentTask()* are marked "deleted" or "obsolete," and you're referred to the new API. (Yes, you'll find *GetCurrentProcess()* instead.) Of course, the compatibility constraints that govern Windows 95 mean that the system must still support the older task API calls, so they aren't really "deleted" in the true sense of the word. Even though

---

8. The 2-GB low address boundary of the shared memory region moved from 1 GB to 2 GB in successive test releases of Windows 95. (Although such a move wasn't contemplated, it may even have moved again by the time you read this.) It isn't an address you should depend on for any reason.

Microsoft doesn't expect anyone to develop new 16-bit applications, you could still do that, and the task APIs would be available to you. Once you enter the 32-bit world, though, a "process" is what you have and the process APIs are what you use.

Virtual Machine Management

The virtual machine concept that was so important in the very first implementation of Windows on the Intel 386 is alive and well in Windows 95. The Virtual Machine Manager is truly the heart of the Windows 95 base system. The efficiency of the VMM has a major impact on the performance of the whole system, and some of the most complex components of the OS live there. The code for the VMM consumed some of the best efforts of the development team, and they've added a lot of new functionality:

- 32-bit Windows applications are preemptively scheduled within per-process private address spaces.

- Many new system primitives related to the preemptive scheduling environment are available to VxDs.

- VxDs can be dynamically loaded and paged, which reduces the working set for the system.

Also, within the Windows User module, each 32-bit application obtains a private message queue—eliminating the possibility of a single application's locking up the entire system, which can happen in Windows 3.1.

Windows 95 uses the same two basic types of virtual machine that Windows 3.1 did:

- The system VM, in which the Windows Kernel, User, and GDI components as well as all the Windows applications run

- The MS-DOS VMs that run a single MS-DOS session each, with applications running in either virtual 8086 mode or protected mode

Real MS-DOS

Despite earlier statements to the contrary, MS-DOS is still alive and well in Windows 95. (You didn't really think it had gone away, did you?) The code and data for the current release of MS-DOS (version 6.22) will be present on the Windows 95 disks at shipment, although it's not clear exactly how the packaging and pricing issues will be resolved. Here's why MS-DOS is still around:

- Windows 95 supports a *single MS-DOS–based application mode*— to give it its official title. This mode is for MS-DOS applications that can't run under Windows—typically, game programs that have stringent timer control requirements.

- The software in the "hidden" VM, where Windows sets up the global MS-DOS context for all other VMs, has to come from somewhere. MS-DOS itself is the obvious candidate for providing the MS-DOS context.

Earlier in the development of Windows 95, the intention was to use MS-DOS as the bootstrap loader for the system. Rather than reinvent the code that brings the system to life, processes the CONFIG.SYS and AUTOEXEC.BAT files, and then runs Windows proper, Microsoft planned simply to use MS-DOS. Eventually, the boot process was put into the WINBOOT.SYS module. The module contains a lot of MS-DOS code, but it's tailored to the job of getting Windows 95 into memory and starting it.

The big difference in Windows 95's relationship with MS-DOS is that if you run only Windows applications, you'll never execute any MS-DOS code. As successive versions of Windows have appeared, each has supported more and more of the MS-DOS INT-based software services, and Windows applications have had an ever decreasing need to switch in and out of virtual 8086 mode to execute MS-DOS code. The big exception to this (up to Windows for Workgroups version 3.11) has been support for the filesystem services. Windows 95 finally breaks all ties with the real mode MS-DOS code, and with few exceptions even the existing 16-bit Windows applications follow a protected mode path through the new File Management System to the disk and back.

Virtual Machine Scheduling

Process scheduling in Windows 95 is so closely tied to the management of virtual machines that it's appropriate to examine scheduling as part of the VMM discussion. The Windows 95 scheduling algorithms deal with virtual machines, processes, timeslices, and priorities similarly to the way Windows 3.1 did. Windows 95 also introduces *threads,* the principal objects that the system scheduler deals with. The thread is now the basic unit of scheduling in Windows 95. If you're familiar with Windows NT or OS/2, you're accustomed to dealing with threads. A thread

- Is an execution path within a process.

- Can be created by any 32-bit Windows application or VxD running on Windows 95.

- Has its own private stack storage and execution context (notably processor registers).

- Shares the memory allocated to the parent process.

- Can be one of many concurrent threads created by a single process.

Threads are sometimes called "lightweight processes" because creating and managing them are relatively simple operations. In particular, the fact that threads share all the code and global data of the parent process means that setting up a new thread involves only minimal amounts of memory allocation. When Windows 95 loads an application and creates the associated process data structures, the system sets up the process as a single thread. Many applications will use only a single thread throughout their execution lifetimes. But an application can (and many do) use another thread to carry out some short term background operation. Under Windows 3.1, waiting for a word processor to load a large document can be tedious. If you change your mind halfway through, you still have to sit and watch the hourglass cursor for a while before you can do anything else. Under Windows 95, the application can create one thread to load the document and another to manage a dialog with a Cancel button. Any time you want to, you can interrupt the document loading operation with a single click.

Thread services are available only to 32-bit applications and VxDs under Windows 95. MS-DOS VMs and the older 16-bit Windows applications can't call the thread APIs. An MS-DOS VM represents a single thread: in simple terms, an MS-DOS VM is a process is a thread. Every 16-bit Windows application uses a single thread of execution, and the cooperative multitasking model for older Windows applications is preserved. Any 32-bit Windows application or VxD can create additional threads, and Windows 95 can schedule all these threads preemptively—adding a whole new facet to Windows multitasking.[9]

The Windows 95 Schedulers

There are two schedulers within the Windows 95 VMM: the *primary scheduler,* which is responsible for calculating thread priorities, and the *timeslice scheduler,* which is responsible for calculating the allocation of timeslices. Ultimately, the timeslice scheduler decides what percentage of the available processor time to allocate to different threads. If a thread doesn't receive execution time, it's *suspended* and can't run until the schedulers reevaluate the situation.

Here's how the scheduling process works:

1. The primary scheduler examines every thread in the system and calculates an *execution priority* value for the thread, an integer between 0 and 31.[10]

2. The primary scheduler suspends any thread with an execution priority value lower than the highest value. (The highest value doesn't necessarily mean the value 31. If two threads have the execution priority value 20 and every other thread has a priority value lower than 20, then 20 is the highest value until the next priority recalculation.) Once a thread is suspended, the primary scheduler pays no further attention to the thread as far as priority calculation during this timeslice is concerned.

3. The timeslice scheduler then calculates the percentage of the timeslice to allocate to each thread using these priority values and knowledge of the VM's current status.

4. The threads run. By default, the primary scheduler will reevaluate the priorities every 20 milliseconds.

In the example in Figure 4-3, two of the five active threads (B and D) have execution priority values of 20 and the other three threads

---

9. Although these threads can correspond to radically different program types, the system represents each thread using the same data structure. Thus, the scheduler, along with other 32-bit system code that uses these internal data structures, could be implemented without the team's having to worry about 16-bit to 32-bit translation idiosyncrasies.

10. That this is the same priority model as Windows NT's reflects a design guideline for Windows 95: "where it makes sense to, be the same as Windows NT."

have lower priorities. The timeslice scheduler will therefore divide the next timeslice between threads B and D.

Three control flags maintained for each VM also play into this process. *VMStat_Exclusive* tells the scheduler that the VM in question must receive 100 percent of the next timeslice; neither of the remaining two flags is set. One of the remaining two flags—*VMStat_Background* and *VMStat_High_Pri_Background*—must be set if the scheduler is to

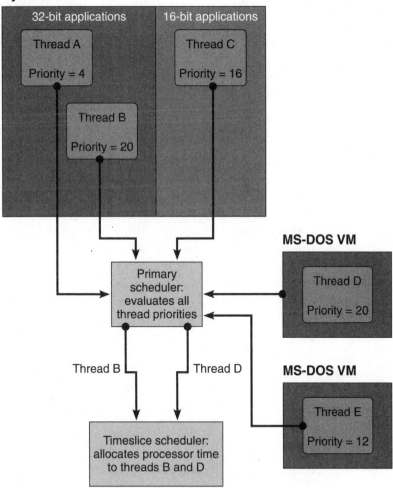

Figure 4-3.
Windows 95 thread scheduling.

grant a background VM any allocation of the next timeslice; otherwise, the foreground VM gets the entire allocation.

Scheduling Within the System Virtual Machine

All the Windows application threads run within the System VM context. The System VM is the only VM that supports multiple threads: one for each 16-bit application and at least one for each 32-bit Windows application. As you can see from the discussion of the scheduling algorithm, it's possible (in fact probable) that the System VM will frequently contain multiple nonidle threads with equal high priorities.

To handle this situation, the timeslice scheduler adopts a *round robin* scheduling policy to ensure a fair allocation of execution time among threads of equal priority. Once a thread within the System VM consumes its allocated execution time, the scheduler puts it at the end of a queue of threads with equal priority. This classic technique ensures that each thread at the highest priority level has an equal opportunity to consume processor time. If the chosen thread fails to consume all of its allocated processor time, the scheduler hands the processor to the next thread of equal priority in the System VM and allows it to use the remainder of the timeslice.

Controlling the Scheduler

Two different influences control the scheduler. One is its own internal algorithms that try to provide a smooth multitasking environment with each thread receiving an equitable share of processor time. "Smooth" in this context is really a user perception—the goal is to provide a thread with enough processor time to get work done but not so much time that other threads are locked out for long periods. Erring on the side of providing too much processor time to a thread will give the user an impression of slow response as he or she waits until the system switches to the new thread. Providing too little processor time to threads will give the user an impression of jerky response as the system switches among threads. The other influence on the scheduler is the direct calls on system services that VxDs might make.

Internally, the scheduler uses three techniques to help it meet its goal of equitable distribution of processor time for an impression of speedy and smooth response:

Dynamic priority boosting allows the primary scheduler to briefly raise or lower the priority of a thread. For example, a keystroke or a mouse click indicates that the receiving thread's priority should be boosted.

Timed decay causes the boosted priority of a thread to gradually return to its usual value.

Priority inheritance rapidly turns a low-priority thread into a higher-priority thread. Typically, a thread's priority is inverted to allow a low-priority thread to rapidly complete its use of an exclusive resource that high-priority threads are waiting for.[11]

The VMM includes a large number of services available to VxDs. The operating system uses these services extensively to control multitasking operations. For software authors brave enough to dive in, the multitasking services are all available from within user installable VxDs. These services allow a VxD to inquire about current scheduling conditions—priorities, timeslices, VM focus, and other parameters—and to adjust those conditions.

Threads and UAEs

One of the problems facing the Windows designers has always been how best to deal with applications that fail during execution. Whether you call such a crash a UAE or a general protection fault, it comes from a bug—probably in the application itself, although the user tends to blame Windows. It's unlikely that any generation of Windows application designers will deliver totally bug-free software, so Windows itself has to be able to deal with application crashes. This involves two things:

- Handling the program failure gracefully—meaning allowing the user to close the application with a minimum of fuss and no lost data.

- Cleaning up afterwards. Apart from open files, the application undoubtedly owns handles to system resources such as memory segments, pens, and brushes. If the system can't free up the memory these resources occupy, the available free resources are reduced.

The most common application program error resulting in a crash is an addressing error. Typically, the bug causes the program to try to use an invalid pointer to some object. A 0 address is the most common case, which is why address 0 is always an invalid address for every Windows

---

11. Windows 95 immediately adjusts the inherited priority back to its normal value once the contention condition is past.

95 application. Such an addressing error causes a *general protection fault* on the 386, and eventually the user sees a dialog box that provides the name of the program module that caused the fault and the option to close the erring application. Of course, this information and the option to close the application don't help the user very much, and often the system behaves very strangely even after the user closes the application and dismisses the dialog box.

Windows 95 addresses this problem in two ways. First, the general protection fault handler runs as a separate thread within the system. Thus, rather than having the fault and the closing of the application handled from within the application context, which may by now be in a hopelessly messed-up state, Windows 95 has the fault dialog and program termination managed by a thread in a known (good) state.

The system has already tagged every allocated resource with a thread identifier, so if a thread terminates abnormally, the system can search its tables for any resources the thread owned and return them to an unused state. All global memory, window resources, logical brushes, device contexts, and other resources are available for reuse after this postmortem cleanup. The cleanup goes into immediate effect if a 32-bit thread fails. Amazingly, one of the "techniques" used by some existing Windows applications relies on allocated resources remaining available even after the application quits. For this reason, the resource cleanup can't take place until the system notices that there are no 16-bit applications running. Then any remaining allocated resources can be returned to the free pool.[12]

Threads and Idle Time

Another use of the thread mechanism is to schedule background activities that can run when the system is quiescent.[13] Waiting until the system is quiescent ensures that the maximum number of processor cycles remains available to applications.

---

12. This technique works also when an application simply "forgets" to release a resource, such as a display context, before exit.

13. In Windows 3.1, there was a background VxD that wrote modified memory pages out to the swap file. When no applications were running, this process woke up and ensured that the swap file images matched the memory images of the currently executing programs. Experiments showed that this really wasn't a big performance win, and the technique was dropped in Windows 95.

Application Message Queues

The event driven nature of all Windows applications calls for the system to provide an effective means of delivering messages to every application. A message is sent at the behest of a device driver (representing the occurrence of some external event such as a mouse click), by another Windows application, or by the system itself (for example, the system will notify other processes when a new application starts). The system puts all the hardware-initiated messages into a data structure called the *raw input queue.*

A classic problem with Windows 3.1 is that every Windows application draws messages from a single systemwide message queue. This message queue contains a processed form of the raw input messages suitable for application consumption as well as all the other messages that flow through the system. Whenever a process asks for a message (usually with a *GetMessage()* call), the system simply delivers the message at the head of the queue. Until the process yields control of the CPU, the system doesn't try to deliver any more messages. Since there is no preemption in Windows 3.1, if an application fails, the flow of messages—and consequently the system—comes to a halt. No doubt you've seen this phenomenon when an application puts up the hourglass cursor and goes to sleep—sometimes forever. Clicking the mouse on other windows doesn't help the situation in the least.

Unfortunately, even if Windows 3.1 were to provide a preemptive multitasking environment, a single message queue would still cause the same problem. For example, suppose that two messages (A and B) destined for the same process were at the head of the queue and that the process accepted message A and then failed, looping endlessly. The timeslice would expire, and the system would reschedule and grind to a halt—unable to deliver message B to the recalcitrant process.

To prevent this kind of situation, Windows 95 supports multiple message queues, a design improvement it shares with Windows NT. Since the efficient flow of messages is vital to good response times and smooth multitasking, this design technique is key. It ensures that a single errant application can't lock up the entire system.[14] The multiple queue technique is called *input desynchronization,* and Figure 4-4 on the next page shows how it works.

---

14. For the most part. There's still a design problem associated with the 16-bit application subsystem that we'll look at later in this chapter.

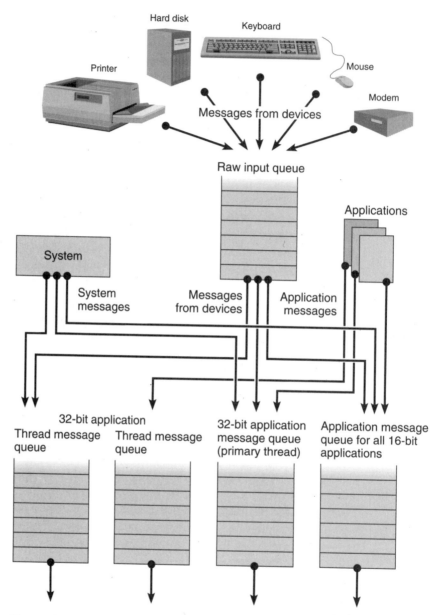

Figure 4-4.
Multiple queue message delivery under Windows 95.

Under Windows 95, new messages are put into the raw input queue only briefly. An execution thread within the system regularly empties this queue and moves the messages to one of these queues:

■ A single queue for all 16-bit applications—meaning that the behavior for these applications is exactly as it was under Windows 3.1

■ A private per-thread queue for 32-bit applications

Messages generated by the system itself or by other processes move straight to the private queues. There's a small amount of internal buffering if the system is extremely busy, but most of the time that isn't necessary. When a 32-bit process first runs, it has a single message queue associated with its primary thread. If the process creates another thread, the system doesn't immediately create another message queue, though. The system creates another message queue only when the second thread makes its first message queue–related call. If a thread doesn't need a message queue, the system doesn't waste any resources building one.

Physical Memory Management

Underlying the virtual machines and the virtual address space supported by Windows 95 are the confines of the physical memory present on the host system. Managing physical memory is the process of choosing which pages within the system's 4-GB virtual address space to map to physical memory at any instant in time. The system swaps the remaining active pages in the virtual address space to and from the hard disk, reassigning physical memory pages as it needs to. Many physical pages—for example, those occupied by the memory resident components of the kernel—have their use determined during system startup. These pages never change roles and don't figure in the memory management process. On a system with 4 MB of RAM and a small (probably very small) disk cache, you can expect roughly 1 MB of memory to be locked down this way. Several software components contend for the remaining physical memory: dynamically loaded system components, application code and data, and dynamically allocated regions such as DMA buffers and cache regions for the filesystem.

The Windows 95 physical memory manager is brand-new code. The main reason for rewriting the existing memory manager was the proliferation of memory types that Windows 95 has to deal with. Along with all the memory page types that Windows 3.1 has to manage, Windows 95 memory page types include 32-bit application code and data, dynamically loadable VxDs, memory mapped files, and a dynamic filesystem cache.[15] This increase in complexity was enough to dictate a rewrite.

Unlike the design of a multiuser system, in which the operating system has to worry about equitable sharing of the precious memory resource, the Windows 95 design allows you to fill your memory as you wish. All available physical memory pages are created equal, and both the system's dynamically loaded components and running application programs compete for available memory pages. You want an application to run as fast as possible, so the application is allowed to fill as much physical memory as can be made available. Over an extended period, machines with 8 MB or less of memory are likely to gradually fill all the available memory and have to start paging.[16] Note that the system imposes a restriction on the total amount of memory an application can lock—if this weren't controlled, it would be possible to reach a deadlock situation. Once physical memory is full, the next page allocation request starts the paging process. An interesting side effect of this design is that there is no reliable way for an application to determine how much memory is available in the system. The *GlobalMemoryStatus()* API reports various statistics about the system's memory, but the report is a snapshot of current conditions, and calling the API again will probably yield different results.

The paging algorithm in Windows 95 is a standard *least recently used (LRU)* technique that re-allocates the oldest resident pages when new requests must be satisfied.[17] Pages come and go from different places: most pages are either directly allocated in memory (as a result of a request for new data pages) or loaded initially from an application's .EXE file. Subsequently, these pages travel back and forth between physical memory and the swap file. The system always loads pure code

---

15. The VCache filesystem caching VxD interacts with the physical memory manager, claiming and releasing chunks of memory that can then be allocated to the individual filesystem drivers for cache usage.

16. Windows 95 remembers what it loaded, and even after an application exits, its code pages may remain in memory for some time. If the pages aren't taken for some other purpose and the user happens to run the same application again, the pages are still there and can be reused.

17. Early test releases of Windows 95 used a simple page-at-a-time paging algorithm. Late in 1993, the developers began experimenting with clumping pages together and paging a block of pages in each operation. At the time of this writing, page out operations were being done in groups, and page in operations were being done one page at a time.

pages for Win32 applications and DLLs from their original executable files. This setup doesn't entirely rule out the possibility of using self-modifying code: if a code page is modified (usually by a debugger), the page becomes part of the process's swappable private memory—so it isn't subsequently reloaded from the .EXE. *WriteProcessMemory()* is the API that debuggers can use to modify an application's memory image. Applications can use this API themselves and achieve the same effect.

To assist in the management of all the different types of memory, every active page—that is, every page that is part of an executing system module or application—has a handle to a *pager descriptor* (*PD*) stored with it. A PD holds the addresses of the routines used to move a page back and forth between physical memory and the disk. Regardless of the type of memory the page contains, to get the page into or out of memory the physical memory manager simply calls the appropriate function as defined by the page's PD. Figure 4-5 shows the structure of a PD. A page is defined as a "virgin" page if it has never been written to during its lifetime. (Win32 application code pages are usually virgin pages, for example.) A page is "tainted" if it has been written to at least once since it was originally allocated, and a tainted page is either "dirty" or "clean" depending on whether it has been written to since it was last swapped into physical memory—in which case its contents must be written out to the swap file before the physical memory page can be re-allocated.

```
typedef ULONG FUNPAGE ( PULONG ppagerdata,   // Page data word
                        PVOID ppage,          // Pointer to page
                        ULONG faultpage);     // Page #
typedef FUNPAGE * PFUNPAGE

struct pd_s {
    PFUNPAGE pd_virginin;      // Swap in a virgin page
    PFUNPAGE pd_taintedin;     // Swap in a tainted page
    PFUNPAGE pd_cleanout;      // Swap out a clean page
    PFUNPAGE pd_dirtyout;      // Swap out a dirty page
    PFUNPAGE pd_virginfree;    // Free a virgin page
    PFUNPAGE pd_taintedfree;   // Free a tainted page
    PFUNPAGE pd_dirty;         // Mark a page as dirty
    ULONG pd_type;             // Page is swappable or not
};
```

Figure 4-5.
Pager descriptor structure.

For a Win32 code page, only the *pd_virginin routine* is needed—all others are null operations. For a Win32 data page, the PD functions would be set up this way (a null entry denotes, esssentially, a no-op):

pd_virginin	Load the page from the .EXE file.
pd_taintedin	Load the page from the swap file.
pd_cleanout	Null.
pd_dirtyout	Write the page to the swap file.
pd_virginfree	Null.
pd_taintedfree	De-allocate the page's space in the swap file.

The functions for an initialized swappable data page would be the same as this except that the *pd_virginin* routine would point to a routine that zero fills the page.

In Windows 3.1, the system allocates the swap file during system setup. This allocation involves the user in responding to a few rather obscure questions, and once it is created, the swap file occupies a sizable chunk of the hard disk. Regardless of what the system actually ends up using, the swap file stays the same size, and Windows 3.1 doesn't offer the user much help in tuning its size to the minimum necessary amount of memory. Windows 95 fixes these deficiencies by using a normal disk file (not hidden, not contiguous) that expands and contracts to the required size during system operation. The swap file gets only as large as it has to, and the user is never involved in either setting it up or adjusting its size.

The bad news about this technique is that under certain conditions the swap file can become much larger than it has to be. For example, if you run one application, get a lot of its data pages dirty, and then run a second application, the first application's data pages will swap to the front of the swap file. Now, if you dirty up plenty of data pages in the second application, switch back to the first application (forcing those data pages out to the end of the swap file), and quit the first application, there will be an unused hole at the front of the swap file.[18] One feature of the Windows 95 design that helps reduce this fragmentation problem is that a physical memory page doesn't always

---

18. Although it wasn't implemented in the test releases, Microsoft planned to incorporate a background swap file compaction process to prevent the swap file from growing too large.

occupy the same page in the swap file. Unlike in Windows 3.1, if a dirty page has to be swapped out in Windows 95, it's swapped to the first available page in the swap file. This tends to push pages toward the front of the file.

Virtual Memory Management

Virtual memory management in Windows 95 did get considerably more complex. Windows 95 puts several new demands on the virtual memory manager:

- The new Win32 application type with many new API functions that support a number of different shared and dynamically allocated application memory types

- Dynamically loadable system components

All of these demands require changes to the 32-bit protected mode virtual memory manager, although no changes are required to support the older Win16 applications. First, let's examine the new virtual memory types that Windows 95 must support for Win32 applications. As you can see in Figure 4-6 on the next page, Windows 95 allows a Win32 application to consume an enormous virtual address space—and there are plenty of new features available to Win32 programs to encourage the consumption of all that space, including true shared memory and a number of new dynamic memory allocation capabilities. The base OS allocates all Win32 application private virtual memory regions within the lower 2 GB of the virtual address space. All shared memory objects—for example, shared memory regions created by the application—reside within the 2-GB to 3-GB region. Originally, the design had the Windows subsystem DLLs living within this shared memory region. A later change moved these DLLs above the 3-GB boundary, mapping them into the System VM's address space as necessary. Notice that a Win32 application has a true 4-GB address space. Calls to system DLLs are direct calls with no ring transition and no context switch. The advantage of this approach is its speed—there's no overhead beyond the overhead of the function call itself. The disadvantage is that an application can obtain a pointer into the system address space and start poking around—possibly to no good effect. Under Windows NT, the system address space is truly protected and no application can obtain a pointer into it. In this particular instance, the Windows 95 designers went for performance over security.

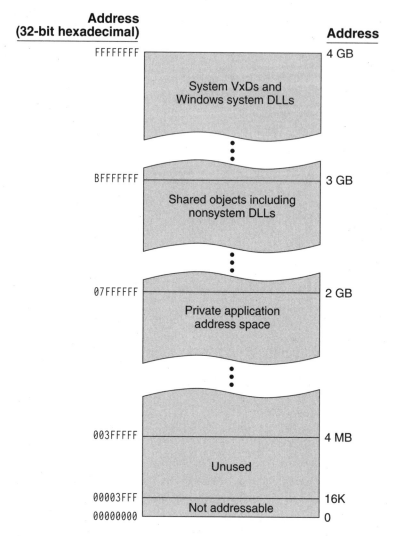

**Address
(32-bit hexadecimal)**

Address

FFFFFFFF — 4 GB

System VxDs and
Windows system DLLs

BFFFFFFF — 3 GB

Shared objects including
nonsystem DLLs

07FFFFFF — 2 GB

Private application
address space

003FFFFF — 4 MB

Unused

00003FFF — 16K
Not addressable
00000000 — 0

Figure 4-6.
Win32 application virtual memory map.

Within the shared memory region, the different objects will appear in the address space of every Win32 process. This means that whenever the system allocates a shared object, that piece of the address space is reserved in the memory map of every Win32 process—regardless of whether the process cares about the particular shared object. Suppose, for example, that you have two processes A and B that need to communicate with each other by means of a 64K shared memory region.

Process A allocates the shared region, and process B attaches to it. The system determines where in the shared region the memory actually exists. Let's say that the system allocates address 0x8000000 to 0x800ffff. Now suppose that processes C and D run and do some similar allocation and sharing. C and D don't care, or even know, about A and B and their shared memory area. This time the system will allocate a shared region for C and D between 0x8010000 and 0x801ffff. The first 64K has already been reserved across all memory maps, so it's unavailable to C and D. You might object that the disadvantage here is the possibility of filling up the shared region. But seriously? One gigabyte of shared memory? The huge advantage is the performance benefits gained by mapping a shared region to the same address in every process that uses it. A process can access the region by simply using the 32-bit pointer the system hands back—there's not even any system call overhead.[19]

The memory management services within the base OS must support the creation of many different memory object types within the application's virtual address space. Managing their allocation and deallocation efficiently is a key aspect of the system's memory management capabilities. Many virtual memory management functions require that the system back up the virtual memory by allocating physical memory at some point (although there are functions that simply reserve never-to-be-used regions of virtual address space). However, actual physical memory allocation (that is, RAM allocation) may not occur immediately since there's no need to back up the virtual memory until the application touches the memory page. But the system does have to take steps to make sure space is available in the swap file.

Memory Mapped Files

Perhaps the most important new memory management feature for a Windows programmer is the support of shared memory operations through memory mapped files. In fact, this is the recommended way of allocating and using shared memory regions. Typically, applications will use this facility to enable access to large memory resident data structures. To access a memory mapped file, an application must obtain a handle to a *file mapping object* using the *CreateFileMapping()* API function. Once the application has a handle to the file mapping object, it can use the *MapViewOfFile()* API shown in Figure 4-7 on the next page to obtain a memory address for the memory region. Other applications

---

19. Again, this approach differs from Windows NT's, in which a shared region can appear at different virtual addresses within the memory maps of the processes that use it.

```
LPVOID MapViewOfFile(hMapObject, fdwAccess, dwOffsetHigh,
                     dwOffsetLow, cbMap)

HANDLE hMapObject;      // File mapping object to map
DWORD fdwAccess;        // Access mode
DWORD dwOffsetHigh;     // High-order 32 bits of file offset
DWORD dwOffsetLow;      // Low-order 32 bits of file offset
DWORD cbMap;            // Number of bytes to map

LPVOID MapViewOfFileEx(hMapObject, fdwAccess, dwOffsetHigh,
                       dwOffsetLow, cbMap, lpvBase)
    //
    // First five parameters same as MapViewOfFile
    //
LPVOID lpvBase;         // Suggested starting address
                        //  for mapped view
```

Figure 4-7.
Mapping a file into memory.

can access the same file mapping object using the *OpenFileMapping()*
and *MapViewOfFile()* APIs.

The pointer returned by *MapViewOfFile()* is a virtual address somewhere within the 2-GB to 3-GB region. As you'd expect, there's no predicting where the memory object will be within this region, but the
shared memory region will appear at the same virtual address within
different processes.

The *MapViewOfFileEx()* API, also shown in Figure 4-7, is usable in
Windows 95. This API tries to force the system to allocate a shared region at a particular address (and it will fail if some part of that address
space is already in use). Under Windows NT, this explicit request is necessary since the system won't guarantee the same virtual address for the
shared region in each process. Under Windows 95, *MapViewOfFileEx()*
is redundant.

Reserving Virtual Address Space

An application can reserve a region within its virtual address space using
the *VirtualAlloc()* API (Figure 4-8). The address the application passes
as a parameter may be a specific address, or the application may simply
request a region of a certain size at any available address. The application can simply reserve the virtual address space—meaning that no
physical memory is ever allocated to back up the virtual memory. The
application can also set certain conditions on the region, such as read-
only protection.

```
LPVOID VirtualAlloc(lpvAddress, cbSize, fdwAllocationType,
                    fdwProtect)

LPVOID lpvAddress;          // Virtual address of region
DWORD cbSize;               // Size of the memory region
DWORD fdwAllocationType;    // Type of allocation
DWORD fdwProtect;           // Type of access protection
```

Figure 4-8.
Reserving a virtual address region.

Private Heaps

An application can take advantage of the existing memory allocation capabilities of the system by creating private heap space using the *HeapCreate()* API (Figure 4-9). Once the application has a handle to the heap area, it can allocate memory from the private heap in the same way it allocates memory from the Windows global heap. The system reserves the memory for the heap within the private virtual address region of the application and won't allocate physical memory to back up the virtual memory until it's needed.

```
HANDLE HeapCreate(flOptions, dwInitialSize, dwMaximumSize)

DWORD flOptions;        // Heap allocation flag
DWORD dwInitialSize;    // Initial heap size
DWORD dwMaximumSize;    // Maximum heap size
```

Figure 4-9.
Private heap allocation.

Virtual Machine Manager Services

The Virtual Machine Manager is the single most important operating system component in Windows 95. As distributed, the VMM is actually a VxD that lives in the DOS386.EXE file together with a number of other VxDs, such as the Plug and Play subsystem and the filesystem drivers. This combination of VxDs forms the base operating system for Windows 95. Once it is loaded during system initialization, the VMM is permanently resident. Although the VMM uses the binary format of a VxD, it certainly isn't a virtual device driver in the sense in which you normally regard VxDs.

Every VxD can define a *service table* to identify entry points to functions within the VxD that provide a *service* to other VxDs or applications. You can think of the services provided by a VxD as an API that's internal to the operating system. Since you can add VxDs to a system and write applications that call on VxD services, for some purposes you can consider these services as an extension to the Windows API. No, that doesn't mean that the Windows 95 API suddenly grew by several hundred functions. The services are for use by other VxDs when they're running at ring zero. Calling them indiscriminately from an application guarantees a system crash. VxDs don't have to provide any services, though, and there are standard system VxDs that don't. However, Windows 95 does include a documented interface that allows applications to call VxD services, and therein lies the major difference from Windows 3.1, which included only an undocumented and nonportable interface.

The VMM actually provides a central core of services callable by any VxD and doesn't deal specifically with any device. Windows 95 contains over 700 services within the base OS. The fact that the VMM provides close to half of these is an indication of the relative importance of the VMM.[20] Normally, the use of VMM services is the domain of device drivers, debuggers, and other system-level extensions to the base OS, and the scope of VMM services covers the lowest level of OS requirements, such as

- Memory management—meeting the physical and virtual memory allocation requirement details

- Scheduling—dynamic priority management and timeslice administration

- Interrupt handling—hardware device and fault management

- Event coordination—notification and thread supervision

As its name suggests, the VMM controls Windows' virtual machines. It keeps track of each VM using a *VM control block* and a 32-bit handle that identifies the specific VM. (The handle is actually the virtual address of the VM control block.) The VM control block contains information about the current state of the VM, including the VM's execution status (idle or suspended, for example), the VM's scheduling

---

20. A normal Windows 3.1 system includes a total of about 400 services, and the Windows 3.1 VMM offers 242 services.

priority, and copies of the VM's registers. Discussions of VMM services refer to VMs as *clients* of the VMM, and you'll often see references to "client" data structures such as the *Client_Reg_Struc* area used to save the VM's registers.

Calling Virtual Machine Manager Services

Before looking at how VxDs and applications interact with the VMM, we should look at how the OS supports the various code paths in the system, noting at the same time several new features of Windows 95. Developing a VxD is not a trivial task. The VMM and every other VxD is always 32-bit protected mode software running at ring zero, and you have to use assembly language to call upon VMM services. The Microsoft Windows Device Driver Kit tells you why you might want to do this and how to go about it.

Figure 4-10 shows an example call to the VMM's *Call_Global_Event* service. As you can see, the *VMMcall* macro masks the true nature of the call to the VMM service. A *VxDcall* macro is used in a similar way. In fact, both macros generate the same sequence of instructions, so the difference in name is more for documentation than for any other reason.

```
include    vmm.inc                    ; All the basic
                                      ;  definitions
        ; Start of fragment
mov    esi, OFFSET32 CallbackProc     ; Address of callback
mov    edx, OFFSET32 CallbackData     ; Address of data
VMMcall      Call_Global_Event
        ; End of fragment
```

Figure 4-10.
Calling a VMM service from a VxD.

VMM Callbacks

One of the important techniques used by the VMM and other VxDs is a *callback* mechanism that allows a VxD to register the address of a procedure for the VMM to call when certain conditions hold. The technique is similar to the way an application registers window procedures that the Windows subsystem calls for message processing. The VMM uses callbacks extensively to notify VxDs of system events such as hardware interrupts and general protection faults and for scheduling related events. Usually, every VMM service that allows the registration of a callback is matched by another service allowing the caller to cancel the callback.

The *Call_Global_Event* service illustrated in Figure 4-10 is one of the services that use a callback procedure. When the VxD makes the call to this service, the VMM will make arrangements to call the procedure whose address is supplied to the VMM service (*CallbackProc* in the example) and pass it the other parameter (*CallbackData*) supplied in the original request to *Call_Global_Event.* In this particular example, the callback from the VMM may happen immediately, or if the VMM is busy with a hardware interrupt, it will defer the callback until the interrupt processing is complete. Thus, when the VMM calls the VxD's callback procedure, the VxD knows the current status of the system and has a reference to some data that identifies the purpose of the call.

An important point to note about the VMM in general and the callback mechanism in particular is that many VxDs can call the same service. If the VMM registers more than one callback for a particular service, it simply works its way through a list, making each callback in turn. If you need exclusivity, you have to arrange to get it some other way.

Another example of a callback is the VMM's *Call_When_Idle* service. When the system is completely idle—that is, when there is no Windows action and no VMs are running—the VMM will call every VxD that registers itself with the *Call_When_Idle* service. Idle time is a good time to consume processor cycles for housekeeping chores. Windows 3.1 used it for writing modified memory pages out to the paging file. Windows 95 uses it for swap file compaction. Other VxDs could register a callback for their own idle purposes. But on a busy system there are only small amounts of idle time and no guarantee of when they'll occur or which other VxDs they may have to be shared with. This indeterminance is an aspect of many callback services—so design accordingly.

Loading VxDs

Windows 3.1 loads VxDs at only one time: during system initialization. There's no provision for loading VxDs while the system is running, as there is for loading application DLLs. Even if a VxD provides only infrequently used services, it must be loaded at startup and remain resident while Windows runs. Since Windows 3.1 uses the SYSTEM.INI file to specify the VxDs to load, installing a new VxD requires the addition of an entry to SYSTEM.INI. Another shortcoming of using VxDs in earlier versions of Windows was the identifying mechanism used by the system. Every VxD had to have a unique identifier, and VxD developers had to apply to Microsoft for this magic number.[21] The developer then

---

21. Internet e-mail to *vxdid@microsoft.com* will get you the information you need. One ID actually gives you the ability to create up to 16 unique VxDs.

embedded the so called VxD ID within the VxD, and the system used this number at runtime to connect VxD service callers to the correct VxD. There's nothing sinister about having to apply for an identifier; it's simply an artifact of a rather primitive method for guaranteeing uniqueness.

Windows 95 solves most of these problems. VxDs are dynamically loadable and unloadable, and for most VxDs a new naming convention does away with the need to acquire a private identifier. Microsoft's shorthand for dynamically loadable VxDs is "dynaload VxDs," or simply "DL VxDs." For brevity, we'll call them "DL VxDs." The operating system loads DL VxDs into the system's private virtual address space (above the 3-GB boundary), and the DL VxD author can identify the regions of the VxD's code and data that are pageable. This identification of pageable regions allows the developer to optimize the DL VxD's working set. Also, in Windows 95, applications can cause the system to load DL VxDs by name, which eliminates the need to edit the system's configuration files. You need a unique VxD ID from Microsoft only if the VxD offers VxD services or other API functions. If your VxD doesn't do this, you can simply use the constant *Undefined_Device_ID* as its identifier. Windows 95 will happily load multiple VxDs with this identifier.

For compatibility, you can still load VxDs during system startup. In fact, that's what happens with the VMM and most of the base system VxDs. If you write a VxD for disk device support, for example, you'll probably want it to be loaded during system boot. If the presence of your VxD is required only occasionally, the dynamic loading technique is the one to use. Network support is a good occasion for the use of DL VxDs, notably for the large components such as network transports. The Windows 95 Plug and Play and installable filesystem components are themselves dependent on DL VxDs. The dynamic loading of VxDs is the domain of the VXDLDR module—itself a (static) VxD. VXDLDR offers six services callable by other VxDs or indirectly by application programs.

The general rules for a VxD in earlier versions of Windows specify both its executable format and a number of interfaces it must support.[22] The system uses the mandatory interfaces to allow VxD initialization and to call the VxD with certain systemwide events the VxD must respond to. There are several events associated with system initialization and shutdown, for example, that each VxD is asked to process.

---

22. The only substantive change to the executable format of VxD in Windows 95 is that you can now define both memory resident and pageable code and data sections.

The rules for DL VxDs don't change very much in Windows 95. The format is a little different, and there are some restrictions on what a DL VxD can do. Only one restriction is significant: if a DL VxD offers any VxD services, it can't be dynamically unloaded. One reason for this restriction is the difficulty of notifying other VxDs or applications that a service they're using is about to disappear. Consider the problem associated with removing a DL VxD that provides a callback service that other modules might yet try to use.[23]

The Shell VxD

The final piece in the VMM puzzle is the module called the *Shell VxD,* or sometimes the *shell device.* Note first that the Shell VxD has absolutely nothing to do with the user shell, the application that manages the desktop. Once again, overloaded terminology can lead to confusion. The Shell VxD is the last component of the base system that gets loaded, and it's responsible for loading the Windows subsystem (Kernel, User, and GDI). As the user shell is to the user, so the Shell VxD is to the ring three software.

There's a Shell VxD in earlier versions of Windows as well. One of its main functions was the display of dialog boxes on behalf of a VxD. It's the Shell VxD that generated the *System has become unstable* dialog that came up frequently in Windows 3.0 and only occasionally—rarely—in Windows 3.1. Windows 95 expands the Shell VxD services considerably, adding functions in two areas that are relevant to this discussion.

The Shell VxD manages to do its dialog box work by running briefly within the context of an application. Its memory mapping and resources are those of the System VM, and in some senses the Shell VxD masquerades as a Windows application to display a dialog. Windows 95 generalizes this facility and adds Shell VxD services that allow a VxD to run at application time. A VxD entered at application time can do anything an application can: open files, load DLLs, and send messages, for example. VxDs achieve application time execution by scheduling an event using the Shell VxD's *_SHELL_CallAtAppyTime* service.[24] Windows 95 implements application time by providing an application thread that the VxD runs on during the callback. Application time isn't

---

23. No doubt those who probe around in the depths of Windows will soon come up with ways to overcome this restriction.

24. The service mnemonic gives away the name genealogy. Its originator called this context "appy time"—a play on "application" and "happy." Unfortunately, Windows isn't allowed to be whimsical, so "application time" is what the name became.

always available: during system initialization and shutdown, for example, the system is in a state in which it can't support application time processing. One use of application time is to post a graphical Windows dialog informing a user of the options when he or she has pressed Ctrl+Alt+Del to close a nonresponding application. In Windows 3.1, the system could only display a character mode blue screen.

Right about now you're probably beginning to see the expanded possibilities in Windows 95 for applications to interact with the base OS. It gets better yet. The Windows 95 Shell VxD also offers three new services that deal directly with Windows messages:

_SHELL_PostMessage posts a message to a specified window.

_SHELL_BroadcastSystemMessage sends a message to a specified list of windows and VxDs. This service is the same as the Windows 95 *BroadcastSystemMessage()* API.

_SHELL_HookSystemBroadcast allows a VxD to monitor calls to the *_SHELL_BroadcastSystemMessage* service, so that even if a particular VxD is not a target of the broadcast, it can still observe the message.

The windows and messages involved in these new services are exactly what you'd expect: application window handles (the *hWnd*s in an application) and the message identifier and message parameter (the *wParam* and *lParam* in an application message loop). Because the Shell VxD doesn't constrain the message parameters in any way, you can use the *_SHELL_PostMessage* service to set up private transactions between a VxD and an application. It's essentially a clean way for system components to send messages to applications.

Getting Around in Ring Zero

OK, enough discussion of the superstructure. It's time to see how all these pieces collaborate. Of the more interesting paths in the Windows code, the hyperspace jumps between ring three and ring zero and some of the trails within ring zero are among the most revealing. Figure 4-11 on the next page illustrates the variety of different call and return transitions. All are code paths executed as a result of a function call—either a Windows or an MS-DOS API or a call to a base system service. Other paths, taken as the result of hardware interrupts or page faults, aren't illustrated in Figure 4-11.

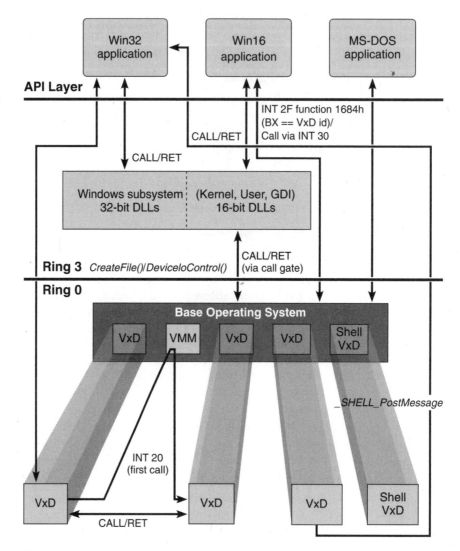

Figure 4-11.
Calls and returns among applications and VxDs in Windows 95.

In Windows 3.1, both MS-DOS applications and the Windows DLLs issued INT 21 software interrupts to call on system services as a result of API calls from applications. Ultimately, these INT instructions caused a general protection fault that the Windows 3.1 VMM picked up in ring zero. In the case of the system virtual machine, the base OS would then switch the VM to virtual 8086 mode and—for all VMs—the MS-DOS operating system code would run to process the API call.

Also illustrated in Figure 4-11 is the INT 2F interface supported by Windows 3.1. For compatibility's sake, the INT 2F interface still works under Windows 95. But that isn't the way you should do it anymore. The Windows 3.1 INT 2F function 1684h interrupt allows an application to retrieve an entry point address for a VxD service. The additional parameters in the call have to specify the VxD identifier. The INT 2F call results in a fault that the VMM intercepts. Using the VxD identifier, the VMM searches for a matching VxD and if successful returns an address that allows the application to directly call the VxD, requesting one of its services. Windows 3.1 actually implements this call by giving the application the address of an INT 30 instruction within a memory segment full of INT 30s. When the application calls the INT 30, there's a fault. The VMM picks up the fault, recognizes it as an INT 30 request, figures out the offset of the particular INT 30 within the segment, and, lo and behold, there's the index to the requested VxD service. Barring some trickiness in returning to the application, this interface works the same for both Windows and MS-DOS applications.

Calling Windows 95 Base OS Services

Obviously, Windows can't do anything about the fact that MS-DOS applications use INT 21 to call system services. File I/O–related calls now get handed directly to the protected mode filesystem INT 21 handler, and the entire filesystem transaction executes in protected mode. The Windows subsystem no longer issues software interrupts to initiate the trap from ring three to ring zero—the subsystem now uses a 386 call gate, passing parameters that identify the required ring zero service. This is a faster operation than trapping and unraveling a GP fault and results in a small performance gain. The return from ring zero to ring three is similarly elegant, simply using a return via the call gate. In the case of the System VM, there is no excursion into virtual 8086 mode—the processor remains in 32-bit protected mode throughout.

Although Windows 95 still supports the INT 2F interface for compatibility's sake, the recommended interface now uses the Win32 API functions *CreateFile()* and *DeviceIoControl()*. If you're familiar with Windows NT, you may already have seen these APIs. *DeviceIoControl()* in particular is intended for use as a general purpose interface that allows private communication between an application and a device driver. Windows 95 uses the interface both for device control and for communication between applications and VxDs.

To initiate communication between an application and a VxD, the application must obtain a handle to the VxD. You use the *CreateFile()* API function to do this (Figure 4-12). The naming syntax for the VxD is a little unusual. To get a handle to the Shell VxD, for example, you use the string "\\.\SHELL" as the filename in the *CreateFile()* call. This naming syntax works for any VxD registered with the system.

```
HANDLE CreateFile(lpszName, fdwAccess, fdwShareMode, lpsa,
                  fdwCreate, fdwAttrsAndFlags, hTemplateFile)

LPCTSTR lpszName;                  // Pointer to filename string
DWORD fdwAccess;                   // Access mode (read/write)
DWORD fdwShareMode;                // Share mode
LPSECURITY_ATTRIBUTES lpsa;        // Address of security
                                   //  descriptor
DWORD fdwCreate;                   // Creation mode
DWORD fdwAttrsAndFlags;            // File attributes
HANDLE hTemplateFile;              // Handle to file with
                                   //  attributes to copy
```

Figure 4-12.
The CreateFile() *API function.*

Figure 4-13 shows the API definition for the *DeviceIoControl()* function. In its normal mode, the API uses the device control code to initiate a device-specific operation—formatting a floppy disk, for example. When the function is used for communication with VxDs, the device control code and the contents of the input data buffer and the output buffer are entirely application defined. To fully support a VxD interface for general application use, the VxD developer will have to publish the supported control codes and the other details of the data exchange protocol. But if you write both the application and the VxD, you can use *DeviceIoControl()* as a private interface for communication between ring three and ring zero software.[25] Within the system, the VMM System Control service, which is called with a W32_DEVICEIOCONTROL message, dispatches the *DeviceIoControl()* call to the target VxD.

Calling from One VxD to Another

The last interaction we'll look at is the call and return mechanism between VxDs that's used within the base operating system. The method

25. The *DeviceIoControl()* interface also has the advantage that, for published functions, it's portable between Windows and Windows NT. An INT 2F interface definitely isn't.

```
BOOL DeviceIoControl(hDevice, dwIoControlCode, lpvInBuffer,
                     cbInBuffer, lpvOutBuffer, cbOutBuffer,
                     lpcbBytesReturned, lpoOverlapped)

HANDLE hDevice;                    // Handle of the device
DWORD dwIoControlCode;             // Operation control code
LPVOID lpvInBuffer;                // Input buffer address
DWORD cbInBuffer;                  // Input buffer size
LPVOID lpvOutBuffer;               // Output buffer address
DWORD cbOutBuffer;                 // Output buffer size
LPDWORD lpcbBytesReturned;         // Address of actual output data
LPOVERLAPPED lpoOverlapped;        // Address of overlapped
                                   //  structure
```

Figure 4-13.
The DeviceIoControl() *API function.*

relies on the system's ability to create a unique 32-bit number formed
from the VxD identifier and the VxD's service number. In Windows 3.1,
the VxD identifier had to be assigned before link time. In Windows 95,
the dynamic VxD loading mechanism allows the VxD identifier to be determined at runtime. Both the *VMMcall* and *VxDcall* macros generate
code that contains an INT 20H instruction followed by the 32-bit number
identifying the required VxD and service. At runtime, the INT instruction causes a fault that's picked up by the VMM. The VMM examines the
VxD service identifier embedded in the code and replaces it with a direct CALL to the VxD service entry point. Subsequent calls to the VxD
then go directly rather than cause a fault.

Dynaload VxDs use a similar mechanism in Windows 95, but there
are some subtle differences:

- At compile time, the *VMMcall* macro generates a CALL instruction. The target of the call is an external symbol in the
  target VxD indexed by the service identifier.

- At load time, VXDLDR replaces this call with an INT 20
  instruction followed by a 32-bit word containing the module
  identifier and VxD service number. VXDLDR also sets the
  high bit in the 32-bit word to denote that this is a call from
  a dynaload VxD.

- At runtime, the VMM patches the INT instruction, using the
  32-bit word in the code to map the module identifier to a VxD
  identifier.

You can see another reason for the no-services restriction on dynaload VxDs. Since the VMM patches the calls to VxD services to actual CALL instructions, if a target VxD were unloaded the VMM would have to go around changing all the CALLs back to INTs.

VMM Service Groups

The VMM is by far the dominant provider of base operating system services, and many of the services are either new or improved for Windows 95. Base OS support for the new threaded architecture for Win32 applications called for many changes and additions to the services, including thread management, scheduling, and mutual exclusion primitives. The largest single category of VMM services (about 20 percent of the services) deals with memory management. Other services are split among several different categories. In this section, we'll look briefly at the various service groups. All of these services are offered by the VMM.

Event services allow the caller to register callback procedures for global events or events for specific virtual machines. Windows 95 adds support for thread events—allowing a VxD to signal an event for a specific thread.

Memory management services include many different memory allocation and de-allocation functions for both physical and virtual memory. Other services that provide information about memory conditions support the memory management functions. Windows 95 adds services that support the creation and management of memory for Win32 applications.

Nested execution and protected mode execution services provide the ability for a VxD to call software within a specific virtual machine that's running in either virtual 8086 mode or protected mode. The system may need to call an MS-DOS real mode device driver or TSR, for example—both of which are always executed in virtual 8086 mode.

Registry services are new for Windows 95. They allow VxDs to interrogate the contents of the on-disk registry. The VMM registry services are similar to those available to applications via Windows API functions.

Scheduler services let a VxD influence the operation of both the primary scheduler and the timeslice scheduler. The VxD's influence can include creation and destruction of individual threads and VMs and adjustments of the current scheduling priorities and timeslice parameters.

Synchronization services offer a range of functions for managing semaphores and *mutual exclusion objects* (*mutexes*). The VMM also offers a number of associated services related to critical section management. Mutex object management, thread-specific services, and several of the critical-section services are all new in Windows 95.

Debug services have been improved in Windows 95, toward the goal of providing better base OS support for system-level debugging tools.

I/O trapping services provide a way for VxDs to collaborate with the VMM to manage the processor's I/O ports. Using these VMM services, a VxD can control access to individual I/O ports.

Processor fault and interrupt services allow VxDs to involve themselves in the system's handling of specific global conditions such as page not present faults and NMI interrupts.

VM interrupt and callback services interface a VxD to the software and hardware interrupt status of an individual VM. For example, a VxD can acquire and modify current interrupt vector settings within a specified VM.

Configuration manager services interface a VxD to the Plug and Play subsystem incorporated in Windows 95.

Miscellaneous services cover a host of other functions used to support VxD execution, including queries about system initialization, error handling, linked list manipulation, time-outs, and even internal versions of the faithful *printf()* function.

Application Support

Although the details of an operating system can be a fascinating study in and of themselves, the OS must ultimately be judged on how well it runs application programs and the associated subsystems. In Chapter

Six, we'll look at the details of the subsystem that supports the graphical environment for Windows applications. Here we'll examine the underpinnings for this support. Earlier we looked at the various code paths between the ring zero and ring three components of Windows 95 and at how an application calls directly on the services of a VxD. Windows 95 introduces support for 32-bit Windows applications using Microsoft's Win32 API while it continues support for existing 16-bit applications (nowadays referred to as "Win16" applications).

Unlike Windows NT, which began life as a 32-bit operating system, Windows has evolved slowly toward full 32-bitness. Ever since the release of Windows/386 in 1988, Windows has included 32-bit code that exploited the 386. Initially, this code was confined to the ring zero system components. Then, in the era of DOS extenders, we saw the first 32-bit applications. Third party VxDs followed. The Win32 API is the next step toward full 32-bit operation for Windows. Win32 is Microsoft's strategic system interface. Its first appearances were with Windows NT and in the subset Win32s API introduced for Windows 3.1. In Windows 95, we see the implementation of this 32-bit API for a product that will most likely sell millions of copies—so, yes, it's pretty important to learn about it. But Windows 95 doesn't support a 32-bit API exclusively. Microsoft hopes that every new Windows application will be a 32-bit application. However, given the sheer number of Windows applications now available, even the most optimistic marketeer has to acknowledge that 16-bit application support is going to be a feature of Windows for some time to come.

The API Layer

The code path from a Windows 95 application to the supporting system code and back is very similar to the one traveled by an application running on Windows 3.1. The system makes extensive use of dynamic link libraries to provide the necessary code paths between the application and the Windows subsystem. Earlier the interface between Windows applications and the Windows subsystem was characterized as a simple call and return interface (Figure 4-7). It might be simple if every system module and application were 32-bit code, but it's actually a lot more complex.

If you think about the Intel processor architecture for a moment, you'll realize that the internal code structure of 32-bit Windows applications and the system code to support them has to be fundamentally different from the existing 16-bit environment. In particular, the variation in addressing modes means that you can't easily mix 16-bit and 32-bit code. For Windows 95 applications, this means new compilers, assemblers, and linkers to enable 32-bit development. The system itself must at least provide co-resident 32-bit versions of the Windows subsystems (Kernel, User, and GDI) to support the new 32-bit API—alongside the 16-bit API for the older applications. And of course all the code must be small, fast, well tested, and well documented. No problem? Let's see about that.

Mixing 16-bit and 32-bit Code

The problem of mixing 16-bit and 32-bit code has occupied many developers at Microsoft. They have tried various implementation techniques in various forms in earlier versions of Windows and OS/2 and in Windows NT. The Windows 95 implementation certainly represents the state of the art. Whether it's the final word on the subject is a different matter. Here are the problems: [26]

- 32-bit code deals in 32-bit linear addresses (usually called *0:32 addressing*). 16-bit code uses a 16-bit segment selector and a 16-bit offset (known as *16:16 addressing*). There has to be a translation between the two address formats so that the 16-bit code receives valid pointers originally passed as 0:32 parameters—for example, an address parameter that points to a C structure. The solution to this problem involves a technique called *tiling*, in which the system allocates a new 16-bit segment descriptor to describe memory that overlies the memory containing the parameter. (Think of tiles on your roof, and you'll get the idea.)

- In C, the language of choice for Windows, an *int* data type is 32 bits wide in a Win32 application and only 16 bits wide in a Win16 application. When a 32-bit function calls 16-bit code, the 32-bit *int* parameters must be narrowed to 16 bits and then widened on return; this is a relatively easy operation if the parameters are in registers, but many Windows function calls will also push parameters onto the stack.

---

26. Omitted from this list are some tricky problems associated with the different executable file formats that Windows 95 supports. Essentially, these problems involve the different relocation information contained within the files. There are people who live and breathe object file format issues. We're not going to join them in this chapter.

- 16-bit code will return a 32-bit value (for example, a pointer) in the DX:AX register pair. 32-bit code expects this value to be in the EAX register.

- 32-bit code uses the 386 SS:ESP register pair for stack addressing. 16-bit code uses the SS:SP registers. There has to be a stack switch back and forth and possibly some parameter copying.

An implementation device called a *thunk* is central to the ability to mix 16-bit and 32-bit code effectively.[27] Every call and return from 32-bit code to 16-bit code, or the reverse, requires a thunk. Whenever an API call has to use a thunk, the execution time for the thunk code is pure overhead. If the thunks are slow, application performance suffers. The implementation challenge is therefore to make the thunks consume the smallest amount of memory (remember, there are hundreds of APIs) and the shortest possible execution time. Thunks are always written in assembly language. Figure 4-14 illustrates the different API execution paths in Windows 95 and shows the position of the *thunk layer* relative to the better-known subsystems.

The system handles the stack management issues by building a new stack frame during the transition between the different code types. A call from one code segment type to another will translate parameter formats as the parameter values are pushed on top of the existing stack frame. The addressing of this new frame will then be set up to conform to the rules of the target code type.

Some of Microsoft's previous efforts at thunk design have been documented as parts of various product releases. Windows NT uses a "generic thunk" method whose details you can find in the Win32 Software Development Kit. The Win32s subsystem for Windows 3.1 uses a "universal thunk" mechanism that is an integral part of the subsystem. The Windows 95 thunk method is another iteration and incorporates further execution speed improvements.[28] Some of the speed improvements result from using as much 32-bit code as possible within the

---

27. The term *thunk* came to Microsoft with one of the original designers of Windows 1.0, courtesy of his college research. It's been around ever since and is now in use as noun, verb, adjective, and insult. Those who were there way back when remember its original definition as "a piece of code that gets you from one place to another."

28. During the development project, the Windows 95 method was sometimes referred to as the "extensible thunk" mechanism, although it may end up with a different final name.

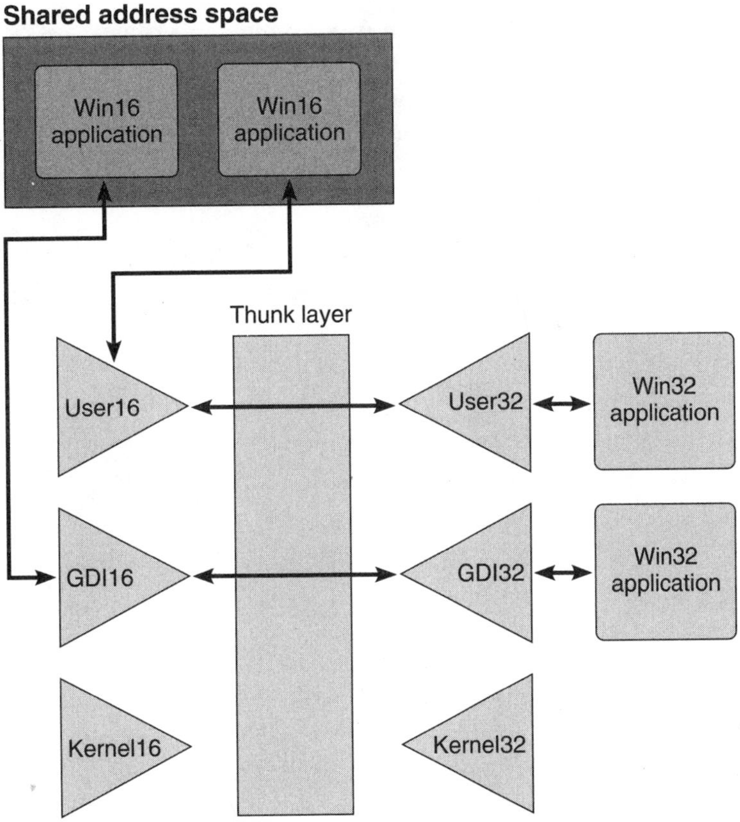

Shared address space

Figure 4-14.
32-bit API support using thunks.

thunk layer. (Microsoft calls this the "flat thunk" mode.) Other speed improvements come from very careful coding of the thunk handler—in particular, minimizing the number of selector loads. (Remember that selector load operations are expensive on the Intel processors since the hardware must validate the new selector against the program's current privileges and memory map.) Late in 1993, the Windows 95 team had a thunk transition down to just seven selector loads and they were still thunking—er, thinking.

Generating large numbers of thunks by hand is a waste of effort, so Microsoft developed some tools to help automate the process.[29] This

---

29. The thunk compiler toolset became part of the Windows 95 SDK in early 1994.

automation requires the programmer to prepare a description of the source and target APIs in a language that's very close to C, and the result is a sequence of assembly language instructions that form the thunk for the particular API. Figures 4-15 and 4-16 illustrate the input and output for the thunk compiler using the GDI *LineTo()* API function as an example.

```
//
//  LineTo() thunk compiler input. LineTo is:
//
//         BOOL LineTo(HDC hdc, int X, int Y)
//
typedef int INT;
typedef unsigned int UINT;
typedef UINT HANDLE;
typedef HANDLE HDC;


     // 16-bit target followed by 32-bit target
BOOL LineTo(HDC, INT, INT) = BOOL LineTo(HDC, INT, INT) {}
```

Figure 4-15.
Example thunk description input.

```
; 16-bit side
externDef     LineTo:far16

FT_GdiFThkTargetTable:
    ...
    dw     offset     LineTo          ; Entry #59 (say)
    dw     seg        LineTo
    ...

; 32-bit side
public LineTo@12
LineTo@12:
    push     ebp
    mov      ebp, esp
    sub      esp, 40                  ; Workspace for Kernel32
    push     word ptr [ebp+8]         ; Push 3 DWORD to WORD
                                      ;  parameters
```

Figure 4-16.   *(continued)*
Example thunk output.

Figure 4-16. *continued*

```
    push    word ptr [ebp+12]
    push    word ptr [ebp+16]
    mov     cl, 59                      ; Thunk index
                                        ; Call 16-bit code and
                                        ;  widen result
    call    QT_Call16_ShortToLong
    leave
    ret     12
```

Note that although Microsoft made the thunk compiler tools available, this technique for mixing 16-bit and 32-bit code is not recommended as a long-term solution. For one thing, the code isn't compatible with Windows NT. If you do choose to use thunks as an interim solution, make sure that the associated code is isolated and easy to replace.

The Win32 Subsystem

You can find the code for Win32 application support in four files in the \WINDOWS\SYSTEM directory:

GDI32.DLL contains the API entry points and support code for the 32-bit graphics engine functions.

USER32.DLL contains the API entry points and support code for the 32-bit window management functions.

KERNEL32.DLL contains the API entry points and support code for the 32-bit Windows Kernel functions.

VWIN32.386 contains a VxD that's responsible for loading the other 32-bit DLLs.

Within these modules lies the complete Win32 subsystem. To get it running, the 16-bit Windows Kernel module will load the VWIN32 VxD the first time there's a call to any 32-bit API. VWIN32 loads the three DLLs and returns to the 16-bit Kernel, which then calls the KERNEL32 DLL initialization function. Once this call is complete, the Win32 subsystem is ready for use.[30]

---

30. Given that the Windows 95 shell is a 32-bit application, the loading and initialization of the Win32 subsystem will actually occur during the system startup phase.

Most of the code in the 32-bit User DLL is little more than a layer that accepts 32-bit API calls and hands them to its 16-bit counterpart for processing.[31] Although that sounds simple, it's where all the thunk trickery comes in. It's also a sensible way of using tried and trusted code—after all, the 16-bit API implementations have to be there for compatibility reasons. The 32-bit GDI DLL contains a lot of new code and embodies some significant performance improvements. Consequently, the 32-bit GDI handles a lot of API calls directly. The Kernel32 module is completely independent of its 16-bit ally. There is some communication from the 16-bit side to the 32-bit side, but the 32-bit Kernel never calls across to the 16-bit side. This is as you'd expect since most of the code—memory allocation and thread management, for example— is quite different.

Since the call and return between the 32-bit and 16-bit code is a relatively expensive function call, the designers had to look carefully at each API before committing it to the thunk technique. The design guideline was that if the time to execute a 32-bit to 16-bit call and return was a significant proportion of the total execution time for the API call, the API should be replicated in 32-bit code. Examples of these replicated functions are the *Get* functions in GDI such as *GetBrush()* and *GetStockObject()*. These functions simply collect some data and return it to the calling application. Very few instructions are necessary within the API routine. Of course, code replication is out of the question if the API might need to modify a global data structure since the system has to guard against reentrancy problems.

The development team's emphasis on putting their efforts into the new 32-bit code meant that 16-bit applications could pick up many of the benefits. But there had to be a way to get from the 16-bit side to the 32-bit side, so the thunk mechanism also supports calls in this direction. The 32-bit GDI code is in some cases so much better than the 16-bit code that the 16-bit application still runs faster despite the thunk overhead. An example of this benefit is the more efficient 32-bit TrueType rasterizer. Also, to ensure memory allocation consistency, the 16-bit User code calls its 32-bit counterpart to allocate heap storage for 16-bit applications. All the dynamic memory allocation is thus efficiently satisfied from a single 32-bit region.[32]

---

31. There are actually about 25 User APIs that also exist as 32-bit code. Again, this is for performance reasons.

32. This memory allocation technique supersedes the use that Windows 3.1 made of DPMI in order to get 32-bit memory chunks.

The team was also conscious of the debate that would arise when observers began to analyze the mixture of 32-bit and 16-bit code, so high performance was a priority. The lowest thunk overhead for a Win32 application runs to just over 60 clock cycles, with the average overhead at about 90 clock cycles. For a very expensive API function such as *CreateWindow()*, which has 11 parameters, the overhead is about 100 clock cycles. Windows NT, with its security requirements that call for a ring transition and careful validation of all parameters, imposes a much larger overhead even in a pure 32-bit system call.

Internal Synchronization

One of the biggest design debates inside the Windows 95 development team was over how to deal with system reentrancy.[33] The 16-bit Windows subsystem wasn't originally designed to deal with the possibility of process preemption. Consequently, there are many places in the 16-bit GDI, User, and Kernel modules where the system will fail if one thread is allowed to execute reentrant code concurrently with another. Every operating system has to deal with this problem. Windows NT handles it by blocking threads that try to access the same object at critical times. UNIX and OS/2 contain sections of code that block every thread but one for the duration of a critical section. Windows 95 absolutely required support for the preemptive multitasking of Win32 applications, and since many 32-bit APIs call 16-bit code, the development team had to address the preemption issue. To solve the problem, the team looked at a number of possibilities:

- Develop a new subsystem to support the existing 16-bit applications.

- Use the new Windows subsystem (particularly the GDI module) that the Windows NT team had developed.

- Adopt an approach similar to that of OS/2 2.0, in which each 16-bit Windows application runs as a separate VM—somewhat as the MS-DOS VM support works.

- Use one or more system semaphores to ensure that no more than one thread at a time can run within the 16-bit subsystem.

---

33. Not only within the development team. During late 1993, this topic became by far the most popular topic of debate in the Windows 95 CompuServe forums and at the various developer events organized by Microsoft.

■ Revise the old code to enforce mutual exclusion on system resources within the appropriate critical sections of the 16-bit subsystem (a design technique referred to as "serializing the kernel").

As you can probably imagine, the debate over reentrancy swirled around issues of compatibility, performance, timescale, implementation effort, and long-term value. The different approaches to the reentrancy problem broke down to a question of new code, new architecture, or protection of old code. Let's look at just a few of the specific trade-offs the development team had to take into account as it considered adopting one of the new approaches:

■ The nonpreemptive nature of Windows 3.1 and its predecessors has meant that some Windows applications could depend on the ordering and timing of certain system messages. Preempting one of these applications at the wrong time would cause such a program to fail. Breaking this compatibility constraint was simply not an option.

■ Application-registered callbacks are another difficult compatibility issue. If the team used a semaphore approach, the procedure for correctly setting the appropriate flags during a callback to a 16-bit application would be a tough one to develop and test; this is a soluble problem, but the solution would have involved huge amounts of testing.

■ Rewriting the entire Kernel, User, and GDI subsystems as 32-bit code would have dramatically increased the memory required for the system's working set. The User and GDI modules alone require a working set of about 800K.[34] Measurements indicated that a conversion to 32-bit code would have increased the memory requirement by close to 40 percent, which would have raised the working set requirements for User and GDI to well over a megabyte. Given the goal of running Windows 95 well on a 4-MB system, this increase in memory consumption wasn't acceptable.

---

34. Out of a planned total working set of around 3 MB for the product—similar to that of Windows 3.1.

■ Using the Windows NT subsystem looked attractive but would have required extensive adaptation work for the Windows 95 architecture and a lot more memory to run in. (The Windows NT code is written predominantly in C++, whereas Windows 95 is written in C and assembler.)

■ A similar problem would have arisen from adopting the multiple VM solution used by OS/2—more memory would have been needed on the host system. And the OS/2 solution fails to address some critical compatibility issues that the Windows team weren't prepared to ignore.

With radically new approaches disqualified, it came down to figuring out how to introduce protection (by way of mutual exclusion) into the Win16 subsystem. The new 32-bit code designed for the Win32 subsystem simply didn't have this problem: from the outset it was designed to support a multithreaded environment. Each of the potential solutions for the protection of old code traded implementation time off against overall impact:

■ A single semaphore guarding the Win16 subsystem against reentrancy would have been the simplest solution. It would have been quick to implement and easy to test, and it would have had no associated compatibility problems. However, under certain conditions it could have had a big effect on the system's multitasking performance.

■ Multiple semaphores guarding related groups of Win16 functions would have reduced the adverse effects of a single semaphore on multitasking performance; but when the benefits were weighed against the implementation and testing effort it would require, this design didn't seem to be a compelling solution. Using multiple semaphores to reduce the granularity of a critical section would have imposed a performance overhead. In one measurement, the execution time for a single API increased by 10 percent. Providing the user with a new system that was slower than Windows 3.1 was, again, an unacceptable trade-off.

■ The team also looked at a solution somewhere between the single semaphore approach and the multiple semaphores approach. In this solution, two semaphores would have been used: one for Win16 applications and the other for the 16-bit User and GDI modules. This arrangement would have allowed calls from 32-bit code into the 16-bit User and GDI whenever a Win16 application was doing something else. Unfortunately, this solution would have involved modifying over 1000 entry points within Windows, as well as required modifications to system DLLs and many third party device drivers. Compatibility constraints disqualified this solution too.

■ Serializing the Win16 subsystem would have been the most effective solution. Shared resources would have been locked only briefly—minimizing the impact on the system's multitasking performance. Unfortunately, the estimates for implementing this solution indicated that it would have taken a significant amount of time to complete the development work and would have added a massive testing burden to the project. The team realized that the serializing approach would have involved them in one of those software tasks that's virtually impossible to accurately estimate the timescale for until a lot of work has already been completed. Certainly, they knew, months of elapsed time would be involved—enough time to push the product release beyond acceptable limits.

Microsoft decided to adopt the single semaphore solution for Windows 95. Figure 4-17 shows a revised version of the diagram in Figure 4-13, one that depicts what really goes on when 16-bit and 32-bit applications run concurrently. The semaphore that guards the Win16 subsystem against reentrancy is called *Win16Mutex*[35]. This semaphore is set whenever the scheduler hands the processor to any 16-bit Windows thread. The setting of the semaphore has several implications:

■ Win32 application threads set and clear the semaphore as they pass through the thunk layer. A concurrent Win32 thread blocks on this semaphore while another thread is executing Win16 code.

---

35. The awesome power of marketing. *Win16Mutex* used to be *Win16Lock*. After the early technical debates about Windows 95 multitasking effectiveness, the marketing group decided that *Win16Mutex* had fewer negative connotations than *Win16Lock*, and the name was changed.

- A Win32 thread that does not thunk to the Win16 subsystem never blocks on *Win16Mutex*.

- Whenever the scheduler hands control to a Win16 thread, it sets the semaphore. *Win16Mutex* remains set until the Win16 thread yields control.

- The behavior of a 16-bit Windows application will be exactly the same as under Windows 3.1: no preemption and no changes in message ordering, timing, or any other system-dependent operation.

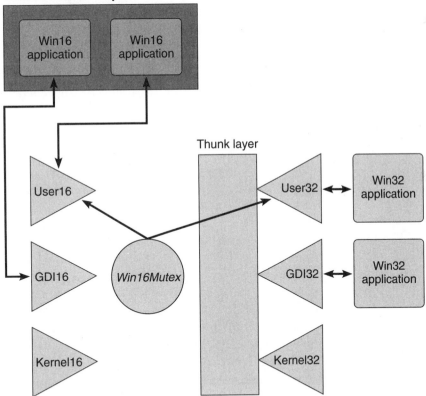

Figure 4-17.
Serializing execution of the Win16 subsystem.

The *Win16Mutex* operations warrant more explanation since they are also the drawback to this solution. Setting *Win16Mutex* prevents a Win32 thread from entering the Win16 subsystem whenever a Win16 thread is active. *Win16Mutex* has to be set because there are non-reentrant Win16 components, such as the common dialog library, that a Win16 application calls directly rather than via an entry to the Win16 subsystem. Setting and clearing *Win16Mutex* as a Win16 thread enters the system won't account for this case, so the semaphore has to remain set whenever a Win16 thread is active. Under normal operation with well-behaved 16-bit applications (that is, with applications that regularly yield control as they should), the effects on the system's multitasking are minimal. At worst, there might be a brief delay in a window repaint for a Win32 application. (And "brief" here is on the order of microseconds.) If a 16-bit application actually hangs up, the system will gradually come to a halt as the Win32 threads block on *Win16Mutex*. When the user hits Ctrl+Alt+Del to get rid of the offending application, the system will reset *Win16Mutex* as part of its cleanup procedure—and everything will proceed normally. If a 16-bit application actually crashes—with a GP fault, for example—then again *Win16Mutex* will be cleared during cleanup. The *Win16Mutex* semaphore is a less than perfect solution—no question. And no doubt critics searching for flaws will pounce on this shortcoming. It is the best solution Microsoft could come up with to the most obvious problem brought about by the compatibility constraints placed on Windows 95. Having examined the trade-offs inherent in each possible solution, I'll happily argue that the Windows 95 designers made the right choice. Ignoring compatibility constraints would have been the worst decision the design team could have made, and the additional constraints of performance, memory occupancy, and project timescale make the single semaphore solution the best one. Windows 95 offers a scheduling mechanism that's markedly better than the one in Windows 3.1 today. Your existing 16-bit applications will run as well as or better than they ever have, you'll get full preemption with new Win32 applications, and in everyday use the combination of the two really won't have a detrimental impact on performance:

■ The 32-bit and 16-bit kernel components are independent, so a Win32 thread requesting a potentially lengthy operation, such as file I/O, won't have to call into the 16-bit code.

■ The User and GDI calls that do have to grab the *Win16Mutex* semaphore are predominantly ones that have very short execution times, so Win32 threads will need to own the semaphore only briefly. This means that separate Win32 threads will rarely compete for the semaphore.

■ Both the shell and the print spooler are 32-bit applications, so the most commonly used components will avoid the problem altogether.

The possible drawbacks to this solution when the user runs a mix of 16-bit and 32-bit applications are another incentive for application developers to concentrate their efforts on Win32 applications. And don't forget: if you truly, absolutely, require a system that provides guaranteed preemption of both 32-bit and 16-bit applications, Windows NT is the product for you.

Conclusion

For students of operating system design, Windows 95 is interesting for its practical implementation of some modern techniques, such as threads. And the base system now fully exploits the 386 processor architecture, with its core components retaining no dependence on 16-bit code or 16-bit processor modes. The ugly practicality of running applications designed for the world's most popular piece of software has meant that some design compromises had to be made. For the purist, the compromises may detract from the major improvements implemented within the base operating system introduced with this version of Windows. For the user and for the developer who's in the business of selling software, the compromises mean compatibility—to this day the only feature guaranteed to increase the popularity of an operating system.

Windows 95 provides the application programmer with some major new opportunities, including the prospect of developing with a full 32-bit API and memory model and the ability to exploit preemptive scheduling. The user will benefit from 32-bit applications in terms of performance, robustness, and increased functionality. Those enhancements won't be the user's first impression, however. That will be provided by the major changes in the appearance of Windows 95, and they're our next topic.

References

Microsoft Corporation. Win32 Software Development Kit. Redmond, Wash.: Microsoft, 1993.

Microsoft Corporation. *Win32s Programmer's Reference Manual.* Redmond, Wash.: Microsoft, 1992.

Microsoft Corporation. Windows 95 Device Driver Kit. Redmond, Wash.: Microsoft, 1994. If you really want to grope around inside Windows, you must have this product. Simply studying the header files reveals a lot of information about the internals of Windows. There are also reams of sample VxD source code if you want to get very serious.

Nu-Mega Technologies, Inc. *Soft-Ice/W Reference Manual.* Nashua, N.H.: Nu-Mega, 1993. If you program seriously for Windows and you don't use this debugger, stop everything and go buy it. Clearly, Microsoft itself was impressed—a preliminary version of Soft-Ice/W for Windows 95 came with the very first external test release. Apart from being a great tool, Soft-Ice/W offers a lot of interesting information about Windows in its product manual.

Oney, Walter. "Mix 16-Bit and 32-Bit Code in Your Applications with the Win32s Universal Thunk." *Microsoft Systems Journal,* November 1993: 39–59. A useful discussion of some of the issues surrounding mixed memory models and thunking techniques.

Pietrek, Matt. *Windows Internals.* Reading, Mass.: Addison Wesley, 1993. If you really want to know how Windows 3.1 does its work, this is a book you have to read. I imagine Matt as he wrote this book as a lone spelunker, flaming torch held high as he crawled through the world's latest and largest heretofore undiscovered system of caves. I hope that Matt is already at work on the version for Windows 95.

 Start

CHAPTER FIVE

THE USER INTERFACE AND THE SHELL

Microsoft's introduction of Windows 3.0 in New York on May 22, 1990, was the cornerstone upon which the Windows product line has built an ever increasing market share over the last few years. Although there were many notable new features in the Windows 3.0 release, the product introduction and a large proportion of the product's reviews focused on the improved visual appeal of the Windows interface. Many small, simple improvements to the interface, such as buttons that appeared to move when the user clicked them with the mouse, enhanced the product's immediate appeal—perhaps out of all proportion to their actual importance. The product's eventual success was a function of the other major new features of Windows 3.0 plus Microsoft's intense marketing campaign and the availability of some important new Windows application products. But in the first flush of the product's success, its visual appeal counted for a great deal.

Windows 95 looks as dramatically different from Windows 3.0 (and 3.1) as Windows 3.0 did from its predecessors. From the moment you start Windows 95, you can see that the appearance of Windows has been completely altered. Figures 5-1 and 5-2 on the next page illustrate the difference. Each shows one of the first screens a user sees after initial installation.

So why change a winning formula so completely? Aren't there some major business risks associated with asking a loyal base of users to accept change one more time? Of course there are some risks, and the reception of Windows 95 will determine whether Microsoft's gamble pays off.[1] In this chapter, we'll look at all the new elements of the Windows interface

---

1. Late in the project Microsoft decided to retain versions of the Windows 3.1 Program Manager and File Manager as desktop accessories for Windows 95—no doubt to lessen the initial shock for experienced Windows 3.1 users.

and in particular at the new Windows 95 shell—itself significantly different from the Windows 3.1 Program Manager.

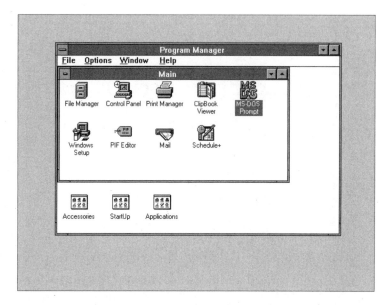

Figure 5-1.
The initial default user screen for Windows 3.1.

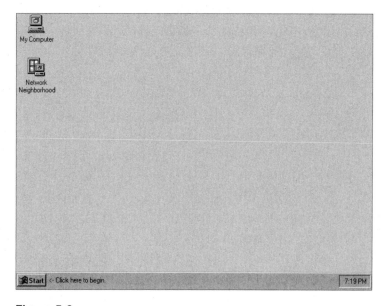

Figure 5-2.
The initial default user screen for Windows 95.

If you're familiar with the UNIX or the OS/2 operating system or with any one of the many products available for MS-DOS or Windows, the term *shell* is no doubt also familiar to you. Generally speaking, the shell is a program that provides the user with a means of control over the system. The shell is the program the user generally considers to be "the system." In MS-DOS, both COMMAND.COM and the MS-DOS Shell provide user control and the system interface. In Windows 3.1, it's hard to point to "the shell." The Program Manager fulfills some of the shell function and the File Manager some more. Neither provides all of the functions that the sophisticated user has come to expect of a good shell program. The new shell is the component that realizes a lot of the user interface improvements in Windows 95. The success of the shell, as the average user's means of controlling the system, will by and large indicate the success of the user interface improvements in Windows 95.

Given that Microsoft rarely alters a successful product simply for the sake of change, you can conclude that there were good reasons for the extensive revision of the interface in Windows 95. One was the desire to take a step toward a fully *document-centric* interface, one in which users concern themselves only with their documents and not with files, programs, directories, disk volumes, and the other odd paraphernalia of operating systems. Microsoft's work on OLE technology laid the foundation for a lot of the thinking that went into Windows 95 and also into Cairo. Windows 95 doesn't quite reach the goal of being a completely document-centric system, but it is a major step forward. It's up to the Cairo team to pull off the final jump.

The other major reason for revising the Windows 3.0 and 3.1 interface was to fix some of its problems—problems either that Microsoft knew about from the beginning or that had become apparent as more and more people began to use Windows. The goal of making Windows 95 easy for users and the desire to attract more new users to the Windows platform warranted a major effort to eliminate these problems.

We'll return to document-centric thinking a little later. Let's take a look at the perceived problems in Windows 3.0 and 3.1 first.

Improving on Windows 3.0 and 3.1

Criticism of Windows became a popular sport shortly after the success of Windows 3.0 began to pick up speed. The continued success of Windows has muted many of the more strident critics, but some critics made valid points that Microsoft paid close attention to. Within the company, the extensive degree to which Windows served as an application platform created a lot of requests for modification or enhancement of the product. As most reviewers are quick to point out, Microsoft's first release of a product is rarely perfect. But Microsoft does strive to get things right, and most of its products improve dramatically from one release to the next. Windows is no exception, and regardless of whether you consider Windows 95 to be the third or the eighth release of Windows, it does include some major improvements to the user interface.

Windows 95 benefits from the effort invested in the following:

- More unified configuration and control of the system. The plethora of manager programs and other control functions is reduced.

- Improved consistency of the user interface. Similar functions look and feel the same.

- Improved visual details.

System Configuration and Control

Of all the criticisms of Windows 3.0 and 3.1, the most frequent one concerns the confusing variety of managers and control functions.

Program Manager, File Manager, Task Manager

The Windows Program Manager plays a notoriously inconsistent role as a tool for controlling the system. Windows 3.0 and 3.1 include both a Program Manager and a File Manager. The fact that the two different managers allow the manipulation of, in some cases, the same items compounds the confusion many users experience over the relationship between the items displayed in one and in the other. A novice user finds it difficult to grasp the concept of an application program and its separation from data. Even the expert user, for whom the distinction between application programs and files is a known, gets frustrated with the primitive methods Windows 3.0 and 3.1 provide to form an association between applications and documents.[2] Here are a few instances of the shortcomings and inconsistencies in the standard Windows 3.1 managers:

---

2. Several Program Manager replacement products, such as Symantec's Norton Desktop for Windows, have been very successful by virtue of carefully papering over some of these cracks in the Windows veneer.

- Double-clicking on a filename in the File Manager will start the associated application only if the user (or an installation program) has specifically listed an association between a filename extension and a particular application. If no association has been defined, getting at your data means first running an application and then loading the appropriate data file. This involves a number of steps and a number of names to know or locate.

- The initial Windows desktop shown in Figure 5-1 offers the user no clue as to how to begin working. It displays a confusing collection of icons and names and offers the naive user very little help.

- Application icons can appear on the desktop (the background screen) only when they're running. Otherwise, the icons must reside in one of the Program Manager windows.

- Using the Program Manager to delete the icon that refers to an application or a file is a traumatic experience for many users. The fact that only the icon and the reference to the file get removed is not well understood.

- Similarly, the true meaning of Move and Copy operations for program icons is obscure.

- Filenames composed of 8.3 character strings, with some characters having assigned meanings, are completely inadequate for virtually all users.

The other major deficiency of the Windows 3.1 Program Manager is that it really isn't even a complete program manager. The Task Manager provides some control over running programs. Unfortunately, the Task Manager is confusingly implemented and provides the user with very little actual control over the system. See how many Windows users you know who routinely double-click on their desktop wallpaper to bring up the Task Manager and its list of running applications.

Although it may not happen to you, most Windows users routinely lose windows on their desktops. Because application windows obscure others, a user tends to start the same application twice—thinking that the first instance somehow failed or stopped running. Or the user may believe that his or her document is completely and irretrievably lost. The Program Manager itself can disappear, causing further consternation. The obscure nature of the Task Manager and of the method for switching between full screen windows compounds the inadequacy of the Program Manager as a mechanism for fully managing every program regardless of its current state.

Control Functions

Although the Control Panel program incorporates most of the components used to effect setup, configuration, and control of a particular Windows system, several other system control functions are hidden away in other corners. Perhaps the best-known example is printer control. Windows 3.1 includes a printer control function in the Control Panel program and an entirely separate Print Manager program. And most applications include a printer setup function accessible from their menu bars. Exactly when to use which control function, and what the results will be, remains something of a mystery even to experienced Windows users. Windows 95 tries to reduce the proliferation of control functions, locating all of them in only two places: one for printer control functions and the other for all other control functions.

Consistency

Another aspect of Windows 3.1 that is treated inconsistently is the particular properties of a control or configuration object. The definitions of how particular items are set up or of how they will respond in certain situations are inconsistent. For example, Windows 3.1 allows you to get to the printer setup option either by choosing Printer Setup in the Print Manager Options menu (see Figure 5-3) or by choosing the Printers icon in the Control Panel (see Figure 5-4).

Both routes lead to the same dialog (see Figure 5-5 on page 164), but neither could be described as a swift or direct route to the most pertinent information. Windows 95 introduces the concept of *property sheets*—a feature aimed at resolving this problem. We'll look at property sheets in some detail later in this chapter.

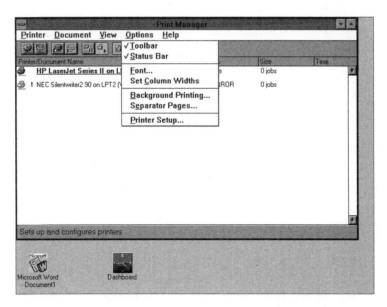

Figure 5-3.
Getting to Printer Setup via the Print Manager in Windows 3.1.

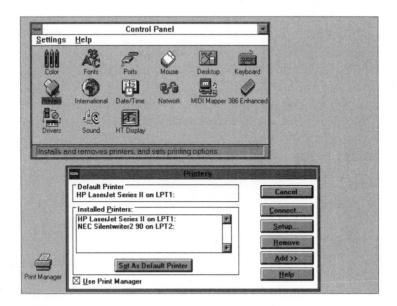

Figure 5-4.
Getting to Printer Setup via the Control Panel in Windows 3.1.

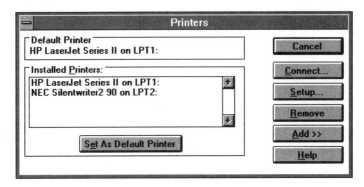

Figure 5-5.
Windows 3.1 printer setup dialog box.

Visuals

The appearance issues the Windows 95 team addressed are minor when you take them up individually. But by carefully eliminating all of the perceived problems and improving the visuals, the team improved the look and feel of Windows dramatically. Essentially, each change amounts to a great deal of attention devoted to every visual detail of the interface. In particular, the team took care to improve the consistency of the screen display and to reduce visual clutter. Take a look at the dialog box from Windows 3.1 in Figure 5-6. Notice that the different controls and buttons are all different sizes and differently aligned. Look at the Screen Saver and Wallpaper groups of controls. In one, the drop-down list box has the arrow button firmly attached to the text box. In the other, the arrow button stands alone. Does this difference have any significance? Actually it does, but this particular visual cue doesn't really help the user at all. The Windows 95 designers were intent on removing such small discrepancies.

Scalability

One other visual design issue also received attention: allowing the user interface to scale better on different display hardware. If you've ever seen Windows 3.1 on a large, high-resolution monitor, you'll have seen that a number of the visual elements don't scale up very well. The system font is one example. With higher-resolution displays becoming more commonplace on popular systems, Windows 95 had to do a better job.

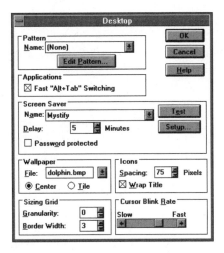

Figure 5-6.
Windows 3.1 desktop control dialog box.

Concepts Guiding the New User Interface

Many of the new user interface ideas for Windows 95 came from the visual design group at Microsoft. These are the people who define, refine, and improve the user interface for all of Microsoft's products. Over the last few years, Microsoft has used more and more visual design expertise on its projects, and Windows 95 is perhaps the first product in which the efforts of the visual design group have had a high level of impact on the appearance and operation of the product. Involved in more than pure visual design, the group works with the development team to define how a product is to respond to user actions. Their goal is to get all of Microsoft's products appearing and behaving in similar, obvious ways. If you know how to use one product, your learning time for another should be greatly reduced. Among other influences, the visual design group uses real people to test hypotheses about interface design—the input often coming from controlled usability testing. Does the user actually respond the way you think he or she should? If not, why not? One team goal for the revised interface in Windows 95 was to reduce the level of knowledge a novice needed in order to begin using the system. The usability tests helped validate whether the design innovations really did accomplish that goal.

In Chapter One, we looked briefly at Microsoft's other major operating system effort—the Cairo project. The initial design for the Windows 95 shell and for many of its interface elements was done by the Cairo group. Throughout the Windows 95 development project, there was a lot of interaction between the Windows 95 and Cairo groups to ensure the consistency of Windows 95 with the evolving Cairo design.[3]

The other major influence on Microsoft's operating system design efforts during 1992 and 1993 was OLE technology. OLE was originally developed by Microsoft's Applications Division as a way of providing a consistent basis for complex data interchange and other application interaction features. OLE rapidly became a more and more important component of Microsoft's evolving software architecture, and in the late fall of 1993, the OLE group moved from the Applications Division to the Systems Division—a move that confirmed OLE's central role in Microsoft's plans. In many ways, OLE can be viewed as the first implementation of Cairo's design concepts. The Windows 95 shell and user interface would be the next major step. Central to all of this work was the evolution of the user interface to a document-centric model, replacing the application-centric view implemented in Windows 3.1.

The Document-Centric Interface

The document-centric interface is the main theme of much of the conceptual work for OLE, Windows 95, and in the future, Cairo. The document-centric approach is derived from the object-oriented concepts that are now increasingly popular in the software industry. Unfortunately, *object orientation* has become an overused marketing term. There are real examples of its use, as in Next's NextStep system, but the proponents of many a system claim that theirs is an object-oriented approach without really implementing one. OLE and Windows 95 are major steps toward a full object-oriented system, although neither of them is complete in that regard. Microsoft intends that Cairo will be.

A document-centric approach means that the users concern themselves only with documents and not with programs and files. The system itself is responsible for maintaining the relationship between data of a particular format and the application that can manipulate the data. Putting the responsibility on the system ties in with the usability information

---

3. And, of course, one thing the Cairo group did not want was for Windows 95 to appear with features that Cairo would not or could not be compatible with.

that Microsoft has gathered from users of Windows. Many users, particularly those introduced to the PC via Windows, not MS-DOS, find it difficult to separate the concepts of programs and of files. To these users, the item of concern is the document they work on—whether it be a letter composed with a word processing application, or a chart of recent sales results prepared with a spreadsheet application. For many people, the application program and the file containing the specific data are conceptually indivisible.

The document-centric approach contrasts with the approach implemented in most systems today, including Windows 3.1. Today you use an application-centric model. To carry out some operation—for example, redrawing a sales graph in light of the latest month's results—you must first run the appropriate application, then load the data file, then change the numbers, and then redraw the chart. If you want to include the chart in a report, you also have to know how to run the application that handles your report and then cut and paste the chart from its native application into the report file.

OLE introduced the concept of a *compound document.* With OLE, many different types of data can be held and edited within a single document. Editing one element of the document involves simply double-clicking on the object. The application appropriate for manipulating that type of data is loaded without any further action from the user. You see and work with only a single document but possibly several different application programs.

The Windows 95 shell provides a document-centric approach to the system. Everything that can be conceptualized as a document has been. Collections of documents form *folders* (just like file folders), and you can organize folders and documents just as you would organize them in a real filing cabinet.

Look and Feel

The designers and developers of any graphical user interface, such as the Windows GUI, speak of the *look and feel* of the interface. This term refers to two aspects of the interface: the visual appearance of the interface and the behavior of the interface in response to a user action such as a mouse click or a keypress. The appearance and the behavior of the interface are closely intertwined. Many user actions are the direct result of a visual cue. A user who is unfamiliar with the details of a particular operation will seek visual guidance while navigating through a sequence of actions aimed at producing the desired result. Windows, and other graphical interface products, tend to reduce the learning task associated with a new application by presenting access to many standard operations in the same way. For example, opening a data file within a Windows application always requires clicking on the File menu and then on the Open option on that menu.

Designers of these graphical interfaces worry constantly about a few very important characteristics, asking themselves whether the interface can be described in these ways:

Consistent. Does the user always do the same thing in the same way? Does the user gain access to similar operations using the same keyboard or mouse inputs, guided by similar visual cues?

Usable. Does the interface allow the user to do simple things simply and complex things within a reasonable number of operations? Forcing the user to go through awkward or obscure input sequences leads to frustration and ineffective use of the system.

Learnable. Is every operation simple enough to be remembered easily? What the user learns by mastering one operation should be transferable to other operations.

Intuitive. Is the interface so obvious that no training or documentation is necessary for the user to make full use of it? This aspect of a GUI is the holy grail for interface designers.

Extensible. As hardware gets better or faster—for example, as common screen displays achieve higher resolution or new pointing devices appear—can the interface grow to accommodate them? Similarly, as new application categories become popular, does the user interface remain valid?

Attractive. Does the screen look good? An ugly or overpopulated screen will deter the user and reduce the overall effectiveness of the interface.[4]

In Windows 95, Microsoft addresses many of the issues involved in ensuring compliance with the guidelines set down in *The Windows*

---

4. Judging by the sales of screen saver software and the semiunderground proliferation of Windows wallpaper and icons, we might conclude that the average computer user is fairly keen on the entertainment value of the interface as well. Designers might not admit to spending a lot of time on this aspect of the interface, but Microsoft introduced a plan to include animated desktops in Windows 95 quite late in the project. Obviously, the Windows 95 designers believed in the value of entertainment.

Interface: An Application Design Guide (Microsoft Press, 1992). This book describes how the appearance and behavior of a Windows application ought to leverage the user's earlier learning. Microsoft is always at pains to point out that the book provides guidelines, not absolute rules. If someone comes up with a better or simpler way to provide a feature, as far as Microsoft is concerned it's fine to go ahead and use it.[5]

The Windows 95 Shell

A lot of design and development effort has gone into the new shell for Windows. During development, one of the major shell functions was referred to by the name Explorer. Whether this name will be used in any form when Windows 95 ships is unknown, but as of mid-1994, the term Explore still appeared on the shell's Start menu. The name does embody one important aspect of the shell's function. The Windows 95 shell is intended to be the program you'll use to explore the system— not just your own desktop system, but also the network system you're connected to. The Windows 95 shell replaces the Windows 3.1 manager programs such as the Program Manager, the File Manager, the Task Manager, and the Print Manager. The Windows 95 shell consolidates the manager functions into a single program that is always accessible and, at least by intent, will be the means by which most users will view and use a Windows 95 system.

One of the more popular terms in Microsoft's Windows group in recent times has been *browsing*. Sometimes it sounded as though all anyone ever wanted to be able to do was to browse around a network, locating files, programs, printers, and whatever. It began to seem as though actually doing something with one of these resources was incidental. That's stretching the truth a little, but Microsoft does intend the Windows 95 shell to make browsing (and thus resource locating) an easy and natural operation.[6] If you study your own work patterns, you'll see that you do spend a significant amount of time locating objects: finding old documents in a word processor directory, for example, or removing old unwanted files to free up disk space. Both of these tasks

---

5. One new standardized element of Windows 95 is the application tool bar, an interface element used by several early application developers and subsequently copied very widely. The tool bar is a good idea that has become popular with users, so Microsoft decided to include it as a standard element of the Windows 95 interface.

6. Cairo will take this capability much further by providing a powerful query mechanism that will allow the user to rapidly locate any object, anywhere on the network.

involve browsing operations, and improving the efficiency of browsing is a definite positive.

Folders and Shortcuts in the Windows 95 Shell

The Windows 95 shell implements two new concepts that need immediate introduction: *folders* and *shortcuts*.[7] Folders are a foundation of the shell design, and as you use Windows 95, you'll quickly find that shortcuts are a valuable enhancement. A lot of the examples in the upcoming pages will display the use of folders and shortcuts to one degree or another. We'll take a look at shortcuts in the next section.

Folders   A number of folders and their contents are shown in Figure 5-7. A folder is a logical container that allows you to group any collection of items you choose—a set of documents produced with your word processor, for example. The items, or objects, a folder can hold include

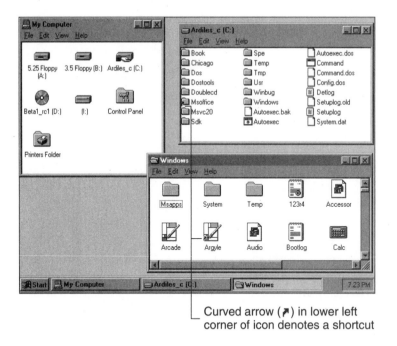

Curved arrow (↗) in lower left corner of icon denotes a shortcut

Figure 5-7.
Folders in the Windows 95 shell.

---

7. Microsoft originally used the name "link" to refer to this feature. As expected, it did change before product release. Among other candidate names, "nickname," "remote control," "jump," and "post it" were under consideration. The term "shortcut" was chosen in early 1994. Whether it will be the final term remains to be seen.

individual files, other folders, or shortcuts. (Notice the curved arrow mark used to visually denote a shortcut.)

The shell provides a view of both the local and the network system that is an exact replica of the filesystem—that is, an object shown in one of the shell's windows is actually a file or a directory residing on a disk somewhere. Folders are directories, and even shortcuts are stored as files. This design is different from that of other implementations in which some objects really are files and others exist in another universe. In Windows 3.1, for example, the icons in the Program Manager groups exist physically either as individual files or as resources within executable files; entries in a .GRP file in the \WINDOWS directory link the icons to the program groups. When you try to track down the icons outside the Program Manager, you need special knowledge to do so. Windows 95 makes everything a file or a directory, so most special files (such as the .GRP files) disappear. If you know how your desktop looks, you know how your files are organized, and vice versa.

The generalized folder mechanism, with its ability to contain any other object, is a big step on the way to a completely document-centric system. Operations such as printing, copying, and searching through a document require no knowledge of the particular program used to implement the operation. Any operation is available in a completely general way for any document. And one of the most important design goals for the shell is to provide a fully consistent environment. An operation on one kind of object achieves predictable results based on what you know about the behavior of the same operation with a different kind of object. The use of the folder concept is key to achieving this consistency.

Shortcuts   The Windows 95 shortcut concept is a very powerful one. It allows you to create a reference to an object without having to make a copy of the object. For example, you might create a folder containing several word processing documents together with a shortcut to the printer you use for output. Figure 5-8 on the next page is an example of how this folder might appear. To print a document, you'd simply open up the folder, click on a document icon, drag the icon to the printer icon, and drop it. Access to the appropriate printer would be immediate, and the document would be printed without your needing to specifically run the application you used to create the document. The shell would take care of loading the appropriate application and informing it of the operation (printing) and the chosen document.

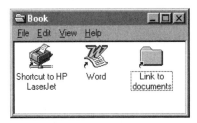

Figure 5-8.
Shortcuts in the Windows 95 shell.

Windows 95 uses shortcuts extensively, and you'll see several other examples of their power in this chapter.[8] Although Windows 95 continues the use of a hierarchically organized filesystem, the availability of the shortcut mechanism makes it possible for you to organize your documents the way you want them, without having to make multiple copies of particular files or programs. For example, if you keep several folders of documents that require the use of a calculator while you're working on them, you can store a shortcut to the calculator in each folder. The calculator is then immediately accessible, and you don't have to make multiple copies of the calculator program. Although purists might frown at the ability of shortcuts to muddle a pure hierarchical filesystem structure, usability tests have shown that very few people are comfortable with the constraints of a strict hierarchy. People don't work hierarchically, and they dislike the hierarchical filesystem for forcing them to try to.

Windows 95 implements shortcuts in the shell by recording their existence in a .LNK file. Each shell folder that contains shortcuts, and thus each disk directory associated with a folder, contains a .LNK file for each shortcut.[9]

Desktop Folders

Desktop folders in Windows 95 are very dynamic, and thus the contents of the associated disk directories change frequently. A \DESKTOP directory on the system's boot drive contains all the items that define

---

8. Something akin to links is in use in the Windows 3.1 Program Manager: icons in program groups are links to the executable program. Other desktop utilities extend the capability. However, Windows 3.1 neither formalized nor generalized the link concept.

9. Originally shortcut information was stored in a DESKTOP.INI file that also held window placement information for shell folders. DESKTOP.INI eventually disappeared in favor of directories collected under the Windows \DESKTOP directory.

the initial layout of the user's desktop. As items are moved on and off the desktop, the physical contents of the \DESKTOP directory change. Figure 5-9 shows a desktop layout and a listing of the associated disk files that track this configuration. Notice the default SHORTCUT.LNK files that contain the shortcuts to the printer object.

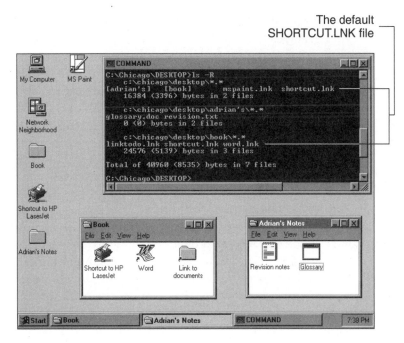

Figure 5-9.
Desktop folders in the Windows 95 shell.

System Setup

System setup in Windows 95 is considerably improved over Windows 3.1 setup. As part of the overall goal to make the system easy to use, system setup makes it simple for the new Windows user to install the system and get it running for the first time. If you know what you're doing, you can still customize your system as you install it. But if Windows is a new adventure for you, the answers to a few simple questions are sufficient to get you going. Microsoft's Plug and Play technology is central to the improved setup process.

Microsoft's usability tests uncovered the difficulty new Windows users had with getting the system to do something—anything—the very first time they tried to use it. In retrospect, it's perhaps easy to see why. Look at the Windows 3.1 screen display in Figure 5-1 back on page 158. Nothing on the screen provides a hint about how to start—and the StartUp icon can even mislead. There's a lot of information, but no discernible first action. The problem is compounded by the physical difficulty many beginning users have with the mouse double-click action. In Windows 3.1, unless you can double-click after installation, it's very hard to get the system to do anything for you. This isn't a problem limited to Windows. Most graphical systems today still require users to possess quite a lot of information and skills before they can start to use the system.

Microsoft addresses these problems early on in Windows 95. The single "Start" button on the screen (see Figure 5-2 back on page 158) is a good hint. To make sure that the user doesn't miss the Start button, the status message alongside bounces against the button when the user first starts the system—like a finger pointing to the correct path. As the user continues to work with the system, other helpful hints appear as status messages.

The Initial Desktop

With the initial default desktop in Windows 95 (see Figure 5-2), there is but a single obvious point of access to the system—the "Start" button in the lower left corner. The area at the bottom of the screen is called the *system taskbar*.[10] In the initial configuration, the empty desktop and the message on the taskbar telling you exactly what to do leave you with only one real choice. In fact, double-clicking on the desktop computer icons also gets the user going. Clicking on the "Start" button will get the user to the screen shown in Figure 5-10. Selecting any items with continuation menus offers yet more possibilities. Figure 5-11 shows one of these possibilities.

To get this far, the user must at least have mastered the single-click operation with the mouse. Simply moving the mouse to one of the items shown on the menu in Figure 5-10 means that you're almost home. One more click, and you're running an application. Microsoft believes that this simplified setup and first time operation of the system will quickly get users to the point at which they're doing real work, rather than fooling around with the system. It's hard to come up with a

---

10. Another term that may yet change. "Tray" was the term used for a long time.

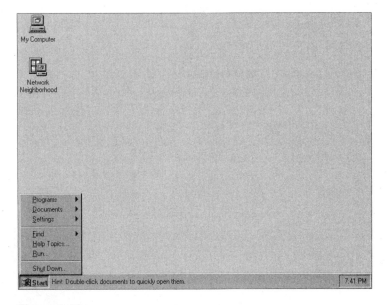

Figure 5-10.
The default Start menu.

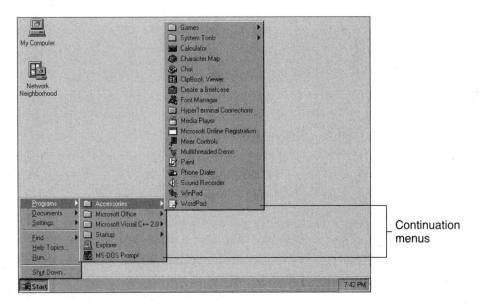

Figure 5-11.
Continuation menus.

general purpose scheme that's faster than two prompted mouse clicks from startup to application, so the expectation appears to be justified.[11]

The only other access points on the initial desktop are "My Computer" (which the user will promptly rename) and "Network Neighborhood" (which appears only if Setup detected a network connection). Figure 5-12 shows these folders after double-clicking has opened them. The user can explore the local system further by double-clicking on the disk icons and can explore the network by double-clicking on the other systems that are active.[12]

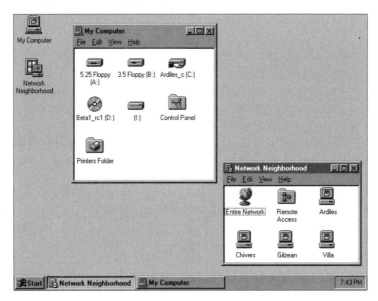

Figure 5-12.
Other access points on the initial desktop.

11. If you think this is an at all unreasonable amount of effort to get users to the point of running an application, Microsoft's usability testers have some videotapes for you. The tapes show novice users taking several minutes (and in some cases giving up the attempt) to locate and run Notepad under Windows 3.1. In the same test under Windows 95, the time was reduced substantially.

12. Early versions of the shell allowed access to the entire network from this point. On a large network (such as the Chicago development group's), accessing the entire network produced a lengthy and nonuseful list of network resources. The neighborhood concept allows you to constrain the network resources you view to the resources you're interested in.

The Desktop

In Windows 95, a number of new design ideas underlie the new look and behavior of the desktop. In Windows 3.1, the user's conceptual desktop consisted of the Program Manager and its program groups and to some extent the background. Beyond holding minimized windows and providing a display area for the user's favorite screen wallpaper, the background didn't do much. Windows 95 changes that significantly. The Program Manager is gone, and the background becomes an important part of the overall shell design.

On the desktop, Windows 95 implements a look and feel that is consistent across all objects. Drag and drop operations are supported everywhere. You can move folders by means of drag and drop operations, and as we've already noted, you can print documents by dragging them to the printer and dropping them. The screen background itself becomes an integrated part of the desktop. You can drop objects on the desktop for storage. You can create storage objects and put them on the desktop for safekeeping. Conceptually, the Windows 95 desktop is intended to serve just as your own real desk in your own real office does—even to the extent of allowing you to put pictures of the family dog on it.

As you gain experience, your desktop will probably look something like those shown in Figures 5-13 and 5-14 on the next page after you've been using Windows 95 for a while. The desktop itself acts as a storage medium for any objects you put there: folders, shortcuts to objects, and additional access points to the system such as the local system and the network. Some of the icons will probably appear on every desktop because they represent specific points of access to the system. Other objects on the desktop will reflect the user's personal customization of his or her working environment.

The computer icon provides access to your local disk storage. Your opening this object is intended to convey an impression of your "opening" your computer to inspect the information it contains. Earlier on, we looked at some of the system folders and at some aspects of the shell's facilities for browsing as you deal with folders. The network neighborhood is the point of access to the systems you have connections to. Figure 5-15 on page 179 shows an example of the hierarchy of folders opened across the network as the user looks for a particular file.

Figure 5-13.
A user's desktop in Windows 95.

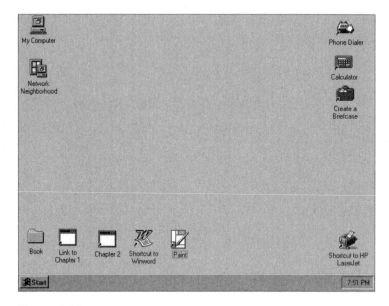

Figure 5-14.
Another user's desktop in Windows 95.

The system taskbar at the base of the screen represents a permanently available "home base," or anchor point, for the user. By default, the system taskbar is always visible and accessible. The Windows 95 designers intend the system taskbar to keep the novice user from losing his or her place in the system. Even when an application maximizes its window, the taskbar is still visible and the user can access it.

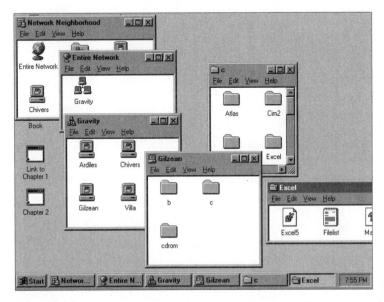

Figure 5-15.
Browsing the network from the desktop.

The Taskbar

Losing windows on the desktop has been an all too common problem with Windows 3.1, notably when minimized windows got hidden behind other windows. To solve this problem, Windows 95 introduces the taskbar—a user interface element that serves as a common storage point for several different types of objects. As you'll have noticed from the earlier figures in this chapter, you'll see the taskbar on the screen nearly all the time. The default taskbar behavior is to always be visible. Windows 95 applications must content themselves with the physical screen dimensions that are left. A maximized window occupies the entire physical display except for the area used by the taskbar. If you turn off the *always on top* property for the taskbar, a maximized window can obscure the taskbar. This is not quite the same behavior as that of contending windows under Windows 3.1. The *always on top* attribute in

179

Windows 3.1 would cause a window to obscure some of the maximized window underneath. The apparent screen dimensions did not change as they do in Windows 95. Microsoft has added an Auto hide option for the taskbar. Setting this option will cause the taskbar to appear only when you move the mouse cursor to the edge of the screen at which the taskbar rests. The taskbar will disappear when the cursor moves away from that edge of the screen.

In the taskbar, you'll see the following:

■ The single button that provides immediate access to some common system functions: help or system shutdown, for example.

■ A resting place for active windows. The system will put a button representing each active window into the taskbar. This refuge solves the Windows 3.1 problem in which minimized-window icons disappeared when they were hidden behind other windows.

The user can configure the location and size of the taskbar. Figure 5-16 shows an alternative layout. This particular layout makes it easy to demonstrate the various uses for the taskbar, but it probably isn't one you'd choose because it significantly reduces the screen space left for applications. And the shell does limit the configuration possibilities. You can adjust the size of one dimension of the taskbar, but the taskbar must rest against one physical screen boundary, and its larger dimension is always the same as that of the chosen edge.

One major function of the taskbar is to provide a consistent "home position," or anchor point, for the user. If you accept the taskbar's default behavior, the taskbar is always visible. Then, if you get confused or the desktop gets thoroughly messed up, the taskbar is always there as a place to return to for help or other system functions and to reorient yourself.

Application compatibility issues in relation to the system taskbar are quite interesting. Ultimately, the designers decided to treat the area occupied by the taskbar as if it were off the edge of the screen. Thus, Windows 95 clips the window in Figure 5-16 much as if the user had moved it past the right-hand physical edge of the screen. In Figure 5-17, the application believes it is running in a maximized window and occupying the whole screen. Windows has actually reported the screen dimensions to the application so that it excludes the area used by the taskbar.

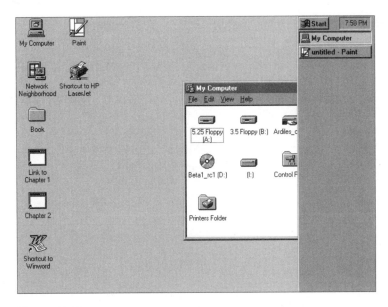

Figure 5-16.
The system taskbar in an alternative layout.

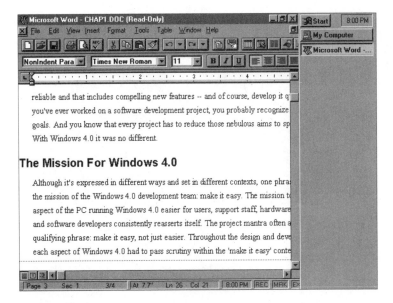

Figure 5-17.
The taskbar and a maximized application window.

On-Screen Appearance

In the example screens we've already looked at, you've no doubt noticed many of the innovations in the on-screen appearance of Windows 95. A lot of effort went into refining the overall appearance of the product. Some changes, such as the introduction of the system taskbar, are obvious, but there are many subtle design changes throughout the product as well. And many specific visual elements have changed in Windows 95. You may have noticed already the changes in the minimize and maximize icons on the application title bar. We'll look at several other changes later in this chapter.

The example screen detail in Figure 5-18 shows some of the subtle aspects of changes in the Windows visual elements. This part of a screen shows a Windows 3.1 application alongside the Windows 95 system taskbar. If you examine the application buttons closely, you can see that the alterations are very slight: in the system taskbar, some of the black outline disappears, and the shading details change. As you look at an individual element, the change doesn't seem very significant. However, when replicated in every element of the Windows 95 interface, this level of detailed change does produce a much softer, more visually pleasing, and consistent appearance. You can see this attention to visual detail throughout Windows 95—a case of the whole amounting to more than just the sum of the parts.

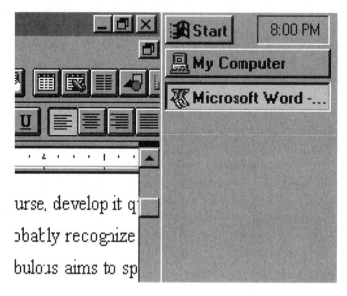

Figure 5-18.
Windows 95 screen detail.

Figure 5-18 also highlights an interesting side effect of the redesign. The buttons on the application's menu bar show the new-style minimize, maximize/restore, and close icons, and their appearance follows the Windows 95 conventions. The application's button bar, on the other hand, retains its "older" style. The button bar wasn't a standard control in Windows 3.1, so the application has to draw its own buttons. Under Windows 95, an unmodified application will continue to do that, whereas the standard controls are drawn by the system itself, so they adopt the new style and appearance.

Another theme in the redesign for Windows 95 is the provision of visual cues to the user as often as possible. In earlier examples, you may have noticed that the minimize and maximize buttons convey the appearance of minimized and maximized windows and that specific application icons are embedded within document and folder icons. Figure 5-19 shows screen detail from a more obvious example, in which the user is examining a disk drive. The type of the drive (the hard disk graphic), the space used in comparison to the available free space (the pie), and the fact that it's a network drive (the connecting cable) are all shown pictorially.

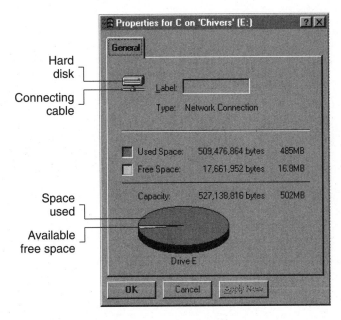

Figure 5-19.
Visual cues in Windows 95.

183

Light Source

Another theme of the design for all the visual elements of Windows 95 was the adoption of a consistent light source. The imaginary source "shines" from high and wide over your left shoulder as you look at the screen. All the shading for the three-dimensional effects uses the same light source. The screen detail shown in Figure 5-20 demonstrates this consistency. The sunken field containing the LPT1: string, for example, is shaded on the left and upper edges, and the raised New... button is darker on the bottom and right edges. In Windows 3.1, the light source isn't entirely consistent, and you can find examples in which the light "shines" from different places. Again, this is an apparently trivial attention to detail taken in isolation, but it does add a lot of polish and coherence to the product as a whole.

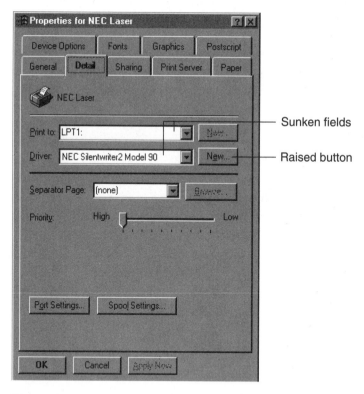

Figure 5-20.
The Windows 95 light source made consistent.

Property Sheets

Windows 95 attempts to introduce a much higher level of consistency for access to object properties by making use of the secondary, or right, mouse button (yes, finally a use for the other button!). Clicking the right mouse button on any object will produce a popup menu that includes a Properties item. Selecting the Properties item leads to a new control called a *property sheet*. A property sheet is similar to a dialog box in many respects and can include checkboxes, buttons, and editable fields—in fact, any kind of control. Within the property sheet lies all the information about the configuration of the selected object. Figure 5-21 on the next page, for example, shows the property sheet for the desktop. Note a few points about objects and property sheets:

- The popup menu for the object appears when you right-click on the object itself.

- An object's property sheet can have multiple pages marked by tabs—much as a book might have its sections separated by tabbed dividers. This provision for multiple pages allows a single property sheet to include a lot of information that doesn't have to be jammed into one enormous dialog box.

- You make page selections in a property sheet by simply clicking on the appropriate tab.

- Consistent with the Windows 95 theme of providing visual cues, the property sheet that controls the monitor configuration provides a representation of the display and its screen appearance, the property sheet for printer configuration provides a representation of a printer, and so on.

The obvious intent is to persuade all application developers to adopt the same conventions with respect to use of the right mouse button and the property sheet control. If that happens, object property inspection and modification will be completely consistent under Windows 95. Windows 3.1 applications won't respond to the right mouse button click or display property sheets since an application must be modified to do so.

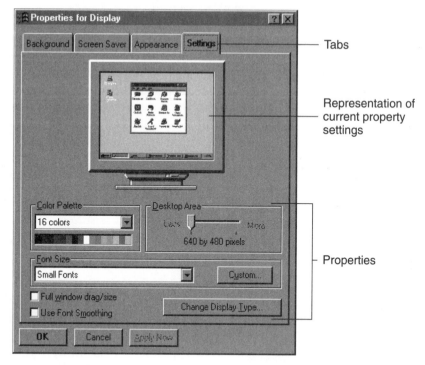

Tabs

Representation of current property settings

Properties

Figure 5-21.
Desktop property sheet in Windows 95.

Online Help

If you've ever tried to find your way to some deep, dark Windows secret, chances are that you found the online help system rather tedious and frustrating to use. You probably found that there was a lot of information to browse through, and you probably had to do a lot of backtracking before you finally unveiled the secret. You weren't the only one. Microsoft's usability studies showed that this was a common problem. Windows 95 adopts a much more direct approach to online help presentation. The help text is shorter, more explicit, and more context sensitive. Microsoft is encouraging application developers to adopt similar guidelines for revisions to online help in application products. The Windows 95 help system is unlikely to be perfect, though. There always has to be a compromise between simple, direct instructions that satisfy 90 percent of the user's needs and lengthier treatments of the more obscure details. No doubt we'll see more improvements in future releases of Windows.

Here are some of the changes to the Windows 95 online help:

- Keeping a persistent access point available to the user. The "Help Topics" item on the Start menu is always available.[13]

- Taking a task-oriented approach to the online help text. The text describes explicitly the steps the user must take to accomplish his or her goal instead of providing a general description of the topic. Figure 5-22, below, and Figure 5-23 on the next page include examples of this new format.

- Making sure the help window remains visible throughout. There's no need to click back and forth between the window you're trying to work with and the obscured help window that describes what you're supposed to do. As you can see in Figure 5-22, the active window is the Find File window but the help window is still visible.[14]

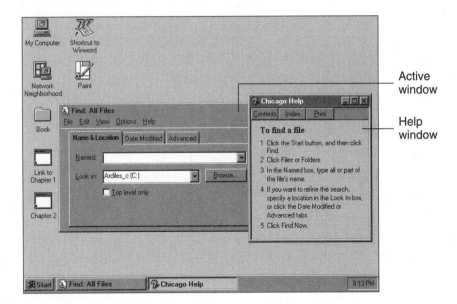

Active window

Help window

Figure 5-22.
A Windows 95 help window.

---

13. For a long time, the shell included a help button on the taskbar.

14. This example also points up one of the problems in keeping the help screen visible. The help window obscures the Start button in the Find File window.

■ Reducing the help verbiage and the steps you have to take to complete an operation for which you need help. The text is simpler and more direct, and the help windows include shortcut buttons that take you directly to the system function that will complete the operation. Figure 5-23 shows an example. Clicking on the button will immediately display the desktop properties screen saver sheet.

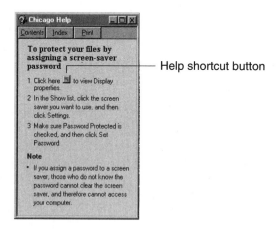

Figure 5-23.
A help shortcut in Windows 95.

■ Heightening context sensitivity. The help for an individual field within a dialog box is for that field, for example, and not simply a link to the help text for the entire dialog.

Implementation

Apart from enabling the shell as an OLE client, the Windows 95 team introduced three other features of the shell implementation worth noting:

■ 32-bit code. The shell is a 32-bit application that makes full use of the Win32 API.

■ Multithreaded processing. The shell takes advantage of the threading capabilities of the system. Each window opened by the shell runs as a separately scheduled thread. You'll see this innovation in action if you move the hourglass mouse cursor outside a window boundary. The cursor will change back to the normal arrow pointer, and, yes, you can actually continue working, moving to another task.

- ■ Shell extensions. Acknowledging its competitors' desire to extend and improve the Windows interface, Microsoft has included a lower-level interface that allows other vendors to integrate extensions of the basic Windows shell.

Design Retrospective

We've now looked at each of the major new concepts introduced with the Windows 95 shell. Of course, some of the concepts come from much earlier work on user interface design outside Microsoft, and many have evolved from earlier versions of Windows and Microsoft application products. The Microsoft designers didn't simply sit down one day and draw up the design for the Windows 95 shell. During the course of development (and indeed, during the preparation of this book), the design of the shell has changed quite a lot. It's worth looking at how and why these changes came about.

The Outside Influences

Throughout the history of Windows, Microsoft has taken vociferous criticism of the user interface. Some of the criticism is attributable to the product's success, some of it to the detailed legal scrutiny the interface underwent during the long-running dispute with Apple Computer, and a great deal of it to the simple fact that people tend to be opinionated about interface issues. Very few people care a lot about the names of Windows API calls or about the order of parameters passed to a function. But everyone has an opinion about the user interface. So whether they wanted to be or not, the Windows 95 designers were the focus of a lot of attention when they began to show prototypes of the shell.

By the time of Microsoft's first major Windows 95 design review—a meeting in Redmond in July 1993 that hosted about 25 people from the leading PC software development companies—most of the shell's features were in place, ready for the product's first external release. Much animated discussion at this meeting, and much more on the private CompuServe forum that hosted the early testers of Windows 95, helped shape the thinking behind the next release.

Although Microsoft sought and received a lot of expert opinion on the shell's design, one principal influence was the series of usability tests it conducted throughout 1993 and 1994. In some 30 separate tests involving as many as 12 people at a time, Microsoft observed a mix of users trying to complete tasks using the new shell. The users included people who had never used Windows (although they had used MS-DOS) as well as Windows 3.1 and Macintosh users. Microsoft augmented these tests by interviewing people who trained Windows users.

Among the user difficulties identified by the usability tests, these seemed to consume most of the design thinking during the development of the Windows 95 shell and user interface:

- Window management—dragging windows and sizing them, and the implicit ordering of the windows on the desktop.

- The difference between the windows supported by multiple document interface (MDI) applications and single document interface (SDI) applications. (Try to explain to a novice why the Windows 3.1 Program Manager apparently clips some windows and not others, and you'll see the problem.)[15]

- The concept of hierarchical containment. Experienced computer users have learned to live with hierarchy, but putting a folder in a folder inside another folder is certainly not the way most people organize a filing cabinet.

- The mouse double-click action. If you are innocent of experience and receive no instruction, it's almost impossible to guess that you need to double-click.

The Development of the Shell

The design work for the shell really began back in 1990, although at the time the effort wasn't even thought of as Windows 95 interface design. Later a lot of the Windows 95 shell design work was done in conjunction with the Cairo team's work to ensure long-term consistency between the two products.

These days Microsoft uses Visual Basic to prototype almost every screen display. The shell has been no exception. In addition to the obvious advantage that people can see and show each other what they're

---

15. MDI vs. SDI was a hot topic during Windows 95 design reviews. Ultimately, the team decided that Windows 95 would be an SDI system because they believed SDI to be easier for users. But since many software developers had invested in it, MDI support would still be there.

talking about, VB prototyping makes it possible to develop an early working model of the design. Although most operations won't have any effect yet, you can put together a prototype sufficiently rich that you can get real users to come and try it out. This kind of prototype is what was used most often in Microsoft's usability tests.

Microsoft released the first external test version of Windows 95 in August 1993. This so called M4 release was a major milestone for the development group since it represented the beginning of the end of the project. The subsequent M5 release was scheduled for the huge Win32 software developers conference Microsoft hosted in Anaheim in December 1993. In between M4 and M5, the shell development team concentrated on transforming the shell from its 16-bit state into a true 32-bit application. The design team in the meantime went back to thinking and usability testing.

Immediately after the M4 release, Microsoft undertook a six-week design project that put members of the Windows 95 and Cairo teams together to refine the shell design in light of current knowledge. This design effort focused largely on

- Learnability—how to get people doing productive work in the shortest possible time

- Usability—how the observed tests should guide refinement of the shell to make common tasks easier than in Windows 3.1

- Safety—how to achieve an environment in which no user should ever have to worry that his or her actions might destroy data

- Appeal—how to get people to like the Windows 95 shell; how to harness the naturally polarized opinions of the users to foster an emotional attachment to the shell

The result was a new prototype presented in an internal design review meeting with Bill Gates in late September 1993.[16] In this meeting, the team introduced the changes to the shell's folder mechanism, a new design involving novice and expert modes of the shell, and animated desktops. As they came out of that meeting, the shell design

---

16. Such meetings are a standard ingredient of Microsoft's development process. Always approached with much energy and not a little trepidation, a "BillG review" continues to have a significant influence on every Microsoft product.

team believed that pending a final decision on the transfer model (which we'll look at a little later in this chapter) and a host of small details, they were close to a final design. All they had to do, they thought, was wait for the programmers to finish the 32-bit conversion for the M5 release, and they could have the user interface they really wanted. This didn't turn out to be true since the novice and expert modes were later dropped and the detailed operation of the system taskbar underwent further changes.

Changes in the Shell

The biggest change in perspective that took place during the course of the shell development project was seeing that the novice user and the experienced user should be treated differently. Figure 5-24 shows the default startup screen used in the M4 and M5 releases of Windows 95.

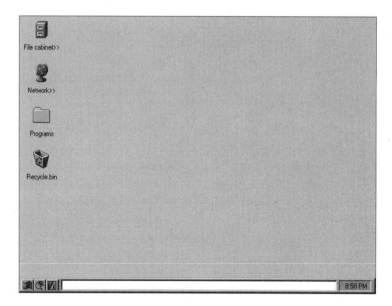

Figure 5-24.
Prototype default startup screen for Windows 95 M4 and M5 releases.

Contrast this prototype with the eventual design we've seen in Figure 5-2 back on page 158, and you can see some big changes:

■ The default startup screen in the prototype shown in Figure 5-24 offers several points of access to the system. The taskbar, for instance, includes three buttons rather than one, and the Network icon, the Programs folder, and the File Cabinet icons on the desktop seem to suggest even more avenues of approach.

■ There's no hint to the user about how to begin.

After the M5 release, the design introduced the explicit notion of a novice mode and an expert mode. Users who acknowledged themselves to be novices would see a shell configuration that painstakingly guided them through the system.

Figure 5-25 shows an example of the novice interface. Eventually this separation of users was dropped, and it never was a feature in any of Microsoft's external test releases. [17]

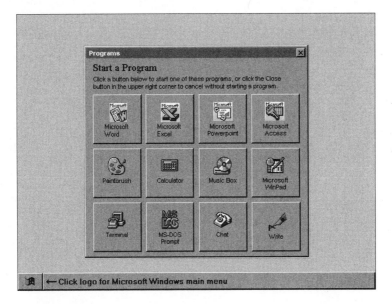

Figure 5-25.
The prototype for the novice shell.

With the final design, you end up with a personal desktop that looks a lot like the older default desktop. The changes to achieve the final default desktop guide the novice into being able to use the system quickly.

---

17. As of the Beta-1 release, some form of graphical buttons for augmenting the Start menu was still under consideration.

The Taskbar

A number of issues shaped the final design for the taskbar. The main issue was the behavior of minimized windows. The original design, shown in Figure 5-26, had windows shrinking and parking themselves on top of the default taskbar area—although it was still possible to move a minimized window to a different location on the desktop. Then the taskbar buttons became directly related to minimized windows. The final design, shown in Figure 5-27, provides for the creation of a button in the taskbar that corresponds to any window. (Ingeniously, the shell gradually shrinks the buttons as you add more and more of them to the taskbar—the change is almost imperceptible.)

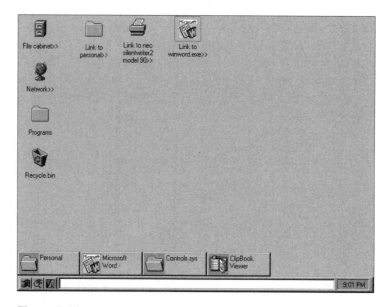

Figure 5-26.
Minimized windows on top of the taskbar area in the early shell.

This final design addresses the user's problems: losing minimized windows and having trouble differentiating among minimized windows, executing applications that simply have very small main windows, and other desktop objects. The user can always go to the taskbar to find an application that is running.

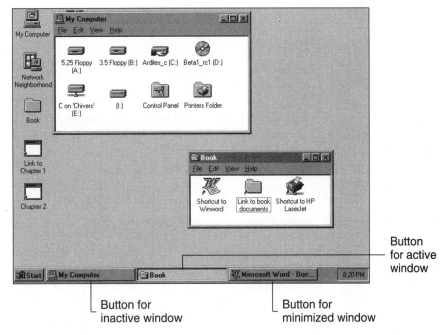

Button
for active
window

Button for
inactive window

Button for
minimized window

Figure 5-27.
*Buttons on the taskbar correspond to all open windows in the final
version of the shell.*

Folders and Browsing

As you can see in Figures 5-24 and 5-26, the old desktop design in the M4
and M5 releases incorporated a File Cabinet icon intended to be the
point of access to local file storage. Not surprisingly, experienced Windows 3.1 users assumed that this was the familiar File Manager application. It wasn't. Under Windows 95, it's the shell that allows you to open
folders on the desktop, and the folders can contain any kind of object—
not just files. The Windows 3.1 notion of a separate application—the
File Manager—that you must run in order to inspect files doesn't really
exist in Windows 95.

This subtlety proved difficult for many Windows 3.1 users to grasp,
so the designers simplified the shell by altering the file cabinet icon so
that it looks like the computer icon you see in Figure 5-27, thus breaking
the association with the old File Manager.

The default behavior of the shell resulted in folders opening on top of other folders. Quite soon the desktop would get pretty full, as in Figure 5-7 back on page 170. The modified shell behavior in the final release introduces the explicit Explorer program you see in Figure 5-28). The default Explorer behavior displays a two-pane window. Moving through the hierarchy causes the contents of the right-hand pane to be replaced with the contents of the next folder window you open. So more often than not, you'll have just one open folder window on the desktop.

When you browse directly using the shell, there's also an option that allows you to choose either to have a new window for each folder or to replace the current window contents with the new folder. The level of desktop clutter is thus controllable.

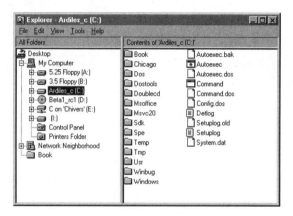

Figure 5-28.
Exploring the system.

Animation

The use of animation in Windows 95 isn't purely frivolous—though it may appear so at first. On the desktop background, the animation effects are there purely for user appeal, it's true. The device was introduced during one of the usability tests, and a lot of people liked it. The popularity of animated screen savers and animated desktop wallpaper seems to lead naturally to animated desktops. (Of course, a whole new third party industry segment will debut, providing replacement desktops for Windows 95.)

The more serious use of animation in Windows 95 is as an indicator of the relationships among objects: a window that shrinks to a minimized state gives the user a pointer that indicates where the application went. A folder that expands into a window showing a list of objects provides a hint that the different objects share something in common. This use of animation is actually quite important to the shell's "explorer" mode. One problem identified in Microsoft's usability tests was the difficulty people had in relating the contents of the left and right panes of a folder view—the tree and the individual folder. Animation helps users relate the contents of the two different panes.

The Transfer Model

Transfer model is the term applied to the user's conceptual view of what's involved in moving information from one place to another. If you know Windows, you'll usually think of information transfers as the Cut/Copy and Paste options found on an application's Edit menu. It's rare to find a document-oriented application for Windows that doesn't support cut and paste operations. Over successive Windows releases, system support for cut and paste operations has been improved both for Windows applications (with the Clipbook introduced with Windows for Workgroups) and for MS-DOS applications in the Windows environment.

Unfortunately, many novice Windows users have difficulty grasping the cut and paste metaphor. A strange hidden application called "Clipboard" is involved, and the user must understand the notion of different data formats to use cut and paste proficiently. With OLE-enabled applications starting to appear, the user's reliance on cut and paste ought to shrink, but there will still be a need to support cut and paste operations for a long time to come.

Microsoft's designers wrestled with introducing a different transfer metaphor, one involving the verbs *move, copy, link,* and *put here.* As you can probably guess, the *move, copy,* and *put here* operations would have effects similar to those of Cut/Copy and Paste, whereas the *link* operation would exploit the new OLE-based ability to support dynamic connections between objects. In fact, OLE uses the new *link* term together with the older cut and paste terms. During the July 1993 design review, these ideas sparked some of the most heated discussions.

Ultimately, the shell designers came to view the problem of redesigning the transfer model as insoluble. Some believed that the new metaphor was conceptually easier for users to deal with, but they also acknowledged the investment to date in code, documentation, and training that existed for the cut and paste school of thought. The September 1993 internal design review resolved to let Bill Gates decide, with most people leaning toward retaining the cut and paste model.

Other Changes

The most notable change in the shell was the elimination of the "Wastebasket"/"Recycle Bin" feature present in the early test releases. For a number of reasons, this feature was, unfortunately, dropped. Perhaps next time.[18]

The New Appearance

We've already looked at the design concepts that underlie the new look of Windows 95, and you've seen many of the individual elements in the examples. The new look has four main components:

- A more thoroughgoing use of three-dimensional effects. Windows 3.1 does include some 3-D effects on buttons, but Windows 95 uses the 3-D look extensively.

- New system colors and fonts.

- New controls. Windows 95 features several new controls, and these are all available to application programs as well.

- New system dialog boxes. Several of the common dialogs, such as File Open, have been revised.

We're going to take a brief look at all of these items, concentrating on their use in the system. As it did for earlier versions of Windows, Microsoft will publish an *Application Design Guide* book that describes more precisely when, where, and how to use the new visual elements in applications. Many of the new guidelines are manifest in the system itself, and you can find lots of examples in the system of dialogs that have been simplified and generally cleaned up.

Screen Appearance

From the screen shots all through this chapter, you can see that many elements of the Windows 95 interface adopt a 3-D appearance. In Windows

---

18. Stop press: it's back in, together with a comprehensive Undo feature for all shell operations.

3.1, use of the 3-D effect was limited: most buttons got the treatment, but that was about all. In Windows 95, the 3-D effect is used just about everywhere: for menus, buttons, dialog fields, and more. Of course, this is a 3-D *effect,* not a magical new screen display technology. The main contributor to the effect is the use of different colors around the edges of a screen element.[19]

Figure 5-29 shows how Windows 95 uses outer and inner border color pairs—light gray with black, and white with dark gray—to produce 3-D effects in keeping with the idea of a consistent light source. When a button is not pressed, the top and left edges of its outer and inner borders are in lighter colors than the bottom and right edges of its outer and inner borders. When a button is pressed—as depicted by the outer and inner borders shown in Figure 5-29 at right, by the button shown in Figure 5-30 on the next page, and by the top button shown in Figure 5-31—the top and left edges of its outer and inner borders are in darker colors than the bottom and right edges of its outer and inner borders, and the color pairing of the outer border becomes the color pairing of the inner border and vice versa.

The system augments the basic effects by sometimes reversing the color pairs—pairing black with white, and dark gray with light gray. The outer and inner borders of the pressed button shown in Figure 5-30 are composed of such reversed color pairs. Or the system might pair black

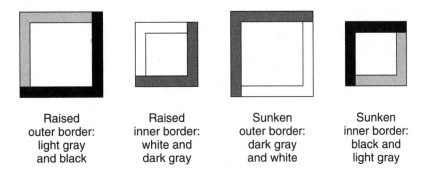

Raised	Raised	Sunken	Sunken
outer border:	inner border:	outer border:	inner border:
light gray	white and	dark gray	black and
and black	dark gray	and white	light gray

Figure 5-29.
Using the outer and inner borders to create unpressed and pressed buttons in the default color pairs.

19. Exactly why the human eye accepts this simple device as three dimensional is way, way beyond the scope of this book.

with dark gray, and light gray with white. In all, the four colors in three different pairings, combining to show both pressed and unpressed buttons, produce six variations.

Figure 5-31 shows an example of a pressed button as it appears on the screen in the company of unpressed buttons. The user can change the default gray color of the button and the default shading color. If the user changes the default colors, the system supplies the colors it needs to complete the 3-D effect.

Button pressed:
Sunken outer (top and left edges in darker color)
Sunken inner (top and left edges in darker color)
Colors of outer and inner borders exchanged
Color pairings reversed

Figure 5-30.
Using reversed color pairs and creating a pressed button effect.

Figure 5-31.
A pressed button.

The other major contributors to the new screen appearance are the different system color scheme and the new treatment of system fonts. Everything is more subtle: gray is often chosen over the stark black and white of Windows 3.1, and fonts are no longer bold.[20] The menus shown in Figure 5-32 exhibit the way in which a Windows 3.1 application automatically inherits these system improvements when it runs under Windows 95. And the new color scheme all actually works on gray scale displays—you don't have to have a 256-color SVGA adapter to realize the benefits of the new look.

---

20. Microsoft's early test releases of Windows 95 used Arial 8-point regular for the system font.

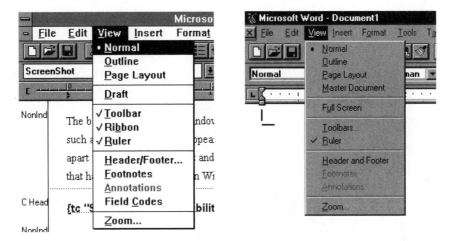

Figure 5-32.
Changes in system fonts between Windows 3.1 and Windows 95.

Visual Elements

The basic elements of the Windows 95 screen are those you're already familiar with from using Windows and applications for Windows. Some of them, such as the tool bar control, appear as standard Windows components for the first time. But you won't find, apart from the property sheet and the new controls it uses, any elements that haven't appeared before, either in Windows or in popular applications for Windows.

Scalability

As part of the overall revision of the Windows screen appearance, the Windows 95 designers did pay a lot of attention to the issue of how to scale the Windows interface. As very high resolution screen displays and adapters have come down in price, their use has grown. Unfortunately, Windows 3.1 doesn't handle this hardware particularly well. Your work might occasionally demand that you use 1280 by 1024 pixel resolution on a 14-inch monitor, for example—at which point, in Windows 3.1, the system font becomes so tiny as to be unreadable and grabbing a window border with the mouse becomes an exercise in patience and dexterity. Similarly, running Windows 3.1 on a very large display tends to result in unnecessarily large amounts of screen real estate devoted to scroll bars and the like. And, of course, the issue of personal preference can't be ignored.

Included in Windows 95 is a control panel for window metrics. You can change the size of every element of a window—even to the extent of making the window's appearance a little ridiculous, as in Figure 5-33.

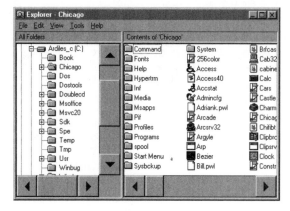

Figure 5-33.
New window metrics in place.

The user can make these changes dynamically: there's no need to restart Windows to have them take effect. One issue application developers have to deal with is the possibility that such changes will occur while an application runs. This problem is similar to that of the user's resizing the system taskbar or to that of dealing with hardware that allows the user to rotate the monitor between portrait and landscape orientation. The video device drivers in Windows 95 also allow screen resolution changes on the fly.

Menus

In addition to the refinements to their colors and fonts, menus have changed in a few subtle ways and a couple of obvious ways. There is also one new menu type: the *popup menu.* The user accesses a popup menu by using the right mouse button (or, more correctly, mouse button two) as he or she selects an object. The popup menu appears next to the object, and the design guidelines recommend that the menu be context sensitive so that it can change according to the current state of the object. Figure 5-34 illustrates the popup menu for a printer that is in the midst of a print operation.

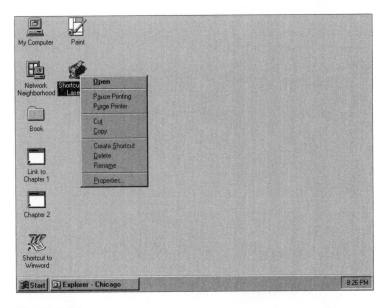

Figure 5-34.
*A popup menu brought up by a press of the right mouse button
(mouse button two).*

The *window menu* is the new name for what you used to call the
system menu. The design guidelines add a standard "View" menu that
affects the displayed view in the window. Figure 5-35 on the next page
shows an example in which the status bar and the tool bar have been
turned on using the View menu options.

Of the more subtle changes to menus, the most noticeable is
their behavior once you have a menu displayed on screen. Simply
moving the mouse along the menu bar will cause other menus to drop
down from the menu bar or cascaded menus to unfold from within
the current menu. You don't need to click or hold down the mouse
button after the first click. This behavior contrasts with that of Windows 3.1, where access to any other menu required at least one more
mouse click.[21]

---

21. Sometimes called a "hot mouse," this behavior has been incorporated into
other graphical systems. (It was considered for OS/2 back in 1987 but never implemented.) Most implementations of a hot mouse don't even require the first mouse
click—simply passing the mouse cursor over the menu bar makes the menu appear.
Some people find this behavior irritating, and others love it.

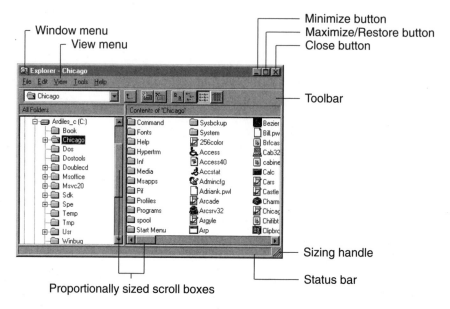

Figure 5-35.
The window display with Tool Bar and Status Bar options.

Window Buttons

The Minimize, Maximize, and Restore buttons located on the upper right of a window's title bar have also changed. The icons depicting the three operations are different. See Figure 5-35 for an example. And a third icon has been added. Clicking this button is the same as doing a Close operation on the Window menu.[22]

Icons

The visual designers have applied the same principles to icon design that they have applied to the rest of the system. The apparent light source for an icon is now the same as for all other controls, and the subtler shading and outlining techniques are used for icons too.

Applications now have to provide two icons: a 32 by 32 pixel icon and a new 16 by 16 pixel size. Windows 95 uses the larger icon to represent the application itself—for desktop shortcuts, for example. The smaller icon appears as a visual aid that can be embedded within a document icon, within a folder's small-icon view (see Figure 5-35),

---

22. Personally, I disagree with the design decision to place the Close button where Maximize used to be. After you've run a few applications that start with a nonmaximized window, you'll see what I mean.

and within a window's title bar. If the application doesn't provide the smaller icon explicitly, the system will try to create one by scaling down the application icon. Depending on the complexity of the original icon, this may or may not result in a recognizable image.

Proportional Scroll Box and Sizing Handle

To see more or different information in a window, you can do one of two things: scroll the window or resize it so that it has a larger client area. The information Windows 95 displays to help you do this includes a proportionally sized scroll box within the standard scroll bar control and a new sizing handle in the bottom right corner of the window. You can see an example of each of these in Figure 5-35. The position of the box within the scroll bar still provides an indication of your current position in the document. The size of the scroll box shows you how much of the total document is shown in the window. A scroll box that fills the entire scroll bar would tell you that you were looking at the whole document.

The sizing handle is simply a visual cue. Window sizing behavior is the same under Windows 95 as it was under Windows 3.1. If there's no sizing handle, the window is a fixed size.

New Controls

The new Windows 95 controls are available only to 32-bit Windows applications. A 16-bit application can't call the common control DLL that implements the new controls. Many of the new controls are simply standardized system implementations of elements you've seen before in applications for Windows.

Tool Bar Control

With the *tool bar* control, Windows 95 implements perhaps the most popular visual device seen in applications for Windows 3.1. Somewhat as in the garish early days of desktop publishing, applications, including Microsoft's, have sprouted strips of buttons and edit controls that purport to provide a shortcut to every function in an application. Like them or loathe them, they're here to stay. If the Windows 95 tool bar control becomes the preferred method of deploying this shortcut feature, at least we'll have a degree of consistency among different applications.[23]

---

23. Microsoft's long-term stated direction is to merge the menu bar with a system tool bar. I hope we'll all have 35-inch monitors and excellent pattern recognition capabilities by then.

The tool bar control assists in the management of the buttons on the control. The edit fields, if any, are separate windows. The programmer can add, delete, move, raise, and lower buttons within a tool bar control. The control also supports a customization feature, allowing the user to add his or her favorite buttons to the tool bar. The system arranges for the tool bar control to be automatically resized when the window size changes. Figure 5-36 shows the details of an example tool bar. Figure 5-35 back on page 204 shows an example of how the Windows 95 shell uses the control.

Figure 5-36.
Example tool bar control.

Button List Box Control

The *button list box* control shares some of the tool bar's properties. It allows the programmer to create a horizontal or vertical row of buttons that display application-specific bitmaps. The button list box control might be used to create the floating palettes of buttons popular in some existing applications.

Status Window Control

The *status window* control implements another very popular Windows application and tools user interface component.[24] Figure 5-37 shows an example of a status bar at the bottom of the folder view window. Microsoft Word for Windows used the status bar concept in a very early revision. The status window control allows the programmer to divide a screen area into multiple windows and display text in each of them. Usually, the status bar appears at the bottom of the window, although early API definitions also allowed it to appear at the top of the window. Typically, the text provides helpful information about the current document—the present cursor position, for example. Another common use of a status window control is for a brief prompt to indicate the likely outcome of choosing the current menu item.

---

24. The Microsoft Foundation Classes for Visual C++ actually included an implementation of the status window control under Windows 3.1.

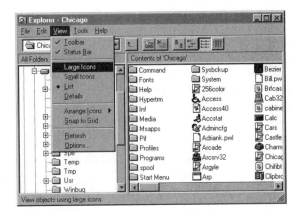

Figure 5-37.
Example status bar.

Column Heading Control

The *column heading* control implements a horizontal window that can include column titles. The programmer positions the column heading window above columns of related information. The user can grab the column dividers within the header window control and drag them to adjust the widths of individual columns. The Windows 95 shell uses the column heading control extensively. Figure 5-38 shows an example of the column heading control's use while the contents of a folder are displayed—the user has substantially increased the default column width for filenames by dragging the column delimiter to the right.

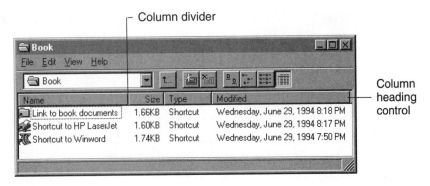

Figure 5-38.
Example column heading control and status window control.

Progress Indicator Control

The *progress indicator* control (sometimes called simply a *progress bar*) standardizes a visual device already used in many applications. It provides the user with an indication of how far a lengthy process is from completion. The application programmer can set the range of the control and the rate of the advance of the current position indicator. If a label for the control is present, it will either show the percentage of the process that is complete or otherwise indicate the current position. Figure 5-39 shows a progress indicator control. You can see an example of its use as Windows 95 scans the disk when you open a new folder.

Figure 5-39.
A progress indicator control (progress bar).

Slider Control

The *slider* control is now the preferred control for setting values within a continuous range (as opposed to a series of discrete values). Many applications have used scroll bars for this purpose, but that use was a little misleading since there is no information to scroll through.

The programmer can set the minimum and maximum positions for the control, the tick marks, and the position of the slider. Figure 5-40 illustrates the basic design of the slider control.

Figure 5-40.
A slider control.

Spin Box Control

The *spin box* control (Figure 5-41) implements a common input device often called a *spin button* or a *spin control*. Clicking on the arrows in the control will alter the value displayed in the associated edit field. As the designers originally defined it, the new control was termed an *up-down* control, and the application programmer had to associate the control with a particular edit control (its "buddy window"). Later discussion seemed to indicate that this division of controls wouldn't come about and that the edit control and up-down controls would be combined into the single spin box control.

Figure 5-41.
A spin box control.

Rich Text Control

The *rich text* control implements an oft-requested feature: an edit control that allows for the input of multiple lines of text with word wrap and other formatting features.[25]

Tab Control

The *tab* control implements a device that allows the user to navigate among logical "pages" of information. Figure 5-42 shows an example tab control for three pages of information. The most common use for a tab control is within the property sheet control we saw in Figure 5-21 back on page 186. The tab control is meant to suggest to the user a peer relationship among the different pages. If the information is really hierarchical, the dialog organization should reflect that.

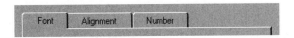

Figure 5-42.
An example tab control.

Property Sheet Control

The *property sheet* control implements the mechanism the shell uses to display object properties. Providing the property sheet as a basic control within the system makes it readily available for applications to use. Figure 5-43 on the next page shows a page of the property sheet for an MS-DOS virtual machine control. You can think of each page in the property sheet as if it were a separate dialog box. The buttons at the bottom of the page are global—they relate to the property sheet as a whole, not to a specific page. Every property sheet includes an Apply Now button. Clicking on the Apply Now button will alter the properties to match their new settings but will not dismiss the property sheet (as would happen if you clicked on the OK button). The absence of a strict hierarchy is the major difference between a property sheet and

---

25. This innovation single-handedly reduces much of the implementation of the Wordpad accessory to the creation and management of a solitary rich text control.

a cascading series of dialog boxes. In a property sheet, you can flip back and forth between pages and leave the property sheet from within any page.

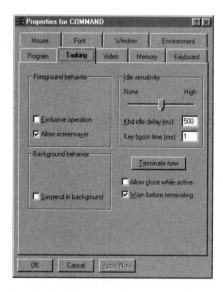

Figure 5-43.
Example property sheet for the MS-DOS virtual machine control, open to the Tasking properties page.

List View and Tree View Controls

The *list view* and *tree view* controls provide the ability to display a collection of items to the user. The shell uses these controls when it displays folders. Figure 5-28 back on page 196 shows examples of both a tree view control and a list view control.

The tree view control provides hierarchical information about items and allows the programmer to expand or collapse parts of the tree. The list view control supports a single-level list of various types: large and small icons and a details view.

New Dialog Boxes

When Microsoft introduced the notion of common dialog boxes for standard operations such as File Open, their actual implementation required the application vendor to ship the DLL that supported the functions. In fact, every Windows application you've installed in recent years probably came with a copy of the COMMDLG.DLL file. Using the common dialogs meant consistency for the user and less effort for the application developer.[26] These common dialogs gradually became a part of the Windows product. Windows 95 introduces some improvements and some new dialogs.[27]

A few of the common dialogs haven't changed beyond adopting the Windows 95 visual style: the Find and Replace dialog and the Fonts dialog are essentially the same as in Windows 3.1. At least initially, Microsoft planned to make only minor revisions to the Print and Print Setup dialogs. At Microsoft's early user interface design review meetings, however, the audience greeted this plan with something less than tacit agreement. The Windows 95 product release may well include larger scale changes to the print dialogs.

Windows 95 does revise the file management and color dialogs, adds a page setup dialog, and includes all of the OLE dialogs as standard components. Naturally, all of these dialogs exhibit the new visual style, and Microsoft's application design guidelines encourage developers to always use the common dialogs. The Windows 95 common dialogs also use the standard controls (including the new ones we've looked at). Earlier versions of the common dialogs were often built separately instead of making use of the standard controls, and they included some subtle incompatibilities as a result.

File Open Dialog

You'd think that the amount of time and brainpower that have been applied to the apparently simple task of opening a file would long ago have produced the ultimate File Open dialog. Not so. The Windows 95 File Open dialog adds a number of new features to the state of the art:

- The dialog looks very much like a shell folder window, displaying a tree view and a small icon list view of the files and directories.

- You can browse the network directly. You no longer need to understand the concept of network drives to cruise for a file.

---

26. For a long time, one of Bill Gates's better known complaints was "Why on earth does everyone have to write file open code?" He would usually put it a little more strongly than that.

27. Early examples of most of these dialogs are shown in this section. Some, such as the OLE dialogs, weren't available in time to be included here.

■ The dialog includes a document preview window that provides an indication of the file's contents.[28]

■ Links and long filenames are understood and handled correctly.

■ The dialog provides direct access to an object's popup menus.

Figure 5-44 shows the design for the Windows 95 File Open dialog, which was presented in the first design review meeting. You can see the tree and list views of the folders and documents, the long filenames, and the document preview window.[29]

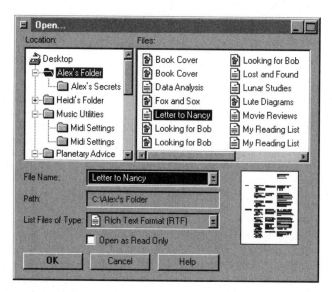

Figure 5-44.
One design for the new File Open dialog box.

---

28. The intention is to provide a preview window for a very wide range of file types. This goal implies a large number of specialized file viewers and a lot of work—not all of which might get done for the Windows 95 release. One easy file type to display is an OLE compound file, in which the dialog can use the embedded thumbnails directly.

29. The first test release of Windows 95, in August 1993, did not include this dialog.

Page Setup Dialog

Page Setup is a function you see in many applications for Windows. It's not used as frequently as a simple file open operation, but in Windows 95, it makes the cut and becomes one of the common dialogs. Figure 5-45 shows the original design for this dialog. It includes paper orientation and margin setting features, as well as paper handling facilities that used to be part of the Printer Setup dialog.

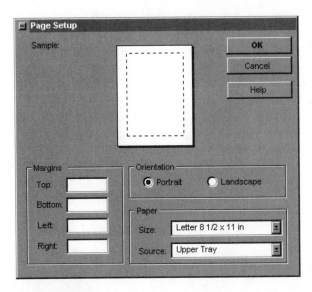

Figure 5-45.
The new Page Setup dialog box.

Long Filenames

In Chapter Seven, we'll look in detail at the new filesystem for Windows 95. The filesystem's biggest impact on the user interface is its support for long filenames. It took a lot of development work to get the shell and other visual elements to fully support this new capability. And if someone chooses to call a file My letter to Aunt Winnie about the dahlias, displaying the name and allowing it to be easily edited becomes a nontrivial task. One new feature of the shell allows document renaming in situ. Figure 5-46 on the next page illustrates the creation of the new filename.

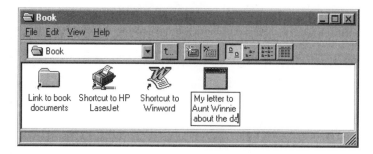

Figure 5-46.

Long filename creation.

Windows 95 and any application written for it will handle the long name quite happily. This is not the case for Windows 3.1 and MS-DOS applications, and Figure 5-47 illustrates how the long filename will appear in Windows 95. The system creates a short name (using the old 8.3 naming convention) that references the same file. If you know the alternative name, you can get at the file. The Windows 95 implementation of COMMAND.COM helps out by listing both the short name and the long name. Figure 5-48 shows the short version of the long filename as it will appear in an earlier Windows application running under Windows 95.

Figure 5-47.

COMMAND.COM in Windows 95 provides a directory listing that shows both the 8.3 version and the long version of a filename.

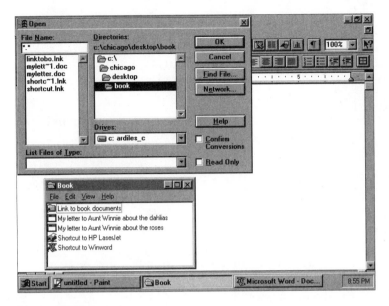

Figure 5-48.
The directory listing in an earlier Windows application running under Windows 95 shows a shortened version of the long filename.

Obviously, with every user's initial mixture of old and new Windows applications, there are going to be some user interface difficulties. This is an unavoidable price that has to be paid if we are (finally) to get the extra functionality of long filenames.

Windows 95 Support for MS-DOS Applications

As one well-known advertising slogan put it, "He's back," or in this case, they're still here. Around the world, beloved MS-DOS applications continue to take up a lot of disk space and CPU time. Acknowledging the obvious, Windows 95 includes some significant improvements to Windows support for MS-DOS sessions—notably:

■ COMMAND.COM supports long filenames (as shown in Figure 5-47).[30]

---

30. Windows 95 also includes new INT 21 API calls that allow the use of long filenames in MS-DOS applications. It will be very interesting to see how many developers revise their applications to support these functions.

■ The MS-DOS window is sizeable—just as most other application windows are.

■ You can choose the font size for the MS-DOS window. Windows adjusts the font size automatically when you resize the window.

■ Windows supports cut and paste operations for any rectangular area within the MS-DOS window.

■ The MS-DOS session supports a tool bar control that provides quick access to most of the window functions just described.

Figure 5-43 back on page 210 illustrated part of the MS-DOS VM property sheet you can use to control the behavior of the session. All of the many configurable options are there, along with several new ones. In Figure 5-49, an MS-DOS session window shows part of the tool bar control and one use for the automatic font sizing capability. The font has shrunk so small it's unreadable, but if you're interested only in being able to see when a long series of commands have finished executing (during program compilation, for example), it's sufficient. (After all, you've probably watched that same sequence of commands often enough that you could recite it verbatim.)

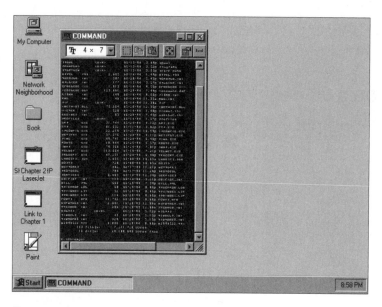

Figure 5-49.
MS-DOS application support in Windows 95.

Application Guidelines for Windows 95

Given all the revisions to the Windows 95 user interface, it's not immediately obvious to an application designer what the most important aspects of the new interface are. And for users, there are a lot of new features that require exploring and learning. The success of the product alone will tell whether Microsoft has met its goal of providing a solid transition path for existing Windows users. For the application implementer, Windows 95 includes plenty of new technology to exploit: the 32-bit API and Plug and Play support, for example.

Microsoft recognized the potential bewilderment of the application interface designer and early on in the Windows 95 preview process began to provide design guidelines.[31] The guidelines fell into two categories:

- The user interface style guidelines that had appeared in book form for previous versions of Windows were updated continually throughout the Windows 95 project. The guidelines present a detailed series of recommendations on when and how to use various interface elements: dialog boxes vs. property sheets, for example.

- Guidelines were made available for exploiting the Windows 95 interface to the extent that an application can truly showcase the capabilities of the system.

In each case, there's an interesting question of the lines you have to draw between what you, as an application designer, ought to do or could do as opposed to what Microsoft really wants you to do. Using the common File Open dialog that the user is familiar with is something you ought to do. It makes sense from both a consistency and a cost viewpoint, and the user is likely to consider your application a little strange if you don't use it. Adding support for long filenames is probably a good idea. It costs you implementation dollars, but it's a great feature that enhances any application. OLE support is a feature Microsoft definitely wants to see you add to your application. And it does add an impressive set of features. Unfortunately, it's an expensive addition, and

---

31. Actually a presentation entitled "How to Be a Great App in the Chicago Shell," which remained fairly consistent throughout 1993.

whether OLE is the way the world will use objects isn't entirely clear yet. Enough speculation—let's take a look at what Microsoft recommends to Windows 95 application designers.[32]

Follow the Style Guidelines

It goes almost without saying that presenting a consistent, predictable environment helps enormously in the user's learning and using applications. It's really what Windows is all about. As we noted earlier in this chapter, Microsoft always points out that their recommendations are just recommendations and not rules. However, many of the guidelines are entirely noncontroversial and make the application design process a lot simpler.

Support Long Filenames

Long filenames are probably destined to be the most immediately popular feature of Windows 95. Given that the system provides much of the basic support for this capability, it looks like a great thing to support in your applications.

Support UNC Pathnames

The number of PCs attached to networks continues to grow at an impressive rate, and Windows 95 is inherently a networked system. Both of these points argue for making applications fully network capable. Support for the *Universal Naming Convention* (UNC) style for filenames is built into Windows 95, and the shell depends on it also for network browsing. Microsoft recommends the support of UNC-style names rather than the drive letter convention. For example, a file open of \\DocsMss\Book\Chapter 5 is preferable to G:\Book\Chapter 5. The preferred title bar caption is Chapter 5 On Docs rather than simply the UNC pathname.

Register Document and Data Types, and Support Drag and Drop

The Windows 95 shell can do a lot without any assistance from the application, provided the application makes the correct resources available, usually by adding information to the Windows registry so that the shell can get at it. In particular, the application helps by

---

32. In July 1994 Microsoft began to disclose the requirement that an application support many of these features in order to qualify to display the Windows logo. Be warned.

- Incorporating and registering icons for document types to allow the shell to display them correctly when the user opens a folder

- Registering data-specific commands to allow the shell to display the commands in popup menus

- Supporting drag and drop print capability

Use Common Dialogs

The intent of the common dialogs is to provide consistency across applications for frequent operations. The user expects to see the same interface when carrying out one of these operations in any application. The Windows 95 common dialogs also add a lot of features, such as network browsing, that are "free" to applications that use them.

Reduce Multiple Instances of an Application

The perennial lost window problem is exacerbated when an application allows the user to start multiple instances of it rather than simply becoming the foreground application and opening successive document windows.

Be Consistent with the Shell

The Windows 95 shell shows off many of the new Windows features: property sheets, the new controls, popup menus, and so forth. The user will spend a lot of time with the new shell and will come to expect applications to have features similar to the shell's. Providing such features for an application will provide consistency for the user.

Revise Online Help

The style for help in Windows 95 is quite different from the Windows 3.1 help style. Revising the help text for an application so that it will conform to the Windows 95 model is a nontrivial task—a task that may take some time to complete. As part of the revision of online help, Microsoft strongly advocates the incorporation of much more context sensitivity—help popups available in dialogs and help on menu items, for example. As far as the overall revision of help systems is concerned, the general philosophy of Windows 95 help is for task orientation and brevity. So don't use a request for fonts help to embark on a discussion of scaling technologies; tell the user how to choose a font.

Support OLE Functionality

The move to objects is on, and Microsoft wants you to view the object-oriented world through the capabilities of OLE. Although OLE is not without its competitors, the support for it from Microsoft's (extremely successful) operating system platforms gives it a definite edge. In particular, Microsoft has based a number of concepts for the Cairo system on work originally done by the OLE group.

Several applications have already incorporated OLE technology, and the resultant functionality is impressive. Right now, adding full OLE support to an application is an extremely complex engineering project. New development tools and methods will no doubt reduce the cost of OLE implementation. If you do use OLE within an application in combination with Windows 95, you'll get these features:

- The OLE compound file as the application data type allows the shell to display the document properties such as the thumbnail view. This compound file format will be the native format for Cairo, so there's another incentive to support OLE now.

- OLE drag and drop will allow users to move and hold documents anywhere in the shell's workspace—the desktop will be the most common place in which to hold them.

- The OLE in-place editing capabilities preview the move to component software and the document-centric interface that Windows 95 promotes.

OLE is leading edge technology. Using it now is expensive but could also give you a competitive edge in the Windows 95 applications market.

Conclusion

In this chapter, we've taken a lengthy tour through the most visible part of the system. As the Windows 95 visual designers are wont to remind people: details count. Many details of the interface have changed, and several new or improved concepts make their debuts in Windows 95. The biggest change from Windows 3.1 is evident in the shell itself. Given Microsoft's intention to provide Cairo with the same user interface, it will be interesting to see whether the new shell achieves the dual goals of making the system easier for novices to use and providing a natural transition for experienced Windows users.

We haven't looked at some components of the shell in this chapter—the desktop accessories, for example. And you'll have to take your own tour of Windows 95 to see a lot of the more detailed revisions to specific dialog boxes and utility programs. But we did look at all the important new pieces with the exception of the pen interface. Windows 95 includes support for pen computers within the basic system—pen support no longer comes from an add-on module as it did for Windows 3.1.

Now we have to dive a little deeper into the system. In Chapter Six, we'll look at the details of the graphical environment supported by Windows—at how applications harness the graphical environment and how devices are commanded to display it.

Reference

Microsoft. *The Windows Interface—An Application Design Guide.* Redmond, Wash.: Microsoft Press, 1993. This book appeared as part of the Windows Software Development Kit and as a separately published volume. It's the final word on how a Windows 3.1 application should look and contains a lot of useful insight into user interface design. The Windows 95 team produced an updated version of this book under a new name, *User Interface Design Guide,* for the Beta-1 release and planned to update it for the Beta-2 release. Microsoft Press will publish a final version titled *The New Windows Interface.*

CHAPTER SIX

APPLICATIONS AND DEVICES

In Chapters Four and Five, we looked in detail at two of the major Microsoft Windows enhancements that appear in Windows 95: the 32-bit protected mode base operating system and the new user interface exemplified by the shell. The improvements in the base OS help support many collateral enhancement details in the Windows subsystem, and the shell with its new features is but one manifestation of the new capabilities you'll see in Windows 95 applications. To realize these enhancements, applications call on the Windows API, and when the user interacts with an application, a requested service is translated into some device-specific operation, such as the manipulation of visible objects on the display screen or the reading of information from a disk file.

Many different software modules are involved in the translation of user and application actions to specific hardware operations. In this chapter, we'll look at some of the most important components: at the Windows 95 API and its implementation in the Windows User and GDI modules and at a few of the device drivers and subsystems associated with the User and GDI modules. If you need a primer on the basics of how Windows implements its graphical environment, see Chapter Three. Our concentration in this chapter will be very much on the new and different features of Windows 95:

- The Win32 API implementation in Windows 95

- Enhancements in User, the window management subsystem

- Improvements in GDI and the associated graphical device subsystems that control the display and the printer

In later chapters, we'll look at the major product enhancements for local and network filesystem support. This chapter is biased in the direction of what Windows is best known for: its graphical application environment.

The Win32 API

During 1993 and 1994, Microsoft invested enormous amounts of its developer relations time and effort in promoting two specific elements of its operating system products: the Win32 API and OLE. If you left any of the company's systems software presentations with any doubt about what Microsoft wanted you, as an application developer, to develop for, the incessant Win32/OLE chant must have put you to sleep. Naturally, business reasons were at the base of this promotion: if most of the industry's applications are written for your operating system interface, you get to sell the most operating systems. The history of MS-DOS and Windows bears this out. But as the histories of UNIX, OS/2, and indeed early versions of Windows attest, convincing developers to invest resources in a new API is extremely difficult. So Microsoft put everything it could in gear to sell the Win32 API, starting with Windows NT and now with Windows 95.

The Win32 API has one big advantage in its favor: it is by and large compatible with today's most popular API, the Windows 3.1 API. The Win32 API is also extensive. With well over 2000 functions and macros and having undergone a few years of field trials, Win32 offers a wealth of features.

Microsoft's first implementation of Win32 was released in 1992 as the Win32s add-on for Windows 3.1. Recognizing that the rate of adoption for Windows NT would be governed largely by the availability of true 32-bit applications, Microsoft released the Win32s subset to give developers an early opportunity to begin porting their code to the Win32 API. With the release of Windows NT in mid-1993 the first full implementation of Win32 came to market. During the rest of 1993 things got a little more confusing. Later in that year Microsoft began to talk about Win32c—that "c" initially meaning "Chicago" and later spun to "compatible." Eventually the "c" was dropped and Microsoft began to talk simply of different implementations of the Win32 API—each particular to the underlying operating system.

As a practical matter, the Windows 95 implementation of Win32 will probably come to be seen as the "standard" implementation—if only because of the size of the Windows 95 market. As a numerical matter, the Win32 APIs implemented in Windows 95 account for 95 percent of the total defined Win32 interface. The APIs missing in the Windows 95 implementation are specific to capabilities that Windows NT has and Windows 95 does not—the rigorous security features in Windows NT, for example. But the Windows 95 implementation introduces features that the Windows NT version 3.1 implementation doesn't include—for example, the new device-independent color capabilities. No, this doesn't mean another round of subset and superset confusion. Microsoft plans to promptly update Windows NT so that it will retain its position as the provider of the full Win32 API.[1]

In addition to the API compatibility issue is the issue of binary compatibility: the different operating system products must be able to load and run the various flavors of Win32 application. Both Windows 95 and Windows NT will load Intel format Win32 binaries and run them as full 32-bit applications. Windows 95 will never have a non-Intel processor implementation of Win32. Only Windows NT will run applications compiled for other processors.

What's a developer to do? If you believe in the continued success of Windows, you have to develop for that platform. With Windows 95 we'll see the arrival of full 32-bit support for a mainstream operating system, so if you're starting from scratch, Win32 is the way to go. Since the new features of Windows 95 are available only to Win32 applications, porting your 16-bit Windows code to the Win32 API is an obvious first step. Fortunately, the tools Microsoft provides to assist in the porting task make it less than onerous. Beyond that, the OLE mountain looms—although improved versions of Microsoft's Visual C++ (among other language products) are making that assault a little easier.

All of this begs the question of whether Windows really is the right platform to develop for. It's hard to argue against the current commercial success of Windows, and all of the pieces are falling into place to ensure a continuation of that success. No doubt the debate will continue in many quarters, however. In the meantime let's take a look at what Microsoft is trying to achieve with the Win32 API.

---

1. Some of the new color facilities will appear in the next release of Windows NT—the so called "Daytona" product. Others will appear as add-on libraries when Windows 95 ships.

Goals for Win32

Microsoft's overriding desire is to concentrate both its own efforts and those of other developers on a single, long-lived API. As candidates for the base API, the existing APIs for both MS-DOS and Windows 3.1 fell short in several ways: they weren't portable, they weren't 32-bit, and they were functionally deficient. At one time the OS/2 API was supposed to be "the API for the future," but for many reasons that prediction didn't work out too well.

A single API does accelerate the market. More people write more software, resulting in more users finding satisfactory solutions to buy. This is one of the reasons MS-DOS was so successful. The PC world had gotten very complex since the first release of MS-DOS, though, and Microsoft decided it was time to try to re-introduce a little more order. Enter Win32—an API aimed at meeting the following goals:

- Broad support. Meeting this goal entails developing plenty of developer momentum and getting lots of applications released in as short a time frame as possible. The best way to do this is to make Win32 as closely compatible with Win16 as possible.[2] Porting applications from Win16 to Win32 will thus be simplified, and momentum will quickly build.

- Portability. Windows NT was designed as a portable operating system—specifically to allow it to run on RISC processors. The debate over whether and when the Intel processor architecture will finally be outperformed by RISC technology continues. Irrespective of the outcome in the hardware battle, Microsoft aims to establish Win32 as the preferred API.

- Room for growth. As PC technology continues to improve, the operating system must be able to offer access to the improvements. Whether the technology be high-speed video on demand or radio-based networking, Microsoft wants an API that can be extended to support the new technologies without modifications to the existing interfaces.

---

2. The fact that the OS/2 Presentation Manager API differed so widely from the Windows API (both conceptually and syntactically) was a major factor in the slow adoption of OS/2. The Win32 developers, many of whom were involved in the PM effort, were careful not to make the same mistake twice.

■ Scalability. Windows NT supported multiprocessor machines in its first release. There's already news of processors that operate with a native word size of 64 bits. The era of the PDA has begun. Developing software for all of these hardware platforms would be impossible if the software platform were different for each. One API suitable for supersetting and subsetting for different hardware platforms will help a lot.

Components of the Win32 API

Before we examine the details of the Win32 API, it should be worthwhile to look at a few of the statistics and then to group the functions. Bear in mind that the statistics deal with a prerelease of the product some months before its expected release. The absolute numbers will probably change, but the proportions should stay roughly the same.

As of this writing the total number of Win32 APIs, macros, messages, and defined constants is 2246. Of these members, 1350 were included in the Win32s subset and only 114 are not in the Win32 API set supported by Windows 95. Of the 114 members supported only by Windows NT, almost all relate to the security features or the service control and event logging subsystems available under Windows NT. Of the 2246 total, 546 of the interfaces are macros, messages, and predefined constants, so the API total drops to a very manageable 1700 interfaces!

The major components of Windows 95 remain the Kernel, User, and GDI modules that provide the interface to the base OS, window and application management, and the graphics facilities, respectively. Each of these modules supports about 300 APIs.[3] In Windows 95, these APIs are the major extensions to the three basic modules:

■ OLE. The OLE APIs, numbering only (!) 66. They are perhaps the most complex and, for Microsoft at least, the most important extension of the core Windows system.

■ Controls. The support for the standard user interface elements described in Chapter Five.

■ Common dialogs. Dialogs such as "File Open" that are shared by applications.

---

3. To be precise, in the M5 version it was 346 in Kernel, 262 in User, and 300 in GDI.

- Decompression. File decompression capabilities commonly used during installation.

- DDE. The Dynamic Data Exchange facility. DDE was Windows' first popular application information interchange capability. Over the course of time OLE is expected to replace the use of DDE.

- RPC. The support for remote procedure calls relied on for distributed application development.

- Sockets. The so called "WinSock" interface. Sockets has grown in importance for Windows networking. Originally developed simply for TCP/IP network support, Sockets is now seen as the best way to develop non-RPC network applications for Windows.

- Networking. Network-specific APIs outside the RPC and socket interfaces. Of course, many of the Kernel APIs ultimately find their way to the network subsystem for file input/output and other operations.

- Communications. A set of APIs designed to support reliable wide area communications applications such as electronic mail and remote network access.

- Shell. A set of APIs supported by the shell itself that enables the extension of the shell's capabilities through installable libraries.

- Multimedia. Extensions to the core system for audio and video management. The multimedia extensions number close to 200 APIs—interestingly the largest single set of extensions.

- Pen. Extensions to the core system that support the specific needs of pen-based applications.

As mentioned earlier, that won't be the end of the Win32 API story. Already, Microsoft has begun to describe its plans to implement the OpenGL 3-D graphics library for Windows NT—a component that will add another 300 or so APIs to Win32. But for the purposes of this chapter's discussion we'll concentrate on the core components that we haven't yet examined: User and GDI.

The Win32 API on Windows 95

Developing a Win32 application for both Windows 95 and Windows NT requires that you recognize two basic kinds of issues: those inherent in porting existing 16-bit code to the 32-bit interface, and the Win32 APIs that aren't supported on Windows 95. In addition you can observe some general programming guidelines that help prepare an application for future improvements—after all, someday you may actually have to worry about 64-bit interfaces.

Porting to the Win32 API

You'll find extensive documentation describing the details of the 16- to 32-bit porting process in the Windows SDK products, so there's little value in a regurgitation of all of it here. A few of the more important aspects are worth reviewing, however: notably,

- The mechanics of the porting process
- API syntax changes
- Memory management
- Version checking

Note too that if you're tempted to try to mix 16-bit and 32-bit code (using the Microsoft thunk compiler tools) to help speed up the porting process, you'll end up with an executable program that will run only on Windows 95 and that won't even load on Windows NT. You'll also create the potential for many bugs because of the different sizes of integers (and thus of many Windows data types). Microsoft's recommendation is simply don't mix 16-bit and 32-bit code segments. If you have to mix them, make sure that the 16-bit code is carefully isolated and plan to replace it as soon as you can.

Porting Tools

If you're starting with a 16-bit Windows application, there's some mechanical help at your disposal. Included in the Windows SDK is a source code analyzer called PORTTOOL.EXE that will examine each and every Windows interface and suggest changes you may need to make. This porting tool isn't foolproof, but it's a good way to start the process. Another mechanical aid is to define the *STRICT* constant when you compile your code. Then the strictest level of type checking will be applied to Windows functions. Your fixing the ensuing stream of warning messages can often remove subtle bugs before they have a chance to bite.

The WINDOWSX.H header file included in the SDK also contains many macros that cloak API calls in a single portable interface. If you have to maintain both 16-bit and 32-bit versions of an application, that's some help.

API Changes

As successive versions of Windows have appeared, more and more parameterized types have appeared in the declarations of Windows interfaces. Most programmers are familiar with declaring device context handles as *HDC*, for example, but the "before" and "after" declarations of the main window procedure shown in Figure 6-1 illustrate just how pervasive the technique has become with Win32. Admittedly, the person who wrote the "before" declaration must not have touched the code in a very long time, but the new types in the up-to-date version affect every part of the declaration.

```
    /* The old declaration of the window procedure */
long far pascal WndProc(HWND, unsigned, WORD, long)
    // ...and the new
LRESULT APIENTRY WndProc (HWND, UINT, WPARAM, LPARAM)
```

Figure 6-1.
Using predefined types in Win32.

Modifying the code this way assists in compiler type checking and also masks the actual word size of the underlying system. Unsigned integers that were 16-bit quantities are now 32-bit values—and can become 64-bit values with no further code modification. This *widening* of many 16-bit values can be seen in a lot of the Win32 APIs. It's really an artifact of the extensive use of C integers: they were 16 bits on Windows 3.1, and they become 32 bits on Win32. But the changes aren't purely syntactic. There are some semantic issues as well.[4] Figure 6-2 illustrates

---

4. There's also the subtle issue of alignment: structure fields that lined up neatly on 16-bit boundaries may not do the same when integers widen to 32 bits. On the 386 this results in only a slight performance overhead, but on some RISC processors it causes a hardware fault.

one of the porting problems engendered by the Win32 API that can't be fixed simply by careful use of the predefined types.[5] Here the data supplied with the WM_COMMAND message has been packed into the *wParam* and *lParam* parameters differently, necessitating code that differentiates between API versions. This sort of change between Windows 3.1 and Win32 is not uncommon. The porting tool helps you find the occurrences, but even so this is one area in which careful checking is necessary.

```
    ...
case WM_COMMAND:
#if defined(WIN32)
    UINT nID = LOWORD(wParam);
    UINT nCode = HIWORD(wparam);    // NOTE!
#else
    UINT nID = wParam;
    UINT nCode = HIWORD(lparam);    // NOTE!
#endif
    switch (nID) {
        case IDC_BUTTON1:
        ...
```

Figure 6-2.
Message parameter passing in Win32.

You'll also see many Win32 APIs with names similar to those of Windows 3.1 APIs but with an *Ex* suffix. Microsoft has used this convention to signal that it's extending the functionality of an existing Windows 3.1 API in some minor way.[6] The recommendation for porting code to Win32 is to use only the APIs with the *Ex* suffix. You'll find the superseded function marked "deleted" or "obsolete" in the Win32 documentation. Figure 6-3 on the next page shows one example, the GDI function for setting a window origin. The old version has been modified to return the coordinates of the previous window origin differently.

---

5. *#ifdef*'d code never was the best way to handle this sort of problem. You can write portable code to handle either situation. The *#ifdef* method makes for a better illustration, though.

6. Unfortunately, neither the extent of the extending nor the name signal are entirely consistent. A few of the extended functions incorporate major additional functionality. And some extended functions have *Ext* as the *prefix,* not a suffix, for the old name. The Windows API naming story continues.

```
     // The obsolete version. Coordinates returned
     //  as the result of the function
DWORD SetWindowOrg(HDC, int, int)
     // ...and the Win32 version. Function result now
     //  denotes success or failure, and the previous
     //  origin is stored in the LPPOINT parameter
BOOL SetWindowOrgEx (HDC, int, int, LPPOINT)
```

Figure 6-3.
Similar function changes in Win32.

Most of the extended APIs are GDI functions, and the *Ex* form of the API was actually included in Windows 3.1. The difference is that the older form of the function call is unavailable in Win32. Windows 3.1 actually supported both. The GDI functions also mask one important difference between Windows NT and Windows 95: the difference in their graphics coordinate systems. On Windows NT you identify a point using 32-bit coordinates. Windows 95 retains the older 16-bit coordinate system. For graphics-intensive applications this is an important difference that is syntactically manageable by means of the predefined types (predominantly POINT and SIZE structures). But the associated semantics are a different matter, with no easy solution for developers who would like to exploit the capabilities of the 32-bit coordinate system on both Windows 95 and Windows NT.

Memory Management

We looked at many of the new aspects of Windows 95 memory management in Chapter Four. Apart from the new features, from the application programmer's viewpoint, the Win32 API makes things a whole lot easier. Segments are now a relic, so it's good-bye to far pointers, and any other vestiges of Windows' 16-bit past, such as having to lock and unlock memory objects, can be dispensed with.[7]

The fact that the system is now entirely virtual memory based means that the absolute addresses or contiguous locations of certain segments are no longer the same under Windows 95. The addresses and locations were never published and ought not to have been assumed, and under either Windows 95 or Windows NT, the rules change. You absolutely must use the defined memory management APIs if your code is to work correctly.

---

7. If you did atrocious things with direct segment arithmetic, it's payback time.

Version Checking

Microsoft chose to handle the Win32 API subset issue on Windows 95 by actually implementing the full set of Win32 APIs and then returning an error if a call is made to an API not supported by Windows 95. This strategy allows a Win32 application to always load under either Windows NT or Windows 95—references to missing DLL entry points don't stand in the way. But if you call an API that exists only in the full Win32 set on Windows NT, you must be prepared to deal with an error return on Windows 95.

Calling the *GetLastError()* API in response to the error return indicating a failure and getting the ERROR_CALL_NOT_IMPLEMENTED error code will tell you that you've called an unsupported API. A *GetVersion()* API enables you to identify the particular version of Windows that you're running on.

In a very few cases, an API that isn't really supported by Windows 95 will run without the return of an error. One example of such an API is the *GetThreadDesktop()* API that under Windows NT will return a handle to the desktop window associated with a particular thread. Windows 95 has only one desktop, so it's always the same handle that gets returned. Since no undesirable side effects of using this API on Windows 95 are possible, it's easier to allow the call to succeed than to insist that the application handle an error return.

Nonportable APIs

Although some of the older Windows APIs have vanished, the presence of their direct descendants in Windows 95 ensures that porting existing 16-bit Windows code will be a manageable chore. The only snag comes from the use of MS-DOS functions within Windows-based applications—by means of the provided *Dos3Call()* API of Windows 3.1 or by means of embedded assembly language code that calls MS-DOS directly. Win32 doesn't support a direct MS-DOS interface, and it never will. Even if translating 32-bit parameters to 16-bit equivalents weren't an issue, the fact that the base operating system in Windows 95 is entirely call based and makes no use of the Intel software interrupt mechanism other than for compatibility when Windows 95 is running older MS-DOS applications means that Win32 applications that issue MS-DOS software interrupts will fail. If you have code that calls MS-DOS directly—for file I/O, for example—you have to replace the call with the appropriate Win32 API.

Win32 on Windows 95

We'll look at some details of the API changes and enhancements a little later, when we take a closer look at the User and GDI modules. First let's see what Windows 95 doesn't implement that Windows NT does implement. Remember, it's all Win32. As the design of Windows 95 progressed, the Win32 specification changed to accommodate new features that would come to market for the first time with Windows 95. Whether the Windows NT API comes to be regarded as a superset of the Windows 95 API, or the Windows 95 a subset of the Windows NT remains to be seen.

Faced with the prospect of turning all of the new ideas and the enhancement requests into specific Win32 APIs, Microsoft had to consider a couple of factors over and above the basic design and implementation challenge. Was the underlying operating system capable of fully supporting a proposed feature? Was the feature appropriate for the intended market? By and large, you can see these criteria reflected in the eventual choice of APIs that would not be fully supported by Windows 95.

Security APIs

The collection of Win32 APIs that deals with system security issues is merely the most visible aspect of the security capabilities embodied in Windows NT. The system implements stringent authentication and privilege checking features that allow it to be used for secure applications: in a network server role or as a C2-compliant desktop system.[8] For the system to be fully secure, you must use the NTFS filesystem with Windows NT—since the FAT filesystem is provably insecure.

The Windows NT internal system architecture is dramatically different from the Windows 95 architecture in order to meet the secure system goal. This difference translates into a need for more system memory and more processor horsepower—more than the average target Windows 95 machine would have. Since the underlying operating system can't fully support them, Windows 95 does not implement the Win32 security APIs. Microsoft's reasoning: why try to provide two products to meet the same need? If you really need the security capabilities, you'll know it—and you'll use Windows NT.

---

8. Windows NT on its own cannot be C2 certified. The certification process requires a complete system—the hardware, the operating system, and applications—to undergo verification.

Console APIs

The Win32 console APIs provide an environment for applications that require character mode I/O facilities. For applications with simple user interface requirements—a compiler, for example—the console APIs offer an easy way to run using Win32.

Windows 95 supports the console APIs but provides support for only a single console subsystem. Whereas Windows NT allows the management of multiple console sessions by means of the *AllocConsole()* and *FreeConsole()* APIs, Windows 95 supports only a single console session.

32-Bit Coordinate System

There is no *world transform* coordinate transformation capability in Windows 95, and neither the associated *SetWorldTransform()* and *GetWorldTransform()* APIs nor the XFORM data structure is supported in Windows 95.[9] Their absence is tied to the decision to retain a 16-bit coordinate system in GDI. Implementing 32-bit coordinates really requires a full 32-bit GDI, which, partly for memory consumption reasons and partly for timescale reasons, Microsoft chose not to implement for Windows 95.

Unicode APIs

The first release of Windows NT was unusual in that it supported the Unicode character set specification not only for applications but also as its own internal character set representation. Every Unicode character requires 16 bits for storage—which expands the system's memory requirements—and in addition many compatibility considerations are associated with existing character strings: filenames on disk, and 16-bit Windows application resources, to name just two.

Supporting Unicode would have been a big leap of faith for the Windows 95 team to take. They chose not to, so the system retains its ANSI character set roots and doesn't support the Win32 Unicode APIs. However, some new aspects of the Windows 95 system do use Unicode internally: its long filename support in the filesystem and its 32-bit OLE subsystem, for example. And Windows 95 has far more extensive support for international versions of applications than any of the earlier Microsoft operating system products.

---

9. If you use world transforms, be sure to read up in the Win32 documentation on how the *SetGraphicsMode()* API works under Windows 95.

Server APIs

The Windows NT role as a highly capable network server means that there are groups of Win32 APIs supporting server operations: notably, server-side named pipes and RPC facilities and tape backup APIs. The server-side named pipes allow a server process to create a pipe that multiple client processes can connect to. The RPC facilities you won't find in Windows 95 include the locator and endpoint mapper features.[10] These features relate to the name service facilities provided by the full Win32 API. (Windows NT supports an endpoint mapping service, RPCSS, and a locator service that don't exist on Windows 95.)

Printer Support

Windows 95 doesn't include the entire gamut of print APIs defined for Win32. There is no forms support (all the APIs with *Form* in their names), and the *AddJob()* and *ScheduleJob()* APIs available on Windows NT aren't supported either.

Service Control Manager APIs

Windows NT supports a *service control manager* facility that allows a subsystem, such as a network server, to register itself as a *service*. Once the subsystem is registered, the system itself takes care of starting the service and maintaining information about currently running services. Under Windows NT, the service control manager is actually accessible across the network by means of RPC, so it's possible to manage networkwide services from a single machine.

In an oversimplification, you could say that the Windows NT service control manager is a highly structured form of the capabilities inherent in the startup files you're familiar with, such as AUTO-EXEC.BAT and WIN.INI. The general philosophy of the service control manager doesn't really fit a personal system such as Windows 95, so the service control subsystem and the associated Win32 APIs aren't supported.[11]

Event Logging

Associated with the service control manager are the event logging facilities. Under Windows NT, these facilities allow subsystems to record

---

10. The full Win32 RPC also includes some Unicode and security related APIs. As you'd expect, these aren't supported on Windows 95.

11. Service control APIs are generally recognizable by virtue of the *Service* or *SC* in their names. For once there's some orderly naming going on.

information about interesting occurrences: unexpected errors, configuration changes, and the like. The Windows NT administrator can inspect the event log when trying to diagnose problems or simply to verify the health of the system. Windows 95 doesn't support the Win32 event logging APIs.

Detailed Differences

Within the Win32 API a number of details have been changed or enhanced and that will affect some applications. Later we'll look at some of the brand-new Win32 features and at Microsoft's recommendations for application developers. Here are just a few of the lower level modifications:[12]

- Most application resource limits have been substantially raised: memory, handles, and other resources are all plentiful under Windows 95. There are 32,767 window handles, for example, compared to only 200 in Windows 3.1. Similar improvements have been made for COM and LPT devices, with Windows 95 providing many more logical ports than physical ports. Total available memory rather than individual resources now becomes the limiting factor.

- Windows 95 tags every application resource with the thread identifier of its owner. When an application quits, the system automatically frees all resources that have been allocated to the application. Some Windows 3.1 applications assume the continued allocation of a resource even after an application terminates. Such an assumption is not valid with Win32 applications.

- Windows 95 includes yet more parameter validation. Whereas Windows 3.1 concentrated on validating the parameters supplied to the published APIs, Windows 95 also validates the so called "undocumented" interfaces that have been discussed in various books and journals. If you use undocumented interfaces, beware.

---

12. Naturally, the detailed information about these changes tends to be spread around in the documentation. One way of pointing yourself in the right direction is to look for the string *#if (WINVER >= 0x400)* in the Windows SDK header files. The Windows developers have used this string to bracket all the new definitions.

■ There are several new Windows messages, ranging from generalized application notification for the Plug and Play subsystem (WM_DEVICEBROADCAST) to the support for multiple keyboard layouts (WM_KBDLAYOUTCHANGE) required by fully international applications.

■ Windows 95 presses into service some previously unused parts of existing data structures. New capabilities, such as automatic centering of a dialog box (the new DS_CENTER style bit), are supported. If your code "borrows" reserved or previously unused regions of Windows data structures, you may need to make some changes.[13]

Programming for Windows 95

Now that we've looked at some of the things you can't do on Windows 95, let's turn our attention to a more interesting topic: the new capabilities you can exploit as you create your next million-copy seller. The new features are accessible only by 32-bit applications,[14] so the first task is to port existing code to Win32. Together with all the new possibilities for Win32 applications come new rules and considerations. We'll look at those as we examine the new features.

There are many small enhancements to the Windows API, and we won't look at them all in any detail here. Reference works that analyze the new features will probably address this extensive topic. Checking the specification for all the APIs with the *Ex* suffix is one way to begin an investigation.[15]

Multitasking

As you saw in Chapter Four, the Windows 95 multitasking environment is dramatically different from the Windows 3.1 environment. If you've

---

13. To preserve compatibility, Windows 95 includes several internal version checks to preclude any attempt to interpret "old" data structures with new semantics. An executable with a version number of 3.1 or lower won't see any of this new behavior.

14. The DPMI challenge was met by a band of developers determined to prove that real mode code could use protected mode facilities. It'll be interesting to see whether someone comes up with a trapdoor for 16-bit Windows applications. But don't try this at home.

15. For example, there's even an *ExitWindowsEx()* API. Though you're unlikely to use it, on machines that support the feature, you can close down Windows *and* turn off the power.

programmed for other multitasking systems—Windows NT, UNIX, or OS/2—you're already familiar with some of the issues you'll have to deal with in the Windows 95 environment:

- Synchronization and sharing. You can never be sure that the operating system isn't going to preempt your application and take the processor away from you, so any use of shared objects, such as memory mapped files, must be synchronized with other applications' use. Assumptions about the timing of arriving window messages are also invalid for Win32 applications under Windows 95.

- Multithreading. Using additional execution threads to manage different windows or background operations such as file searching adds complexity to an application's code. But users will quickly come to expect such capabilities. The Windows 95 shell, for example, uses a separate thread for each visible window. If your application simply puts up the hourglass cursor during a lengthy operation and refuses to respond quickly to mouse clicks, it will suffer in comparison with applications that do allow the user to interrupt the operation or get on with something else.

A plethora of Win32 APIs are available to assist in thread synchronization. Many of them look similar to one another, but study of the details will reveal subtle but significant differences. Windows 95 supports all of the Win32 synchronization APIs. One group—made up of the *InterlockedIncrement()*, *InterlockedDecrement()*, and *InterlockedExchange()* APIs that allow manipulation of a single 32-bit word—was originally designed to help support Windows NT multiprocessor operations. Even though you'll never see Windows 95 controlling a multiprocessor system, the APIs are still valid on Windows 95.

Win32 synchronization primitives deal with *critical sections, events, mutexes,* and *semaphores.* Here's what's important about each:

A **critical section** is used by threads belonging to the same process. One thread declares a CRITICAL_SECTION variable and initializes it using the *InitializeCriticalSection()* API. Thereafter, any thread can call *EnterCriticalSection()* and *LeaveCriticalSection()* to protect code sequences in which it must be the only thread of the parent process allowed to run.

Any thread can create a named **event** object and obtain a handle to it using *CreateEvent()*. Other threads belonging to any process can obtain a handle to the same event by specifying the same event name. Any thread with a valid handle can then use the *SetEvent()*, *ResetEvent()*, or *PulseEvent()* API to signal an occurrence of the event. Threads waiting for the event are then free to continue execution, and multiple threads may become eligible to run when the event is signaled. These event APIs send a "one to many" signal, unlike the other synchronization APIs.

A **mutex** is a named object that you acquire a handle to by means of *CreateMutex()* or *OpenMutex()*. Again, any thread in any process can obtain a handle to the mutex if it knows its name.[16] Only a single thread can gain control of the mutex object—so this implements critical sections for cooperating processes. The *ReleaseMutex()* API relinquishes control of the object.

A **semaphore** object is controlled in a way similar to control of a mutex object by means of *CreateSemaphore()* and *OpenSemaphore()*. The difference between the two is that the semaphore can have a value. For example, if you have an application controlling an eight-line telephone dialer, you can set up a semaphore with a value of *8* to help manage line allocation. The first eight threads that ask for a line get one, and the next thread blocks, awaiting a line release by another thread, which uses the *ReleaseSemaphore()* API to increment the count.

All of the interprocess synchronization APIs use handles to identify the object in use, be it an event, a mutex, or a semaphore. When a thread wants to synchronize with another thread, it uses an API that allows it to wait for a single object (*WaitForSingleObject()* and *WaitForSingleObjectEx()*), or for one of possibly many objects (*WaitForMultipleObjects()* and *WaitForMultipleObjectsEx()*). The two multiple objects APIs can use an array of object handles supplied by the caller—plus a time-out—to simplify the synchronization procedure. The *MsgWaitForMultipleObjects()* API allows you to synchronize with any of these objects, or with a time-out, or with a Windows message arriving in the thread's input queue.

---

16. The *DuplicateHandle()* API allows you to pass the handle to another process. The receiving process doesn't have to know the name of the mutex object. This works with all the handle-based Win32 synchronization APIs.

Memory Management

In Chapter Four, we looked at the Win32 memory management APIs and at some aspects of their implementation. Remember:

- The need to lock resources and memory objects is gone. All objects exist within a huge 32-bit flat virtual address space. Assumptions about actual addresses of objects are probably wrong, and they're definitely nonportable. You have to address objects using only system-supplied handles or pointers.

- The system protects the private address space of each Win32 application. You can't get a valid pointer into some other Win32 application's address space.[17] To exchange information, cooperating applications must use the defined interprocess communication methods and synchronization APIs. The *WriteProcessMemory()* API is the only controlled way of modifying somebody else's address space, and this API is really meant only for use by debugging tools.

- You can't pass handles back and forth between Win32 applications except by using the *DuplicateHandle()* API. Just as actual memory pointers aren't valid in different processes, neither are handles. You have to use the *DuplicateHandle()* API to get a valid handle to pass to another process.

- Of the various shared memory allocation methods, using the *CreateFile()* and *MapViewOfFile()* APIs is the recommended method for sharing. The performance with this method is good, and the method is fully portable to Windows NT.

Plug and Play Support

Chapter Eight deals with the Plug and Play subsystem in detail. Much of the Windows 95 Plug and Play support involves device drivers, not applications, but there is one new Windows message specifically associated with Plug and Play operations. The WM_DEVICEBROADCAST message informs an application of changes to the system's hardware configuration. If your application or device driver is the controlling party, you can use the *BroadcastSystemMessage()* API to send this message.

---

17. But you can get a pointer into the shared region used by all of the Win16 applications and the 16-bit subsystem DLLs. Again, this is an artifact of the strict compatibility requirements for Windows 95.

Perhaps unusually, this particular message is important to both applications and system components, although the information the message sends is often of interest only to device drivers. At the application level, the device event code the message sends can provide, for example, information about the addition and removal of logical disk drives.[18] This would allow an application to respond sensibly to docking and undocking operations, for instance.

The Registry

The registry in Windows is a structured file that stores indexed information describing the host system's hardware, user preferences, and other configuration data. In Windows 3.1, the registry is used by applications to specify a limited amount of information, such as OLE document types.[19] In Windows NT, everything goes in the registry. Use of the registry in Windows 95 falls somewhere between these minimalist and all-embracing approaches.

The purpose of the registry is to reduce the proliferation of configuration files that can plague a Windows machine. In Windows 3.1, the CONFIG.SYS, AUTOEXEC.BAT, WIN.INI, and SYSTEM.INI files all contain information related to the system configuration. Some of the information is vital to the system's operation—specifying device drivers to load, for instance—and most of the remaining information describes other important aspects of the system's configuration. Add to these files the private .INI files set up by applications and the .GRP files used by the Program Manager, and it gets harder and harder to know where to look when diagnosing a problem or searching for a configuration setting.

Apart from the proliferation of these files in Windows 3.1, their integrity is a problem. Since the files contain plain text, the user can edit them directly, perhaps messing them up, and Windows has no way to figure out what might have happened. Incorporating all the configuration information into a registration database file and providing controlled access to it would preclude many of these potential problems.

---

18. This much was true in July 1994. It's clear that the device broadcast message could be extended to cover many different occurrences.

19. To be precise, Windows 3.1 supports a *registration database,* which the purist will argue is different from the Windows NT registry. It's a rather academic point.

Windows NT does away with all of the plain text files that Windows 3.1 uses and, in addition to the system's own use of the registry, allows applications to use the registry for storing private configuration data.

Windows 95 continues to process the configuration files you're familiar with—AUTOEXEC.BAT for example. Windows 95 also supports the registry. The principal user of the registry in Windows 95 is the Plug and Play subsystem, and all device-related information moves to the registry. Although this might seem to simply expand the file proliferation problem, you can use your own Windows 3.1 system as an example to measure the effect of putting this information in the registry. Count the number of lines in CONFIG.SYS, AUTOEXEC.BAT, WIN.INI, and SYSTEM.INI, subtract the lines that relate to hardware configuration, subtract other lines such as "BUFFERS=" that have no relevance under Windows 95, and you'll see that a lot of data disappears.[20] Although the development team would have preferred to adopt the registry mechanism in its entirety, the compatibility issues associated with upgrading the installed base of Windows 3.1 systems and their 16-bit applications were too great. The old style configuration files thus survive, but no doubt more and more use of the registry will be made in the future.

Figure 6-4 on the next page shows the arrangement of the registry database with its principal keys. Notice that the keys are hierarchically related, meaning that entire subtrees can be isolated and indexed with subkeys.

A particular software vendor might use the registry database to store application configuration information under the key HKEY_LOCAL_MACHINE\SOFTWARE\VENDOR\APPLICATION. In Figure 6-4, information about Exotic's spreadsheet application is registered this way. Typically the HKEY_LOCAL_MACHINE branch of the hierarchy describes non-user-specific information about the host system. The HARDWARE branch of this subtree is where the Windows 95 Plug and Play subsystem stores all of the system's hardware configuration information.

As you might expect, the registry APIs supported by Windows 95 don't include the security-related interfaces. Windows 95 does support

---

20. On my machine, CONFIG.SYS and SYSTEM.INI disappear altogether, and AUTOEXEC.BAT and WIN.INI shrink substantially.

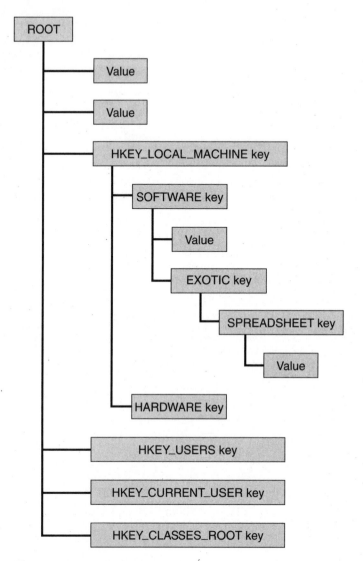

Figure 6-4.
Registry hierarchy in Windows 95, showing the principal keys.

a number of interfaces for VxDs that allow access to the registry, however. A subset of these interfaces is available for read-only access during the system's real mode initialization procedure.

The User Interface

In Chapter Five, we looked at the new visual elements of the Windows 95 user interface and at some of the Microsoft guidelines for making Win32 applications consistent with the shell and its behavior. Underlying the new appearance are many new and enhanced APIs. Two aspects of the new interface have an impact on existing applications:

- The minimum hardware supported by Windows 95 is a VGA display with 16 colors. The system itself operates internally with a palette of 256 colors, mapping the 256 to 16 if the hardware has only 16. The new 3-D appearance and the improved use of color mean that you should avoid hard coding colors, particularly for owner drawn items such as buttons. The *GetSysColor()* API helps you use the currently selected color palette within an application.

- The ability for the user to resize every visual element—scroll bar widths, caption bars, and the like—means that your code must not make assumptions about the size of standard items. User resizing coupled with the system's ability to change display resolution on the fly[21] plus the overall Plug and Play environment means that an application that truly exploits the Windows 95 capabilities must be able to react well to dynamic configuration changes.

The enhancements to the APIs you're familiar with cover many areas: menus, keyboard accelerators, icon management, and new capabilities that allow you to exploit the new visual appearance just as the shell does. Since this isn't an attempt to teach Windows 95 programming, we won't look at the details here. Suffice it to say that if Windows 95 is successful, its users will rapidly come to expect updated applications that exploit its new appearance and interface capabilities.

OLE

OLE has been the most widely promoted aspect of Microsoft's system software products over the last couple of years. Viewed initially as simply a "better DDE," OLE has evolved to become the cornerstone of

---

21. You'll receive a WM_DISPLAYCHANGED message both before and after this happens.

Microsoft's object-oriented system efforts. Windows 95 is the first operating system release that incorporates OLE as a standard function, although add-on libraries for Windows 3.1 have been available for developers to ship with their applications for some time. OLE's importance to developers is underlined by Microsoft's plans for the Cairo operating system to provide support for distributed object-based systems and an object-oriented filesystem—both of which are derived from the current OLE object model and compound file format. OLE today is a complex subsystem, but support for it within C++ class libraries continues to grow, somewhat simplifying the developer's task.

OLE has been dealt with extensively in other books. And doing justice to OLE would merit at least an entire chapter in this book. Nevertheless, it's important to at least look at some of the fundamental features of the technology.

OLE deals with collections of objects that make up *compound documents*. A compound document is a grouping of data prepared by several different applications. A letter prepared by a word processor, for example, might include a numeric table generated by a spreadsheet program. The Windows DDE capability offered limited facilities for using multiple applications to prepare and maintain such compound documents, but more often than not, the act of preparation involved simply copying a final version of the spreadsheet table, pasting it into the letter, and printing it. OLE aims to provide the framework wherein the user can prepare and maintain compound documents without losing any of the attributes of the data objects or precluding the possibility of manipulating the data objects in their original forms. This capability involves either maintaining a *link* in the compound document to the object in the original application, or *embedding* the data object directly within the document. In either case, when the user selects the data object, the originating application runs and provides the user with all of its data manipulation capabilities. The user can not only resize the spreadsheet as it sits in the document but also change the numbers and recalculate the contents.

An application that supports this architecture is called an *OLE server*, and an *OLE client* is any application that allows the inclusion of OLE objects within its supported document formats. Selecting an embedded object may cause the server to use an *in-place activation* technique whereby the server takes control of the client application's menus and of the redrawing of the screen area occupied by the data object. There's no apparent switching to another application such as we're used to. The user just has a different set of operations available for that particular data object.

OLE-enabled applications support *drag and drop* operations, in which the user can select a graphical representation of a data object and deposit it on some other object, whereupon the target object does something useful with the data. The Windows 95 shell, for example, allows the user to drag an object onto the desktop and leave it there or to drag a document to a printer and have it be printed with no further interaction.

Since the client application in the printing drag and drop example would know nothing about how to print the document, it would rely on the *programmability* of the server application. Simply put, this means that the client can determine which application created the document and send the server application a print command together with the document data. The server will expose possibly many interfaces to its functions, and any client can call the server functions at will. A page layout program, for example, could call on the text justification function available in a word processor. No user actions would be required to make this happen—it's the OLE subsystem that initiates and controls the interactions among all of the components.

Microsoft calls the core of the OLE design the *component object model,* and under this broad heading lists all the programming interfaces, data structures, and protocols that control OLE operations. OLE relies completely on object-oriented programming techniques and in particular on C++. The written OLE specification is based entirely on C++ conventions. The implementation of OLE on Windows 95 requires the presence of several DLLs in the Windows directory.

The OLE *compound file format* specifies a storage mechanism for OLE objects and their associated data. Within one compound file, it's possible to create multiple *streams*—each of which can contain collections of logically separated objects. A compound file allows its contents to be indexed efficiently, and the index is permanently retained—just as a database index is. Windows 95 implements an OLE compound file by storing the streams and the index in a single disk file. To the operating system, the file is just a collection of bits. Only the OLE subsystem knows how to interpret the index and the data streams. All of that will change with Cairo, and the interfaces offered today by the OLE libraries will become part of the operating system proper. With Cairo,

Microsoft plans to offer a new *object filesystem* as the native storage format. Multiple stream support, indexing, and object storage and retrieval functions will be an inherent feature of this filesystem. Whereas today we have APIs that simply read and write data, Cairo will provide APIs to load and store entire compound documents.

Of course, Microsoft faces healthy competition from various quarters in its bid to establish OLE as the preferred object model for PC-based applications. But OLE is gradually establishing itself, and its ready availability in Windows 95 and Windows NT is a good way to approach the contest.

International Support

Over the years Microsoft has invested an enormous amount of effort in the process of translating its products for use in overseas markets. It isn't just a matter of translating program text and documentation. Issues of local currency and date formats and other cultural considerations abound. For the Far East and Middle East markets, the complex character sets and right to left parsing issues further increase the work required to make a software product truly international.

Windows 95 will represent Microsoft's largest investment yet in the internationalization of a product. The plan calls for Windows 95 to be released simultaneously in seven languages (English, French, German, Italian, Swedish, Spanish, and Dutch) and for many other language versions to follow in the subsequent six months. To achieve these goals, Microsoft has restructured its development methods. Whereas Windows 3.1 had been localized by having a variety of small teams modify the source code and carry out the language translation, the rule for Windows 95 has been no source modifications for localization purposes. Whatever changes were necessary for localization were done just once, in Redmond, and then the individual translation groups worked with binary resources only.

Apart from the effort it has invested in the localization project itself, Microsoft has also enhanced Windows 95 considerably for foreign language support. Among the design decisions that the team had to make, determining whether to use the Unicode character set, as Windows NT does, was one of the major ones. For compatibility and size reasons, Windows 95 is not a Unicode system, although a number of its components, such as OLE, use Unicode as their internal character representation.[22] A range of Windows 95 features are aimed at simplifying the challenge of producing software that deals with many foreign languages:

■ Support for multiple keyboard layouts, allowing dynamic switching between character sets. This means, for example, that more than one foreign language can be used and displayed within a single document.

■ The so called *locale* APIs that handle issues such as string sorting, code page management, and localized date and time formats. A locale implies both a language dialect and a location.[23] So, for example, the issues associated with software for a multilingual country such as Switzerland can be correctly handled. Windows 95 allows you to control some 110 different locale items.

■ Extensions to existing APIs, such as *MessageBoxEx()*, that allow an application to specify the language resources to be used for display of the text in buttons.

Structured Exception Handling

Although not specific to Windows, structured exception handling is a feature that Windows 95 supports. Together with operating system support, you have to have a compiler that supports the capability. One without the other won't do it. Windows NT with the Microsoft 32-bit C compiler was the first Microsoft environment to support structured exception handling, and now it's in Windows 95.

Structured exception handling allows the programmer to bring order and simplicity to the usually onerous chore of error handling. A condition such as an error code returned by a system API, or a memory fault caused by an invalid pointer, can be handled in one place rather than with code scattered throughout an application. Figure 6-5 shows

---

22. The principal problems were the growth in the size of the system's working set (remember that 4-MB requirement) if Unicode were to be used and the compatibility testing issues associated with modifying close to 500 individual APIs for Unicode support.

23. Even to the extent that American English can now be properly viewed as a dialect of the Queen's English!

an example of how you might handle errors the "old" way (including an "old" bug), and Figure 6-6 is the same code modified to use structured exception handling. Some of the obvious declarations have been omitted for brevity, and the code is a little artificial—but it serves to illustrate the technique.

This code fragment opens a file, reads the first word of the file to determine the size of the subsequent data record, allocates memory for

```
      // Open a file, read a word, allocate that many
      //  bytes, and read the data in. Scan for a pattern.
      //   Return TRUE if it's found; FALSE otherwise.
hFile = OpenFile(lpszName, lpFbuff, nMode);
if (hFile == HFILE_ERROR)
      return FALSE;               // Failed
bFlag = ReadFile(hFile, &lSize, 4, &lCount, NULL);
if ((bFlag == FALSE) || (lCount != 4)){
      CloseHandle(hFile);         // Any error ignored
      return FALSE;               // Failed
}
lpMem = VirtualAlloc(NULL, lSize, MEM_COMMIT, PAGE_READWRITE);
if (lpMem == NULL){
      CloseHandle(hFile);         // Any error ignored
      return FALSE;               // Failed
}
bFlag = ReadFile(hFile, lpMem, lSize, &lCount, NULL);
if ((bFlag == FALSE) || (lCount != lSize)){
      // Deallocate memory. Ignore any error.
      (void) VirtualFree(lpMem, lSize, MEM_DECOMMIT);
      (void) CloseHandle(hFile); // Any error ignored
      return FALSE;               // Failed
}
lpScan = (DWORD *)lpMem;
      // Scan buffer--bug: no bad pointer check
bFlag = FALSE;
while (TRUE)
      if (*lpScan++ == lPattern){
          bFlag = TRUE; break;
      }
      // Ignore errors on deallocation or closing.
(void) VirtualFree(lpMem, lSize, MEM_DECOMMIT);
(void) CloseHandle(hFile);
return bFlag;                     // Failed
```

Figure 6-5.
Handling errors the old way, without structured exception handling.

the data, and reads the data in. Errors can occur while the code tries to open the file, while it reads the file, while it tries to allocate the memory buffer, or when it searches the buffer for a given value—when the pointer steps past the end of the buffer. The code shown in Figure 6-5 laboriously tests for error conditions. The code in Figure 6-6 handles all possible errors by embracing the code in a single *try* block, defining an *except* block that will be called if any errors occur, and then cleaning everything up in a *finally* block that executes regardless of success or failure. Note that the *except* block in Figure 6-6 will execute in

```
try {
    hFile = OpenFile(lpszName, lpFbuff, nMode);
    (void) ReadFile(hFile, &lSize, 4, &lCount, NULL);
    if (lCount != 4)    // Bad file format:
                        //  raise private exception
        RaiseException(BAD_FILE_DATA,
                       EXCEPTION_NONCONTINUABLE, 0, NULL);
    lpMem = VirtualAlloc(NULL, lSize, MEM_COMMIT,
                         PAGE_READWRITE);
    (void) ReadFile(hFile, lpMem, lSize, &lCount, NULL);
    if (lCount != lSize)    // Bad file format
        RaiseException(BAD_FILE_DATA,
                       EXCEPTION_NONCONTINUABLE, 0, NULL);
    lpScan = (DWORD *)lpMem;
        // Bug still present
    bFlag = FALSE;
    while (TRUE)
        if (*lpScan++ == lPattern){
            bFlag = TRUE; break;
        }
}
except (EXCEPTION_EXECUTE_HANDLER) {
    // Do the exception analysis here.
    bFlag = FALSE;       // Set error indication;
                         //  cannot return from here
}
finally {
    (void) VirtualFree(lpMem, lSize, MEM_DECOMMIT);
    (void) CloseHandle(hFile);
}
return bFlag;            // Return the result
```

Figure 6-6.
Using structured exception handling.

the event of a memory access fault when the code scans past the end of the allocated memory buffer (with the pattern not found). Neither example tests for this condition, and in the first case you'd get a program failure with little useful qualifying information.

Exception handlers are frame based, meaning that their scopes nest just as declaration scopes do, so it's possible to handle errors on either a global or a local basis. There are also facilities for specifying the context in which the exception is handled.[24] The structured exception handling feature also allows a program to initiate an exception (the *RaiseException()* API) and specifies the protocol for interacting with a debugging tool if one is in use. Within an *except* block, you can determine the cause of an exception so that you can carry out appropriate error recovery. You shouldn't replace every error test in your code with an exception sequence, but it is a great way to manage a multitude of possible error conditions diligently and efficiently. After all, how many times do you test for every possible error in your code?

The Graphics Device Interface

GDI is the heart of the Windows graphics capabilities. All of the drawing functions for lines and shapes are in GDI as well as the color management and font handling functions. Many aspects of Windows performance are tied closely to GDI performance, and a lot of the GDI code is handcrafted 386 assembly language. At the application level, Windows provides logical objects known as *device contexts* (DCs) that describe the current state of a particular GDI drawing target. A DC can describe any output device or representation of a device. An application will obtain a DC for printer output or for completely memory-based operations, for example. Applications manage DCs by means of Win32 APIs only. The actual DC data structure is always hidden from the application. At any instant a DC contains information about objects such as the current pen (for drawing lines), the current brush (for filling regions), the color selection, and the location and dimensions of the logical drawing target.

The key to the use of Windows and Windows applications on a widely disparate range of target hardware is the device independence

---

24. Reminiscent of, but much better than, the C language *setjmp()/longjmp()* facility.

embodied in the Windows API. An application uses DCs and other logical objects when calling GDI functions. It never writes data directly to an output device. GDI itself manages the process of transforming the data into a format suitable for use by a particular device driver, and the driver handles the task of placing a representation of the request on the output device. For example, an application may call the system asking for its main window to be repainted. During the repainting operation, among many other requests, GDI may tell the driver "on the screen draw a one-pixel-wide black line from position (0, 48) to position (639, 48)." If the device—a dot matrix printer, say—can't perform operations such as line drawing, GDI will break the request down into simpler operations. The device driver will receive a series of calls telling it to draw individual dots, for example. This architecture frees applications from device-dependent problems and allows Windows to make use of even the simplest hardware as an output device.

With this device-independent capability come several problems. In addition to simply choosing and managing an appropriate device-independent representation of all the graphics objects, you need to have a plethora of device drivers available to interface GDI to the target hardware. Issues such as handling complex fonts through a range of point sizes and then being able to draw the font legibly on both a 1024 by 768 pixel display screen and a simple dot matrix printer involve many complex algorithms and a lot of very clever code.

Over successive releases of Windows, the capabilities of GDI have improved considerably, and the underlying structure of the system has adapted to the experience gained from earlier versions and to the prevailing market forces. The vast majority of Windows users nowadays tend to have fairly capable hardware: VGA displays and laser or high-resolution dot matrix printers. The hardware will probably get even more powerful, with higher resolution and color-capable devices abounding. It's therefore important to get the best possible performance out of a few core components rather than expend effort on hundreds of device drivers, each with a limited installed base. It has also been important to look ahead at the likely effects of hardware trends. Two of the major changes in the Windows 95 GDI subsystem reflect hardware trends: the *device-independent bitmap* (DIB) engine and the *image color matching* (ICM) subsystem.

Windows 3.1 successfully introduced the concept of the *universal printer driver*—a device driver that does much of the work for all the other system printer drivers. The so called *printer mini-drivers* support only the hardware-specific operations of a printer and rely on the universal driver for most printing-related functions. This allocation of responsibility allowed Microsoft to invest heavily in a high-performance, high-quality universal printer driver and in some good example mini-drivers for devices such as the Hewlett-Packard LaserJet. From the printer manufacturer's perspective, Windows printer driver development became a much simpler and much less error prone project.

Windows 95 takes up this design concept by incorporating the DIB engine and a *display mini-driver* capability. If the display hardware matches what the DIB engine can do, what was once a very complex, performance-sensitive development effort is considerably simplified.[25] Write a display mini-driver, and rely on the DIB engine as (in Microsoft's phrase) "the world's fastest flat frame buffer" display driver. The DIB engine design also recognizes the level of effort that hardware manufacturers now put into hardware assists for Windows-based systems. If you have hardware acceleration or other capabilities, the display mini-driver can use these instead of calling the DIB engine.

Image color matching is a new capability that addresses device-independence issues for applications that deal with color, such as photo retouching applications. Although color has always been part of Windows, earlier releases didn't have to worry too much about the issue since color-capable peripherals were relatively rare. But now that the price of good color scanners and color printers has fallen to the $1,000 range, Windows has to take careful note of color management.

Here are the other improvements to GDI in Windows 95:

- Performance. A lot of code has been tuned, and some important components have been converted to 32-bit code.

- Relaxation of resource limitations. In parallel with what's been done to the User subsystem, many of GDI's resource limits have been raised significantly.

- Win32 support. Windows 95 fully supports many graphics APIs unavailable in Windows 3.1.

- TrueType enhancements.

---

25. One simple code count shows the VGA display driver in Windows 3.1 to be over 41,000 lines of assembler (for a 16-color–only display). In Windows 95, it's only about 5000 lines for the full 256-color driver.

■ Metafile support enhancements compatible with Windows NT's metafile support.

■ Printing subsystem enhancements, including bi-directional printer support and a new 32-bit print spooler.

GDI Architecture

Figure 6-7 illustrates the major components of the GDI subsystem. It also shows the breakdown between 16-bit and 32-bit code modules—with one caveat: the DIB engine is actually 32-bit code running with a 16-bit (segmented) view of system memory—so the code makes use of the fast 386 instructions for memory move operations, for example. There's considerable trickery involved in efficient address manipulation, but it means that existing 16-bit applications can realize the performance improvements of the new DIB engine and that the engine itself can call into the 16-bit GDI code with no additional overhead. If the DIB engine were placed on the 32-bit side of the fence, either the

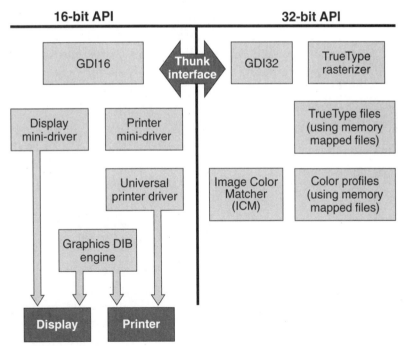

Figure 6-7.
The components of GDI in Windows 95.

32-bit GDI module would have to replicate much of the GDI functionality, or the DIB engine would incur lots of thunk overhead calling back to the 16-bit side.

Before looking in detail at the new DIB engine and the ICM subsystem, let's review the smaller improvements in the Windows 95 GDI.

Performance Improvements

The performance of the GDI subsystem is critical to the performance of Windows. Many benchmarks of Windows 3.1 tend to focus attention on video performance. Although video performance is only one element of the overall performance of the system, it's certainly a huge factor in perceived performance.

The Windows GDI code has been worked on for a sufficiently long time that there really aren't any huge undiscovered performance gains to be made. But Windows 95 includes quite a few incremental improvements:

- The new DIB engine is handcrafted assembler. The effort invested in this will improve the performance of many video display drivers as well as the print subsystem.

- The TrueType rasterizer is the component responsible for turning a description of a font into the actual image you see on the screen or on the printed page. The Windows 95 rasterizer is new 32-bit code.

- The print subsystem spools print metafiles, reducing the amount of data movement and hence speeding up the print process. The print spooler itself is new 32-bit code that can run as a true background process.

- A lot of new 32-bit code in key components makes use of the improved instructions available on the 386 processor. Also the duplication of some GDI components in 16-bit and 32-bit code avoids thunk overhead.

Limit Expansion

Along with the move partway to a 32-bit subsystem comes access to the 32-bit memory pools used by Windows 95. Under Windows 3.1, the GDI subsystem allocated all resources from a single 64K heap—which limited the total number of available resources significantly on systems that were capable of running several applications at once.

In Windows 95, GDI still keeps many logical objects in a heap limited to 64K. The data structures that describe brushes, pens, and bitmap headers, for example, stay in this smaller heap. Display context structures also remain in this pool. However, GDI now allocates the objects that can really eat up space from a separate, 32-bit memory pool. GDI regions, font management structures, and physical objects all move to this pool, which considerably reduces the pressure on the 64K heap. For example, the collection of rectangles used to describe an elliptical region can consume up to 45K. Decisions over which objects to move out of the 64K heap were also influenced by performance considerations. Since both 16-bit and 32-bit code has to manipulate the structures, the designers had to be careful not to incur too many selector loads when switching between the different heap areas.

New Graphics Features

Windows 95 incorporates almost all of the more advanced graphics APIs defined by Win32. Their inclusion increases the suitability of Windows for use as an application platform by graphics-intensive applications. The new APIs encompass

- Support for *paths,* allowing an application to describe a complex arrangement of geometric shapes that GDI will outline and fill with a single function call

- *Bézier curve* drawing, in which an application describes a curve using a series of discrete points and GDI figures out how to draw the curve

Applications such as high-end drawing packages and CAD products have to concern themselves with the very accurate representation of geometric objects. One of the differences between Windows 95 and Windows NT is in the drawing algorithms that define the pixels used when an application draws lines or fills shapes. Internally, an application can draw anywhere within the 16-bit coordinate space ($-32,767$ to $+32,767$ in both the x and y directions). GDI may have to scale this image dramatically to allow its display on a 640 by 480 pixel screen and, regardless of scaling issues, drawing a diagonal line on a video screen is always problematic. Essentially, GDI and the display driver have to figure out between them which pixels become black and which stay white. For most of us (and most applications), the differences between lines drawn according to the two algorithms won't be discernible. There are similar subtle differences between the ways the two GDI subsystems fill shapes on the screen. The algorithms differ as they determine which pixels to include or exclude around the edge of the shape.

TrueType

The new TrueType rasterizer is implemented in C. It's an adaptation of the C++ module developed for Windows NT.[26] The new code also implements an improved mathematical representation of a font, using 32-bit fixed point arithmetic with a 26-bit fractional part. Windows 3.1 uses a 16-bit representation with a 10-bit fraction. This led to some rounding error problems (leading to reduced fidelity on high resolution devices) and difficulties in handling complex characters such as those in the Chinese language (the Han characters).

The rasterizer now uses memory mapped files to access font description files (all those .TTF files in your Windows system directory), and the associated .FOT files are gone. During the system boot process a private record of an installed font is written to disk and used during the next boot. This improves the speed of system startup considerably if you have a lot of fonts installed.

Metafile Support

Metafiles contain sequences of graphics operations written in a device-independent format. An application can obtain a device context to a metafile and draw a picture using the DC. GDI generates the metafile records that correspond to the GDI function calls made by the application. Metafiles can be reprocessed with the drawing output directed toward any capable device. The recorded picture will appear with the original sizing, proportions, and colors intact.

Windows 95 adds support for the enhanced metafiles defined for Win32, including limited support for world transforms (scaling operations only). There are some Win32-generated metafile records that Windows 95 won't understand, so it skips them when reading the metafile. This means that a metafile generated on a Windows NT system using the full range of graphics capabilities can't be completely reproduced on a Windows 95 system.

---

26. The Windows NT operating system code uses C++ extensively. There's none in the Windows 95 operating system.

Image Color Matching

The problem of producing a completely device-independent color capability for Windows remains an intractable one. There doesn't yet exist a recognized solution to the problem—for any general purpose computer system. Accurate color reproduction is the subject of many research projects, and a number of international standards try to solve subsets of the problem. Interestingly, all color standards in use today are derived from a 1931 definition known as the CIEXYZ standard. Apart from the fact that color reproduction involves issues of human perception, the basic problem is that even if you can define a completely adequate internal color representation system, no two devices will reproduce a given color identically. Thus, a "red" on the printed page will look different on the screen, and many colors that you can choose for your latest Van Gogh knockoff on screen can't be accurately matched by the colors your printer can produce. Given the inability of a device to produce a particular color, what do you do? Adjust that color to the nearest one available on the output device? Or adjust every color in the image in an attempt to maintain the original contrast? It doesn't seem likely that anyone will ever solve the problem to the complete satisfaction of every expert.

Color management systems that do exist today are built around specific hardware, so the controlling software knows what colors are available and what transformations it must use to render accurate color output. This of course runs counter to the Windows philosophy of always maintaining device independence. Yet the need for a good color management system is apparent. For a few thousand dollars, you can set yourself up with a very high quality color production system, and the prices will no doubt fall further. Thus, the Windows designers were faced with the challenge of integrating a color management system that meets the nonexpert needs (and budgets) of most of us while still supporting the stringent requirements posed by professionals in magazine publishing and photographic reproduction.

Image color matching (ICM) is Microsoft's name for the solution incorporated into Windows 95:

- ICM defines a *logical color space* for Windows that is defined in terms of the RGB (red, green, blue) triplets already used in Windows 3.1. The use of the existing RGB mechanism is really a convenient implementation detail. The logical color space is actually calibrated with reference to the CIEXYZ standard.

- ICM uses a *color profile* that defines the color capabilities of a particular device. Manufacturers of color output peripherals can ship a color profile with their devices, much as they might ship a Windows device driver today. If a device has no associated color profile, the system chooses a sensible default profile.

- The color profile allows the ICM to build a *color transform* that defines how to map colors from the logical color space to the colors reproducible on the output device. For an input device such as a scanner, ICM uses the profile to transform the device colors to the logical color space.

- ICM thus allows device drivers and the system itself to perform color matching and color transformation operations in support of scanning or reproducing images involving a specific device. ICM aims to be consistent—giving you predictable results each time you scan, display, or print an image.

- ICM is implemented as a replaceable DLL, and it's possible to load more than one ICM at a time.[27] This means that for environments with different color management needs the system's default processing can be replaced or circumvented.

- Windows 95 adds support for the CMYK color standard that's widely used in applications that produce color separations for printing and publishing. If an application chooses CMYK as its color space, Windows stays out of the way and the application can pass color coordinates to the device driver without further transformation by the ICM.

Microsoft also realized early on that there were people who knew a lot more about color management than they did. The specification and development of the Windows 95 ICM was done in conjunction with Eastman Kodak, a company that does indeed know quite a lot about color. The default ICM DLL planned for inclusion with Windows 95 was written largely by Kodak.

---

27. Loading a new ICM is under application control. Two new APIs—*LoadImageColorMatcher()* and *FreeImageColorMatcher()*—manage the procedure.

Color Profiles

Microsoft will publish the format of a color profile in the Windows 95 SDK and DDK products. The definition will describe both the file and in-memory formats for color profiles. No doubt some standard profiles will be included with Windows 95 when it ships—just as you get most of your printer drivers "in the box" today. The contents of a color profile have been determined by efforts involving several different companies, and it's freely acknowledged that there are application areas that will need further extensions of the information embodied in a color profile. But for most applications, these color profiles are sufficient.[28]

As you'd expect, color profiles will be available for scanner devices, display screens, and color printers. The profile definition also enables the specification of profiles that describe abstract devices (allowing color effects) and color space conversion (from the internal logical color space to a different standard) and the specification of *device link* profiles. A device link profile caters to a system with a fixed configuration, allowing the color transformations to be fine tuned so that, for example, the particular "red" generated by your Hewlett-Packard ScanJet becomes exactly this "red" on your HP DeskJet printer.

Don't imagine that you'll be generating color profiles the same way you change your desktop colors with the Windows Control Panel, though. Color profiles are real science and may involve device calibration, temperature correction, and the handling of different paper and ink types, among other complexities.

Communicating Color Information

Figure 6-8 on the next page illustrates the flow of color information among the various components in the system. The color information communicated among the components is always expressed in either RGB or CMYK values, or in some transformation of these values according to the way the application has defined its color space.

At the application level, GDI provides several new APIs that allow a specific color space to be defined and manipulated.[29] An application uses a device-independent bitmap (DIB) to store an image, and the

---

28. If you don't already believe that color management is a tough problem, note the way in which the ICM designers acknowledged the difficulty. They listed one of their goals as specifying a system that's "simple enough to implement in our lifetimes."

29. If you're interested in the details, look for all the ICM-related APIs—those that have the string *Color* somewhere (!) in their names.

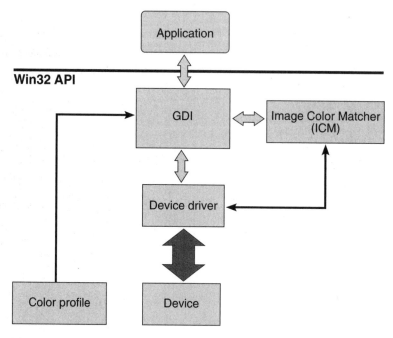

Figure 6-8.
Color information handling within the system.

color matching APIs operate directly on the bitmap. The DIB structure itself has been extended to incorporate color information, and, as with other device-related operations, color manipulation is specific to each Windows device context.

The Display Subsystem

Although Windows allows only a single system display device to be active, several different software components are involved in controlling the display. Figure 6-9 illustrates most of these components, together with the boundaries between them—the API layer and ring zero components vs. ring three components. The example in Figure 6-9 assumes a configuration that uses the new device-independent bitmap engine. The DIB engine assumes a major role in the control of the video display under Windows 95. In a configuration that doesn't use the DIB engine, the engine and the associated display mini-driver won't be present, and the system components such as GDI interact with a single

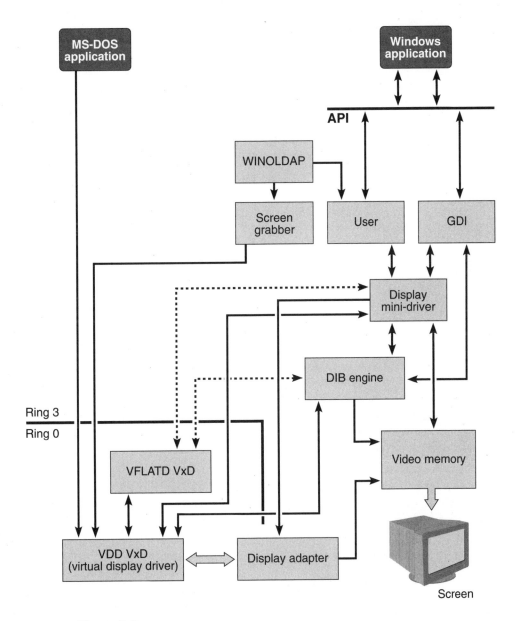

Figure 6-9.
Display subsystem components in an example configuration.

display driver module. That's essentially how Windows 3.1 works today, but in a very large percentage of Windows systems, the video hardware will be appropriate for use of the new DIB engine and the display mini-driver architecture introduced with Windows 95. For most purposes, you can think of the DIB engine and the mini-driver as a single display driver. Windows always assumes that the video display is directly addressable as a memory region. Display adapters that don't allow this aren't usable by Windows for graphics operations.

Video system performance is critical to Windows, so, in terms of the length of instruction sequences, bringing the video memory and the video display adapter as close as possible to GDI is an overriding consideration. The device-independent nature of GDI means that it has to go through a device driver to get to the hardware and, in fact, two device drivers are involved. One is the VxD responsible for virtualizing the video hardware and controlling the switching of the screen between different virtual machines. (This is the VDD in Figure 6-9.) The other driver is a ring three DLL that always runs in the context of the system virtual machine. (This is the combination of the display mini-driver and the DIB engine in Figure 6-9.) So when the Windows desktop is on the screen (meaning that any MS-DOS applications are either not running or running in the background), the path from a Windows application to the screen is fairly efficient: a call to one of the Windows system DLLs, which in turn calls the display driver. No ring transition is involved, and the display driver has direct access to the video memory.

If Windows needs to initiate a hardware control operation—for example, to switch the screen resolution—it does rely on the display driver VxD. Normally, the ring three display driver will use the INT 10 video services interrupt to do this. The INT causes a fault, which initiates a ring transition. The kernel unravels the cause of the fault and hands control to the display driver VxD. Typically the display VxD will be the only component that mucks with the display adapter hardware.

The *grabber* module in Windows 95 is the same as in Windows 3.1. To support MS-DOS applications, the system's WINOLDAP module relies on a screen grabber for the purpose of saving and restoring the state of the video hardware and the video memory. The grabber has to match the display hardware type, so the grabber, the display VxD, and the display mini-driver are developed in concert. The VxD services used by the grabber include functions for copying data back and forth between video memory and a memory buffer, and various synchronization primitives that assist in critical section management and switching between virtual machines.

The DIB Engine

In Windows, a *bitmap* is a memory-based representation of a completed sequence of GDI operations. The resulting object is suitable for immediate display on a compatible output device, and, in the case of a device-independent bitmap, minimal additional processing will prepare the object for output to a different device. Bitmaps appear in files (the desktop wallpaper, for example), as application resources (the pictures on toolbar buttons, for example), and in main memory, where applications and device drivers can build and manipulate them directly. The entire Windows desktop display is itself a large bitmap, and the code that deals with updating the screen is critical to the system's performance.

The Windows 95 DIB engine recognizes the current state of display hardware by implementing a bitmap management capability that deals very efficiently with color flat frame buffer devices. In hardware terms, this would mean that the output device provides a large linear memory space with each screen pixel directly addressable as a memory location. Associated with each pixel is a color, represented by a number of bits. The DIB engine handles 1, 4, 8, 16, or 24 bits per pixel color, giving it a range from simple monochrome displays to high-end output devices with the ability to display millions of colors.

The DIB engine architecture assumes that it can set a particular pixel to a particular color by simply storing the appropriate number of bits in the correct memory location in the device's frame buffer. If the hardware doesn't have a frame buffer, the DIB engine is usable only for assistance in manipulating memory resident bitmaps: it doesn't try to allocate some huge chunk of memory and pretend it's the display device. Although the principal use of the DIB engine is for managing the video display, its bitmap manipulation capabilities lend themselves to other operations as well. Printer drivers can call the DIB engine for assistance when preparing a page, and GDI can use the DIB engine for operations on memory resident bitmaps.

Associated with the DIB engine is a display mini-driver called by GDI. This driver is still responsible for managing hardware-dependent operations in collaboration with the display driver VxD. GDI never calls the DIB engine directly, and, ordinarily, the DIB engine will rely on the mini-driver for hardware-dependent operations.[30] Also, if the

---

30. Among other enhancements such as color cursors and 32-bit color devices, Microsoft is already thinking about extending the use of the DIB engine so that GDI can indeed call it directly.

display adapter has additional capabilities, such as hardware acceleration for text output, the mini-driver is responsible for directly using these features and the DIB engine won't be called to perform that function. As part of its effort to get complementary hardware designed for Windows, Microsoft has been lobbying display adapter manufacturers to build devices with flat frame buffers, local bus video memory, and hardware acceleration for text output and bit blt operations.

Both the display mini-driver and the DIB engine are dynamically loadable libraries. Display drivers that rely on the DIB engine will cause it to be loaded during initialization. If the display driver doesn't use the DIB engine, it won't be loaded. The bitmap memory manipulated by the DIB engine is shared with GDI. For performance reasons, there's an attempt to minimize any back and forth copying of bitmaps.[31] The design of the DIB engine also tries to recognize the needs of multimedia applications with very high speed video data transfer requirements.

The Display Mini-Driver

The display mini-driver uses two major data structures to interact with the DIB engine and GDI. The GDIINFO structure is central to all of GDI's device-related operations. The structure defines, for example, the capabilities of the device in terms of its ability to draw lines, circles, text, and so forth. Many calls between GDI and its device drivers pass a pointer to the appropriate GDIINFO structure as one of the parameters. Information common to all devices is collected in the GDIINFO structure.

The other data structure is the DIBENGINE shown in Figure 6-10. Every GDIINFO structure specifies the size of the device descriptor structure associated with the device. Usually referred to as the PDEVICE structure, this data structure is entirely device dependent. Its size and contents vary according to the type of the device. For a display mini-driver, the PDEVICE structure is a DIBENGINE structure. Taken together, the GDIINFO structure and the DIBENGINE structure describe everything GDI needs to know about a display device that uses the DIB engine.

---

31. There's an analogous *CreateDIBSection()* API in Windows 95 that allows an application to reserve a directly addressable memory region for a bitmap that it shares with GDI.

```
struct DIBENGINE {

    WORD            deType;                 // 'DI' when GDI calls;
                                            //   0 or ScreenSelector
                                            //   when mini-driver calls
    WORD            deWidth;                // Width of DIB in pixels
    WORD            deHeight;               // Height of DIB in pixels
    WORD            deWidthBytes;           // No. of bytes per scan line
    BYTE            dePlanes;               // No. of planes in bitmap
    BYTE            deBitsPixel;            // No. of bits per pixel
    DWORD           deReserved1;            // Reserved
    DWORD           deDeltaScan;            // Displacement to next scan
    LPBYTE          delpPDevice;            // Pointer to associated
                                            //   PDevice
    WORD            deBitsOffset;           // Offset to DIB
    WORD            deBitsSelector;         // Selector to DIB
    WORD            deFlags;                // Additional flags
    WORD            deVersion;              // Version 0x0400
    LPBITMAPINFO    deBitmapInfo;           // Pointer to BitmapInfo
                                            //   header
    void (FAR *deCursorExclude)();          // Cursor Exclude callback
    void (FAR *deCursorUnexclude)();        // Cursor Unexclude callback
    DWORD           deReserved2;            // Reserved

};
```

Figure 6-10.
The DIBENGINE data structure.

Bank-Switched Video Adapters

Another important component of the DIB engine architecture is a VxD
called VFLATD, the flat frame buffer VxD. This VxD caters to display
adapters that possess large amounts of video memory but have to use a
memory window to switch back and forth between different 64K blocks
of it.[32] The VFLATD VxD will manage up to a 1-MB logical frame buffer.
The display mini-driver initially contains the code for switching the
physical frame buffer to a different region of the logical frame buffer.
When the mini-driver calls VFLATD to register this bank-switching
code, the VxD actually copies the code into its own memory. Whenever
the video memory window needs to be moved, VFLATD simply

---

32. If you remember expanded memory, that's exactly what this is like.

267

executes the switching code by running through it—not even a function call to get in its way as it comes steaming through!

Providing the bank-switching support as a standard part of the system (and making sure it runs as fast as possible) makes the mini-driver solution applicable to a much broader range of display adapters, so the likelihood of your system's using the DIB engine is pretty high.

Interfacing with the DIB Engine

When Windows 95 first loads a display mini-driver and calls the driver's DLL initialization routine, the driver simply collects information about its own configuration from the SYSTEM.INI file. Later on in the system's initialization process, GDI calls the driver's *Enable* interface twice. The first time through, the driver calls *DIB_Enable()*. The DIB engine hands back a pointer to an appropriate GDIINFO structure. The driver fills in some of the device-dependent fields (for example, the number of bits per pixel) and returns the GDIINFO structure pointer to GDI. The second call to *Enable* is where the rest of the initialization work gets done, including calling the display VxD to set the hardware into the correct graphics mode (using an INT 10) and if necessary handing the bank-switching code to the VFLATD VxD.

Once all the initialization is over, GDI, the mini-driver, the DIB engine, VFLATD, and the display VxD are all hooked together and ready to actually put something on the screen. The display mini-driver provides a standard set of about 30 or so interfaces that allow GDI to interact with the driver. Many of these functions are the same as those defined for existing Windows 3.1 display drivers, such as those for managing the cursor. All of them are exported entry points from the driver DLL. Several functions simply accept the call from GDI and hand it directly to the DIB engine. For example, GDI will call the driver's *BitmapBits()* function whenever an application creates or copies a bitmap. The mini-driver can turn around and call the DIB engine's *DIB_BitmapBits()* entry point with no transformation of parameters or, indeed, any other processing.

Management of the cursor is handled largely by the mini-driver, and, as with Windows 3.1 display drivers, the mini-driver must define the set of standard cursor resources used by GDI. This includes objects such as the standard arrow pointer, the I-beam cursor used in text fields, and the cursor we all hope we'll see a lot less of, the hourglass.

The Printing Subsystem

Much of the Windows 95 printing subsystem architecture (and indeed a lot of the code) is shared with Windows NT, so much of the new terminology and the new components of the print subsystem will be familiar to you if you've studied Windows NT. Apart from the new Image Color Matching capability, Windows 95 doesn't introduce any dramatic changes into this printing architecture, although across the board there are a number of significant improvements over the printing subsystem in Windows 3.1:

- A new spooler, implemented as a fully preemptive Win32 application. Print spooling can thus be a true background activity under Windows 95.

- Support for PostScript Level 2—the version applicable to color output devices.

- Bi-directional communication with the printer, which enables good Plug and Play support and the possibility of other enhancements.[33]

- Use of the new device-independent bitmap engine for high-performance bitmap manipulation.

- A new "quality of service" mechanism that allows the system to manage the simultaneous operation of more than one printer driver for a particular device.

- Improvements in the tools used for developing printer mini-drivers.

The Windows 95 printing system also expands the use of the printing APIs in preference to the printer escape functions used in Windows 3.0. An escape function (generated using the now-obsolete *Escape()* API) allowed an application to make a direct request to the printer driver. Windows 3.1 and Windows NT have replaced more and more of these escapes with APIs, and the recommendation now is to always use the API.[34]

---

33. A sample of these enhancements is already available in Microsoft's Windows Printing System product for Hewlett-Packard LaserJet printers.

34. The documentation for the *Escape()* API describes the details.

Printing Architecture

Three groups of components collaborate to print pages under Windows 95:

- GDI and its supporting modules, such as the DIB engine and the printer driver, which are responsible for translating drawing primitives issued by applications into a data stream suitable for the target printer.

- The local print processors and the print spooler that accepts the data stream and either writes it to a local disk file for subsequent printing or hands it to a local printer *monitor* for output to the physical printer.

- The despooler process and the *print request router* (PRR) that takes a print job and dispatches it to the correct target printer. This printer may be either a locally connected device or a network-attached printer.

Figure 6-11 illustrates these components and their interaction. In Chapter Nine, we'll look in more detail at the PRR and at the management of network printing. Essentially the PRR determines where a print job is headed and passes it to either the local printing system or the appropriate network subsystem for printing on a remote machine.

The Printing Process

An application produces output for a printer as it does for any other graphics device: it asks GDI for an appropriate device context and then draws its output using the DC. Obtaining the DC is a little different because the application must use the *CreateDC()* API, naming a target printer rather than simply requesting one of the available display device contexts maintained by Windows. Once it has the DC, the application uses the *StartDoc()* and *EndDoc()* APIs to identify the beginning and end of a discrete print job. Within a single job, the *StartPage()* and *EndPage()* APIs identify page breaks within the document.

Within the system, GDI, the printer driver, the DIB engine, and the local spooler combine to generate a disk file containing the data destined for the printer and an information file used to describe this *print job*. Both Windows 3.1 and Windows NT use a series of *journal records* as the basis for the print data file. The despooler is responsible

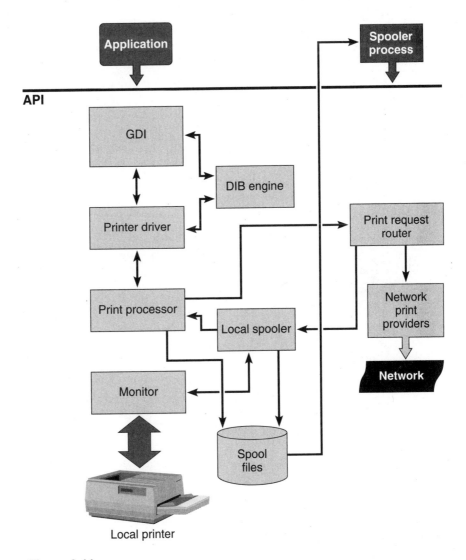

Figure 6-11.
Components of the Windows 95 printing architecture.

for subsequently handing the print job to the print request router for actual printing.

If the print job is for a local printer, the local spooler hands the data to a *print processor* that converts the journal records to a printer-specific format. Ultimately, the data stream goes to a *monitor*, and it's the monitor that actually controls the physical printer. Although it might seem that the monitor is yet one more level of indirection in this process, it enables much more intelligent handling of a printer device. The monitor handles all bi-directional communication with the printer so that conditions such as paper out can be reported to the local spooler. This allows the user to see a useful error message, such as *paper out* or *cover open*, rather than the generic *printer not responding*. The monitor also implements the Plug and Play support for printers, enabling automatic identification of the printer, for example. The monitor design also provides a general interface that allows devices such as direct network-attached printers to function properly. As far as the spooler is concerned, the monitor is dealing with a directly connected printer. If the monitor chooses to talk NetBIOS commands to a laser printer plugged in down the hallway, so be it—the spooler doesn't care.

Rather than a print job, the application can choose to directly produce a metafile by requesting a DC using the *CreateEnhMetaFile()* API. GDI generates a metafile on disk that describes a *reference device*—a basis for the metafile contents—and a series of metafile records. Metafiles remain device independent, and an application can replay their content and direct the output to a specific device at some later time.

Microsoft plans to use enhanced metafiles as the basis for the contents of the print job data file, so all print processors will convert metafile records to device-dependent data during the despooling operation. Windows 95 will implement this for only locally attached printers, but in the future metafiles will be used for network printing. Apart from the fact that much less data gets sent across the network, the printing subsystem on the local machine is a lot simpler. It doesn't need to know much about the target printer, and the printer driver and print processor need only exist on the target machine.

Using the Universal Printer Driver

Windows 3.1 introduced a major enhancement into the printing subsystem—the universal printer driver. Like the DIB engine–mini-driver combination for display drivers in Windows 95, the universal printer driver recognizes the fact that most printers work pretty much the same way. Thus, the universal driver can encapsulate much of the printing workload, leaving the printer manufacturer free to concentrate on developing a much simpler printer mini-driver to handle the hardware-dependent interactions. Windows 95 shares the design of the printer mini-drivers with Windows NT, and a particular mini-driver will work on either system.

The universal printer driver approach has been extremely successful, and Microsoft predicts that support for over 700 different printers will be included with Windows 95 when it ships. The driver has been enhanced for Windows 95 in a few small ways, including support for 600-dpi devices and the ability to download TrueType fonts to the target printer. The mini-driver design is largely unchanged, and the philosophy remains to offload the majority of print output processing to the universal driver with the mini-driver providing only device-dependent functionality.

The world of printing is a highly complex one, and the quality of font reproduction is one of the most carefully scrutinized aspects. Adobe Systems has built a very successful business by evangelizing both its fonts and its PostScript printing technology. For many years Adobe fonts and PostScript output devices have set the standard for computer-based printing and publishing. The majority of printers deal in data streams interspersed with printer commands (the basis for the universal printer driver design), but PostScript is a page description language. The PostScript printer driver generates the description of the page to be printed with very little knowledge of the actual output device.[35] This device independence has allowed PostScript to span the range of printing devices, from $500 laser printers to high-end color film production systems costing tens of thousands of dollars. A PostScript interpreter, which resides on the output device, translates the PostScript data stream into actual hardware operations that place dots on paper or film. The universal printer driver model doesn't suit the needs of PostScript, so no use is made of the mini-driver architecture for PostScript printers.

By far the most popular laser printers for Windows systems are those in the Hewlett-Packard LaserJet series. Microsoft and Hewlett-Packard have collaborated closely on Windows printing design for several years, including the design of the TrueType font subsystem. Hewlett-Packard also has its own printer language—PCL—that is common to all the LaserJet models. Many printers feature "LaserJet emulation"—essentially meaning PCL emulation. PCL is closer to the model of the world implemented by the Windows universal printer driver, so this class of printer can use the mini-driver architecture.

---

35. Should you be so inclined, you can actually read the PostScript driver's output by directing it into a file.

Conclusion

Windows 95 finally makes 32-bit Windows programming a mainstream activity. In addition to improved ease of development and compatibility with Windows NT, Windows 95 adds a number of new features to Windows. Some, such as the color matching capability, are long-awaited responses to features previously available only in competing operating systems. Other features, such as OLE and RPC, have existed before Windows 95 but never as standard components of an operating system that will be used on millions of PCs. Once again, we can all look forward to the amazing inventiveness of the software industry as it harnesses these features in new application products.

Between the API layer and the device drivers that translate application requests into operations on the bare metal, Windows 95 includes several radically new or revised subsystems. The rest of this book isolates some of these subsystems and examines them in detail. The next chapter looks at one component that everyone uses: the filesystem.

References

Microsoft Corporation. Windows 95 SDK documentation. Redmond, Wash.: Microsoft, 1994. No doubt Microsoft's product documentation will be augmented by dozens of new or warmed-over books that deal with the details of the Windows API and Windows device drivers, but I haven't seen any yet. If you program for Windows and you don't yet have a CD ROM drive—invest now. The online help files in the SDK and the CD distributed as part of the Microsoft Developer Network product are about the only sane way to approach this volume of information.

Brockschmidt, Kraig. *Inside OLE 2.0.* Redmond, Wash.: Microsoft Press, 1994. This is an intimidating book, nearly 900 pages in length. It is, however, the single most comprehensive treatment of OLE available. If OLE development is in your future, this is a book you have to tackle.

CHAPTER SEVEN

THE FILESYSTEM

Although the 32-bit API and the shell are likely to attract the highest initial interest from programmers and users, the new filesystem architecture of Microsoft Windows 95 is the base operating system component that has the most widespread impact on the system. Windows 95 continues to use the MS-DOS FAT filesystem as its default on-disk structure, but the code implementing the filesystem organization is completely new. In Windows 95, the FAT filesystem code—referred to as VFAT—is merely one piece of an entirely fresh design. These new features supported by the Windows 95 filesystem architecture affect both end users and application developers:

- Support for long filenames finally addresses the number one user complaint about earlier versions of MS-DOS and Windows. The new API support for long filenames requires developers to modify their applications, but there is an immediate and significant payback for the effort invested.

- Network support relies on the new installable filesystem architecture to allow the concurrent use of different network systems. Support for multiple network connections means that users can simultaneously access different networks without suffering through a complex setup and configuration procedure. Network software providers can develop Windows 95 network support using an interface designed to allow the integration of multiple high-performance connections.

- Users will see improved performance resulting from the implementation of the standard FAT filesystem as multithreaded 32-bit protected mode software.

■ Developers specializing in the support of new hardware devices will realize the benefit of the layered filesystem design as the effort required to implement new disk device drivers is significantly reduced.

These features reflect the goals of the filesystem effort—add long filename support, improve performance, and dispense with the poorly suited MS-DOS INT 21H mechanism in favor of a properly architected interface that supports multiple filesystems. The reliance on MS-DOS has been the major weakness in every release of Windows through version 3.1. Apart from significant user frustration with the limited filenaming capabilities, there have been a number of system-level problems stemming from continued reliance on MS-DOS:

■ MS-DOS[1] contains a lengthy critical section that prevents efficient multitasking of applications—particularly during heavy disk access. Retaining such a bottleneck is simply not acceptable in an operating system intended to support multithreaded applications.

■ Every access to the filesystem from a Windows-based application requires the System VM to switch between protected mode and virtual 8086 mode in order to execute MS-DOS code. This is another performance hit.

■ MS-DOS network support requires the network software to hook the INT 21H software interrupt and reroute the appropriate filesystem requests across the network. Every other disk-related TSR program uses the same basic interrupt hooking technique. The interface was never designed for overloading this heavily. In the case of only one network connection, this technique tends to destabilize the system, and trying to support multiple network connections is yet more problematic.

■ Proprietary solutions have led to a profusion of filesystem interfaces designed to support CD ROM devices, SCSI adapters, tape devices, and other devices. Even when a particular

---

1. Note that references to MS-DOS in this chapter mean MS-DOS releases up to and including version 6.22. If there is an MS-DOS version 7.0, it will incorporate the same filesystem architecture as Windows 95.

interface proves to be popular under MS-DOS, supporting the interface in Windows is by no means a straightforward task.

Elements of the new filesystem have been under development since early 1991, and much of the new filesystem design appeared for the first time with the November 1993 release of Microsoft Windows for Workgroups version 3.11. This release of Windows included the protected mode implementation of the MS-DOS FAT filesystem and support for multiple network connections. However, the Windows for Workgroups release did not include either the long filename capability or the full features of the base OS to be introduced with Windows 95.

In this chapter, we'll examine the features that enable the coexistence of multiple filesystems and the details of the support for what Windows 95 calls *block devices*[2]—principally disk and tape drives that are local to the host system. Network support relies on the new filesystem architecture also, with Windows 95 classifying the higher layer of any network connection software (usually called the *redirector*) as a network filesystem. In Chapter Nine, on Windows 95 networking, we'll revisit this particular filesystem type in more detail.

Overview of the Architecture

There are many individual components of the new filesystem architecture. In fact, to refer to it as "the filesystem" is to be rather inaccurate. The design relies on a layered approach that places the *installable filesystem manager* (IFS) at the highest level and a collection of *port drivers,* or *miniport drivers,* at the lowest level, where they interface to individual hardware devices. Within the boundaries set by these components, the system can support several different active filesystems. Windows 95 supports some—such as the FAT filesystem—directly. Support for non-Microsoft filesystems comes from installable modules supplied by other vendors. If you're familiar with the disk subsystem design of Windows NT, you'll notice a lot of similarities to it in the Windows 95 design. Figure 7-1 on the next page illustrates the principal components of the filesystem architecture.

---

2. Microsoft referred to the complete block device driver subsystem as "Dragon" during development. This subsystem deals only with local block devices and not with network support.

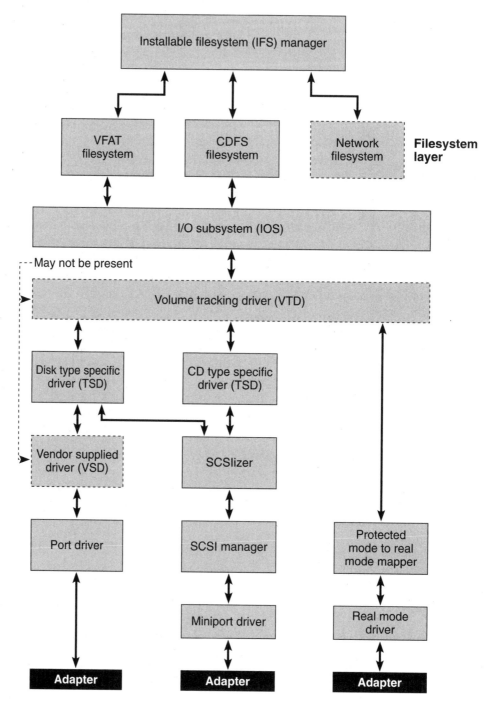

Figure 7-1.
Windows 95 filesystem architecture layers.

The choice of a layered design controlled by the IFS aims to resolve the problems inherent in using the MS-DOS INT 21H interrupt as the solitary interface to every filesystem function. Network systems and other popular products such as caching software and disk compression TSRs all hook INT 21H to inspect every file request for possible rerouting. Since there's no well-defined order for these TSRs, or any published interface between them, the interactions can cause problems. And conflicts among different vendors' products usually highlight any review of an MS-DOS release. Even when various products can be made to work well together, the user might have had to indulge in hand to hand combat with the CONFIG.SYS and AUTOEXEC.BAT files first. The Windows 95 filesystem design fixes this situation by providing many levels in which add-on components can be installed. Each layer has defined interfaces with the layers above and below, which enables each component to collaborate smoothly with its neighbors. The new filesystem architecture relies on the dynamic VxD loading capability of Windows 95 to load many of its lower-level components.

Figure 7-1 illustrates only a small number of the possible layers in the filesystem—although these are the components you'd expect to find in a "standard" system. The filesystem design supports as many as 32 layers from the *I/O subsystem* (IOS) down. Layer 0 is the layer adjacent to IOS, and layer 31 is closest to the hardware. On initialization, a component registers itself with IOS and declares the layers at which it wishes to operate. To operate at more than one level, a module has to supply IOS with different entry points—one per required level. Above IOS are the filesystems themselves and the *installable filesystem manager* (IFS manager). Let's take a brief look, from the top down, at the functions of the common layers and at the components you'd expect to find in them:

The **IFS manager,** at the highest layer, is a single VxD that provides the interface between application requests and the specific filesystem addressed by an application function. The IFS manager accepts both dynamically linked API calls from Win32 applications and INT 21H calls generated by Win16 or MS-DOS applications. The IFS manager transforms the API requests into calls to the next layer, the filesystem layer.

The **VFAT,** in the filesystem layer, is the protected mode implementation of the FAT filesystem. VFAT is an example of a *filesystem driver,* or *FSD.* Each FSD implements a particular filesystem organization. An FSD executes requests made by the IFS manager on behalf of an application. The IFS manager is the only module that calls an FSD; applications never call an FSD directly. VFAT itself is a 32-bit module written as reentrant code, allowing multiple concurrent threads to execute filesystem code.

The **CDFS,** in the filesystem layer, is the protected mode implementation of an ISO 9660–compliant CD ROM filesystem. It's another example of an FSD. Again, it's 32-bit protected mode, reentrant code. In most cases, CDFS will replace the real mode MSCDEX TSR that's currently used to support CD ROM devices, so there'll also be a protected mode execution path all the way to the CD ROM hardware.

The **I/O subsystem,** or IOS, is the highest layer of the block device subsystem. The IOS component is permanently resident in memory and provides a variety of services to the other filesystem components, including request routing and time-out notification services.

The **volume tracking driver,** or VTD, in the layer below the IOS layer, is the component responsible for managing removable devices. Typically, such a device is a floppy disk, but any device that conforms to what Windows 95 calls "the removability rules" can use the VTD services. The most important job of the VTD is to make sure that the correct disk or device is in the drive. If you exchange a floppy disk while an application still has a file open, it's the VTD that initiates a complaint.

A **type specific driver,** or TSD, in the layer below the VTD layer, manages all devices of a particular type—for example, hard disks or tape devices. A TSD validates requests for the device type that it controls and carries out the logical to physical conversion of input parameters. Note that a TSD relates more to devices of a specific logical type—for example, compressed volumes—than to devices of a specific hardware type.

A **vendor supplied driver,** or VSD, is the layer in which another vendor can supply software that intercepts every I/O request for a particular block device. At this level, for example, you could modify the behavior of an existing block device driver without having to supply a completely new driver. A data encryption module is one example of a potential VSD.

A **port driver,** or PD, is a component that controls a specific adapter. On an ISA bus personal computer, for example, there would probably be an IDE port driver. A port driver manages the lowest levels of device interaction, including adapter initialization and device interrupts.

The **SCSIizer** translates I/O requests into SCSI format command blocks. Usually these will be one SCSIizer module for each SCSI device type—CD ROM, for example.

The **SCSI manager** is a component that allows the use of Windows NT miniport drivers in Windows 95. Literally, you can use the same binaries for both Windows NT and Windows 95. The SCSI Manager provides a translation between the Windows NT miniport driver and the upper layers of the filesystem.

A **miniport driver** is specific to a SCSI device. In conjunction with the SCSI manager, it carries out the same function as a port driver, but for a SCSI adapter. Miniport drivers for Windows 95 share the design and implementation rules for Windows NT miniport drivers.

The **protected mode mapper** is a module that enables the use of existing MS-DOS drivers under Windows 95. For compatibility, it's essential to allow existing drivers to run under Windows 95. The protected mode mapper disguises real mode drivers for the benefit of the new filesystem modules—so that they don't have to take account of the different interface.

A **real mode driver** is an existing MS-DOS–style device driver that must run in virtual 8086 mode.

Long Filename Support

The widespread ramifications of the new long filename support in Windows 95 guarantee that every user and programmer will have to pay attention to the feature. Microsoft has encouraged (actually exhorted) Windows application developers to incorporate support for this feature as soon as possible. Microsoft's providing long filename support for

MS-DOS applications underscores this level of encouragement—if you have a product that is available in both Windows and MS-DOS versions, there's no barrier to upgrading both versions.

For users, long filenames are a real benefit. The need to learn rules for filenaming essentially disappears, together with the frustrating inadequacy of the current MS-DOS 8.3 convention. Unfortunately, it's impossible to simply throw a switch and have every application and every existing disk in the world suddenly support long names. For some period of time, applications that support only the old filename conventions will live alongside those that offer access to the new naming scheme. In Figure 7-2, you can see again Chapter Five's example of the support that Windows 95 has to provide to applications in order to allow the parallel existence of short and long filenaming. In the first screen, a file created with a long name is visible in both the Windows 95 shell and the Windows 95 version of COMMAND.COM. The second screen shows the Open dialog for a Windows 3.1 application running under Windows 95. The Windows 3.1 application doesn't handle long filenames, so the system has to generate an equivalent short name that allows the unmodified application to access the file.

This creation of short name equivalents is a fundamental feature of the new filesystem architecture. It would be nice to assume that it's going to be a short-lived feature, but it's probably around to stay. A short filename is not simply a truncated or mutated version of the long name—several rules govern both the format of the name and its behavior in response to different filesystem operations. We'll look at those details later in this chapter. First we'll look at the disk structure for storing the new long filename format.[3]

Storing Long Filenames

The compatibility requirements Windows 95 has to meet meant that it was impossible to simply change the existing FAT filesystem disk format. Although most applications deal with the disk by means of the defined operating system interfaces, there are many popular utility programs that directly inspect and modify the disk format. Virus scanning programs, disk repair utilities, optimizers, and many other programs depend on the on-disk structure of the FAT filesystem.

---

3. Late in the project Microsoft began to refer to the long filename as the "primary file name" and to the short name as the "alias" or "alternate name." For clarity's sake, I'll continue to use "long" and "short" in this chapter.

Windows 95 COMMAND.COM
view of the 8.3 short filename

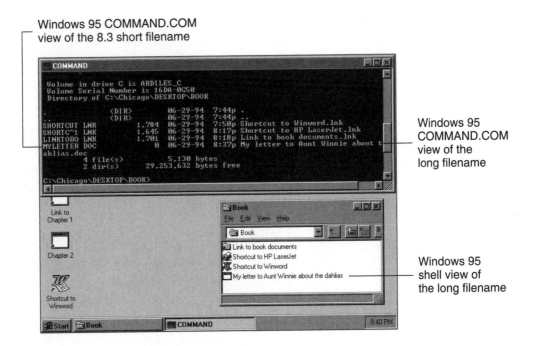

Windows 95
COMMAND.COM
view of the
long filename

Windows 95
shell view of
the long filename

Shortened version of the long filename in a
Windows 3.1 application running under Windows 95

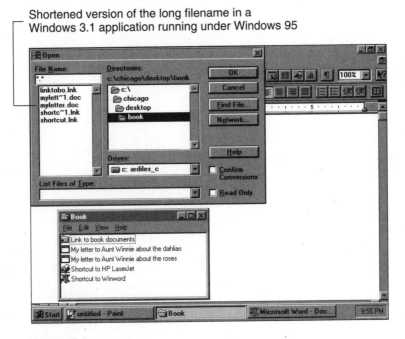

Figure 7-2.
A long filename and the short version.

Modifications to that structure would have caused all of these programs to fail. In some cases, the failure could well have resulted in loss of the user's data—a risk that was obviously unacceptable. The technique for implementing long filename support relies on a little design trickery and a great deal of careful implementation and compatibility testing.[4]

Figure 7-3 shows the format of a FAT filesystem directory entry for a short name (that is, for a filename conforming to the existing 8.3 naming conventions). The new VFAT filesystem supports both long and short names and, apart from its not using the "last date accessed" field, the 32-byte short name directory entry is identical in format to the format supported by previous versions of MS-DOS. Short names in both the FAT and VFAT filesystems have the following rules associated with them:

- The name can consist of as many as eight characters with an optional three character extension.

- Valid characters in the name are letters, digits, the space character, any character with a character value greater than 7FH, and any of the following:

$	dollar sign
%	percent symbol
' and '	open and end single quotation marks
'	foot mark (apostrophe)
-	hyphen
_	underscore
@	at sign
~	tilde
`	grave accent
!	exclamation mark
(and)	left and right parentheses
{ and }	left and right braces
#	pound sign
&	ampersand

---

4. The implementation trick prompted Microsoft to pursue a patent application for the underlying technique. Pursuit of the patent was abandoned, however.

- The full path for a file with a short name can be as many as 67 characters, not including a trailing null character.

- The FAT and VFAT filesystems always convert shortened names that include lowercase letters to uppercase only. This avoids potential problems with matching filenames. For example, the filename Afile.txt is converted to AFILE.TXT and will match the strings afile.txt, afile.TXT, AFILE.txt, and any other possible combination of uppercase and lowercase letters.

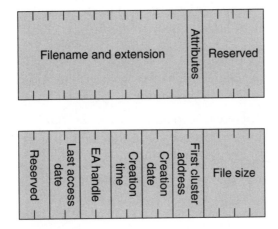

Figure 7-3.
Short name directory entry format for the FAT filesystem.

The implementation technique for long filenames relies on the use of the short name directory entry attribute byte. Setting the least significant 4 bits of this byte (that is, the value *0FH*) gives the directory entry the attributes *read only, hidden, system file,* and *volume.* Adding the *volume* attribute produces an "impossible" combination. Amazingly, Microsoft's testing showed that this combination didn't disturb any existing disk utilities. Unlike other invalid combinations, which cause disk utilities to try to "fix" the problem and thus destroy the data, the *0FH* attribute value protects the directory entry from modification.

Despite the encouraging test results, Microsoft knew there was a possibility that some untested disk utility could destroy data. To avoid such a potential catastrophe, the team came up with an "exclusive volume lock" API that an application must call before Windows 95 will allow direct disk writes (MS-DOS INT 13H and INT 26H).

The "exclusive volume lock" API is accessible either as a new MS-DOS interrupt (INT 21, function 440D, major code 08) or by means of the Win32 *DeviceIoControl()* API. If an application has not been granted exclusive volume access before it tries a direct disk write, the attempted write operation will fail.

To avoid forcing users to get updates to their existing disk utilities, Microsoft planned to include a command-level interface to allow a user to run an older disk utility within a "wrapper" function that obtained and released the volume lock on behalf of the application.

Windows 95 uses multiple consecutive short name entries for a single long name—protecting each of the 32-byte entries by using the *0FH* attribute. The rules for long filenames are different from those for short names:

■ Every long name must have a short name associated with it. The file is accessible by means of either name.

■ A long filename can contain as many as 255 characters, not including a trailing null character.

■ Valid filename characters include all the characters usable in short names plus any of the following:

+	plus sign
,	comma
;	semicolon
=	equals sign
[and]	left and right square brackets

■ Leading and trailing space characters within a name are ignored.

■ The full path for a file with a long name can be as many as 260 characters, not including a trailing null character.

■ The system preserves lowercase characters used in long filenames.

Within a single directory cluster, a long filename directory entry is laid out according to the format shown in Figure 7-4. A long filename component cannot exist without the associated short name entry. If it does, that's an indication that the disk is corrupt.

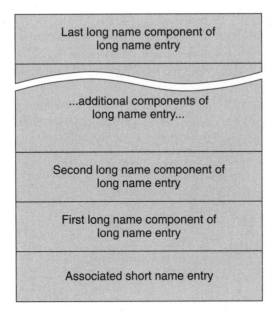

Figure 7-4.
Directory cluster format for a long filename.

Each 32-byte component of the long name entry contains a *sequence* number, the protective *attribute* byte, a *type* value, and a *checksum*. The *sequence* number helps Windows 95 recognize any inconsistent modifications to the directory structure. The *type* field identifies the component as either LONG_NAME_COMP (a component of the long name) or LONG_CLASS (a 32-byte entry that contains class information for the file). If the component is part of the name, most of the 32-byte entry is used to store filename characters. If it's the single class component for that file, the entry holds the class information. Notice that the system stores long filenames using the Unicode character set—meaning that each filename character requires 16 bits.[5] The *checksum* field in each component entry is formed from the short name associated with the file. If the short name is ever changed outside the Windows 95 environment (for example, the file is renamed on a floppy disk using MS-DOS version 5.0), Windows 95 can recognize the long name components as no longer valid. Figures 7-5 and 7-6 on the next page show the name and class component formats for these entries.

---

5. Unlike Windows NT, Windows 95 did not switch entirely to using the Unicode character set for its internal representation. This is one instance in which the change was made.

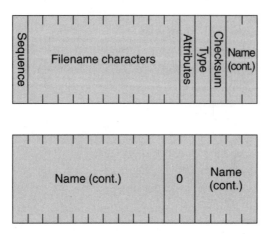

Figure 7-5.
Long filename directory entry format.

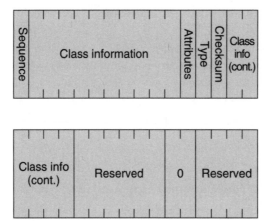

Figure 7-6.
Long filename class information directory entry format.

Generating Short Filenames

A whole series of rules defines how to generate a short filename to associate with a long filename—and we're not going to examine every last nuance of the algorithms. The principal problem is to generate a unique short filename that doesn't conflict with an existing short name. Similarly, if an older application creates a new file with a short name, that name can't clash with an existing short name associated with a long filename. Fortunately, these issues aren't really visible to application programs—employees of companies that produce disk utilities are the only people who will have to delve into the intricacies of the naming system.[6] Here's a summary of most of the important rules used in filename creation:

■ Creating a file by using a short name API (that is, by means of the older INT 21H interface) results in a long name that's identical to its associated short name. If a matching long name already exists, the create operation fails—the same behavior you'd see if you tried to create a file with a nonunique short name.

■ Creating a file by using a long name API always results in the creation of the associated short name at the same time.

■ If the long name is to be a valid short name, it must be unique. For example, if a short name AFILE.TXT already exists, an attempt to create the long name AFile.Txt will fail—this test is always case·insensitive.

■ If the long name is not a valid short name, the system carries out a series of name truncation and translation operations in an attempt to arrive at a valid short name. Note to Kathleen (Review Comments).Document, for example, would successively translate to[7]

    NotetoKathleen_ReviewComments_.Document
    NOTETOKA.DOC
    NOTETO~1.DOC

■ The system would then modify the ~1 suffix to ~2, ~3, and so on until it came up with a unique short name. If a ~9 suffix didn't work, NOTETO~9.DOC would become NOTET~10.DOC, NOTET~11.DOC, and so on.

MS-DOS Support for Long Filenames

To help promote the use of long filenames across all application types, Windows 95 extends the MS-DOS INT 21H interface to allow the use of long names. This extension involves adding new functions that are

---

6. This assumption begs the question of whether application developers will invent schemes to assist users in the translation between long and short names.

7. This is not a description of how the algorithm actually proceeds; it simply serves to illustrate the steps involved.

directly equivalent to Win32 API functions and modifying existing MS-DOS functions that deal with filenames. The calls to the new and modified INT 21H functions continue to use the standard MS-DOS calling conventions with parameters passed and returned in registers. And the functions are still 16-bit code; the fact that the functions are equivalent to Win32 APIs doesn't change the memory mode. Here's a summary of the new functions—all numbers are hexadecimal values:

MS-DOS Function	Equivalent Win32 Function
INT 21 function 4302	*GetVolumeInformation()*
INT 21 function 57	*GetFileTime(), SetFileTime()*
INT 21 function 6C	*CreateFile(), OpenFile()*
INT 21 function 7139	*CreateDirectory()*
INT 21 function 713A	*RemoveDirectory()*
INT 21 function 713B	*SetCurrentDirectory()*
INT 21 function 7141	*DeleteFile()*
INT 21 function 7143	*GetFileAttributes(), SetFileAttributes()*
INT 21 function 7147	*GetCurrentDirectory()*
INT 21 function 714E	*FindFirstFile()*
INT 21 function 714F	*FindNextFile()*
INT 21 function 7156	*MoveFile()*
INT 21 function 716C	*CreateFile(), OpenFile()*
INT 21 function 72	*FindClose()*

Notice that in most cases the functions use new function codes—the other parameters are identical. The new function codes are necessary because the system needs to know whether the application is dealing with short names only or with the extended namespace. For example, an application using INT 21H function 41H to delete a file could pass the filename ABIGBADNAME.TXT as the filename parameter. The filename is illegal under the "old" semantics, although it is a perfectly valid long name. If the INT 21H function 41H call were simply overloaded to allow the use of long names, this semantic error would go undetected. Thus, the new INT 21H function 7141H is the only way to delete a file with a long name, and the same rules apply to the other new name-related functions.

Long Filenames on Other Systems

A file's short name is used by applications that haven't been modified to handle long names, but reading long filenames isn't just an application issue. Long names also disappear on other, otherwise compatible, systems such as Windows NT (versions 3.0 and 3.1), OS/2, and earlier versions of MS-DOS (versions 6.22 and earlier). In most cases, the operating system can't handle the new form of directory entry. In the case of OS/2, the implementation of long filenames is different and incompatible.[8]

The restriction also applies to Windows 95 when the user is in single MS-DOS application mode: the long names are invisible. Access to any file can always be accomplished by using the short name, however—regardless of the host operating system.

Installable Filesystem Manager

The IFS manager in Windows 95 provides features similar to those in other implementations of this type of filesystem design. The development team actually looked very hard at the Windows NT IFS implementation to see whether the code could be adapted for use in Windows 95, but the internal differences between the two operating systems meant that a new implementation was required for Windows 95. Where it made sense to, though, the Windows 95 team used the design of the Windows NT IFS, and they retained the same names for entry points and the like.

The basic role of the IFS manager is to accept all filesystem API calls, convert each to the appropriate IFS interface call, and then pass the request to the target filesystem driver. The target FSD is responsible for interpreting the function call according to its private semantics; the IFS manager simply gets the information to the FSD. The IFS manager is the common target for both Win32 API calls and MS-DOS INT 21H filesystem functions. Once the IFS manager is in control, the execution path for the filesystem call remains a 32-bit protected mode path all the way to the hardware and back, with two possible exceptions.

---

8. Windows NT does support long filenames within the NTFS filesystem, but versions 3.5 and earlier don't support long filenames within a FAT filesystem. The Windows NT and Windows 95 long name schemes are not compatible.

- The filesystem code has to use a real mode device driver to interface with the hardware.

- The filesystem code has to call a real mode TSR that has hooked the MS-DOS INT 21H interrupt.

In either case, the filesystem code calls the real mode component (using virtual 8086 mode) within the context of the VM initiating the filesystem request.

The IFS manager loads during system initialization. It is always in memory, and it must be present before any individual FSD can load. The IFS manager allows several FSDs to execute concurrently.[9] Each FSD registers itself with the IFS manager during its own initialization, passing the IFS manager a table of entry points that will be used in subsequent filesystem calls. Once active, the IFS manager chooses which FSD to call to resolve a particular filesystem request in one of three ways:

- If the API provides a path as a parameter, the IFS manager uses either the embedded drive letter or the whole name to determine the target FSD. For example, a file open call specifying C:\AUTOEXEC.BAT will be passed to the local VFAT FSD.

- If the API passes a file handle obtained, for example, as the result of a previous file open call, the IFS manager uses the handle as an index into a *system file handle* structure. The entry in this structure identifies the target FSD and the FSD-specific handle for the IFS manager to use when it routes the request to the FSD.

- In the event that the IFS manager can't identify the target FSD, it will call each FSD in turn until one of them agrees to accept the request. When the user inserts a new floppy disk, for example, the IFS manager calls each FSD, asking it to *mount* the new volume. To mount the volume, the FSD must recognize the media format; if it doesn't, the IFS manager passes the mount request to the next FSD.

---

9. The initial design allowed as many as 10 local filesystem drivers and 10 remote filesystem drivers to execute at the same time.

Calling a Filesystem Driver

The interface between the IFS manager and an FSD relies on the use of a single data structure called an IOREQ. This structure is a large data object (approximately 100 bytes) containing many individual fields—only some of which are used in each call between the IFS manager and an FSD. Each call to the filesystem code from an application causes the IFS manager to fill in an IOREQ structure and pass it to the target FSD. For performance reasons, the IFS manager passes a pointer to an IOREQ structure rather than the entire data object. The FSD directly modifies fields in the IOREQ structure to return results to the IFS manager. Before returning to the application, the IFS manager examines the IOREQ structure and extracts both the information that it retains internally and the relevant return parameters for the application. Figure 7-7 shows the format of the IOREQ structure.

```
struct ioreq {
    unsigned int    ir_length;  // length of user buffer (eCX)
    unsigned char   ir_flags;   // misc. status flags (AL)
    uid_t           ir_user;    // user ID for this request
    sfn_t           ir_sfn;     // System File Number of file
                                //  handle
    pid_t           ir_pid;     // process ID of requesting task
    path_t          ir_ppath;   // unicode pathname
    aux_t           ir_aux1;    // secondary user data buffer
                                //  (CurDTA)
    ubuffer_t       ir_data;    // ptr to user data buffer
                                //  (DS:eDX)
    unsigned short  ir_options; // request handling options
    short           ir_error;   // error code (0 if OK)
    rh_t            ir_rh;      // resource handle
    fh_t            ir_fh;      // file (or find) handle
    pos_t           ir_pos;     // file position for request
    aux_t           ir_aux2;    // misc. extra API parameters
    aux_t           ir_aux3;    // misc. extra API parameters
    pevent          ir_pev;     // ptr to IFSMgr event for async
                                //  requests
    fsdwork_t       ir_fsd;     // Provider work space
};  // ioreq
```

Figure 7-7.
The IOREQ data structure.

To ease the implementation burden for developers, Microsoft used C language calling conventions to define the interface between the IFS manager and an FSD. So, if you want to get into the business of developing new filesystems for Windows 95, at least you don't have to write them in assembly language. The IFS manager also provides a set of services, callable by FSDs, that fulfill common requirements such as heap memory management, debugging, event signaling, and filename string manipulation.

If the IFS manager is to recognize and use an FSD, the FSD must first register itself using an IFS manager service. The two principal services are *IFSMgr_RegisterMount()* and *IFSMgr_RegisterNet()*, which announce, respectively, the presence of an FSD capable of managing local filesystems or one devoted to the management of a network resource. No meaningful interaction can occur between the IFS manager and an FSD until the FSD has declared its presence using one of the IFS registration services. In each call, the FSD passes a single entry point address to the IFS manager. The entry point address identifies the function called by the IFS manager the first time the manager calls out to the FSD.

Filesystem Drivers

Each Windows 95 FSD is a single VxD responsible for implementing the particular semantics of its native filesystem. Knowledge of a particular filesystem layout exists entirely within the code of an FSD. The IFS manager deals only in handles, and the lower layers of the filesystem deal mostly in byte offsets and counts. Only the FSD knows how to get from an application-supplied name to particular data on a filesystem volume. FSDs can control either local or remote filesystems. Depending on how the FSD registers itself with the IFS manager (local or remote), the FSD must provide a number of individual entry points for use by the IFS manager. Not every FSD must support every function defined as part of the IFS interface—the mandatory entry points depend largely on whether the filesystem type is local or remote. In addition to the two major filesystem types, Windows 95 recognizes a *mailslot* filesystem type that can be used to provide inter-application messaging services.

The single entry point provided by the FSD when it registers with the IFS manager identifies either the *FS_MountVolume()* function (for local filesystems) or the *FS_ConnectNetResource()* function (for remote filesystems). These functions are among the set of standard entry points defined for the IFS manager interface. When the IFS manager calls the single entry point, the FSD will return a pointer to a table of additional entry points. Subsequent calls from the IFS manager to an FSD go directly to the specific function using one of these new entry points. A called function may return yet more entry point addresses. It's all like peeling away the layers of an onion. The FSD returns these function pointers to the IFS manager on what you can think of as an as needed basis, and gradually the IFS manager learns how to call every entry point in a particular FSD. (Until a file is open, for example, the FSD won't provide the IFS manager with a way to call either the file positioning function or the file locking function.)

The IFS manager calls the initial *FS_MountVolume()* entry point for local filesystems as the result of either the first access to a device or a change to the media. The call asks the FSD to try to mount the volume (the VOL_MOUNT operation). It's up to the FSD to determine whether it recognizes the device media format. If it does, it returns a volume handle and a pointer to the initial table of functions to the IFS manager. The handle is used to identify the volume in subsequent calls to the FSD. For disks, the volume handle will identify either a hard disk partition or a specific floppy disk. The IFS manager initiates the removal of all access to a volume by calling the *FS_MountVolume()* entry point, specifying an unmount (the VOL_UNMOUNT operation).

For network filesystems, the IFS manager calls the function *FS_ConnectNetResource()* with a network path for the target resource. As with local filesystem access, the FSD must determine whether it should be responsible for managing the particular resource. If it is, it returns a handle and a function table to the IFS manager. If it isn't, the FSD returns an error and the IFS manager must carry on, looking for the correct FSD to match to the network resource.

FSD Entry Points

The next page contains a summary of all the defined entry points for a filesystem driver.[10]

---

10. There's also a set of entry points used specifically to implement named pipes — Microsoft's preferred network-based, high-level inter-application communication mechanism. Local FSDs don't have to implement these services.

FSD Entry Point Name	Purpose
FS_CloseFile( )	Close an open file
FS_CommitFile( )	Flush any cached data for a particular file
FS_ConnectNetResource( )	Call initial remote filesystem entry point
FS_DeleteFile( )	Erase a named file
FS_Dir( )	Call directory operations (such as create and remove)
FS_DisconnectNetResource( )	Remove a network connection
FS_FileAttributes( )	Set and retrieve file and filesystem information
FS_FileDateTime( )	Perform date and time management on a file
FS_FileSeek( )	Perform file positioning operations
FS_FindClose( )	Close an *FS_FindFirstFile( )*-initiated sequence
FS_FindFirstFile( )	Initiate a filename search sequence
FS_FindNextFile( )	Continue an *FS_FindFirstFile( )* sequence
FS_FlushVolume( )	Flush all cached data for the volume
FS_GetDiskInfo( )	Get information about disk format and free space
FS_GetDiskParms( )	Call the older MS-DOS DPB function (INT 21H function 32H)
FS_Ioctl16Drive( )	Call the older MS-DOS I/O control operations (INT 21H function 44H)
FS_LockFile( )	Call record-locking functions
FS_MountVolume( )	Call initial entry point for local filesystems
FS_OpenFile( )	Call file open and create functions
FS_ReadFile( )	Call input operations
FS_RenameFile( )	Call file rename operation
FS_SearchFile( )	Implement MS-DOS find first and find next operations (INT 21H functions 11H, 12H, 4EH, and 4FH)
FS_WriteFile( )	Call file output operations

I/O Subsystem

IOS is the Windows 95 system component responsible for loading, initializing, and managing all of the lower-level filesystem modules. (Typically, these modules are port drivers directly concerned with the underlying hardware.) IOS also provides services to FSDs to allow them to initiate device-specific requests. IOS must be permanently resident in memory. It's loaded from the IOS.386 file early in the system initialization process.

The IOS and device driver layers rely on the use of a large number of interlinked control blocks[11] coupled with the standard VxD service interface and an implementation technique referred to as a *calldown chain*. An FSD will prepare a request for a device by initializing a control block and passing it to the *IOS_SendCommand()* service. The control block used in such a request is called an *I/O packet,* or *IOP.* IOS uses the IOP to control the passage of the device request down and back up the driver hierarchy. Most other control blocks used by IOS are hidden from the higher layers, and an FSD doesn't have to worry about the allocation or management of device-specific control blocks. We'll look at the role of several other control blocks within the filesystem architecture as we examine the components of the IOS and its lower-level driver modules.

IOS itself operates in one of two roles—as the managing entity when specific device requests are in progress, or as the provider of a number of centralized services that any device driver can call. Here are the three basic VxD services offered by IOS:

IOS_Register() — The service used by device drivers to register their presence in the system. Without the driver's prior registration, IOS can't interact with the driver.

IOS_SendCommand() — The service used to initiate specific device actions such as data transfers and disk ejection.

IOS_Requestor_Service() — The service that provides a small number of individual functions such as the functions that obtain information about a disk drive's characteristics.

In addition, a wide range of services (called *IOS service requests*) are used by drivers to control their interaction with IOS. Calling these services first requires the device driver to register itself with IOS.

---

11. Over 10 different data structures are defined for the I/O subsystem. Many of these data structures appear in multiple interlinked lists.

During registration, IOS provides the driver with the addresses of the entry points to call when making subsequent service requests.

Device Driver Initialization

IOS takes on the job of loading all the device drivers and requesting their initialization. IOS loads a driver in response to a request from the configuration manager (part of the Plug and Play subsystem) or because of the presence of the driver in the SYSTEM\IOSUBSYS directory. Configuration manager–initiated loading occurs when the Plug and Play subsystem detects the presence of a particular device. IOS force loads the remaining drivers in the IOSUBSYS directory. At the completion of the entire boot process, IOS will send every driver a "boot complete" message. If a loaded driver failed to recognize any hardware it can support, it can unload itself from memory at this point. There are provisions for the system to load older (non-IOS-compliant) drivers by simply including them in the SYSTEM.INI file, as Windows 3.1 does today. Drivers that conform to the new design are all dynamically loadable VxDs and must cooperate with IOS in building the layers of the device control subsystem.

Once IOS has loaded all the necessary device driver modules, the initialization process begins. The initialization of a specific driver module occurs when IOS sends to the driver module's control procedure the VxD message SYS_DYNAMIC_DEVICE_INIT. The driver must register itself with IOS by calling the *IOS_Register()* service with the address of a *driver registration packet,* or *DRP*. The DRP is a data block containing information such as the driver name and the driver's particular characteristics. One of the implementation rules for device drivers is that the address of the driver's DRP structure must appear in the VxD header for the driver module. The appearance of the address in the VxD header allows IOS to examine the DRP structure before it sends the initialization message. Three fields in a DRP are vital to the initialization process:

DRP_ilb	Contains the address of an *IOS linkage block,* or *ILB.* IOS fills the ILB structure with the addresses of several IOS entry points used in subsequent calls to IOS.
DRP_LGM	Contains the *load group mask,* or *LGM,* used during the device initialization process.

DRP_aer	Contains the address of the driver's *asynchronous event routine,* or *AER.* This asynchronous event function is called by IOS to notify the driver of any asynchronous event—for example, the completion of a time-out.

The load group mask is a 32-bit quantity defining the levels at which a driver module wants to operate. IOS sends the initialization message to the driver once for each level at which the driver module wants to register—proceeding from level 31 (the lowest) up to level 0. Since IOS can examine every driver's *DRP_LGM* field before any initialization, it's able to figure out the order in which to carry out the initialization process. IOS completes the initialization for every driver at one level before it moves upward to the next layer. So the initialization of all layer 31 drivers occurs first, followed by all layer 30 drivers, and so on. Several standard levels are defined, so almost every driver will simply use one of these level numbers as the value of its load group mask field.

IOS uses the driver's asynchronous event entry point during initialization to allow the driver to carry out private setup operations, so the driver receives control back from IOS at well-defined points during the initialization process. Among other activities, the driver creates *device data blocks* (*DDBs*) that hold control information about the device and may add itself to the device calldown chain. The driver can also specify its requirements for private workspace within an IOP during initialization. Once the initialization is complete, IOS calculates the final size of an IOP for a particular device: the size of a fixed header plus the size of an *I/O request* (*IOR*) structure, plus the sum of the sizes of all private workspace areas. Whenever an FSD subsequently requests the allocation of an IOP, the IOP size is known from this initial calculation. Also, as an individual I/O request proceeds, driver modules at different levels will have access to the necessary private workspaces at known offsets within their IOPs.

Controlling an I/O Request

As we saw earlier, the local block device subsystem deals in terms of volumes—a hard disk partition or a floppy disk, for example. For each active volume, IOS maintains a data structure called a *volume request packet,* or *VRP.* Calling IOS's *IOS_Requestor_Service()* and specifying the *IRS_GET_VRP()* function will return the address of the VRP for a particular volume. Within the VRP are the address of the entry point within IOS that an FSD must use when it initiates I/O requests, and the size of the IOP necessary for requests to this volume.

An FSD initiates an I/O request by allocating an IOP of the correct type and size (this allocation is another IOS service), filling in the IOR structure (contained within the IOP), and passing the IOP to IOS.

IOS itself uses a structure called a *device control block,* or *DCB,* to manage much of its interaction with a particular device. A DCB is a large (256-byte) data structure that contains information about the device, such as the total number of sectors and the number of sectors per track for a disk drive. Whereas an application I/O request initially results in the creation of an IOP that provides a logical description of the request, the DCB holds information about many of the physical aspects of the device that must satisfy the application I/O request. Applications and, indeed, FSDs never deal with the internals of a DCB; it's a data structure used only by IOS and the lower-level device control software.

One of the fields in a DCB is the address of the calldown chain for the device. IOS's successive passing of pointers to the appropriate DCB and IOP to each entry in the device calldown chain defines the path of execution within IOS and its lower-level driver modules.

Calldown Chains

The multiple layers of the filesystem architecture offer a great deal of flexibility to device driver writers. Essentially, you can get control at any point in the path between an application's issuing a file-related API and the lowest-level device driver's poking the controller registers. This flexibility is a far cry from the single INT 21H hooking technique practiced by existing MS-DOS filesystem and device control software.

The calldown chain technique is what Windows 95 uses to implement the multilayer mechanism. During initialization, a device driver module can add itself to the calldown chain for a particular device, specifying the level for the subsequent call. (This is similar to the technique for specifying the initialization level for the device driver module.) IOS inserts the address of the target function into the calldown chain for the device—using the specified level to order the chain correctly. As an I/O request proceeds from IOS down to the hardware, IOS arranges to call each function in the calldown chain for the device.

A driver routine inserted in a calldown chain may elect to pass the request on—either unmodified or not—to the next lower layer, or if able, the routine may simply complete the request and never pass it on down the chain. A driver can also arrange a callback on completion of a device request by the next lower layer. This amounts to a feature equivalent to the calldown chain, but the call occurs after the device operation rather than before.

Asynchronous Driver Events

Asynchronous events notification allows IOS to interact with device driver modules outside the flow of normal I/O requests up and down the driver hierarchy. In some cases, the driver itself asks IOS to signal an asynchronous event at some later time. In other cases, IOS initiates the request.

IOS signals an asynchronous event by calling the driver's asynchronous event entry point, passing it an *asynchronous event packet,* or *AEP*. An AEP has a standard header that specifies the asynchronous function and the associated device data block (DDB). The AEP also has a field the driver uses as a completion code. Beyond the header, the structure of the data block differs according to the type of event and contains additional event-specific parameters. Here's a summary of the function of each asynchronous event that IOS can signal:

AEP_INITIALIZE	Initialize the driver. Sent when a driver is first loaded.
AEP_BOOT_COMPLETE	System boot is complete. The driver can switch to its runtime configuration.
AEP_CONFIG_DCB	Configure the physical device and associated DCB.
AEP_IOP_TIMEOUT	Time-out counter within an IOP has reached 0.
AEP_CONFIG_LOGICAL	Configure the logical device.
AEP_DEVICE_INQUIRY	Retrieve device identification information.
AEP_RESET_COUNTERS	Reset performance counters.
AEP_REGISTER_DONE	Registration processing is complete.
AEP_HALF_SEC	Half a second has elapsed.
AEP_1_SEC	One second has elapsed.
AEP_2_SECS	Two seconds have elapsed.
AEP_4_SECS	Four seconds have elapsed.
AEP_DBG_DOT_CMD	Pass debug parameters to the driver.

Interfacing to the Hardware

Port drivers are the most common manifestations of the hardware control level in the filesystem software hierarchy. Port drivers that control ISA or EISA configuration adapters interface directly to the hardware. In the absence of another intermediate layer, such as a volume tracking driver layer or a protected mode BIOS layer, the type specific driver (TSD) provides the only other software layer between IOS and the hardware. The port driver is, therefore, what you would typically think of as the "device driver" for the filesystem.

The port driver is hardware specific, and although layers such as the TSD's reduce the driver's workload, the port driver still has the job of translating I/O requests into hardware commands. As with the development of most drivers for devices with similar characteristics, developing a new port driver will typically involve the modification of an existing example rather than the creation of entirely new code. A port driver is a dynamically loaded VxD that provides no VxD services. Figure 7-8 illustrates the declaration of a port driver together with the driver registration packet (*DRP_Port*) used by IOS during the driver's initialization phase. Notice the inclusion of the pointers to the port driver asynchronous event routine (*PORT_Async*) and to the ILB structure (*PORT_ilb*) that IOS needs to complete the initialization process.

```
DECLARE_VIRTUAL_DEVICE PORT, MAJOR_VER, MINOR_VER,
    PORT_Control,, UNDEFINED_INIT_ORDER,,, DRP_Port

DRP_Port DRP <EyeCatcher, DRP_MISC_PD,
    offset32 PORT_Async,
    offset32 PORT_ilb,
    PORTname, PORTRev, PORTFeature, PORT_IF>
```

Figure 7-8.
Port driver and DRP declaration.

We've already looked from the IOS perspective at what happens within the filesystem hierarchy. Turning this around, let's look at a summary of an individual port driver's responsibilities during different execution phases.

Initialization

IOS first sends a SYS_DYNAMIC_DEVICE_INIT message to call the port driver. The port driver uses the *IOS_Register()* service to register itself. During registration, the port driver has to respond to callbacks to its asynchronous event routine:

AEP_INITIALIZE requires allocation of a DDB, retrieval of configuration information, initialization of the hardware, and definition of the device's interrupt handler.

AEP_DEVICE_INQUIRY messages are sent for each possible drive attached to the adapter. (The design accommodates drive numbers 0 through 127.) The port driver must respond with an indication of the presence or absence of a particular drive.[12]

AEP_CONFIG_DCB allows the driver to add its normal I/O request entry point to the calldown chain.

AEP_BOOT_COMPLETE allows the port driver to confirm or deny that it has detected hardware it can control. IOS will remove the driver from memory if no applicable hardware is present in the system.

Execution

Normal execution for the port driver involves processing and queuing IOPs passed to the driver via its normal I/O request function. For actual device I/O operations, if the device isn't busy, the port driver starts the operation. The port driver must also respond to time-out events (AEP_IOP_TIMEOUT) signaled by IOS.

Interrupt

If the device interrupts as the result of its completing an I/O operation, the port driver finishes processing the associated IOP. If there are other IOPs queued for the device, the driver starts the next I/O operation.

Other Layers in the Filesystem Hierarchy

Of the other available levels within the IOS managed hierarchy, a few are used by components that are standard modules within the Windows 95 filesystem architecture. In general, the modules installed at these intermediate levels are designed to provide services commonly required by port drivers. The installation of these modules relieves a

---

12. The port driver can also respond with an indication of *no more devices present* to avoid processing 128 separate inquiries.

driver developer from having to re-implement private versions of functions needed by every driver. The type specific driver (TSD) for disks, for example, will perform some error checking and logical to physical parameter translation, relieving the individual port drivers of this chore. Supplying standardized components such as these is also a means for Microsoft to avoid problems with device driver bugs. The more complex a single device driver, the more likely it is to contain bugs and the more likely it is that Microsoft's technical support group will get a phone call. A user will regard the problem as a bug in Windows—rare is the user who would call Exotic Disk Drive, Inc., if Windows crashed because of a bug in the device driver that came with the drive.

The most highly developed use of the IOS layering capabilities is for the support of SCSI devices. Microsoft Windows NT placed a lot of emphasis on the support of SCSI peripherals—partly because the market for these devices was growing rapidly during the development of Windows NT and partly because SCSI peripherals were a good match for the Windows NT performance and automatic configuration goals. The SCSI design also standardizes many device interface issues, making SCSI devices a perfect match for the layered device architecture.

Windows 95 standardizes other existing features of block device drivers by including modules that manage the issues associated with exchangeable media and by providing a generalized interface to data caching. New in Windows 95 are the support for Plug and Play capabilities and the continued support of real mode device drivers within a fully protected mode operating system.[13]

Volume Tracking Drivers

The volume tracking driver, or VTD, is at the top of the calldown chain for a device. Its role is to ensure that the medium in a particular drive (usually a floppy disk or a tape) is the medium that the I/O request actually refers to. Obviously, in the case of a read operation, a medium that doesn't match what the application previously referred to will probably be only confusing to the user; in the worst case, though, the mismatch could cause an application to fail. In the case of an output operation, the effect of writing on the wrong medium could be disastrous.

---

13. Windows NT ducked this particular challenge by not providing MS-DOS device driver support. Given its compatibility requirements, this was not an option for Windows 95.

The VTD maintains its knowledge of the current medium by matching a volume handle retained in the current DCB for the device with the volume handle contained in any IOP passed down by the filesystem driver. A mismatch means that the medium present in the device is not the medium previously referred to by the FSD. This may result in the user's being asked to insert the correct medium.[14]

Knowledge of the current volume is maintained by the IOS's asking an FSD to read a volume label each time the medium changes (an event that the device driver will notice) or, in the case of hardware that can't report a medium change directly, whenever the medium may have changed. It is up to the FSD to read volume labels because the other components of the filesystem have no knowledge of how to do this. The FSD retains information about a volume label from the time the medium is first mounted.

Type Specific Drivers

In Windows 95, a type specific driver (TSD) currently exists for a disk device in order to provide a mapping from logical to physical device parameters. Using handles and offsets, an FSD will typically translate application requests to requests for logical block numbers within a logical drive—for example, *read block 93 of drive C:* (where a numeric handle would represent C:). The TSD will translate such requests for logical block numbers into physical block numbers. This translation may involve a mapping of logical blocks into physical blocks (where the device's sector size doesn't match the filesystem's block size) or the translation from a logical drive to a specific physical disk partition. The TSD checks every request it processes, ensuring that the lower-level drivers don't have to perform any validation.

During initialization, the TSD is responsible for allocating and building a device control block for each logical device present on a physical device (for each hard disk partition, for instance). The TSD adds each logical DCB to a list that is associated with the DCB previously allocated to describe the physical device. Within the logical DCB is all the information describing the geometry of the drive device—sectors per track and bytes per sector, for instance.

---

14. Volume tracking requirements may change according to the environment. If a file is left open with data still to write out, a different medium is usually an error. For a multivolume backup operation, though, it's an expected condition.

One valuable contribution to flexibility this architecture affords is the ability it gives the system to adapt to the different geometry on high-capacity exchangeable media. Several manufacturers now offer drives with removable media that can store 100 megabytes of data or more. Most of these drives can read older, compatible but less densely packed media. The Windows 95 filesystem participation in the dynamic reconfiguration of the device characteristics for specific partitions helps to support these devices properly.

SCSI Manager

Windows 95 builds on the SCSI device architecture developed for Windows NT by making use of the same low-level device drivers (the so called *miniport* drivers). By providing a method for interfacing existing Windows NT miniport drivers to the Windows 95 filesystem architecture, Windows 95 gains immediate support for a wide range of SCSI peripherals with almost no new code having to be developed. This method for interfacing drivers between the two systems is another manifestation of the Windows compatibility goal. For a device manufacturer, the fact that a single miniport driver will support two different operating systems is a definite benefit.

The SCSI manager, or SCSI port driver, is the upper layer of this support. The SCSI driver offers a range of functions common to any SCSI device, including error logging, cache management, and logical to physical address translation. Essentially, the SCSI manager and the miniport drivers associated with it split the functions of a normal port driver, with the hardware-specific aspects isolated in the miniport driver. Three main data structures are used for communication between the SCSI manager and the miniport drivers:

SCSI_REQUEST_BLOCK contains information describing an individual SCSI device I/O request.

HW_INITIALIZATION_DATA contains the miniport device driver's entry points called by the SCSI manager for a specific device.

PORT_CONFIGURATION_INFORMATION contains data that describes the properties of an individual SCSI host adapter, including, for example, its DMA capabilities.

The entry points provided by each miniport driver allow the SCSI manager to call for hardware-specific operations during various phases of device control: initialization, I/O request initiation, and interrupt processing.

For the ultimate efficiency in implementation, use of the existing Windows NT miniport drivers would have been the optimal solution. Unfortunately, the requirements of real mode compatibility made their presence felt once again. The existing miniport drivers for Windows NT have to undergo a few minor modifications for full compatibility with Windows 95. The modifications have largely to do with the real mode to protected mode transitions and with the fact that, in Windows 95, a real mode SCSI device driver can exist in conjunction with the protected mode miniport driver. However, once the driver has been modified to accommodate the need for real mode compatibility in Windows 95, the new version will still run under Windows NT—the new real mode support code will simply never be executed in the Windows NT environment. Note too that as with support for any device under Windows 95, SCSI drivers should participate in the Plug and Play environment and that means other modifications to the miniport driver.

Real Mode Drivers

Continued support for existing MS-DOS real mode device drivers is obviously critical to the success of Windows 95. Despite the advantages of protected mode device drivers, the sheer number of drivers available for MS-DOS means that it will be impossible to replace every real mode driver when Windows 95 first ships. But replacement of the real mode drivers for many widespread devices, such as IDE hard disk controllers and NEC-compatible floppy disks, will happen immediately, so most users will quickly see the performance benefits of the new protected mode filesystem.

The filesystem design in Windows 95 allows a protected mode port driver to take control of a real mode driver and bypass it while the system is running in protected mode—Windows 95 can classify the real mode driver as a "safe" driver, that is. Safe means, essentially, that the protected mode driver can offer functionality identical to the real mode driver's. In such a case, the protected mode driver will simply carry out all the I/O operations and never call the real mode driver. In a number of instances, the protected mode driver's taking over the function of the real mode driver is considered unsafe. The real mode driver may do data encryption, for example, or may interface with a real mode system BIOS to do dynamic bad sector mapping for the hard disk. The standard Windows 95 port driver for the disk adapter, though able to control the hardware, can't replicate this extra functionality, so it arranges to route I/O requests through the real mode driver—executing the driver in virtual 8086 mode in order to do so.

To recognize a safe driver, Windows 95 maintains a list of such device drivers by means of the registry. If the system running in protected mode detects the presence of a real mode driver, it consults the safe driver list to determine whether the real mode driver functions can be subsumed under the protected mode driver functions. The identification for the real mode driver is its name as entered in CONFIG.SYS or AUTOEXEC.BAT. If the driver name doesn't appear in the safe driver list, Windows 95 will use the real mode driver.

Conclusion

From the discussion in this chapter, you've no doubt realized that the new filesystem design for Windows 95 is a major revision to Windows. Although the compatibility constraints imposed on Windows 95 allow a device manufacturer to continue to support hardware using an older real mode device driver, the advantages to be gained in terms of performance, multitasking, and reduced memory requirements are compelling reasons to provide a full Windows 95 protected mode driver. And, of course, the addition of long filename support is a huge benefit to the user.

The new Plug and Play subsystem augments many of the operations of the filesystem components, and that's what we'll look at in the next chapter. The installable filesystem capabilities also dramatically improve networking support in Windows 95, and that will be the subject of Chapter Nine.

References

Microsoft Corporation. Windows 95 Device Driver Kit. Redmond, Wash.: Microsoft, 1994.

Schulman, Andrew. *Undocumented DOS*. 2d ed. Reading, Mass.: Addison-Wesley, 1993.

C H A P T E R   E I G H T

PLUG AND PLAY

If you've ever had to suffer through the experience of opening up a PC system unit to plug in a new device adapter card, you'll immediately understand why Plug and Play is important. The combination of Windows 95 and a PC that supports the Plug and Play specification will reduce your system setup and reconfiguration suffering to a minimum. You'll still have to know how to use a screwdriver, but that's about the only extra skill you'll need. Although the collaborators who developed the Plug and Play specification deliberately avoided tying the standard to a particular operating system or hardware type, Windows 95 has the distinction of being the first system to provide full support for the Plug and Play standard.

Typically, the process of adding a new device to a PC has involved figuring out how to set all the switches and jumpers on the new card, plugging the card in, installing software, rebooting the system, and praying. The amount of time you could spend trying to resolve problems during the installation of a new device could be extensive. Every PC has one or more *bus devices*. Usually, several devices are trying to share the *system bus,* and those attempts to share often lead to conflict. The bus design determines the electrical characteristics of many system components as well as some aspects of the method that device driver software must use to control an individual device on the bus. Most PC buses conform to a specification referred to as *industry standard architecture,* or *ISA* for short. The ISA specification is little more than the formal description of the original IBM PC architecture that was written down long after the PC first went on sale.

Most device adapter cards plug directly into the system bus. The software that controls a device communicates with the adapter by writing commands to the system I/O ports. The command information travels along the system bus to the device adapter. Some devices (often called *memory mapped devices*) also use a memory region in the 640K to 1-MB upper memory area. Both the device and the device driver software can access the data in that memory area, allowing for the high-speed transfer of large amounts of information between the device and the system's memory. Non-memory-mapped devices transfer data by means of the system bus, raising a hardware interrupt when they need attention from the device driver.

When you first plug a device adapter into the bus, it is normally set up to communicate with the system by means of a default set of I/O addresses, interrupt requests, and possibly a shared memory region or a direct memory access (DMA) channel. If some other device on the bus is already using one or more of these control signals or memory areas, a conflict occurs. The system will usually react to the conflict by refusing to boot properly, requiring you to open the box again and try to resolve the conflict by selecting a different configuration. Or sometimes the system will boot but the device will appear not to work when you try to access it, calling for more reconfiguration effort. Once you have working hardware, you have to configure the associated software to match. Over the history of the PC industry, this type of configuration activity has probably consumed the lion's share of the effort put forth by technical support groups all over the world.

What's the solution? Automatic management of the system's low-level hardware resources—IRQs, I/O ports, DMA channels, and memory—seems to be the key. Plug and Play is Microsoft's attempt to provide such an automatic system management capability. Full Plug and Play support will appear for the first time in Windows 95 and, Microsoft says, will appear over time in their other operating system products. In Windows 95, the system setup process relies heavily on the Plug and Play system management capabilities. And once the system is up and running, the Plug and Play subsystem is responsible for managing all hardware configuration changes.

Why Do We Need Another Standard?

Naturally, there have been other attempts to solve system configuration problems, but none of them has achieved the critical mass of support that's necessary to truly eradicate the configuration conflict problem. The two best-known solutions each involved the introduction of a new system bus design: IBM's MicroChannel bus, used only in IBM's PS/2 series, and the EISA (Extended Industry Standard Architecture) bus.

The designers of the MicroChannel bus came up with a new bus design that allowed any card plugged into the bus to identify itself to the operating system. After plugging the card into the bus and installing the device software, you could configure the adapter card using a standard configuration program. Unfortunately, the MicroChannel design suffered from a number of problems. First, the MicroChannel bus was incompatible with the existing ISA bus. You couldn't take your old network adapter, for example, and simply plug it into a MicroChannel bus. Since the PS/2 series never came to dominate the market, the MicroChannel never won wholehearted support from other device manufacturers. The other problem with the MicroChannel bus was that every adapter needed a unique identifying number, issued by IBM, that was hardwired into the adapter. This requirement reduced configuration flexibility somewhat, and the user still had to work his or her way through the device configuration program in the event of a system conflict.

The EISA bus designers adopted some of the better ideas in the MicroChannel design but based their design on the ISA bus. The big advantage of an EISA bus was that you could use any existing ISA adapter in an EISA machine, although the smarter configuration facilities were available only for new EISA adapters. Several PC companies ship EISA systems, and the EISA bus has gathered a reasonable amount of support from device manufacturers, but EISA is by no means a dominant architecture either.

Other, perhaps less ambitious, attempts to reduce hardware configuration problems include the efforts of suppliers who preconfigure systems with network cards, pointing devices, and the appropriate software already set up. Microsoft's Windows "Ready To Run" campaign was based on the expectation that PC vendors would ship preconfigured machines with Windows 3.1 already installed. Some device manufacturers allow devices to be reconfigured without anyone's having to open up the machine and reset hardware jumpers and switches. Intel's EtherExpress network adapter is a good example of this type of relatively easy to configure device. You plug in the adapter, and if the default adapter configuration doesn't work, a software setup program allows you to change the hardware configuration with commands from the keyboard.

All of these solutions share some of the shortcomings itemized on the next page.

- There is still no single, generally accepted standard for device installation and configuration. In particular, there is no standard for the market's leading hardware architecture: the ISA bus. A single standard would help by encouraging every manufacturer to adopt the same solution to the problem. A standard that catered to the ISA bus as well could greatly reduce the problems of hardware setup for the majority of users.

- Whereas a PC used to have just one bus, recent technology improvements have led to PCs that incorporate multiple buses: SCSI, PCMCIA, and various types of local video buses, for example. None of the existing configuration methodologies allows for this mixture of bus types.

- There's a growing need for a dynamic configuration method. Consider the situation in which you might have a modem on a PCMCIA card plugged into your laptop as COM1 and you connect the laptop to its docking station, which has a more conventional serial COM1 device. Or consider the dynamic reconfiguration requirements of a wireless-based network that supports mobile workstations. None of the existing solutions is flexible enough to handle this kind of situation.

The Plug and Play standard tries to address all of these issues, and Windows 95 intends to be the first major operating system to provide full support for the Plug and Play standard.[1]

History of the Plug and Play Project

The Plug and Play standard has its beginnings in the several different attempts to address the problem of hardware configuration—with IBM's Micro Channel and the Extended Industry Standard Architecture (EISA) effort initiated by Compaq among the most well known. Microsoft's Plug and Play effort began in 1991, and the first public specifications appeared during 1993.[2] At first, Microsoft worked on the

---

1. For information about the pieces of the Plug and Play specification, see the "References" section at the end of this chapter.

2. Folklore has it that the initial impetus for the project was provided by the PC configuration problems experienced by the mother of the vice president of Microsoft's Personal Systems Group. Another story cites Microsoft's irritation at the advertising campaign run by Apple Computer—the one that portrayed Windows as hard to set up and use.

specification alone, seeking an ordered solution to an apparently intractable problem. Early discussions with Intel and Compaq helped to steer the design effort, although these companies did not formally agree to support the Plug and Play standard until the spring of 1993.

The deciding factor in wider industry support was the development of the Plug and Play ISA specification—a document that defined a modified hardware design for adapter cards that could be used on existing ISA bus PCs. Also included in the Plug and Play ISA specification was a software-only solution that could be applied to the installed base of "legacy adapter cards" (a new term considered more polite than "old adapters"). These accommodations of the installed base are where the Plug and Play effort differentiated itself from earlier initiatives. Both the MicroChannel and the EISA bus designs did little to help the users of the installed base of PCs. The attention it paid to the predominant ISA bus design moved the Plug and Play effort from a somewhat academic realm into the entirely practical world. And the fact that a Plug and Play compliant adapter card could be produced for only a tiny amount more than it cost to produce existing adapters made the Plug and Play specification immediately attractive to a broad range of manufacturers. (Microsoft had started with a cost target of a few dollars and realized early on that this would be too expensive. Current estimates pin the hardware cost of adding Plug and Play at around 25 cents.) Once the Plug and Play ISA specification was out, support for the standard gained momentum during 1993, with Intel supplying early developer kits, Phoenix Technologies joining the core group to help define a new BIOS for Plug and Play systems, 3Com providing extensive technical input, and companies such as Future Domain releasing early ASIC implementations of the Plug and Play hardware interface.

By the end of 1993, variants of the Plug and Play specification had been produced for several different bus types, including the ISA, PCMCIA, PCI, and SCSI types.[3] The Plug and Play effort began to have other influence as well. Inside Microsoft, the design of the Windows NT registry underwent modification to incorporate Plug and Play capabilities before the shipment of Windows NT. Outside Microsoft, design efforts such as the IEEE's serial SCSI specification began to take Plug and Play requirements into account.

---

3. This effort continued, and specifications for every major bus type (except EISA) and for several specific devices (such as the parallel port) had been produced by mid-1994.

At the time of this writing, the Plug and Play effort has a long way to go before a complete implementation will be in the hands of a large number of users. Microsoft gained early experience with some of the device detection and configuration techniques they deployed in products such as Windows for Workgroups and Windows NT. These systems try to automatically sense the configurations of their host machines. In the case of Windows for Workgroups, it's the video adapter, mouse, keyboard, and network adapter types that the operating system tries to figure out. Windows NT goes much further, sensing SCSI devices and other installed hardware. The benefits during installation are obvious. Windows 95 goes further still, implementing almost automatic installation and dynamic reconfiguration. Regardless of the success of Windows 95 itself, the Plug and Play specification certainly seems to have enough momentum to gain real acceptance in the marketplace.

Goals for Plug and Play

The Plug and Play project identified a number of goals that the specification, and any of its implementations, needed to meet. The overriding goal, though, was simply to make it easier to add new hardware to or change the configuration of an existing system—actually, not just easier, but very, very easy. This ease helps everyone. Users waste less time and get less frustrated when they try to change their hardware. There's less burden on any support groups that users might call. The device manufacturers have a well-specified standard to develop to rather than the prospect of trying to solve all the potential installation and configuration issues themselves. With new hardware developed to the Plug and Play standard, the goal of requiring absolutely no effort beyond plugging in the device and copying the software to the hard disk can be realized. With existing hardware, it's difficult to reach that level of simplicity because the hardware itself doesn't conform to the Plug and Play standard. However, a lot can be done in software alone, and the Plug and Play standard calls for upgrades to existing device driver software. Upgraded device driver software will allow current ISA hardware to be well managed within a Plug and Play environment.

The Plug and Play specification lists five formal goals:

- Easy installation and configuration of new devices

- Seamless dynamic configuration changes

- Compatibility with the installed base and old peripherals

- Operating system and hardware independence

- Reduced complexity and increased flexibility of hardware

Plug and Play is of course the core of one of the major goals for the Windows 95 project: great setup and easy configuration. And the specification's attention to the existing ISA hardware base is a necessary aspect of the compatibility goal set for the Windows 95 product.

Let's look briefly at each of the major Plug and Play goals.

Easy Installation and Configuration of New Devices

With new—that is, full Plug and Play specification—hardware, the installation and configuration process is reduced to plugging in the device and running a simple installation program. Some assembly is required, but the installation program does little more than copy the device support software to the Windows directory. During the boot process, the system can identify the device and locate the appropriate device driver software and load it. The responsibility for identifying the hardware devices and configuring them correctly belongs to the operating system, not the user.

For the reasons we've already reviewed, the Plug and Play standard provides a potential for tremendous savings of time and effort. The drawback is that for the full Plug and Play benefits to be realized, you need a full Plug and Play machine and full Plug and Play device adapters.

Support for a New Hardware Standard

The Plug and Play specification does not define yet-another way of building a PC. What it does specify is what PC hardware must be able to do if it is to support full Plug and Play capabilities. "PC hardware" means the system motherboard, the BIOS, and the plug-in adapter cards. If each of these components complies with the specification, the operating system vendor can implement Plug and Play. To date, draft or final specifications have been completed for the Plug and Play BIOS and for the ISA, SCSI, PCMCIA, and PCI buses. By the time you read this, there will be many other specifications for Plug and Play compliant hardware.

Some current bus designs lend themselves to a very simple implementation of Plug and Play support; the required information and capabilities already exist. All that's needed is the appropriate layer of software to provide the information in Plug and Play format. For the existing ISA bus, implementation of Plug and Play support is a lot harder. However, the low-level operations that the bus and associated devices must support are somewhat similar in every case:

- Isolating a device. There has to be a way for the operating system to interact with one, and only one, device at a time during the system boot process. If two devices respond to the same operating system inquiry, the process breaks down.

- Reading information from the device. The Plug and Play subsystem needs to collect information from the device. For a Plug and Play device, a defined interface allows the device to provide specific information in a standard format. In the case of a legacy adapter with no provision for Plug and Play support, the software has to collect whatever information it can and then play the software equivalent of a word guessing game during the identification step.

- Identifying the device. Whatever information the device provides must be sufficient for the Plug and Play subsystem to correctly identify the device. Identifying a 3Com network adapter as a Hewlett-Packard scanner will obviously lead to problems.

- Configuring the device. Plug and Play devices expect to be told which resources they can use: which IRQ, which I/O ports, which DMA channel, and which memory region. This provision is a key aspect of the Plug and Play specification design. No longer will you enter a deadlock situation in which two different devices absolutely require use of the same IRQ. Non–Plug and Play devices don't have a reconfiguration capability, so the resources these cards consume are reserved first and made unavailable to other devices.

- Locating and loading a device driver for the device. Once the device driver is loaded, it takes over the control of the device, using the allocated resources.

Devices that conform to the full Plug and Play specification make the operations in this process quite straightforward. The various specification documents for Plug and Play hardware describe the requirements and implementation methods in great detail. The more difficult job is making the legacy cards appear to behave like Plug and Play devices.

New ISA Board Standard

Since ISA systems are what most of us own, it's interesting to take a brief look at how the Plug and Play specification augments the ISA adapter design so that ISA systems can support full Plug and Play operations. The Plug and Play specification describes all the hardware and software components in elaborate detail. Essentially, a Plug and Play ISA card must include a small amount of additional hardware logic that implements the following sequence of behavior:

1. At power on, the device remains quiescent until it senses a specific pattern of commands written to a predefined I/O port—the so called *initiation key*.

2. The device then enters a state in which it waits for a "wake" command written to an I/O port. In response to a wake command, the controlling software can either wake up a specific card, if it already has a unique identifier for the card, or move all the cards to the "isolation" state.

3. The Plug and Play software communicates with one and only one card in the isolation state. The device responds to commands sent via the I/O ports by sending data bytes back to the Plug and Play software. The data the device sends back includes a unique identifier that allows the software to identify the device—the identifier includes fields such as a manufacturer ID to ensure unique identification.

4. Once the device has been uniquely identified, the software and the device can exchange information. In this exchange, resource requirements are identified and allocated.

For the cost of redesign and a small increment in manufacturing overhead, an existing ISA card can become a Plug and Play device. Preferably, the host system will have a new Plug and Play BIOS and of course a Plug and Play capable operating system such as Windows 95.[4]

---

4. The Plug and Play BIOS ensures that a system with multiple boot devices will in fact boot. However, if a Plug and Play BIOS is not present, the operating system takes over all the device configuration chores.

Seamless Dynamic Configuration Changes

With this rather grandiose phrase, the Plug and Play standard addresses the increasingly common situation in which a system's hardware configuration changes while the system is running. No, you won't be opening up your desktop machine and plugging new cards in while your C compiler runs, but there are already a lot of systems available that do allow hardware configuration changes while the system continues to run. The currently popular example of this capability is a laptop system that supports the PCMCIA peripheral standard. Other examples include infrared printer connections and wireless-based networks. The hardware specification for PCMCIA cards took quite a while to develop to everyone's satisfaction, but now a wide variety of PCMCIA-standard peripheral devices is available. In addition to the attractions of their small physical dimensions and light weights, these cards allow you to alter a system's configuration by simply removing one card and plugging in another. You might use an Ethernet card connected to the office network, for example, and exchange it for a fax/modem card while you're traveling. During 1993, many more of the manufacturers began to offer systems with PCMCIA slots, including PCs that use nothing but PCMCIA card slots, such as Hewlett-Packard's OmniBook.

Obviously, the convenience of PCMCIA, or other dynamically reconfigurable systems, is lost if users have to go through an extended software reconfiguration process and reboot whenever they change peripheral cards. The Plug and Play standard addresses this sticking point by defining how a system should allow for hardware resources to be both removed and added while the system is operational. Managing the removal process is easily as important as dealing with the addition of new devices. You certainly don't want the user pulling a disk drive out of the system before all the files on the drive have been correctly updated and closed. Windows 95 takes this aspect of Plug and Play to its logical conclusion by having a notification system inform applications of configuration changes. Every significant configuration change causes a message broadcast that applications can either process or ignore. A facsimile application, for instance, can process a message informing it that the user has tried to eject the fax/modem card. The application's response to the message might be putting up a dialog indicating that there are fax messages still to be sent.

Compatibility with the Installed Base and Old Peripherals

Perhaps the most difficult goal for the Plug and Play consortium to realize was the incorporation of support for the billions of dollars' worth of hardware already in use. Previous attempts at improving configuration flexibility had largely ignored this issue. Not even the combined might of Intel, Microsoft, and the other Plug and Play partners could wave a hardware wand and suddenly make the old systems fully Plug and Play. It was up to the software developers in the consortium to create that magic. The partners realized that achieving the compatibility goal would probably make or break the success of the entire Plug and Play effort.

A number of software components of the Plug and Play implementation contribute to its support for current hardware. Each component makes the configuration process a little easier for the end user. Naturally, some situations will require the user's assistance. For example, if an adapter can be hardware configured only—by moving jumpers and switches on the card, that is—or if the device driver software can't report the adapter's configuration, Windows 95 will have to ask the user for help.

Over the last few years, Microsoft has built a veritable library of techniques for isolating and identifying different ISA devices, and the great majority of popular devices can now be supported by the Plug and Play subsystem. Inevitably, there will be exceptions. If you happen to be the proud owner of one of the only three Flashbang 9000 network adapters ever made, you're almost out of luck. Almost, but not quite. The Plug and Play specification recognizes the need for a fallback position: ask the user for device configuration information. In Windows 95 this might happen during system setup, or during some future reconfiguration exercise called for when the user has added a new adapter that the Plug and Play subsystem simply cannot recognize. A series of dialogs will lead the user through the process of specifying the device and the resources it requires. Once the device is identified, Plug and Play will store the information in the registry and re-use it the next time the system is turned on.

The Plug and Play implementation tries to minimize such appeals to the user for information by both supporting extensions to the device driver software—so that some reporting is available—and recording the current hardware configuration on disk. If you think of the number of times you've lost the scrap of paper on which you'd written the IRQ you assigned to the network card when you plugged it in, you'll surely appreciate Windows 95 when the time to add another adapter to the system comes around. In the case of device driver software, a manufacturer can provide some Plug and Play support by simply updating the driver. No hardware changes are needed. Given the fairly efficient driver distribution mechanisms in place—the Windows 95 product itself, the device driver library disk, and bulletin boards—it's reasonable to expect that a lot of manufacturers will try to add basic Plug and Play support to current hardware. And you don't have to have updated device drivers. Even with no changes to the driver, Windows 95 will support the device and do its level best to detect the device and its configuration during installation. All of this will go a long way in making Plug and Play attractive to the installed base.

Operating System and Hardware Independence

Given the collaborative nature of the Plug and Play specification effort, you'd expect the standard to address any hardware or operating system environment. And in spite of competitive issues, the Plug and Play specification does acknowledge the importance of providing a suitable base for future development. After all, the introduction of PCMCIA and local bus systems gathered momentum only recently. And efforts such as the IEEE serial SCSI specification have not yet left the committee room. Few people would be willing to bet that there will be no other fundamental industry developments in hardware interfaces. Given the intensity of competition, we can expect major improvements in operating system technology over the next few years.

All of this demands that the Plug and Play specification be independent of the underlying hardware and software. The basic data structures, naming conventions, and user interface aspects of Plug and Play are defined only to a level that allows a consistent implementation of the specification across different platforms. Specific implementation details are left to the operating system developer.

Reduced Complexity and Increased Flexibility of Hardware

We've looked at a number of the complexities surrounding hardware configuration. As we noted earlier, making hardware configuration easy was the prime goal for the Plug and Play standard. The specification also lists the goal of making hardware "flexible." Meaning what exactly? Flexibility goes back to the goal of reducing complexity. One of the most frustrating problems with current hardware is resolving conflicts between devices. As we've already noted, for example in Chapter Two's history of the Intel processor, two adapters can't share an IRQ or a set of I/O ports. Yet it's asking a lot to expect users to understand this and be diligent enough to check for conflicts as they add new adapters to their systems. Diagnosing conflicts is also difficult: sometimes the system appears to work fine—until it crashes with no warning and no useful diagnostics.

The goal of increased flexibility really amounts to directing manufacturers to produce hardware that can use a range of different device settings and allow the settings to be chosen by the operating system—not by hardwired jumper and switch settings. In practice, this means that an adapter whose default configuration calls for it to use, say, IRQ 3 can be told by the operating system to use IRQ 10 instead. The user will have provided no input to initiate this change and, in fact, will be unaware of it. Such a requirement for flexibility extends to the dynamic reconfiguration of a system, where the system can instruct a device using a particular configuration to change its configuration in situ. Taken to its logical extreme, this flexibility means that any fully Plug and Play compliant adapter could be plugged into any Plug and Play system and be guaranteed to work. No longer will a user need to dismember a system to disable an existing COM port before installing a new fax card.

Although a lot of the burden for implementing this flexibility falls on the hardware manufacturers, it is also good news for them. Hardware that easily adapts itself to any host configuration is likely to massively reduce the technical support a manufacturer will need to provide. Plug it in and it works—with no series of frustrated phone calls to a support technician who must try to figure out how the user can make the device work alongside the other adapters he or she has already installed. Similarly, the documentation for the product will be simpler, and the installation program for the device driver will be trivial.

The Components of Plug and Play

As we've seen, the goals for Plug and Play are ambitious: easy installation, easy reconfiguration, and on-the-fly configuration changes. What's more, achieving the goals involves a number of different people: the operating system supplier, the system manufacturer, the BIOS developer, and the device vendor. Of course, there needs to be a well-defined set of interfaces and clear divisions of responsibility if the goals are to be met. The Plug and Play specification approaches the problem of dividing and coordinating the labor by defining a layered architecture for implementation and carefully separating functions into different components. To fully understand how Windows 95 implements the Plug and Play standard, we need to look at the major elements of the subsystem. Figure 8-1 is a representation of relationships among the various components. The description of the components here is, not surprisingly, for the Windows 95 implementation of Plug and Play. Many elements would be the same for a Plug and Play subsystem supported by another operating system.[5]

A number of components, not all of which are shown in Figure 8-1, collaborate in the Plug and Play subsystem. Here's a summary of the role of each:

- Hardware tree. The database of information describing the current system configuration. The hardware tree is built by the configuration manager and kept in memory. Every node on the hardware tree is termed a *device node* and contains the logical description of either an actual device or a bus device.

- .INF files. A collection of disk files containing information about particular types of devices. SCSI.INF, for example, holds information about every known SCSI device. During the installation of a new Plug and Play device, a new .INF file specific to that device will be used to help complete the software installation. Usually the .INF file will be on the installation diskette that comes with the device.

- Registry. The Windows 95 registry containing as a subtree the hardware tree describing the hardware.

- Events. A set of APIs used to signal changes in the system's current configuration. In Windows 95, the message system is used to signal events. In other implementations, an operating system component could be used to signal events.

- Configuration manager. The component responsible for building the database of information describing the machine's configuration (in the registry) and notifying the

---

5. Windows 95 also uses the Plug and Play subsystem extensively during system setup and subsequent device installation. Other Plug and Play–supportive operating systems may do things differently.

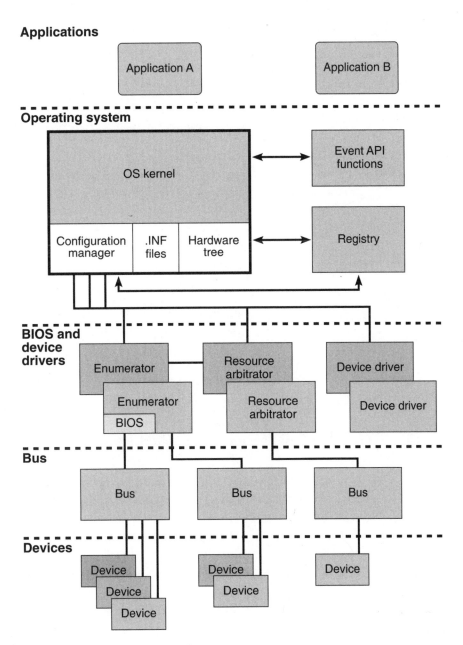

Figure 8-1.
The Plug and Play components.

device drivers of their assigned resources. The configuration manager is the central component of the Plug and Play subsystem when the system is running.

■ Enumerator. A new piece of driver software that collaborates with the device driver and the configuration manager. An enumerator is specific to any device (typically to a bus) to which other devices can be attached.[6] Every bus device in the hardware tree always has an enumerator associated with it. A special enumerator, called the *root enumerator,* is part of the configuration manager. The root enumerator assists in setting up non–Plug and Play devices.

■ Resource arbitrator. A function responsible for presiding over the allocation of specific resources and for helping to resolve conflicts.

■ Plug and Play BIOS. A new system BIOS that supports Plug and Play operations. A device (a video controller, for example) may also have a device-specific BIOS that conforms to the Plug and Play rules. The Plug and Play BIOS is also the enumerator for the motherboard devices and in this guise plays a critical role in managing the docking and undocking operations of portable systems.

■ The Plug and Play device drivers. Protected mode drivers responsible for device control as well as participation in the Plug and Play subsystem.

■ User interface. A collection of standard dialogs used to solicit information when the Plug and Play system needs to get the user involved in configuration information gathering. The user can also examine the system configuration built by the Plug and Play subsystem.

■ Application. In the Plug and Play context, a program modified for improved operation under Windows 95 that can accept and process system configuration change messages.

---

6. Early designs of the Plug and Play subsystem also used the term *bus driver.* Differentiating the roles of enumerators and bus drivers became sufficiently hard that the functions were finally combined.

Remember that the entire Plug and Play subsystem is mainly concerned with the management of four different resource types on behalf of the various devices:

Memory. The physical memory requirements of the device—for example, how many pages of memory the device needs and any alignment constraints.

I/O. The I/O ports the device will respond to. The device configuration information includes a specification of each of the alternative sets of ports that the device can use (if any).

DMA. Any DMA channels the device requires and any alternative channels it can use.

IRQ. The device's IRQ requirements, alternative IRQs, and whether the device can share an IRQ.

How the Subsystem Fits Together

As you can probably guess, the entire Plug and Play subsystem is a lot of C and assembly language code. Fortunately, very little of the code is memory resident and the system will load most components dynamically. Before we look at the detailed operations of a few components, let's take a step-by-step look at how the whole subsystem hangs together. Central to the entire Plug and Play subsystem is the *hardware tree* data structure that describes the current system hardware configuration. We'll look at the hardware tree's components in more detail in the next section.[7] Figure 8-2 on the next page shows the hardware tree structure that corresponds to a typical Plug and Play system.

Although in this example we're fortunate enough to own a real Plug and Play system, we have held onto our legacy network adapter. Although the network adapter is physically plugged into the ISA bus, as a non–Plug and Play device the adapter is logically attached to the root of the hardware tree during system configuration. More on this in a moment. We haven't made any system configuration changes since the last time we used the system. Let's turn our system on and see what happens.

---

7. This simple logical representation of the hardware appeared very early in the software design process and has survived every challenge and attempt at improvement.

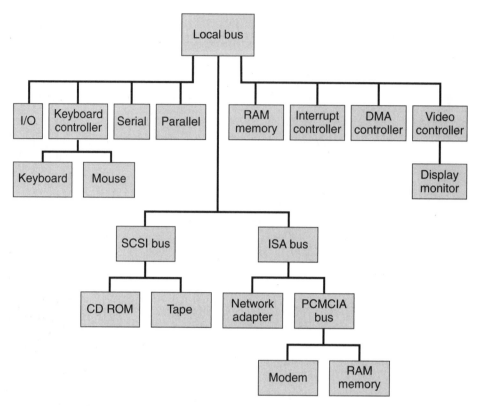

Figure 8-2.
Hardware tree for a typical Plug and Play system.

1. The system BIOS reads nonvolatile memory to determine the machine configuration. The BIOS configures any adapter for which it finds configuration information, notably the motherboard devices. The BIOS disables any adapter for which there is no configuration information.

2. The boot process begins. The system is still in real mode. The configuration manager's root enumerator uses the hardware subtree in the Windows registry as its reference for what the system configuration ought to be.

3. The root enumerator scans the registry subtree looking for all the non–Plug and Play devices. When it finds one, it constructs a device node and adds it to the root of the memory resident hardware tree. This is where you can see the device

node for the legacy network adapter in Figure 8-2's example. The root enumerator also configures the device if the BIOS has not already done so.

4. The real mode boot process continues. The system loader processes SYSTEM.INI, loading the static VxDs that it specifies.

5. Now the next enumerators get loaded. The BIOS has registered the fact that, for example, the system includes an ISA bus. The registry shows which enumerator to load for the particular bus device.

6. The enumerator examines the devices attached to the bus and loads either a static VxD (if one is required) or another enumerator to examine a descendant bus. In the example configuration shown in Figure 8-2, the ISA enumerator would load the PCMCIA enumerator.

7. All the real mode drivers and static VxDs are now in memory. The operating system kernel completes its initialization and switches to protected mode.

8. Now the configuration manager runs. Some of the system's devices are fully initialized, and their drivers are loaded. Other devices simply have their presence on the system recorded with no device driver yet loaded.

9. The configuration manager loads the appropriate remaining enumerators. These enumerators in turn examine the attached devices, build device nodes, and add them to the hardware tree. When this process is complete, the configuration manager will load the device drivers that correspond to the newly created device modes. (During the process, any configuration conflicts will arise and present themselves for solution.)

10. If an unknown non–Plug and Play device is left over, Windows starts the device install process, which asks the user for help in resolving the configuration. Otherwise, the system is now up and running.

Time passes....

After a System Configuration Change

Suppose you automatically load a fax application whenever you start this system. The application uses the fax/modem card on the PCMCIA bus. At some point, you decide you want to transfer the card to another machine, so you press the card eject button.

1. The PCMCIA enumerator receives notice of the button press. It informs the configuration manager. The configuration manager broadcasts the hardware change notification message.

2. Each enumerator sees the change notification message and queries its associated device drivers as to whether they care about your ejecting the card.

3. Eventually, the configuration manager broadcasts a message indicating that the fax card is about to be ejected.

4. The fax application sees the message from the configuration manager and puts up a dialog asking whether you really want to eject the card. You respond Yes. The fax application checks to see whether there are any fax transmissions in progress or pending. If there are no transmissions in progress or pending, the fax application tells the system that the eject operation is OK and returns to a dormant state.

As you can see from this sampling, a lot of interaction goes on among the different Plug and Play components. Much more detail about these interactions would probably overwhelm you. We'll look at a few more implementation details in this chapter, but if you really want every last detail, you need to make the Plug and Play specification itself your favorite bedtime reading.

Hardware Tree

Windows 95 builds the hardware tree during the system boot process, and any subsequent configuration change modifies the tree. The tree is a logical representation of the system hardware configuration. The tree exists as a data structure held in memory while Windows 95 is running. The registry contains a record of every different hardware configuration in the system's lifetime. The memory resident tree is more dynamic, changing as the user adds and removes devices. If you don't change the configuration of your machine from one day to the next, the registry and the memory tree will contain the same (unchanging) information.

Device Nodes

Each node of the hardware tree is called a *device node*. The specification also refers to a node as a *Plug and Play object*, although Plug and Play is not strictly an object-oriented subsystem. The leaf nodes of the tree represent individual devices present in the system—keyboard, monitor, tape, modem, for example. Parent nodes represent *bus devices*—devices that each play a role in the control of at least one other device.

The bus device is fundamental to the design of the Plug and Play subsystem. Plug and Play defines a bus device to be "any device that provides resources." A Plug and Play bus device is also the most common type of parent node for any device node in the hardware tree. In most cases, you can think of the logical Plug and Play bus as the hardware bus in the system. For example, a bus in an ISA system provides interrupt resources (the different IRQs) and I/O port resources. It is also the parent device in the sense that you plug devices into it. In the particular configuration shown in Figure 8-2 on page 326, every node in the tree diagram is a device node, and the *SCSI bus, ISA bus,* and *PCMCIA bus* nodes are bus devices. Take a look at Figure 8-2 again, and note that since the *Keyboard controller* node is also a parent node in the hardware tree, it too is considered a Plug and Play bus device.[8] Every Plug and Play bus device has an *enumerator* associated with it.

Every Plug and Play device node—whether for a device or for a bus device—always contains the following information:

- A unique device identifier—actually a string, not just a number

- A list of resources required by the device node

- A list of resources actually allocated to the device node

- If the device node represents a bus device, a pointer to the descendant device nodes in the tree

Access to the device node data structure is always via a set of system APIs. Device drivers, and other modules, never manipulate the device node data structure directly. Also, it's only the device drivers, enumerators, and other Plug and Play–related modules that use the defined APIs. Application programs never use the APIs.

---

8. This is where the mind's eye representation of a Plug and Play bus as a hardware bus breaks down. Thinking of a Plug and Play bus device as *any* piece of hardware that you can plug something into is perhaps a better visualization.

Figure 8-3 is a more detailed representation of a *Network adapter* and a *SCSI bus* device node data structure. The configuration example shown in Figure 8-3 is similar to the example shown in Figure 8-2 except that the network adapter is a Plug and Play adapter.

- All required resources have been allocated to the *Network adapter* node.

- The resources required by the *SCSI bus* child nodes (*Tape* and *CD ROM*) have been allocated.

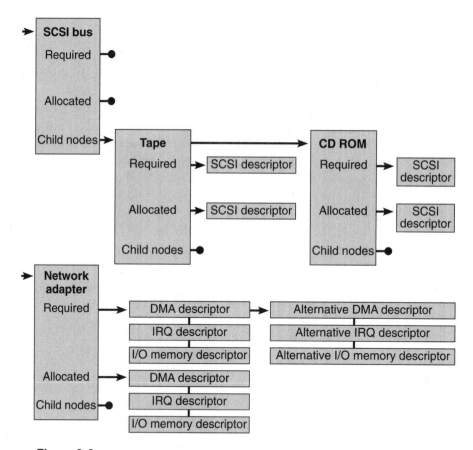

Figure 8-3.
Development of the Network adapter *and* SCSI bus *nodes of the logical hardware tree representation.*

Notice that the *Network adapter* device node depicted in Figure 8-3 has more than one entry in its list for each of the required resources. This provision allows the Plug and Play configuration manager to try to allocate alternative resources when an attempt to allocate an entry in the first set runs into a conflict. For example, if the default IRQ is already in use by another device, the configuration manager will try to use an alternative IRQ. In our example, the registry would have had to contain the information that describes the configuration possibilities for the network adapter.

Device Identifiers

A naming scheme that allows every device on a Plug and Play system to be uniquely identified is a critical requirement for Windows 95. Sensibly, the Plug and Play specification incorporates whatever assistance it can get from currently specified information such as the PCMCIA manufacturer number or the PCI identifier. However, ISA devices have never had a standardized identifying nomenclature, so a new scheme was needed. Rather than trying to evolve an identifier system within the constraints of a 32-bit or 64-bit number, the Plug and Play design uses character strings—sometimes very long character strings. Yes, you can read them, but don't expect to make much sense out of them if you do.

The generation of the device identifier strings is one of the functions of the device enumerator software. The function has to be part of the enumerator since it is this driver alone that is supposed to understand the intimate details of the bus and its attached hardware. Unlike in a static EISA device identifier scheme, the ISA enumerator driver generates the device identifiers dynamically. The algorithm varies from type to type and may involve techniques such as copying company name strings from device ROMs to help. On similarly configured Plug and Play systems with attached ISA devices, the enumerator-generated device name will be the same from one system to the next.

The device identifier for an ISA bus begins with the string *ISAENM*. This beginning at least identifies the enumerator that generated the identifier (and that therefore has control of the device). In our example PC, the modem attached to the PCMCIA bus might end up with a device identifier like *ISAENM\PCMCIAENM\0020071001*— with the trailing digit string's having been generated by the enumerator's reading the manufacturer's ID and part number from the device itself. The enumerator might use just about any naming scheme that ensures uniqueness. If a system had two identical network cards plugged in, for example, the name string might end with ... \0300 and ... \0320 denoting the particular I/O addresses that the cards respond to.[9]

Within the system itself, the device identifiers are very important. Each device node in the memory resident hardware tree contains the device identifier, and the same identifier acts as the registry key the operating system uses to access device-specific information.

Hardware Information Databases

Windows 95 uses four sources of information to determine or record the details of every device on the system:

- The *configuration* files (.INF) held on disk and containing a permanent record of every device ever known. These files arrive already installed on your system.

- The .INF file supplied with each new device (presumably on the installation diskette).

- The user, who has to intercede to solve otherwise unresolvable conflicts or to provide information absent from the databases.

- The Windows 95 registry hardware archive subtree that contains information about the current system configuration. The Windows 95 setup program builds the initial hardware archive in the registry. The registry includes Plug and Play information under three keys:

HKEY_LOCAL_MACHINE	The global settings for the system
HKEY_CURRENT_USER	The current user's personal preferences
HKEY_CURRENT_CONFIG	The current machine configuration—alterable by, for example, whether the system is docked or not

The Plug and Play subsystem draws its information primarily from the hardware archive and the current machine configuration. The user becomes involved only if Windows 95 can't figure out some aspect of

---

9. Note that the I/O port address is only for identifying purposes. Nothing actually parses the string trying to find the I/O address.

the hardware configuration. Such intervention should come into play only for the older ISA devices that don't conform to the Plug and Play specification.

From all this information, the memory resident hardware tree is built and maintained. Windows 95 updates the hardware tree as the system configuration changes. If you change the configuration before turning the machine on again (switch PCMCIA cards, for example, or replace a defective adapter), the detection process has to refresh the hardware tree with the new configuration.

Note that there is a preferred method of hardware installation for manually configured devices—where you must manually change a jumper setting, for instance. You install the software first, and then you turn the machine off to install the hardware. When you switch the system back on, its configuration will be correctly determined.

Plug and Play Events

Early on in the design of the Plug and Play subsystem, there was a distinct software component called the event manager. Later revisions of the design simplified this notion so that Plug and Play events exist as a set of APIs that use the standard Windows messaging system to allow the broadcasting of messages that describe Plug and Play events. Messages describe events such as requests to remove a device from the system and the addition of new logical volumes to the network. The message from a device driver or enumerator is sent to the configuration manager, which may propagate it on through the system—perhaps in a different form. A device level event in particular could be translated and sent to applications as a window message. Any device driver or VxD can call the event API, specifying the event and providing the associated event data. Applications and drivers with an interest in the particular event will receive and process the message in the normal way.

Configuration Manager

The configuration manager is the principal software component of the Plug and Play subsystem. It's responsible for controlling the hardware tree database and linking the other components of the Plug and Play subsystem together. During the system boot process, the configuration manager is the ultimate authority for ensuring that the hardware tree is fully populated and that its information is correct. The configuration manager is also involved, somewhere along the line, whenever a Plug and Play event occurs. If a system configuration change occurs, for example, the configuration manager will control the process through which the various bus and device drivers interact, Plug and Play event messages are sent and processed, and modifications to the hardware tree take place.

Here's an example of what happens if a user runs a word processing application, loads a document from a PCMCIA hard disk card, and then presses the card eject button before closing the document file:

1. The PCMCIA disk driver recognizes the card eject button press and notifies the configuration manager.

2. The configuration manager broadcasts the hardware change notification message, which asks whether the card removal operation is allowable.

3. Each device driver responds, indicating that it's OK.

4. The configuration manager broadcasts a message describing the physical device—the hard disk.

5. The I/O subsystem recognizes that the hard disk card contains an active logical drive and broadcasts an application-level message describing the logical device.

6. The word processing application receives the message, processes it, and recognizes that there is a document file open on the affected drive. It displays a dialog for the user that might present two options: save the document and allow the card to be removed, or cancel the card removal and continue.

7. The user's response filters back to the configuration manager in the form of responses to the various messages. In the case of the user's choosing to save the document and thus allow the card to be removed, the configuration manager will ultimately inform the disk driver that the eject operation can proceed. If the user chooses to cancel the card removal, the disk driver will ignore the button press.

Enumerators

An enumerator is a new type of device driver associated specifically with any device that controls another device. Usually, such a device is really a bus, although a device such as the keyboard controller may also have an associated enumerator. "Enumerator" is an elaborate term for referring to its most common function: walking through each attached device node in its branch of the hardware tree, repeating a particular action. For example, during system startup the enumerator accesses each device on the attached bus, initializing the device and ensuring that the information in the particular device node is complete. The configuration manager calls each enumerator to carry out operations on its attached devices. Using the enumerator this way ensures that the details of the physical bus and the attached devices are hidden from the configuration manager. The enumerator and the associated device drivers deal with the hardware specifics of the device, and the configuration manager deals with device nodes.

The code for a particular enumerator could be implemented by a manufacturer as part of a device adapter BIOS—this is likely, for example, if the system has a proprietary local bus design—or as a protected mode driver that is part of the Windows kernel. For standard hardware, such as the ISA bus, the enumerator is a standard component of Windows 95.

Resource Arbitrators

The other software component that understands the intimate details of a particular hardware device is the resource arbitrator. This kind of function understands the specific hardware resource requirements of a device—for example, the fact that a standard ISA COM device must use either IRQ 3 or IRQ 4. The configuration manager calls an arbitrator function for a device, providing it with the list of required resources from the device node. It is up to the arbitrator to allocate the resources that will satisfy the device's requirements. The configuration manager may also call the arbitrator to inform it that it must relinquish a resource that it is using. Usually, the arbitrator function exists as code within the Windows device driver.

During an attempt to satisfy a hardware resource allocation request, the arbitrator may well come to a dead end. It will need a particular hardware resource, but that resource will already belong to some other device. The arbitrator won't try to resolve the conflict. It will report the error back to the configuration manager and try to provide information that will help the configuration manager resolve the conflict. It's left up to the configuration manager to oversee the process of reallocating resources in an attempt to resolve the conflict.

During this conflict resolution process, arbitrators may be asked to surrender resources they already control. The reallocation process might occur during system startup—the configuration manager reaches a dead end and has to back up—or during a configuration change when a new device requests resources that are already allocated somewhere else.

Plug and Play BIOS

The Plug and Play BIOS is an enhancement of the BIOS that comes in the ROM of every PC. There is a companion document to the Plug and Play specification that describes the details of a Plug and Play BIOS. Every complete BIOS implementation must include both the BIOS functions in use in current machines and the functions that support Plug and Play operation. The design of the Plug and Play BIOS allows both real mode software and 16-bit protected mode software to call BIOS functions. There is no provision for direct calls to the BIOS from a 32-bit protected mode program.

The Plug and Play BIOS extends normal BIOS functionality by

- Maintaining a description of the devices attached to the system board using a data structure very similar to the device node structure used throughout the Plug and Play subsystem

- Supporting a small number of functions that allow an operating system to retrieve and update information about the attached devices

- Providing an event notification mechanism that interfaces with the system configuration manager—this mechanism allowing the operating system to retrieve event information associated with devices that are under BIOS control

- Supporting docking operations on portable systems

The issue of where the BIOS stores the device information is left open to the system and BIOS suppliers. Most systems are likely to use the CMOS memory that the system battery keeps alive. Current PCs already use this memory for storing configuration information, so it's the obvious repository for the Plug and Play information as well. The Plug and Play BIOS specification describes the expected format of the device information that the BIOS must return to the caller. When you make a call to the BIOS function to get device information, the caller provides a buffer for the BIOS to store the information in. Similarly, when updating the device information for a BIOS controlled device, the operating system calls the BIOS with a modified device node. The Plug and Play specification doesn't allow for direct access to the device information, so exactly where and how the BIOS stores the data is left up to the system manufacturer.

The Plug and Play specification also allows for the BIOS event mechanism to be implemented in two different ways. The BIOS can either simply set a flag in a specific memory location whenever an event occurs or allow the operating system to install an interrupt handler that the BIOS will call to notify the operating system of the occurrence of an event. In the first case, the operating system simply checks the memory location regularly to see whether the event flag is set. Either way, the system must then call the BIOS to retrieve information about the specific event.

Plug and Play Device Drivers

One of the issues facing the Windows 95 team was how to build momentum behind the Plug and Play standard. Although Plug and Play has a broader scope, the fact that Windows 95 would be the first major operating system to support it needed thinking about. Apart from simply convincing all the hardware manufacturers that Plug and Play was indeed a really good idea, the team thought that making it easy to conform to the Plug and Play standard would help a lot. One simple way to make life easy for the manufacturers was to limit the software changes necessary to support Plug and Play. Since Windows 95 can use existing Windows device drivers, you don't absolutely need to develop a new driver to support a Plug and Play system. But this is rather passive support for Plug and Play. To actively support Plug and Play, an existing Windows driver needs to incorporate several modifications and extensions. Here's what such a driver needs to do:

- Be dynamically loadable and unloadable. Thus, a Plug and Play driver becomes a dynamically loadable VxD.

- Use the Windows 95 registry for nonvolatile parameter storage. Windows 95 frowns upon system components that store parameter information in private files or other storage areas. Everything should be in the registry. Information stored under the registry key HKEY_CURRENT_CONFIG also defines the current machine state—docked or undocked, for example.

■ Register with the configuration manager at load time and accept the hardware resources allocated by the configuration manager, and then configure the device according to the configuration manager's allocations rather than according to any existing default.

■ Support the release of resources on request.

■ Support the new Plug and Play APIs, including the events notified by the event APIs.

The major manifestation of a philosophical change in a Windows 95 device driver is its acceptance of the configuration manager as the controlling entity for resource allocation. Rather than simply initializing a device to a known configuration, the driver must obey the configuration instructions passed to it by the configuration manager. The driver must also respond to event notification if it is to be a good citizen within the overall event system.

Windows 95 device drivers must support several new APIs if they are to operate within the Plug and Play environment. For example, the configuration manager uses specific APIs to either demand or request that the driver release an already allocated resource. Another API tells the driver to configure the hardware according to the resource allocation specified in the device node parameter. The configuration manager may make this call several times while it attempts to adjust the system configuration to avoid allocation conflicts.

Applications in a Plug and Play System

Any application can involve itself in Plug and Play issues by responding to the events that Windows 95 defines. A lot of applications won't care that the system is Plug and Play. After all, a Plug and Play system with no removable devices probably won't change its configuration from power on to power off. However, for many of the latest generation of portable PCs, there are a number of instances in which applications ought to be aware of dynamic configuration changes. Here are a few examples:

- Applications running on portable systems that use PCMCIA cards for disk storage need to take account of the possibility that the user will try to eject a card when there are files open on that disk.

- User alteration of connectivity options—for example, exchanging a network card for a modem card—is likely to be of interest to both the network subsystem and any communications application. The application ought to try to adapt itself to the new speed of the connection, for example.

- Applications ought to adapt smoothly to changes in display resolution initiated by the user.

- The "disappearance" of network volumes when the user walks out of range of his or her wireless network should not result in inelegant or misleading error messages.

In general, applications need to be event aware, and certainly more hardware aware than they have been. Both the new event system and the use of the Windows 95 registry are key to the implementation of standout Windows 95 applications.

Conclusion

In this chapter, we've looked at the Plug and Play specification from the viewpoint of the general goals and architecture of the Plug and Play subsystem. The details we've gone into are specific to the Windows 95 implementation of the Plug and Play specification, but implementations for other operating system environments will share many similarities with the Windows 95 version. If Plug and Play hardware becomes ubiquitous, it's almost certain that other operating systems will support the Plug and Play specification.

Plug and Play represents a major step forward in the ease of use of personal computers. An Apple Macintosh user might assert that they've always had it that good, but then they've also had a much narrower range of third party hardware to choose from. If you remember the theme of Apple's recent anti-Windows television advertising campaign, you'll appreciate how long overdue an enhancement to the PC environment Plug and Play is. Although it will take time for the industry to catch up and start providing full Plug and Play compliant systems and components, the benefits to users and overwrought support personnel make the effort's wisdom seem compelling.

So far, we've looked at a Windows 95 system from the perspective of a single user. Now that we have Plug and Play, we can fearlessly connect our system to just about anything. The corporate network is probably what occurs first to most of us, so in the next chapter we'll look at the networking capabilities of Windows 95.

References

To receive a copy of the Plug and Play Device Driver Kit (DDK), send electronic mail to *plugplay@intel.com* or fax a request to Intel at (503) 696-1307.

To receive information about future developments at Microsoft on Plug and Play topics, send electronic mail with complete contact information (your name, mailing address, phone number, fax number, and e-mail address) to *playlist@microsoft.com.*

Copies of the various Plug and Play specifications are available for downloading from the Plug and Play forum on CompuServe. Type *go plugplay* at any command prompt. The following specifications are currently available, but others may be added:

The Plug and Play ISA specification

The Plug and Play BIOS specification

The Plug and Play SCSI specification

The Plug and Play PCMCIA specification

The Plug and Play PCI specification

The Plug and Play Advanced Power Management specification

CHAPTER NINE

NETWORKING

Early presentations of the Windows 95 networking strategy characterized Microsoft's goal as "providing the best desktop operating system for networked personal computers." To this end, Windows 95 incorporates full *peer-to-peer* networking capabilities, allowing you to configure self-contained Windows 95 networks with each machine acting as a network server. In addition, Windows 95 aims to provide connectivity to every leading network architecture through a single user interface and a common set of APIs for network applications. Networking under Windows 95 relies on features we've already looked at—most notably on the installable filesystem mechanism discussed in Chapter Seven. In Chapter Ten, we'll look more closely at how Windows 95 handles remote communications; in this chapter, we'll concentrate on Windows 95 support for local area networking.

Although whether or not you'll get networking for free probably won't be clear until the day the product is officially announced, Windows 95 certainly emphasizes networking by incorporating peer-to-peer support, local area network connectivity, and remote connectivity. Windows 95 needed to do a great job of supporting client connections to other networks, and the market positioning for Windows 95 tends to emphasize this connectivity over the peer-to-peer facilities. In fact, most of the newly designed features for Windows networking are more important to client connectivity than to peer-to-peer operation. Microsoft's emphasis on client support is reflected in its development of Novell NetWare support for Windows 95 and its more recent characterization of Windows 95 as "the well-connected client."

Of course, Novell remains the industry's dominant supplier of network products and, at least at the time of this writing, a staunch advocate of the client-server architecture.[1] The Windows 95 team had to be pragmatic about this situation: their goal that Windows 95 be the perfect client operating system meant addressing the NetWare issue as well as client operation on a Microsoft network. As in the recent release of Windows for Workgroups 3.11, Windows 95 incorporates support for a full Novell client. Buy Windows 95, and you can plug straight in to a NetWare network without buying any other software.[2]

Both Windows for Workgroups version 3.11 and Windows 95 go a lot further than just offering Novell NetWare support alongside support for a Microsoft network. In both products, the system provides for the use of multiple simultaneous network interfaces by using the installable filesystem capability to support remote filesystems. Many users question when on earth they'd ever need to take advantage of this feature. But desktop configurations with, for example, a local link to a NetWare server, a wide area link using a TCP/IP protocol stack,[3] and a dial-up terminal connection to some other network are actually commonplace nowadays. Windows 95 allows these three kinds of network connections to be cleanly integrated—a far cry from the earlier trials and tribulations of networking under Windows 3.0.

Windows Networking History

Before we dive into the technology, let's review some of the history of Windows networking. Microsoft has been an active participant in the network market since 1984, when MS-DOS version 3.1 and MS Net were released. For some years, MS Net was outsold by Novell NetWare, and until the release of Microsoft LAN Manager in 1988, Microsoft really didn't have an industrial strength network operating system. During the same period, network support in Windows was weak—a situation that has changed dramatically as Windows has built its market share over the last three years, since the release of Windows 3.0.

---

1. Novell's acquisition of UNIX System Laboratories and its UNIX technology at least raises the question of whether Novell will ultimately provide a mainstream peer-to-peer network product.

2. Since packaging issues hadn't been decided, in this chapter I've treated "Windows 95" as the networkable version of the product. Maybe the product will be in a single package—maybe not.

3. Basic TCP/IP connectivity was another feature under development for Windows 95 that may or may not be "in the box" for free come product release time.

Peer-to-peer networking has leaped to prominence only in relatively recent times. The release of Microsoft's Windows for Workgroups has sparked a heightened interest in what had been, until late 1992, something of an underground movement in the personal computer industry. When Microsoft announced Windows for Workgroups just before the 1992 COMDEX/Fall trade show, peer-to-peer networking joined the technology mainstream. Despite the apparent youth of the technology, peer-to-peer networks had actually been in wide use since the introduction of the Apple Macintosh in 1985. Apple included the AppleTalk networking capability with each and every Macintosh they shipped. Most early users of the Macintosh were unaware of the fact that they were using peer-to-peer networking whenever they printed a document on the Apple LaserWriter. Apple based the design of the AppleTalk networking protocol on the peer-to-peer principle, and AppleTalk continues to be widely used on Macintosh networks today.[4]

In the PC market, products such as IBM's PC Network and Novell NetWare debuted and began building an installed base. Principally because of the overwhelming success of Novell NetWare, *client-server* networking became known as *the* way to set about connecting multiple IBM-compatible PCs. Microsoft's early network products, MS Net and Microsoft LAN Manager, reinforced the notion that it was a client-server world. In fact, until the release of Windows for Workgroups, Microsoft really didn't acknowledge the existence of the alternative model for networking.

There were companies that had built a business espousing the peer-to-peer model. Products such as 10Net, TOPS, and LANtastic built a solid market base and had many loyal and enthusiastic customers. But it was tough going. On the one hand, they had Apple giving away free networking with every Macintosh, and on the other, they had industry heavyweights such as Novell, IBM, and Microsoft advocating a client-server approach. The companies in the peer-to-peer business found that their products were perceived as suitable only for small networks

---

4. In keeping with their habit of promoting benefits rather than technology, Apple never pronounced themselves a leader in peer-to-peer networking; nor did they try to promote their technology as the best way to network personal computers. Many users from the IBM-compatible side of the PC universe as a consequence express surprise when they're exposed to the networking capabilities of the Macintosh.

or for small businesses who employed no PC professionals. Although this positioning belied the capabilities of a peer-to-peer network, this type of environment was where the leading peer-to-peer product companies found their easiest sales and their most enthusiastic customers. Competitive pressures have taken their toll on the peer-to-peer network companies, and today only Artisoft's LANtastic has significant market share. Other early products, such as 10Net, have changed ownership a number of times, and although the other peer-to-peer products still exist, they have fairly small installed bases and the future of the various vendors is uncertain. This sad history doesn't sound like much of an advertisement for peer-to-peer networking, but the lack of success so far comes more from the market issues than from any deficiencies in the capabilities of the underlying technology.

Until late 1991, Novell, IBM, and Microsoft continued to espouse the benefits of client-server networking and either ignore or dismiss peer-to-peer solutions. This market situation was an artificial one, created more by marketing dollars than by technology, but it did make good business sense:

- Server software, for use on a more limited number of machines, allowed the supplier to charge a higher price.

- Server-based application software could similarly command a premium price.

- The buyer was often a DP professional, familiar with the client-server model that had been established by the mainframe and minicomputer network manufacturers.

- Network administration tools were often quite poor, even on a server. A peer-to-peer network could compound the problem by putting poor tools in the hands of an unsophisticated user.

- The technology associated with ensuring the security of a peer-to-peer network was still more a research topic than an off-the-shelf product. In contrast, client-server networks provided more reliable security.

Perhaps ironically, the most popular UNIX-based network solutions had also adopted a peer-to-peer model, but IBM-compatible PCs and mainframes remained the stronghold of client-server networking. The situation began to change when Novell introduced its peer-to-peer product, NetWare Lite, in late 1991. Positioned as a direct competitor to the increasingly popular LANtastic network from Artisoft, NetWare Lite experienced less than spectacular success. NetWare Lite was not a very good product. Novell had tried to ensure that it would not impact upon the continued success of NetWare proper and as a result had introduced a product that was not competitive in its own sphere. The NetWare Lite introduction did put the peer-to-peer concept on many people's radar screens for the first time, however.

In 1992, Microsoft's position on peer-to-peer networking also began to change, as the company began the marketing campaign for its next major operating system product: Windows NT. After years of promotion and successive product releases, Microsoft Windows had become a runaway hit, OS/2 was still selling poorly, and Microsoft had reshaped its plans to promote a Windows operating system product family. At the outset, Microsoft put little emphasis on the networking capabilities of Windows NT. (Remember, Microsoft LAN Manager on OS/2 was the then current solution.) But as more information about the product became available, people began to realize that Windows NT incorporated peer-to-peer networking facilities within the basic operating system. Together with the Windows NT networking news, information about a new version of Windows, called Windows for Workgroups, began to appear. Released for the first time in October 1992, Windows for Workgroups turned out to be a full peer-to-peer network product. During most of 1993, Windows for Workgroups was regarded as a somewhat unsuccessful product, with its critics complaining about slow sales and lackluster features.[5] The "slow sales" charge was unfair; Windows for Workgroups racked up more than a million units in shipments during its first year. And in the fall of 1993, Microsoft released Windows for Workgroups version 3.11—a product that included the debut of a number of features important to Windows 95, such as the protected mode FAT filesystem. Clearly, Microsoft didn't think that peer-to-peer networking wasn't worth further investment. In the summer of 1993, Microsoft had delivered the first production release of Windows NT, with built-in peer-to-peer capabilities, and of course the Windows NT Advanced Server—a product that more closely resembled the client-server architecture of earlier Microsoft LAN Manager releases.

---

5. Even inside Microsoft, the belief that sales were slow prompted company humorists to call the product "Windows for Warehouses."

This is really where our historical diversion began. Although it has taken Microsoft a while to join the advocates of peer-to-peer networking, it appears that the peer-to-peer model provides the direction for the company's own networking products in the foreseeable future—a direction reinforced by the release of Windows 95.

Microsoft's move to a reliance on peer-to-peer networking is hardly unique. Recent developments in distributed systems technology have begun to find their way into commercially available products, with remote procedure call capabilities and distributed object management features[6] moving from the realm of computer science research to production systems. Distributed systems tend to rely on the availability of an underlying peer-to-peer network architecture, and despite what Novell might say, client-server networking seems destined to become not much more than a network configuration issue over the near term.

Of course, the major improvements in Windows networking also allow Microsoft to prevent Novell from establishing any market share in desktop systems. Sure, you may continue to buy Novell servers, but the capabilities of Windows 95 make Microsoft your most likely desktop operating system supplier.

Networking Goals

Microsoft emphasizes the support for multiple network connections over the other goals for networking in Windows 95. You'll hear the term "universal client" used to characterize this particular goal. Here's what the term actually means:

- A set of architected interfaces that enable a network vendor to incorporate proprietary network client support into Windows 95.

- System support for simultaneous operation of a single Windows 95 system on several networks.

- A common user interface for network browsing, resource connection, and printing—regardless of the underlying physical network type.

---

6. Capabilities that Microsoft has already announced as an important part of its Cairo development project.

■ Support for network operations from within the system shell. No longer is networking an "add on" component; it's a fundamental part of the system.

Acknowledging the entrenched position of both Novell NetWare and the UNIX-dominated TCP/IP networks, Microsoft has developed Windows 95 client support for both. Of course, Microsoft would like its own network solutions to become as popular as those of Novell, so Windows 95 has to be a good family member and support connections to Windows NT systems as well as existing Windows for Workgroups networks. Incorporating a peer server with good file and printer sharing capabilities allows Windows 95 to act as a capable, self-contained networking product.

Microsoft chose to develop its own client services for NetWare for Windows 95. This decision was largely a response to Novell's poor track record when it came to providing timely, high-performance client software for Microsoft operating systems. Early tests of Microsoft's client services for NetWare (reported in May 1994) showed some impressive results, with two to three times the performance of the Novell solution for Windows 3.11.

The other major goal for Windows 95 networking was to develop new 32-bit protected mode software for all the network components. Networking is a big winner when it escapes the limitations of real mode, the advantages corresponding to those that were gained by the introduction of a 32-bit protected mode filesystem. Overall performance improves, large software components such as network transports disappear from low memory, and the use of Windows 95's multithreaded architecture gives improved response and network throughput. Naturally, the network team had to obey the laws of compatibility, and Windows 95 still allows the use of older MS-DOS and Windows 3.1 network drivers.

Network Software Architecture

Like the new filesystem architecture, network support in Windows 95 relies on a layered design that separates functionality into several distinct modules. Early formalized approaches to network software design were among the first instances of this technique, and proponents of existing network architectures, such as the OSI model, tend to be quite doctrinaire about the layered approach. As with most aspects of Windows design, though, implementation performance and memory requirements are paramount considerations. Although the designers of Windows 95 networking adopted a layered approach, practical considerations dictated a few design impurities. Figure 9-1 shows the overall network software configuration in a "typical" Windows 95 system that provides access to two networks through a single network adapter.

Many of the component names in Figure 9-1 are probably already familiar to you. We'll look at each of them as we analyze the architecture. Windows 95 networking is one of the best examples of the use of Microsoft's *Windows Open Services Architecture* (*WOSA*), and coming to grips with the networking subsystem is easier if you understand WOSA to begin with.

WOSA

Microsoft came up with the unwieldy WOSA name as an umbrella for a set of software components that, although originating in different projects, exhibited many similar characteristics. Much of the design impetus for WOSA came from the need for applications to interface to different networks, although WOSA can be applied to non-networked environments as well. Essentially, WOSA encompasses a series of interfaces designed to allow multiple software components with similar functionality to co-exist in the operating system. The user's interaction with an application ultimately results in the application's using the system's defined APIs to manipulate data. WOSA introduces the *service provider interface,* or *SPI,* that allows the OS to call system components (called *service providers*) to complete the processing of the data. Whereas the API is independent of the underlying hardware or service, the SPI remains hardware independent but is usually service dependent, and the service provider component itself is intimately connected to its target environment. As far as the user or an application is concerned, a service provider is simply part of the operating system. Figure 9-2 on page 350 illustrates the common components you'll find whenever WOSA is used as the system model. The standard configuration includes the API layer, the *routing* module, the SPI layer, and the underlying service providers. To get its work done, a service provider may call on any operating system functions or use other, lower-level service providers (again by means of a defined SPI).

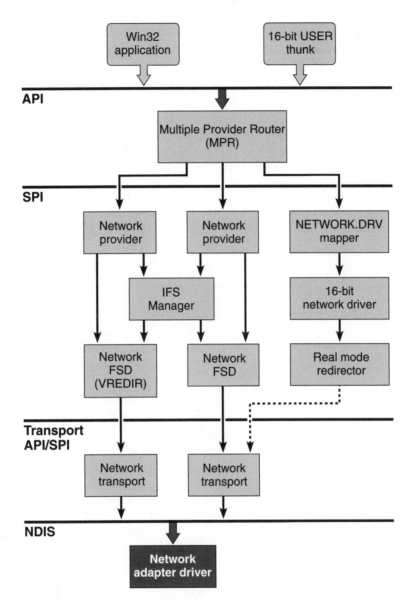

Figure 9-1.
Networking software components in Windows 95.

One good example of the use of WOSA is in an electronic mail application. Most heavy e-mail users today still have to learn at least a couple of different message editors, different mail addressing schemes,

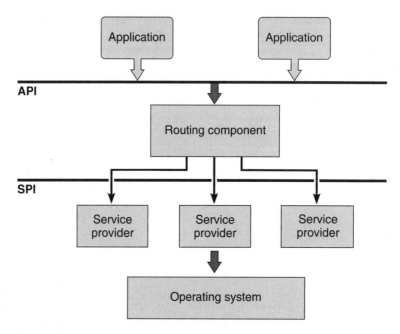

Figure 9-2.
Components in a standard WOSA configuration.

and idiosyncrasies of the underlying mail system. The desirable situation would be to prepare messages using a single application and have the underlying software figure out how to deliver the message—regardless of whether it's to someone in your office, to a CompuServe subscriber, or to a user out on the Internet. There are applications that try to do this, but from the point of view of the application developer, it's a daunting prospect to have to write a single application that knows everything about every electronic mail system. If you write the world's best message editor, you'd like to be able to hand a completed message to the world's best Internet mail delivery program, or to the world's best CompuServe mail delivery program, and so forth. Lower down in the system, the mail delivery programs themselves should have the option of using one of many different network transports to complete the physical transmission of data—and writing network transports is not what an electronic mail application vendor wants to spend resources on.

WOSA is the basis for providing this functional separation within Windows. In an extension of the example we've been considering, a mail message editor would use the Windows API. A mail service provider would implement the appropriate SPI (in this case, Microsoft's

MAPI), and Windows itself would link the components using the routing module. A similar arrangement would exist for other services. Several examples of the WOSA model already exist: the TAPI interface for telephone equipment manufacturers, the WinSock interface that standardizes the TCP/IP socket interface under Windows, ODBC for database access, and others.[7]

Network Layers

Looking back at Figure 9-1 on page 349, you can see the influence WOSA has on the Windows 95 networking subsystem. Networking support in Windows 3.1 was restricted to a single network. Windows for Workgroups expanded this to provide support for its native peer networking plus one other network. Windows 95 makes use of WOSA design techniques to allow you to install support for as many concurrent network connections as you want.[8] *The multiple provider router* (*MPR*) shown in Figure 9-1 is the routing component for Windows 95 networking. Both the *network provider* modules and the *network transports* conform to SPI rules, and at the lowest level, the popular *NDIS* (*Network Driver Interface Specification*) interface provides further support for shared device access and abstraction of the network hardware.

Here's a summary of the functions of each of the components illustrated in Figure 9-1:

API. The API layer is the standard Win32 API. Apart from file-based operations such as file open that happen to address remote filesystems, the Win32 API provides specific network-oriented APIs. These functions allow for such operations as remote resource interrogation and remote printer management. The *WNetGetUser()* API, for example, allows an application to determine the user name associated with a particular network connection. All Win32 network APIs have the *WNet* prefix.

Multiple Provider Router. The MPR is the routing component for Windows 95 network operations. The MPR also implements network operations common to all network types. The MPR

---

7. Each of these interfaces is a service provider. As you can see, marketing requirements dictate that an SPI must also have its own acronym.

8. An arbitrary implementation limit of ten networks was used in early releases of Windows 95. We'll have to wait and see whether ten equals infinity.

handles all Win32 network APIs, some of which may be routed to the appropriate network provider module. The MPR and the network provider modules are 32-bit protected mode DLLs.

Network provider. The NP implements the defined network service provider interface, encompassing such operations as making and breaking network connections and returning network status information. Only the MPR calls the network provider; an application never directly calls an NP.

IFS Manager. The IFS Manager fulfills its normal role of routing filesystem requests to the appropriate filesystem driver (FSD). The MPR won't see pathname-based or handle-based application calls; it's up to the IFS manager to route such calls to the network FSD. Network providers can call the IFS manager directly to perform file operations.

Network Filesystem Driver. Each network FSD is responsible for implementing the semantics of a particular remote filesystem. The FSD may be called by the IFS manager with requests of the same type as for local filesystems (for example, file open or file read), or the NP may call the network FSD directly. Obviously, a network vendor has to develop the NP and the network FSD together since each understands something of the semantics of the underlying filesystem, so these modules aren't interchangeable with others at the same level. Each network FSD is a 32-bit protected mode VxD. (This alone guarantees a substantial performance boost for Windows 95 networking.)

Network transport. The network transport VxD implements the device-specific network transport protocol. Windows 95 allows multiple transports to be in use simultaneously. The network FSD calls upon the transport for the actual delivery and receipt of network data. Given the likely network configurations of Windows 95 systems, each network FSD will probably use a particular transport. However, the separation of functions means that it's perfectly feasible for more than one FSD to use the same transport. Microsoft's NetBEUI and Novell's IPX/SPX are examples of network transports due to be delivered with Windows 95.

NDIS. The Network Driver Interface Specification is a vendor-independent software specification that defines the interaction between any network transport and the underlying device driver. NDIS was originally developed to allow more than one transport to use the same physical network adapter and its associated device driver. NDIS has been revised over time, and Windows 95 networking supports NDIS version 3.0, although Windows 95 also contains provisions for using older 16-bit drivers conforming to either the ODI (Novell's *Open Datalink Interface*) model or earlier versions of NDIS. Both Windows NT and Windows 95 support the NDIS 3.0 interface, which means that network device driver developers only need to follow the appropriate rules to produce a single driver that works under either operating system.

Network adapter driver. The network adapter driver VxD controls the physical network hardware. The NDIS interface allows the driver to remain unconcerned about most network protocol issues— the driver simply works in concert with the network transports to send and receive data packets. Drivers designed for Microsoft's networking products are called *media access control,* or simply *MAC,* drivers. The driver does have to incorporate support for the Plug and Play subsystem in order to participate fully in the Windows 95 environment.[9]

Network Operations

Before we delve into the details of some of the Windows 95 networking software components, let's look at a few of the basic network operations Windows 95 supports and at some of the terminology that pervades Windows 95 networking. The screen in Figure 9-3 on page 355 shows a typical networking action—using the shell to wander around the network looking for something. Such wandering is called *browsing,* and the objects of the user's attention are various types of network *resources.* Here are the terms you'll see as you deal with this type of user action or in descriptions of the software that implements such an action:

A **resource** is a network object available for shared access—usually a printer, a collection of files grouped in a disk directory, or a communications device such as a fax or a modem.

---

9. The network adapter driver supports Plug and Play in concert with the NDIS.386 VxD, which is a standard component of Windows 95.

To **browse** is to wander the network looking for resources. The Windows 95 shell's manifestation of browsing is a series of windows that open to display successive levels of network resources.

To **enumerate** is to list or examine a set of related objects. A server may be sent a command requesting it to enumerate all of its resources, for example. The local shell would then display this list to the user during a browse operation.

A **connection** is a logical link between a local name, such as COM1:, and a network resource. Establishing and maintaining network connections is a principal function of the higher layers of the network subsystem.

A **domain** in Microsoft's networking architecture is a collection of servers and resources. Such a logical grouping allows for easier administration since a user's access privileges to the domain define the user's access to each server. A friendlier grouping concept, the Network Neighborhood, was introduced into Windows 95 early in 1994. Whereas a domain has a formal specification, the neighborhood is simply the network resources you choose to include there.

A **container** is an object that holds other objects. A domain, for example, acts as a container for network servers. Using container objects when browsing a large network is easier for the user, who will at first see a probably small list of container objects rather than a very long list of individual servers.

A **share point** is a disk resource that a remote user can connect to. All directories and files in the share point's subtree become part of the connected network resource.

The connection is particularly significant in Windows 95 networking. A network connection is essentially the ability to have references to the local LPT1: device be replaced with operations on a network printer \\Server1\LaserJetIII or a network file \\Server2\letters\letter.doc take the place of an apparently local file H:LETTER.DOC. Windows 95 formalizes the notion of a *persistent connection,* a network connection that has a lifetime beyond a single session or working day. You'll see persistent connections in use whenever you log in to the network. The shell remembers the connections that were in place the last time you logged

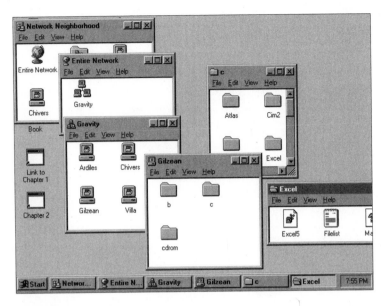

Figure 9-3.
Browsing the network with the Windows 95 shell.

in and restores them. If you use the same network printers and the same network mailbox each day, as most people do, you don't need to explicitly restore the connections every day. Windows 95 networking allows an application to identify a connection to a network resource as a persistent connection, and thereafter the shell will take care of restoring the connection—neither the application nor the network provider needs to worry further about having to set up the connection for each new session.

The Multiple Provider Router

Windows 95 provides the multiple provider router as a standard DLL. Functions within the MPR relieve each network vendor of the need to implement a large amount of common code. Equally as important, the fact that each NP relies on the same code in the MPR means that there will be a consistent treatment of many network issues. The MPR recognizes the fact, for example, that the names LPT1 and LPT1: refer to the same local device. Leaving such details up to each NP would almost guarantee some set of minor differences that would have the potential to confuse the user.

An application (including the system shell) is the principal cause of most MPR service calls. The MPR DLL resolves all the networking APIs defined for the Win32 interface. Microsoft refers to this subset of the Win32 APIs as "WinNet" or "WNet" functions, and every API in the subset uses *WNet* as a name prefix. To avoid any confusion, the functions provided by each network provider use *NP* as a name prefix. Application calls to WinNet functions may well result in the MPR's calling NP services, but applications never call the network providers directly.

The 32-bit WNet API functions are another example of the Windows 95 team's efforts to take advantage of the switch to 32-bit interfaces to improve on the API design. Apart from improvements in the network subsystem proper, enhancements in the Windows 95 base operating system add a lot to the Windows networking capabilities. Changes in the API reflect these improvements in Windows 95:

- Plug and Play technology is a major aid in reducing the complexity of setting up a network. The original release of Windows for Workgroups actually pioneered several aspects of the hardware recognition and configuration capabilities now incorporated in the Plug and Play subsystem.

- Support in the base system for long filenames was previously part of the network subsystem to allow interoperation with Windows NT and OS/2 LAN Manager servers, both of which support long filenames on certain filesystem types.

- Multiple concurrent network support obviates the need for some APIs.

- Common interfaces with Windows NT reduce both the application developer's and the device driver developer's workloads as they try to support both operating systems.

A number of Windows 3.1 APIs, though still supported for 16-bit application compatibility, have disappeared from the Win32 API set and have been declared "obsolete" by Microsoft. All the *LFN* prefix APIs that dealt explicitly with long filenames, for instance, are "obsolete."

Reducing the number of explicit network APIs obviously benefits the application developer, who now has less to learn when incorporating networking capabilities. The API reduction doesn't mean less functionality, however, since improvements in the base operating system also boost the networking capabilities of the average application. For example, using UNC pathnames that reference network locations such as \\Server\Resource\Document_File is now recommended practice for every application. The filesystem supports this naming convention directly (through the *CreateFile()* API), and using full network pathnames is now just plain good programming practice rather than a convention limited to network-aware applications. The new filesystem architecture results in an API call that needs network services being routed to the appropriate network component. The application doesn't need to worry about calling a network-specific API.

32-Bit Networking APIs

Before we look at the services that must be supplied by a network provider, let's look at the APIs that are specific to a network environment. The Win32 network APIs fall into two main sets: the set of functions that deal with network connections, and a set of miscellaneous services that support other network features. Apart from applications' calling these APIs directly, network providers also call these APIs to take advantage of the common code implemented in the MPR.

Network Resources

Several of the WNet APIs use a data structure identified as a NETRESOURCE. This object is central to the interaction of the application and the underlying system and describes the type of the resource in addition to linking the resource to the underlying network provider that supports it. Figure 9-4 shows the NETRESOURCE data structure. Specific API calls may not use all of the fields in the structure, and in some cases, there is a *don't care* or *all* value for a field.

```
typedef struct _NETRESOURCE {
    DWORD   dwScope;
    DWORD   dwType;
    DWORD   dwDisplayType;
    DWORD   dwUsage;
    LPTSTR  lpLocalName;
    LPTSTR  lpRemoteName;
    LPTSTR  lpComment;
    LPTSTR  lpProvider;
} NETRESOURCE;
```

Figure 9-4.
The NETRESOURCE data structure.

357

If you examine the purposes of the fields in the NETRESOURCE data structure, you can begin to see the relationship between the application (particularly the shell) and the underlying network subsystem:

The *dwScope* field, when used in an enumeration function, specifies the scope of the enumeration. The scope can be all resources on the network, currently connected resources, or persistent connections.

The *dwType* field determines whether the resource type is a disk, a printer, or another type.

The *dwDisplayType* field identifies the resource as a network domain, a network server, or a share point for purposes of graphically displaying the network resource.

The *dwUsage* field denotes the resource as one that you can directly connect to or as a container resource.

The *lpLocalName* field points to a string that names the local device.

The *lpRemoteName* field points to a string that names the network resource.

The *lpComment* field points to a string that contains a comment supplied by the associated network provider.

The *lpProvider* field points to a string that contains the name of the network provider associated with the resource. (A NULL value indicates that the name of the provider is unknown.)

Connection APIs

The connection APIs allow applications to create and break access to explicit network resources. The connection APIs appeared in earlier versions of Windows networking, but the latest form of these APIs alters the format of the call parameters slightly, and although older APIs such as *WNetAddConnection()* are still supported, the recommendation is to use the most recent form (in this case, *WNetAddConnection2()*). Here's a summary of the connection APIs:

API Name	Function
WNetAddConnection()	Connect to a network resource using a local device name. Replaced by *WNetAddConnection2()*.
WNetAddConnection2()	Connect to a network resource using a local device name.
WNetCancelConnection()	Break an existing network connection. Replaced by *WNetCancelConnection2()*.
WNetCancelConnection2()	Break an existing network connection.
WNetGetConnection()	Retrieve the network resource name associated with a local device name.
WNetNotifyRegister()	Register a connection notification function.
WNetConnectionDialog()	Start a network connection dialog box.
WNetDisconnectDialog()	Start a network disconnection dialog box.

The connection APIs generally deal with NETRESOURCE structures—passing a structure with the fields necessary to complete the operation filled in. An application can call the *WNetConnectionDialog()* and *WNetDisconnectDialog()* functions directly to allow the user to make or break a network connection. These two functions are the same ones used by the shell for network browsing.

The services of a network provider are called on to help complete the connect or disconnect operation, but the NP doesn't need to be directly involved in the details of network browsing, resource selection, and persistent connections. However, the *WNetNotifyRegister()* API does allow the NP to watch network connections if it wishes. Using this API, an NP can register a callback that occurs before and after each network resource connect and disconnect operation initiated by the MPR. Within the callback, an NP can affect the operation in progress. For example, if a connect operation fails, the NP can use the notification callback to instruct the MPR to retry the connection attempt.

Enumeration APIs

The three enumeration APIs—*WNetOpenEnum()*, *WNetEnumResource()*, and *WNetCloseEnum()*—allow a caller to examine the details of the available network resources. You use these APIs much as you might use an MS-DOS FindFirst/FindNext sequence to search for a file on a disk. The *WNetOpenEnum()* API allows the caller to describe the set of target network resources, and successive calls to the *WNetEnumResource()* API will return NETRESOURCE structures filled in with the details of the matching available network resources. The MPR will involve the NPs in completing the enumeration process, but the Win32 APIs cloak the details of a particular NP's enumeration functions. The user sees the result of a network enumeration as a series of open windows displaying the successive layers of the enumeration, as in Figure 9-3 back on page 355.

Error Reporting APIs

The *WNetSetLastError()* and *WNetGetLastError()* APIs are equivalent to the Win32 *SetLastError()* and *GetLastError()* functions normally used by DLLs. These functions allow a caller to set a specific error code that will be returned to another caller or to retrieve an extended error code. The network versions of the functions are provided for use by a network provider only and not as a general application interface.

Local Device Name APIs

The local device name APIs help an NP to manipulate device names consistently. Again, these APIs are intended for use by NPs only and are not for general application use. The *WNetDeviceGetNumber()* API will accept a device name string and return a local device number—the MPR carries out all the necessary name validation and matching during the call. The *WNetDeviceGetString()* function reverses the procedure, returning a name for a given device number. The *WNetGetFreeDevice()* function simply returns a currently unused local device number.

UNC APIs

The UNC APIs are designed to provide a service to the network providers that allows consistent treatment of UNC pathnames. For example, MS-DOS naming conventions call for the \ character as a pathname component separator, whereas a UNIX system uses the / character. UNC naming support is available for both environments, however. The *WNetUNCValidate()* API function checks a complete pathname, and the *WNetUNCGetItem()* API returns successive components of the name to the caller.

Password Cache API

Windows 95 networking implements a local password cache scheme that encrypts passwords and stores them locally. The administrator can disable this scheme (for extra security), and an NP can prevent its passwords from being retained in persistent storage. *WNetCachePassword()* is the API that provides access to the password cache services.

Authentication Dialog API

The *WNetAuthenticationDialog()* API provides a service that allows an NP to request authentication information—particularly a user name and password—from the user. Again, the intent is to present a consistent network access interface to the user, regardless of the underlying network type.

Interfacing to the Network Provider

The MPR is responsible for loading each NP in turn. The settings in the Windows SYSTEM.INI file determine the total network configuration for a particular machine. Figure 9-5 shows a section of a SYSTEM.INI file that describes a three-network configuration—Windows for Workgroups, NetWare, and the revolutionary NewNet product.[10] The loading and initialization order for network providers will be the order in which they're specified in the SYSTEM.INI file. Each NP can store additional initialization information within its private section of the SYSTEM.INI file, but values for the *NPID, NPName, NPDescription,* and *NPProvider* fields are required, and Microsoft has reserved all strings with the *NP* prefix for its own use. The *WNetGetSectionName()* API allows an NP to find its private section within the SYSTEM.INI file.

```
[BOOT]
Networks=WFWG, NetWare, NewNet
[WFWG]
NPID=0x0002
NPName=Windows
NPDescription=Microsoft Windows Network version 95
NPProvider=wfwnet.drv
[NetWare]
NPID=0x0003
NPName=Novell NetWare
NPDescription=Novell NetWare version 3.11
NPProvider=netware.drv
[NewNet]
...
```

Figure 9-5.
SYSTEM.INI entries for multiple (three) networks.

---

10. The latter product is unlikely ever to see the light of day but is useful for illustrative purposes.

The *NPProvider* field identifies the DLL that implements the network provider interface. The *NPID* field identifies the type of the network. Figure 9-6 shows a partial list of the network products identified for support—which says something for how serious Microsoft is in its intention to allow a Windows 95 system to connect to just about anything you can put on the other end of the wire. Simply adding the name of an existing network driver to the SYSTEM.INI list doesn't magically get you network support, though: the DLL that provides the network interface must be a full Windows 95–compatible network provider, and it's up to the various vendors to produce this software themselves.[11]

Mnemonic Identifier	Supported Network Type
WNNC_NET_MSNET	Microsoft MS Net
WNNC_NET_LANMAN	Microsoft LAN Manager
WNNC_NET_NETWARE	Novell NetWare
WNNC_NET_VINES	Banyan VINES
WNNC_NET_10NET	TCS 10Net
WNNC_NET_SUN_PC_NFS	Sun Microsystems PC NFS
WNNC_NET_LANTASTIC	Artisoft LANtastic
WNNC_NET_AS400	IBM AS/400 Network
WNNC_NET_FTP_NFS	FTP Software NFS
WNNC_NET_PATHWORKS	DEC Pathworks
WNNC_NET_POWERLAN	Performance Technology PowerLAN

Figure 9-6.
Some of the network types supported in Windows 95.

The Network Provider

A single network provider implements the service provider interface for a particular network as a Windows DLL. The NP doesn't have to worry about multiple network issues or about most aspects of interfacing to the user. The MPR and the support that comes from the underlying filesystem architecture take care of all this. In fact, Microsoft's design recommendations for network vendors specifically deter the

---

11. By shipment time, this list may well have changed—not least because some network vendors may no longer exist.

implementer from using private user interface dialogs. This isn't to say that the characteristics of a particular network are totally hidden from the user. In several instances, the NP can register functions that the MPR will call—to extend its default handling of network browsing operations, for example.

The MPR will load the NP if its associated network is listed in the SYSTEM.INI file as active. Since the NP is a Windows DLL, the system will call its standard initialization entry point once the NP is loaded. This allows the NP to carry out any private initialization it needs to. Thereafter, the NP responds to the MPR by means of the defined network provider interface. Many of the defined NP functions are optional—the NP supports them only if it has something to add to the default actions of the MPR. For example, the NP doesn't need to implement the group of functions responsible for enhancing the graphical display of network resources unless it wants to alter the shell's representation of the resources. The MPR also has to determine what the NP can support—for example, whether the NP is able to handle UNC pathnames completely.

To figure out exactly what the behavior of a particular NP is going to be, the MPR calls the *NPGetCaps()* interface. The parameter to this call is a query about a particular NP capability or about an NP characteristic (the supported network type, for example). In the case of a query about a capability, the response from the NP determines whether the MPR will subsequently call the specific interfaces that implement the feature or rely on its own default handling. NPs don't need to implement stub routines or return errors for unsupported interfaces— once the MPR recognizes that an NP doesn't support a particular capability, it won't try to call any of the related interfaces.

There are also times when the MPR calls each NP in turn, trying to find an NP that recognizes a particular resource. An error return from one NP causes the MPR to move to the next, finally returning an error to the caller if no NP responds successfully.

Network Provider Services

Let's take a look at the details of the service provider interface for an NP. Apart from the *NPGetCaps()* interface just described, there are six groups of functions:

User identification. The single *NPGetUser()* interface that allows the caller to determine the current username associated with a particular network resource.

Device redirection. The interfaces that make, break, and manipulate network connections.

Shell interface. Functions that augment the native display behavior of the shell during browsing and other operations.

Enumeration. Functions that an NP must support if it supports browsing operations.

Authentication. Functions that support the network-specific security features.

Configuration. Two optional interfaces: *NPEndSession()*, to notify the NP that Windows is closing down, and *NPDeviceMode()*, to allow network-specific configuration actions, such as choosing a network adapter from among those available.

All of the functions share similar calling and error return conventions.

Device Redirection SPI

The device redirection set of NP interfaces is the eventual target of the WNet connection APIs that form the associations between drive letters (A: through Z:) or device names (LPT1: and so on) and network resources. Some networks don't need local devices for network connections—a characteristic that a network reports through the *NPGetCaps()* interface. The optional *NPValidLocalDevice()* interface allows an NP to restrict the set of local devices that the MPR can use to make connections through the NP. For example, the NP may support only LPT1: and LPT2:, whereas Windows 95 supports additional LPT devices. If the NP doesn't export the *NPValidLocalDevice()* function, that's an indication that the NP can handle any local device name.

NPNotifyAddConnection() is the callback function an NP can use to involve itself more directly with the network connection process. Here's the set of functions it belongs to:

NPAddConnection()	Make a network connection.
NPCancelConnection()	Break a network connection.
NPGetConnection()	Obtain information about a connection.
NPNotifyAddConnection()	Arrange a callback during network resource connection and disconnection.
NPValidLocalDevice()	Indicate whether a local device is valid for use as a network connection (optional).

Shell SPI

The shell interface functions assist the shell in displaying the network layout and the attached resources for the user. Several of these functions are optional. If an NP is happy with the default displays generated by the shell, it doesn't have to support the possible extensions. Here's a summary of the shell NP functions:

NPGetDirectoryType()	Provide information about a network directory.
NPSearchDialog()	Assist in network browsing.
NPFormatNetworkName()	Change the display appearance of a network pathname.
NPGetDisplayLayout()	Customize the appearance of the network layout.
NPDisplayCallback()	Call back during network display.
NPGetEnumText()	Return additional text information during display.
NPGetNetworkFileProperties()	Display file properties.
NPDirectoryNotify()	Notify of directory creation, deletion, and movement.

The *NPSearchDialog()* function extends the standard shell browsing mechanism, allowing an NP to display its own view of the associated network. If an NP supports this extension, the shell enables a Search button in its connection dialog. If the NP doesn't support the enumeration interfaces, the shell will use its private search facility exclusively for browsing.

Enumeration SPI

The enumeration functions are an all or nothing subset—if the NP responds to a query from the MPR by indicating that it supports enumeration, it must support all four functions. If an NP doesn't support network browsing, it doesn't need to implement the enumeration functions. Within an NP that supports them, the open, enumerate, and close functions are the eventual target of the corresponding WNet enumeration APIs. The *NPGetResourceParent()* SPI assists the shell in browse operations by providing a means of moving back up a hierarchy. The enumeration functions are shown on the next page.

NPOpenEnum( )	Begin enumeration.
NPEnumResource( )	Enumerate network resources.
NPCloseEnum( )	End enumeration.
NPGetResourceParent( )	Return the parent of a specified network resource.

Authentication SPI

The authentication functions allow the NP to participate in the network logon and logoff procedures controlled by the MPR. During the logon process (see Figure 9-7), the NP has the opportunity to carry out additional user authentication and to provide the MPR with the name of an executable file it can use as a logon script. The shell will restore the user's persistent connections for the network during the logon. Here are the authentication functions:

NPLogon( )	Log on to the network.
NPLogoff( )	Log off the network.
NPGetHomeDirectory( )	Return the user's personal network directory.
NPChangePassword( )	Notify of a successful change of the user's password.

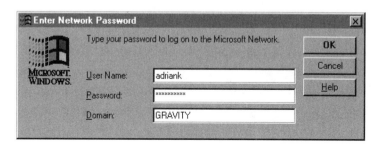

Figure 9-7.
Standard network logon dialog box.

Network Transports

Windows 95 has not revolutionized the world of network transports. Network transports still play the same role: they provide reliable, sequenced, error-free connections among the upper-level network software modules. Windows 95 also has to live within the constraints of compatibility—particularly for existing real mode network device drivers—and the networking subsystem incorporates features that allow the continued use of these drivers by the transports.

The network transport has to play two basic roles within the system: it must act as a communications medium for the network FSDs as they provide support for the file and print services, and as an API usable directly by network applications. In both cases, it's the published transport protocol interface that comes into play. Windows 95 supports both NetBIOS (via Microsoft's NetBEUI transport) and Novell's IPX/SPX protocols. The transports for both protocols are full 32-bit protected mode modules supporting 32-bit and 16-bit application interfaces. These days, network applications such as client-server databases and network management systems tend to make use of higher-level network protocols (named pipes or Microsoft's ODBC, for example) rather than deal directly with the transport interface. But there are plenty of important applications still written to both the NetBIOS and the IPX/SPX interfaces.

In the medium term, Microsoft has begun to recommend use of the Windows Sockets interface for network applications. The project to define the so called WinSock interface was a multicompany attempt to rationalize all of the different versions of the TCP/IP[12] protocol–based socket interface that various vendors had ported to the Windows environment. Originally introduced as a networked interprocess communications mechanism with version 4.2 of the Berkeley UNIX system, the socket interface has become a popular API. Although the sockets lineage goes back to the TCP/IP world, sockets can be implemented on top of other transport protocols. The Windows Sockets project was so successful that, in addition to using Windows Sockets as an interface to the TCP/IP world, Microsoft developed a Windows Sockets module that uses NetBEUI as its underlying transport.[13]

In the longer term, the need for fully distributed applications will make an RPC-based method the preferred network application interface. Windows NT has already begun to emphasize the use of RPC interfaces, and Microsoft's Cairo system will underline their long-term

---

12. TCP/IP is now officially called the *Internet Protocol Suite*.

13. Windows 95 will include a TCP/IP transport and several related utilities such as FTP, Telnet, and Internet access programs.

importance. However, the migration from a simple client-server application model to a fully distributed one is not yet upon us, so the simpler network programming interfaces supported by Windows 95 will remain important for some time to come.

Network Device Drivers

Microsoft defines a *media access control,* or *MAC,* device driver model. A MAC driver is the lowest-level software in the networking subsystem and deals directly with the network adapter. A MAC driver conforms to the *Network Driver Interface Specification (NDIS).* So called clients of the MAC driver—the transport protocol modules—access the MAC driver functions via the NDIS interface (a process termed *binding*). The NDIS specification was originally developed for Microsoft's OS/2 LAN Manager product and has become fairly widely used on network systems that don't use a Microsoft OS. NDIS is now at version 3.0. The development of this most recent version of the specification was done largely by the Windows NT group.[14]

NDIS aims to provide solutions to a number of problems inherent in a complex network environment:

- Hardware independence. The interface between the transport protocol and the MAC driver ought to allow at least source code portability for the transport software.

- Transport protocol independence. The MAC driver has to be hardware dependent, but the NDIS interface ought to allow the use of the driver by any network transport.

- Multiple transport protocols. The interface to the driver needs to allow more than one protocol to share a single network adapter (and a single Ethernet cable).

- Multiple network adapters. NDIS has to allow the simultaneous use of more than one network adapter in the same host machine (possibly using a single MAC driver).

---

14. Along with other general improvements to the specification, Windows NT required that NDIS 3.0–compliant software be usable in a multiprocessor environment. The Windows 95 team didn't have to worry about this particular requirement.

■ Performance. Network vendors strive continually to win benchmark competitions: if using NDIS implies poor performance, it's unlikely to be a very popular interface.[15]

You can think of NDIS as an interface that allows multiple transport protocols to talk to multiple network adapters, possibly on a multiprocessor machine. Despite their graduated degrees of freedom, NDIS-compliant drivers are not that difficult to develop, and any network adapter you buy will probably come with an NDIS driver. Of course, the adapter may not yet come with a protected mode NDIS version 3.0 driver—and that's a problem the Windows 95 networking team had to address directly.

Although the NDIS model has achieved wide acceptance, there's another company in the networking business that has a different way of doing things. Novell's *Open Datalink Interface (ODI)* specification mirrors Microsoft's NDIS in aiming to define a protocol-independent device interface. And there are a lot of ODI drivers available too. In addition to needing to provide compatibility for older NDIS drivers, Windows 95 had to support ODI drivers.

Network Driver Compatibility

To solve the problem of supporting non-NDIS 3.0 network device drivers—specifically NDIS 2.0 and ODI drivers—Microsoft has evolved a series of low-level modules, sometimes called *helper* modules, that act as "glue" between the various interfaces. This allows the Windows 95 protected mode NetBEUI transport to use an NDIS version 2.0–compliant real mode adapter driver, for example, or a real mode IPX/SPX transport and associated ODI driver to operate alongside a NetBEUI configuration.

Essentially, the helper modules present an upper-level interface that complies with the caller's requirements, and they translate the calls to a lower-level interface that matches the capabilities of the available device driver. In some cases, the helper module may simply manage the transition between protected mode and real mode (actually virtual 8086 mode). You can recognize the type of the helper module as

---

15. NDIS is specified as a C language interface, and for performance reasons many of the NDIS function calls are implemented as inline code using macros.

either a protected mode VxD (with a .386 filename suffix) or an MS-DOS TSR (with a .SYS filename suffix). The PROTOCOL.INI file is set up to contain the description of how all the pieces fit together in a running system.

Network Configurations

Putting together the jigsaw of network transports, drivers, and compatibility helper modules yields some interesting configuration possibilities. Figure 9-8 illustrates the simplest case—a single network adapter with a protected mode NDIS 3.0–compliant driver. The additional module illustrated—the VNETBIOS component—virtualizes the access to the transport for the concurrently running virtual machines.

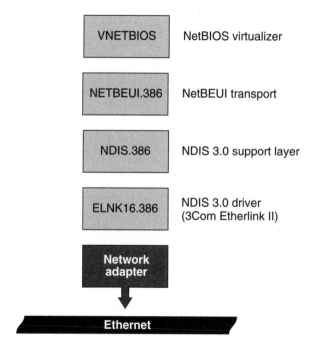

Figure 9-8.
A simple NDIS 3.0 network configuration.

Figure 9-9 illustrates a configuration that supports the NDIS 3.0–compliant NetBEUI transport running together with a real mode NetBEUI transport. At the lowest level, the network adapter driver is an NDIS 2.0 real mode driver (UBNEI.DOS in the example). The helper modules NDIS2SUP.386 (a protected mode VxD) and NDISHLP.SYS (a real mode MS-DOS TSR) merge these different interfaces into a workable configuration.

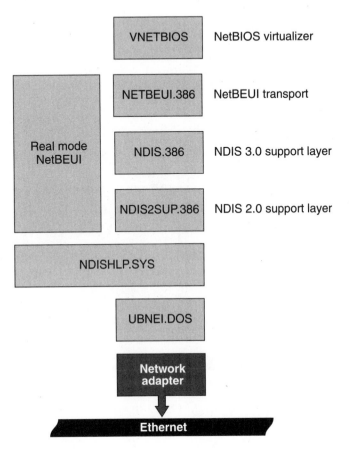

Figure 9-9.
Mixing NDIS 2.0 and NDIS 3.0 in a single network configuration.

Although it seems highly unlikely that the configuration illustrated in Figure 9-10 on the next page would have a life outside Microsoft's test labs, it does serve to show the extent of the compatibility provided under Windows 95. This configuration shows four separate transport protocols in use—Novell's IPX/SPX, the purely illustrative ABC protocol, and NetBEUI and TCP/IP cloaked by the Windows Sockets interface. The lower layers again use a combination of protected mode and real mode helper modules to form the paths to and from the network adapters.

371

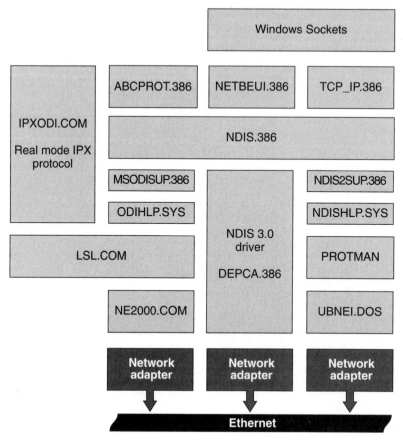

Figure 9-10.
A complex network configuration—multiple protocols and multiple adapters.

The Network Server

The peer-to-peer capability of Windows 95 networking means that there has to be a server available for use on the local machine. Although the Windows 95 networking group is not trying to compete with the high performance and industrial strength of Microsoft's own Windows NT Advanced Server product, they have produced a highly capable server with performance exceeding the levels reached in Windows for Workgroups version 3.11. As in previous versions, the server supports file and printer sharing features, giving you the option to provide other network users with access to files, directories, and printers local to your machine. In response to many customers who want to prevent their users from running desktop systems as network servers, Windows 95 can be configured to run as a client machine only. Figure 9-11 on the next page shows how the Windows 95 server software interfaces with the other network components.

Server Components

The major server component is a ring zero VxD named VSERVER that provides the bulk of the local file and printer access capability. The server utilizes the defined installable filesystem interfaces for access to the real data on local hard disks and CD ROM devices and interacts with the print spooler to support the printer sharing feature. Here's a summary of what each component is responsible for:

Spooler. The print spooler exists at the application level (in ring three) and also as a system component (a VxD running at ring zero). There's a shared memory interface for communication between the ring zero and ring three components, and a ring zero API that allows the server to submit a print job to the ring zero spooler.

MSSHRUI. The Microsoft share point user interface component is a ring three DLL that the shell uses as it satisfies user-initiated operations such as adding new share points to the local machine.

VSERVER. The main server software component itself is multi-threaded, maintaining a pool of threads that it allocates among the different network requests. The server accesses the network directly using the transport level interface and accesses the local file systems through the IFS Manager.

Access Control. The Access Control VxD controls individual file access requests, using the provided username and filename to verify the rights of the particular user to access a shared resource.

Security Provider. The Security Provider component takes responsibility for authentication of network access requests. It uses the combination of the user's login name and supplied password to verify the legality of any access request.

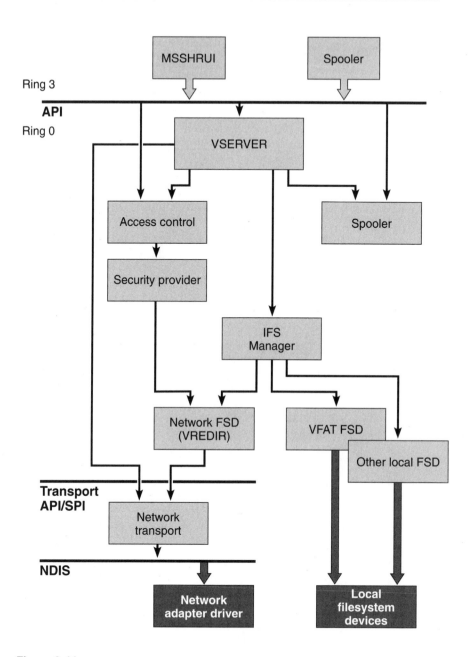

Figure 9-11.
Windows 95 Network Server architecture.

Network Printing

Of all the features of Windows, printing is perhaps the most commonly used and the most difficult for an average user to come to grips with. The complexity inherent in supporting hundreds of different types of printers—each with many configuration possibilities—and the layers of obfuscation added by a network can make printing under Windows 3.1 a painful experience. Even Microsoft's own Windows Printing System product fails to solve the network printing problem, although it does a good job of supporting a locally attached printer. Windows 95 aims to solve these problems with a new printing architecture whose design was borrowed from Windows NT and then adapted. Figure 9-12 on the next page illustrates the major components of the printing subsystem.

In common with the network file access capabilities, the printing system uses a routing component (the *Print Request Router,* or *PRR*) that accepts Win32 API calls and directs them to a *print provider* (*PP*). A single system may host several print providers if there are connections to multiple printers. The PP translates the information in the API call to a form suitable for the underlying network—for example, the printer might be attached to a NetWare server—and passes it on. The PP will convert the returned information to the correct Win32 format and pass it back to the application. The application itself doesn't need to know anything about the printer's capabilities or any network connection details. Although it will include several print providers as standard components, Microsoft's intent is that the printer manufacturers themselves will produce their own print providers. The printing architecture allows for multiple PPs related to a single printer to install themselves. So, for example, the generic PP for an HP LaserJet might be overridden by the better "quality of service" offered by a Hewlett-Packard–produced PP.

Locally attached printers participate in this printing architecture, with the local print provider interfacing to the resident printer driver and the spooling system. The printing architecture also allows for the inclusion of a *monitor* within the chain of modules that collaborate during the printing process. A monitor takes responsibility for low-level interaction with the printer. In the case of a printer attached to a bi-directional port, the monitor enables intelligent error handling and

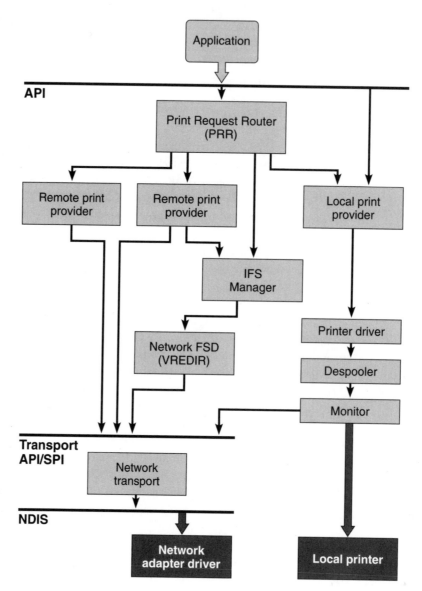

Figure 9-12.
Windows 95 Network printing architecture.

printer management.[16] More recent product innovations, such as printers with built-in network adapters that attach directly to the network, can also be handled by means of the monitor mechanism. The monitor simply talks to the printer via the network transport interface. The upper layers of software don't know and don't care about the specifics of the printer's connection.

One of the design goals of the Windows 95 team was encapsulated in the phrase "point and print," which was used during many early product presentations. What it meant was the ability of the user to print by simply dragging a document icon to a printer icon on the shell desktop and dropping it. Windows then figures out how to print the document, restoring a network connection if necessary and even loading the appropriate printer software dynamically. No longer does the user need to know a printer's exact model number designation and the amount of memory in the printer, which might be fifty yards away—let alone need to have a copy of the right Windows installation diskette handy. The point and print capability is supported by several new APIs that enable the shell to determine the available printers and associated drivers and then to dynamically load a printer driver.[17]

Network Security

Microsoft's emphasis in the design of Windows 95 networking security was on providing good security for the Windows 95 system itself and enabling a Windows 95 machine to participate in the security system implemented in a more complex scheme. The design of the FAT filesystem alone means that a Windows 95 machine is probably insecure—at least not up to the level of security required by the stringent government specifications that Windows NT complies with. In fact, presentations of the Windows 95 network security feature usually include some form of this statement: "if you want something that's small, fast, and easy to use, we have it; if you want something that's bulletproof,

---

16. Microsoft's Windows Printing System was the first product to make use of this bi-directional capability within Windows. Although the Windows Printing System was a great product for locally attached printers, it didn't support network printing. The Windows 95 printing architecture fixes that problem.

17. If you're searching for details, the *EnumPrinters()*, *GetPrinter()*, *GetPrinterDriver()*, *GetPrinterDriverDirectory()*, *GetPrintProcessorDirectory()*, and *LoadLibrary()* functions are those most intimately involved with the point and print capability.

use Windows NT." In the business world, most network administrators have to worry about some level of security protection and only a few have to concern themselves with protection against sophisticated break-ins. Windows 95 aims to meet the majority's need, and Windows NT is there for those who need a higher level of security.

Windows 95 provides two types of security:

- *Share-level security* similar to the security scheme in Windows for Workgroups. An administrator configures each network share point with a particular set of access rights.

- *User-level security.* A user's network name implicitly grants the user a defined set of access rights to each network resource.

Earlier designs for the system allowed for an additional security type— one that made use of a technique called *pass through authentication.* This technique would have allowed Windows 95 to pass a supplied login name and password to another system so that the other system could validate the user's security credentials and return access rights for the user to the Windows 95 host. The feature wasn't greeted with much enthusiasm, and it was dropped from the product. In the current design, a single system can operate under either share-level or user-level security—you can't mix the two types of security on one system. Most likely, every system in an organization will be set up with the same type of security.

Access Controls

A user's access to network resources is determined by what Microsoft calls *access controls,* also referred to simply as ACLs—for "access control lists." The ACL is the system data structure that describes access rights. In Windows 95, access controls can be applied to files, printers and a remote administration capability. Microsoft planned to incorporate security and other administrative functions together in a *System Policy Editor*—a utility aimed at supporting all of the network security and management features.[18]

---

18. This utility had appeared in various incarnations in Microsoft LAN Manager, Windows NT, and Windows for Workgroups. It was a late arrival in Windows 95. It wasn't folded into the product until after the Beta-1 release in June 1994.

Share-Level Security

Share-level security applies a set of permissions to an individual resource—regardless of which user is trying to gain access to the resource. The resource can be either a file (typically a subtree within the filesystem) or a printer. The administrator can protect a resource with a password that allows either full (read and write) access or read-only access. If a user knows the password, he or she has access to the resource.

User-Level Security

User-level security allows you to specify the names of individual users who have access to shared resources. For convenience, you can collect users into groups and give access permissions to an entire group—implying that every user belonging to the group gets the same access permission. To gain access to a resource, the user must belong to the set of users granted the appropriate permissions.

Conclusion

Windows networking has evolved from support for a single network with primitive setup facilities to a complete architecture supporting multiple network connections. The structure of Windows 95 networking relies heavily on Microsoft's WOSA design, and with support from the new installable filesystem interface, the networking architecture ought to be able to stand unchanged for several releases. As we'll see in the next chapter, the implementation of remote communications features is greatly simplified by the underlying support of Windows 95 for network components.

We haven't looked at a couple of features of Windows 95: the remote procedure call (RPC) capability and the collection of administrative features bundled together under the heading "systems management." The RPC facilities in Windows 95 are essentially identical to those available in Windows NT, and although Windows 95 itself doesn't make use of the RPC capability as extensively as Windows NT does, certain Windows 95 components, such as the network printing subsystem, do use RPC. The systems management features of Windows 95 incorporate all the administrative capabilities common to networked systems—assigning users to named groups, granting a user certain administrative privileges, and so on.

The new networking design allows any vendor to provide network access for Windows 95, although it's hard to see why a product that provides out of the box support for Microsoft, Novell, and TCP/IP networks would need to be augmented. Now that the operating system underlying the networking architecture is much more sophisticated, the peer-to-peer capability and overall performance ought to provide competition for the smaller networking companies. Although its security features don't match the rigorous approach taken by Windows NT, for many small to medium-size networks, Windows 95 will probably provide all the networking facilities that are needed. It will be interesting to observe the impact of Windows 95 on the local area networking market.

Sophisticated local area networks are at the upper end of the market Windows 95 addresses. The Windows 95 team also had a mandate to provide very good support for the other end of the market—for the ever-shrinking portable computer now used in a variety of "on the road" situations and for the burgeoning consumer market for multimedia applications. Those markets and Windows 95 support for them are the subjects of the next chapter.

Reference

Tanenbaum, Andrew. *Computer Networks.* 2d ed. Englewood Cliffs, N.J.: Prentice Hall, 1989. The standard tome on networking. If it isn't in this book, either it's not worth worrying about or it's fresh out of the research lab.

C H A P T E R   T E N

MOBILE COMPUTING

Many of the new features of Windows 95—the 32-bit operating system and 32-bit applications, the new rich visuals of the shell, and the built-in local area networking capabilities—call for the use of a fairly high powered desktop system. But the Windows 95 development team also had to address the needs of a large class of users who don't have continuous access to a powerful desktop computer. These users are loosely classified as "mobile," meaning that they use computers in various physical locations at various times. Some users are truly mobile—using only laptop computers and traveling frequently, retaining contact with their home bases or their customers via electronic mail, phone, and fax. Other users may move between only two locations—their offices and their homes—each location having a desktop system with somewhat different capabilities from the other's but the work at hand traveling back and forth and the work task remaining fundamentally the same.

Add to this already established need for mobility the recent market data that shows sales of portable computers growing more rapidly than sales of any other machine type, and sales of modems exceeding even wild expectations—and it's clear that Windows 95 needs to be a good product for smaller machines and for communications. Of course, the much vaunted era of the personal digital assistant (PDA) is now officially upon us too. Although from a practical standpoint the use of general purpose PDAs remains limited and frustration prone, Microsoft has invested considerable effort in the development of handwriting recognition technology and an integrated application, WinPad, targeted at PDAs.

In this chapter, we'll look at a collection of Windows 95 capabilities loosely grouped under the heading "mobile computing": communications support, electronic mail and fax support, and portable system support. A lot of the communications support relies on features of Windows 95 that we've already examined: the layered network architecture and the WOSA service provider capabilities. And there are aspects of other features, such as Plug and Play, that take on even greater importance when smaller portable systems are involved. But to meet Microsoft's goals of great connectivity and what it sometimes refers to as "here, there, and everywhere computing," Windows 95 includes several new software components with important roles.

Remote Communications Support

The design of the communications subsystem in Windows 95 is derived largely from the design of the local area networking subsystem we looked at in Chapter Nine. An important aspect of the Windows 95 network software design is its ability to support many simultaneous connections via different network protocols and network transports. One or more of those connections can go from the user's machine via the communications subsystem to a remote network or to another communications provider such as a bulletin board system or an electronic mail gateway. From the user's perspective, the Windows 95 shell integrates access to remote systems with local area network access, and at least for file sharing and printer sharing purposes, remote communications looks and acts the same as any other network connection.

This consistency is maintained in applications written to make use of remote services: the Win32 API provides a consistent interface regardless of whether the needed resource is a file on the network server down the hallway or a file back at your main office thousands of miles away and accessible only by modem. Applications don't have to take special account of these different physical connectivity characteristics (although some optimization is possible if they do). Windows 95 provides all the glue necessary for the various system components to make each type of connection. And, naturally, for applications that will exploit characteristics of the remote connectivity features, many specific Win32 APIs offer that capability.

New in Windows 95 is the Windows Telephony API—TAPI for short. This new set of Win32 interfaces integrates many of the functions associated with controlling telephone style devices, including fax, answering devices, and the like. Previous versions of Windows didn't have a standard API set to support operations such as dialing and automatic answering, so application developers had to invent their own.

TAPI addresses this problem with the consequent benefits of standardization and the ability to share devices between active applications.

Underlying many of the features that fall into the communications category is the basic device support offered in Windows 95. Whether you're the owner of a venerable 1200-bps modem or the latest cellular fax device, the communications driver—usually referred to simply as VCOMM—is a critical software component of any connection via these devices. The communications (serial port) driver in Windows 3.1 has been much maligned—especially from the point of view of its inability to handle higher-speed connections. As a result, the developers of many communications applications such as fax packages or terminal programs have replaced the Windows driver with their own. This scattered development has often led to conflicts and bugs that a user of two of the applications has been left unable to resolve. For Windows 95, Microsoft has concentrated a great deal of effort on providing a communications driver that will reliably handle extremely high line speeds.[1] The communications subsystem also benefits substantially from the improvements in the Windows 95 operating system kernel— from preemptive scheduling and dynamic VxD loading in particular.

The design of the VCOMM module follows what has become a popular design technique for Windows components—VCOMM itself is shared among individual ports with hardware dependent operations managed by individual communications port drivers. Each of the standard serial and parallel ports of an ISA machine, for example, would have its own port driver and share the functions provided in the single VCOMM module.

Figure 10-1 on the next page illustrates the main software components that would be present in a Windows 95 system configured for remote communications. Some of the components in the illustration are optional or redundant, and others go by yet more acronymic names. Here's a summary of their functions.

RNA. Remote Network Access is the subsystem that allows a user to dial out from his or her local system and log on to a remote network. The connection is set up so that the network appears to the user just as if he or she had logged on from a directly connected network workstation. RNA includes both a client and a server component.

---

1. The stated goal is to be able to handle serial line speeds in excess of 38.4 Kbps.

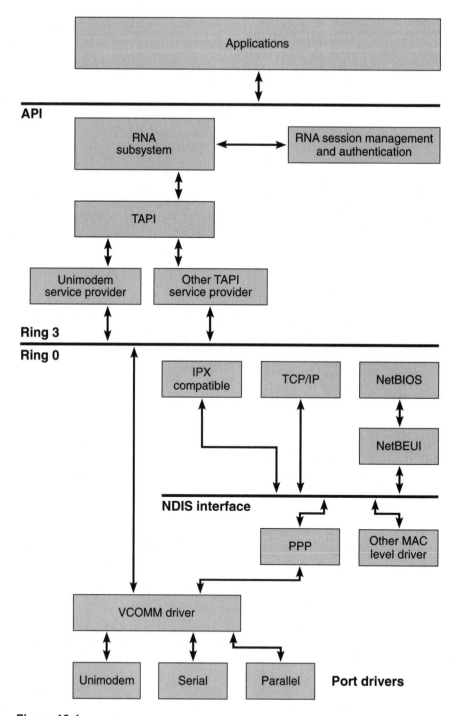

Figure 10-1.
Communications architecture in a Windows 95 system configured for remote communications.

TAPI. The DLL that implements the Telephony API incorporates the new Win32 functions for telephone line management.

Unimodem. The Unimodem service provider is Microsoft's attempt to simplify and unify support for modem devices under Windows. Rather than have each and every communications application developer produce and test its own modem interface, Microsoft has Unimodem use a collection of modem description files to enable every related application to determine a modem's configuration and the appropriate modem control sequences where necessary. In many cases, the application simply uses open and close type API calls and the Unimodem port driver accesses the modem information file.

PPP. The *point to point protocol* driver is for a simple protocol that has been widely adopted. PPP is used for single-session communications over relatively low speed lines (typically telephone lines). The PPP module handles the blocking and deblocking of data packets and simple error correction.

VCOMM. The new communications driver for Windows 95 includes a set of functions intended to be used by the port drivers and other VxD-level clients. The closest equivalent to VCOMM in Windows 3.1 is the serial port driver, but VCOMM addresses additional communication link device types, including infrared and wireless radio connections.

Port Drivers. The port driver components contain the hardware-specific code peculiar to an individual device, such as the serial port, or an infrared connection. Windows 95 will come with standard port drivers for serial and parallel devices. Other port drivers will be supplied by the device manufacturers.

Remote Network Access

RNA refers to the ability of a Windows 95 system to gain access to a remotely located network. The typical scenario features a business traveler equipped with a portable system dialing out from a hotel room to collect electronic mail and other documents from the home office. Many products currently on the market offer this capability. They come in three flavors:

- Dial-in terminal access programs that offer simple point to point connections. On the server side, the software might offer access to a bulletin board system with file transfer capability or to electronic mail. Commercial networks such as CompuServe and MCI Mail offer this type of service.

■ True network access for which the software on the server acts as a gateway to the local network. The remote user can access network resources as if he or she were locally connected. Remote access to network resources is subject to the same security constraints as for a local connection. Microsoft Windows NT offers this feature as part of its Remote Access Services (RAS).

■ Remote control software that allows the user to "take over" the remote machine to which he or she connects. The remote user can make use of the capabilities of the machine he or she connects to and transfer files back and forth between the two machines. Products such as Carbon Copy and PC Anywhere implement this capability.

Windows 95 RNA implements the first two of these flavors. An upgraded Terminal application uses the lower levels of the communications subsystem to provide dial-up access.[2] The full RNA subsystem provides network access for remote users using either a Windows NT or a Windows 95 system that has a local network connection. Figure 10-2 illustrates the various network access configurations RNA makes possible.

On the server side, the Windows 95 RNA subsystem supports a single connection, so the most obvious use of this feature will be for a user at a remote location to dial in to his or her own system back at the office or perhaps call back home from the office. In this case, a network might not be involved and the RNA server might simply provide access to the resources of the machine it's running on.

Types of Remote Access

Windows 95 provides three different ways to go about establishing a connection to a remote network:

■ Making an explicit connection, in which the user selects a remote system and establishes a session.

---

2. The new version of Terminal was developed for Windows 95 under contract to Microsoft by Hilgraeve, the developers of the popular DynaComm product.

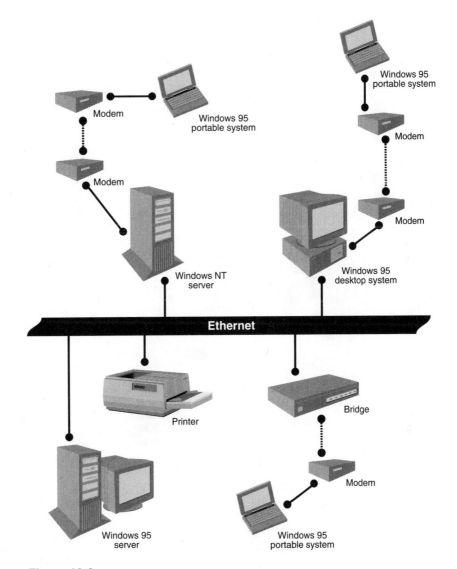

Figure 10-2.
Remote Network Access configurations.

> ■ Making an implicit connection, in which the user tries to access a file or a printer located on a remote system. The Windows 95 shell takes care of establishing the connection with the remote system. Obviously, the local system has to be configured correctly, and the likely delay in getting the connection set up will leave the user in no doubt about what's going on.

■ Using the RNA Session API, a set of Win32 interfaces for applications that will set up and manage remote connections directly.[3]

Figure 10-3 is an example of the shell's screen in the case in which the user has elected to make an explicit connection by double-clicking on the Home System icon in the network Remote Access folder. This particular remote system has already been set up with the appropriate telephone number and device to connect through. Once the user has clicked on OK in the login dialog box, RNA takes care of dialing and completing the connection. At the receiver's end, the called system must be running the Remote Access Server (or an equivalent) and be listening for the incoming call.

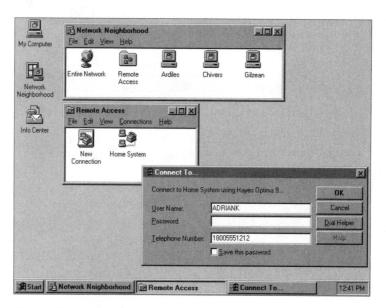

Figure 10-3.
Connecting to a remote network.

Implicit network connections are generally handled by the shell. When the user tries to access a remote resource, the shell initiates the connection attempt with minimal further user input.

The Win32 API associated with RNA provides several functions that allow an application to set up and manage a remote connection:

---

3. All of the functions in the RNA Session API are identifiable by the *Ras* prefix in their names. There are no equivalent Win16 APIs in Windows 95.

RasDial()	Handles the process of making a remote connection.
RasHangup()	Terminates an active connection.
RasEnumConnections()	Returns information about the currently active connections.
RasGetConnectStatus()	Returns information about the current status of the connection initiated by a call to *RasDial()*.

The Telephony API

The development of the Windows Telephony API (TAPI) began as part of Microsoft's At Work office automation initiative. The intent of the At Work initiative is to integrate common office equipment, such as facsimile machines and photocopiers, with the desktop PC. A PC user could send, receive, and print documents in a common digital format under the umbrella of devices supported by the At Work operating system. The most common device in the office is the telephone, and the At Work effort included the specification of an API that allows Windows application developers to control suitable telephone handsets and conforming exchange equipment. The emphasis for Windows 95 is on what Microsoft refers to as personal telephony applications—essentially applications that assume the use of a single PC and a single telephone handset.

Today most telephone equipment that can be connected to a PC offers the application developer a bewildering variety of (often proprietary) interfaces, and most of the available application solutions tend to be either highly specialized or specific to a narrow range of devices. TAPI is Microsoft's attempt to standardize an interface and, in addition to meeting the challenge of developing a suitable API, Microsoft must convince the telephone equipment manufacturers to support the associated service provider interface (SPI) in the WOSA framework.[4] The use of WOSA allows TAPI to remain independent of the specifics of any hardware device. In the Windows 95 product, the philosophy of multiple providers is retained: for example, a service provider can offer access to a shared network device concurrently with a locally attached device.

For the application developer, the success of TAPI would mean that a single Windows application could be developed to control a wide range of telephone hardware. For the user, the incorporation of TAPI

---

4. A full discussion of WOSA and the service provider interface (SPI) appears in Chapter Nine.

into the core Windows 95 product ought to mean that there will be a wide range of telephony-related applications available—either specialized applications (call screening, for instance) or applications that are extensions of the functionality available in mainstream desktop applications (the integration of voice mail messaging within an electronic mail package, for instance). RNA itself uses TAPI when it initiates and controls remote connections made over telephone lines.

Telephony Applications

TAPI identifies two separate connection types: a *phone-centric* connection type, in which the telephone handset is directly connected to the telephone network and then to the PC via a serial interface, and a *PC-centric* connection type, in which an adapter card in the host PC connects to both the telephone network and the telephone handset. In the phone-centric case, the application controls the telephone network by sending commands to the handset for forwarding. In the PC-centric case, the combination of the hardware in the PC and the TAPI application software emulates a phone handset to the network and involves the real handset only when necessary.

In the development of telephony applications, these hardware arrangements manifest themselves as a *line* device class and a *phone* device class. A line device is the connection from the desktop to the telephone network. The line device responds to data objects such as an address (the telephone number) and to state changes such as active and inactive. The phone device is the handset component and provides logical access to components such as the ringer and any buttons or indicators on the handset.

One of the important concepts underlying Microsoft's view of telephony applications is the idea that a single desktop machine might run several concurrent applications that have an interest in the single telephone line. An incoming call might be a facsimile transmission, for example, a voice call, or a connection request from a remote modem. An application that conforms to the TAPI interface has to be prepared to examine an incoming call and, if the call is of no interest to it, hand the call off to the next potentially interested application. Similarly, once the telephone line is active, an application that tries to use the line has to be prepared to gracefully handle the error condition resulting from the line's busy status.

Modem Support

First there was a universal printer driver, and now with Windows 95 come a universal display driver and a universal modem driver. Once again, the intent is to provide a common set of well-tested functions that can control a broad range of similar devices. The Unimodem name is given both to a TAPI service provider and to a low-level driver (implemented as a VxD) that works together with a port driver to directly control an attached modem.

There have been other attempts to standardize a modem control interface—notably on UNIX systems. To some degree, the problem is a more tractable one than it used to be since virtually every modem manufacturer uses the Hayes-defined command strings for direct modem control. In fact, the Unimodem driver assumes the standard Hayes command set as a base and then defines exceptions to the command set for specific modems. The description of a modem appears in a text file that might be supplied by the hardware vendor. Windows 95 comes with a large database of known modems—their descriptions are in the MODEMS.INF file, which is a standard component of Windows 95.

When you set up a modem using the Control Panel, the appropriate command strings are copied from either MODEMS.INF or the manufacturer-supplied .INF file into the registry.[5] Once the command strings are installed, the universal modem driver (UNIMODEM.386) can directly access the command strings. An application never sees the command strings used at the lower levels. It merely issues requests such as open and close. This arrangement hides the peculiarities of any particular modem from the application. Figure 10-4 on the next page illustrates the interactions between the various components when a modem attached to a serial port is in use.

Notice that the upper level of the universal modem driver is a TAPI service provider and that it can co-exist with other service providers. At the lower level, the communications driver (VCOMM) routes modem-related calls to the modem driver, which, alone, deals with the registry. For actual control of the attached modem, the modem driver calls back into VCOMM, which in turn calls the associated port driver (the serial port driver SERIAL.386 in this example).

---

5. You may see references to modem mini-drivers. These are simply the text files that encapsulate the modem commands.

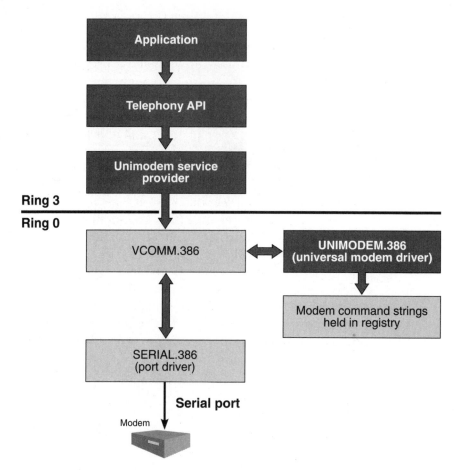

Figure 10-4.
Modem interface.

The Communications Driver

In Windows 3.1, the communications port driver suffered from performance problems engendered by mode-switching back and forth between protected and real modes and by the absence of preemptive multitasking capabilities in the operating system. The VCOMM driver in Windows 95 helps to solve the performance problem by providing a protected mode code path from the application all the way to the hardware. And the improvements in the OS itself assist in meeting the goal of reliable, high-speed communications device support.

Figure 10-5 illustrates the way in which VCOMM interacts with other system components. Notice that the COMM.DRV module is there to provide compatibility for existing Win16 applications. It is simply a thunk layer that translates 16-bit API calls to the Win32 interface. It is not an updated version of the Windows 3.1 communications driver.

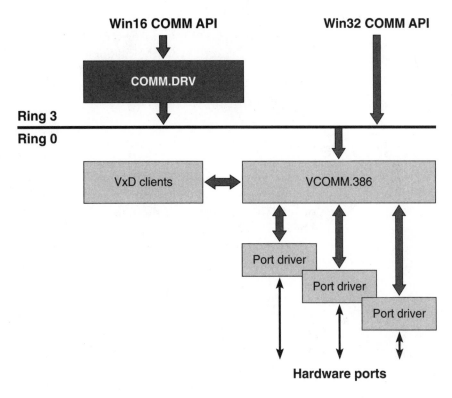

Figure 10-5.
Communications driver components.

VCOMM is a static VxD that is always loaded during the Windows 95 boot process. VCOMM participates in the Plug and Play subsystem by loading the appropriate enumerator and subsequently loading the individual port drivers (which are dynamically loaded VxDs) as ports are first opened. VCOMM is multithreaded, and its code is shared among all of the lower-level port drivers that interact directly with the hardware. The VCOMM services are available to other VxDs, but they are never called directly by an application, only via the defined Win32 APIs.[6]

---

6. All of the VCOMM services can be identified by means of the prefix _VCOMM_.

Windows 95 provides port drivers for both serial (SERIAL.386) and parallel (LPT.386) ports. When VCOMM first loads a port driver, the driver registers its presence using the _VCOMM_Register_Port_Driver service and provides the address of a *DriverControl()* function in the port driver. VCOMM uses the *DriverControl()* entry point to instruct the driver to carry out the function of initializing a hardware port. Once a port is recognized and registered, VCOMM will open it using a *PortOpen()* function in the driver. Subsequent calls from VCOMM into the driver go via a table of functions whose address is returned to VCOMM as a result of a successful *PortOpen()* call.

The Info Center

Quite late in the development of Windows 95 Microsoft decided to group the various information access components under the collective name of Info Center. Although the name has little more significance than to be a simple way to refer to the collection of information access modules, it's an umbrella for a useful grouping. The structure of the Info Center suggests that its capabilities can be broadened significantly in the future. Thus, the early establishment of a "brand name" for these Windows 95 functions seems to have been a good idea. Competitive issues are at work here too. One of the major challenges to Microsoft's dominance of the office software market has been the Lotus Notes product. Positioning the Windows 95 Info Center as a key component of a workgroup application strategy allows Microsoft to begin reclaiming some of the ground it has lost to Notes. Synonymous with the Info Center is what Microsoft calls "messaging," and you'll hear talk of "messaging APIs" and "messaging services." The messaging APIs and services are at the heart of the Info Center.

The Windows 95 Info Center serves as a common access point for the applications and services that deal with office information—electronic mail messages, voice mail messages, facsimile documents, standard forms, and other types of typically textual, loosely structured data. For the user, Windows 95 provides a Microsoft Mail client and the Internet access tools that rely on the WinSock API and the TCP/IP protocol stack.[7] For the application developer, the underlying services provide a standard interface to various messaging systems. The structure of the

---

7. The latest versions of Windows 95 actually have an Info Center icon on the default shell desktop—similar to the local computer and network neighborhood icons. The similarity suggests that the Info Center will be a commonly used information access tool.

Info Center allows applications and service provider modules to be added very easily. Figure 10-6 illustrates the components that Windows 95 groups under the Info Center heading.

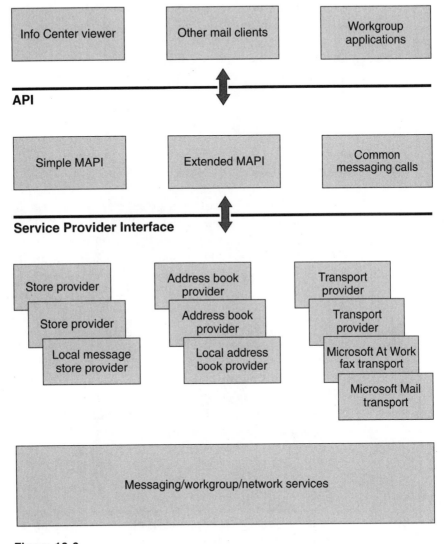

Figure 10-6.
Info Center architecture.

The Info Center breaks into three layers of software: the application level visible to end users, which includes an electronic mail application, for example, and two lower layers. The first of the two lower layers is a collection of Windows DLLs that implement the messaging APIs, and the other of the two lower layers is a service provider layer offering access to different message-related services. Once again, the structure conforms to Microsoft's WOSA model. Below the service provider layer can be any network protocol and transport or, in the case of voice mail handling, for example, some other subsystem such as TAPI.

Info Center Applications

The Info Center viewer is a Microsoft Mail client integrated with the Windows 95 shell. Any time you're using Windows 95 you can send a message—there's no need to start up a separate e-mail application. Microsoft has also announced that Windows 95 will include an interface to the Internet, although by mid-1994 the final form of this application hadn't been determined.[8]

If you're in an organization that has standardized on a non-Microsoft electronic mail package such as ccMail, the inclusion of the Microsoft client application won't really help you. But, as you'd expect, the messaging API is available to all applications, so Windows 95 will no doubt have a variety of electronic mail packages available for it.

Although other kinds of applications don't strictly come under the Info Center umbrella, the inclusion of the messaging API as a standard component of Windows 95 means that other applications—word processors, for example—can make use of the messaging services. An application that deals with documents can add a Send Document option to its standard menu and enable direct document transmission using the messaging APIs. Microsoft refers to this type of application as "messaging aware." This isn't new. Many applications have offered this feature under Windows 3.1. The difference is that the messaging APIs are now a standard part of Windows 95, and any application can rely on their presence.

Messaging APIs

The messaging APIs in Windows 95 are incorporated into three separate modules, two of which implement Microsoft's core messaging effort—the Messaging Application Programming Interface (MAPI). Although Microsoft has gathered support from other companies for MAPI, the

---

8. Including this feature was a late decision, spurred by the growing public interest in the so called information highway.

design and development of MAPI are very much under the control of Microsoft. These are the three components of the messaging API:

Simple MAPI. The basic send and receive functions of MAPI.

Extended MAPI. A superset of Simple MAPI that incorporates message storage, retrieval, and searching capabilities.

CMC. The Common Messaging Calls, a Windows 95 implementation of the functions defined by the X.400 API Association, of which Microsoft is an active member.

Both MAPI and CMC allow an application to use a standard set of functions for messaging. The application developer doesn't have to worry about the details of the underlying message system. The essential difference between MAPI and CMC is that MAPI is defined for Windows systems only—Microsoft hasn't made any attempt to adapt it to other operating systems. CMC on the other hand is defined as OS independent, and if you're planning a messaging application for a variety of different hardware and software environments, CMC is preferable to MAPI. In terms of their basic functions, CMC and Simple MAPI are very similar.

Simple MAPI contains only 12 messaging functions, and it's intended primarily for use in messaging aware applications rather than for the implementation of a full blown messaging application—an electronic mail package, for example. The Simple MAPI functions allow an application to send and receive messages and to manipulate message address information. Simple MAPI also allows files to be attached to messages and OLE objects to be incorporated in messages (hence the Windows dependency).

Extended MAPI is intended for major messaging applications— electronic mail systems, workflow applications, and forms management packages, for example. Functions in Extended MAPI allow the application to access and manipulate the message store and the address books supported by the service providers and to incorporate forms management capabilities.

Messaging Service Providers

Underlying the messaging API is the set of service providers that understand the details of the messaging system they manage. All of the providers support the same service provider interface, but each service provider is written to interface to a particular messaging system. So, for example, one service provider will support Microsoft Mail on the local network whereas another could support dial-in access to MCI Mail.

Common to the design of each MAPI service provider are the notions of a *store provider* (wherein information can be stored and retrieved), an *address book provider* (offering some means of translating a name into an address), and a *transport provider* (which takes information and actually transmits it to the intended recipient via some physical means, such as facsimile transmission or simple file copying). This separation of duties is masked by the messaging API, and, in fact, the underlying service provider can be implemented as a single module.

Microsoft plans to include a personal address book provider and transports for the At Work FAX interface and for Microsoft Mail. The local address book in a Windows 95 system is the single place where user names and associated information are collected. The networking system, for example, uses MAPI as the means for acquiring user information and translating login names.

Portable System Support

Microsoft's standard gee whiz demonstration of Windows 95 portable computer support comes in a segment in which Plug and Play gets the spotlight. The scenario involves an imaginary user removing his laptop system from its desktop docking station and rushing off to another location. This user doesn't bother to turn the laptop machine off, and while he heads out to the waiting taxi, the Plug and Play subsystem dynamically reconfigures Windows 95 so that the user can return to his word processing session as soon as he takes his seat. Do you know anyone who might do this? Neither do I. Nevertheless, as a technology demonstration, it's gripping stuff. Cynicism aside, Windows 95 does include a number of features specifically intended to improve the use of portable systems. Most of these features rely on aspects of the Plug and Play subsystem, and generally the user doesn't have to worry about what's going on—it just works.

Power Management

One of the well-researched technologies in the last few years has been the power supply for portable systems. Low-power chips and displays and improvements in battery technology have combined to make battery-powered machines feasible for even long trips by air. These hardware improvements must work hand in hand with software enhancements that allow the user to control the system, and many portables come equipped with a utility for customizing power consumption. Nowadays, it's the user who controls the length of the interval before the screen blanks or the hard disk spins down to an idle state. In the Plug and Play subsystem, these functions are subsumed under its power management activities.[9]

Docking Station Support

Although portable systems with docking stations haven't sold in the numbers that were first predicted, Windows 95 may be the catalyst to change that. The situation that the Windows 95 Plug and Play subsystem needed to handle is exactly the one described in the earlier example—how do you go about dynamically reconfiguring a system when it moves between a docked state (presumably with access to a network and with a good, high-resolution display) and an undocked state (with a portable display and perhaps a different pointing device)?[10]

Plug and Play is key to solving this problem. The automatic reconfiguration of the system involves unloading and loading the VxDs that control the attached hardware. As a device disappears, Plug and Play will unload the controlling device driver. If a device changes (an external 1024 by 768 256-color display becomes a local 640 by 480 16-level gray-scale LCD screen, for example), the system alters its configuration to suit. The reconfiguration isn't just a system-level activity. Plug and Play will broadcast messages informing running applications that the configuration is about to change. The applications can respond by closing files, blocking the system reconfiguration process, or simply terminating. If the system's FAX card is about to disappear, for example, the background FAX receiver application has no reason to continue to run. For more subtle changes, such as the change of display described above, the application will have to recognize the difference in capability and react accordingly.

---

9. Details of the state of the art in power management are to be found in the *Advanced Power Management Specification Version 1.1,* available from Microsoft.

10. Microsoft also intended to implement deferred printing in Windows 95—so that even if your printer is not currently attached to your machine you can go ahead and print. The physical output will appear when your machine is next connected to the printer. As of the Beta-1 release, this feature hadn't been implemented.

The reconfiguration process is most likely to take place at power on. You'll turn your machine off, pull it out of its docking station, head out of the office, and power the machine on sometime later. The machine will boot up in its new configuration. This won't be the case with PCMCIA peripheral cards: one likely operation is to remove one card and replace it with another of a different type while the system is running. Windows 95 will manage this reconfiguration process the same way it does at power on, and, after a short delay, the system will be reconfigured with no user interaction. You finally have a good reason to fill your pockets with PCMCIA credit cards whenever you head out of the office.

File Synchronization

One irritating problem that comes up when you're using two different systems is needing to ensure that you're always using the most up-to-date version of a file. If you have a single portable computer and docking stations wherever you go, you've solved the problem. But if, like most people, you copy files from one machine onto a diskette and then copy that diskette's contents onto another system, you're always running into the problem of synchronizing the two different physical copies of the file. Windows 95 has a "briefcase" that makes it easy to manage updated copies of files.

The shell allows you to create a briefcase object and drop other objects into it. When you leave the office, you simply copy the entire briefcase to a diskette (or perhaps across the network to another hard disk). You can work on the files in the briefcase and then get the shell's assistance when it's time to return any updated copies to the original system. Typically you'll create a briefcase on the desktop and leave it there, although you can create many independent briefcases if you want to. In the example shown in Figure 10-7, the file CHAP10.ZIP has been copied from the desktop to the briefcase. The original remains in place.

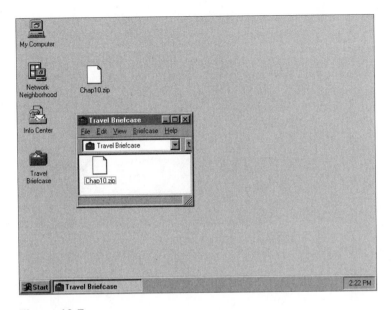

Figure 10-7.
A briefcase on the desktop.

You copy the briefcase and its contents by simply dragging and dropping the whole thing to its destination. In this example, the destination is a floppy disk. Examining the contents of the briefcase on the disk would lead you to believe that only the files you copied to the briefcase are present in the briefcase (see Figure 10-8). In fact, the shell adds hidden files that describe the contents of the briefcase to assist the later reconciliation of different versions of the files you've copied.

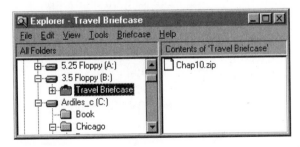

Figure 10-8.
The contents of a briefcase.

When you return to the original system, you copy the briefcase back to the desktop and then initiate an update operation on the contents of the briefcase. The shell compares the versions of the files and recommends the reconciliation action that seems to be appropriate. In the example shown in Figure 10-9, the shell suggests that the updated copy of the file contained in the briefcase ought to replace the original file on the desktop.

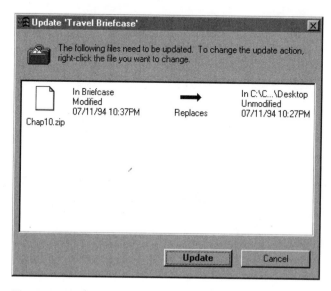

Figure 10-9.
Replacing a file with an updated version from the briefcase.

Of course, if you are only one of a number of people working on a shared document, it's possible that the original will also have been updated in the meantime. In this situation, the shell won't know how to proceed, and you'll see a dialog similar to the one shown in Figure 10-10. At this point the user has to guide the update process.

Although this is a simple scheme, in practice it works well, and naturally there is more to it than simple file modification date and time comparison.

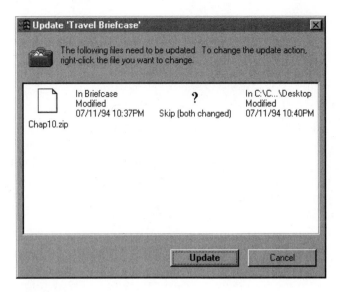

Figure 10-10.
Reconciling a file when both the briefcase version and the original
have been modified.

The Briefcase API

Both briefcases and their contents are controlled by the *AddObjectTo-Briefcase()* API. This API not only copies the physical data associated with the document to the briefcase but also updates the control information associated with the briefcase. Objects copied to the briefcase in some other way won't have this control information incorporated and thus can't be reconciled at a later time.

The *ReconcileObject()* API initiates the process of reconciling two different copies of an object. The shell calls on the services of a *reconciliation handler* to perform the actual updating process. In many cases this will simply mean copying the newest version of the file over the older one. But in cases in which a true merge of the file contents has to take place, the reconciliation handler must understand the details of the file format it's dealing with. Microsoft plans to provide a number of standard reconciliation handlers for common file types.[11] An application can also

---

11. Although this was announced, the exact plans were still vague as of July 1994. Also, an earlier announcement that objects within OLE compound files could not be individually reconciled appears not to be true, so expect this capability as part of the Windows 95 product.

register its own reconciliation handler and thus be called on by the shell to perform the reconciliation action for the associated object type.

Conclusion

If Windows 95 meets Microsoft's dual goals of providing excellent communications capabilities and providing good performance on existing 386 machines with only (sic) 4 megabytes of memory, it will be a strong contender for adoption as the preferred OS for portable and home computer use.[12] If the lower-level communication drivers live up to the advance performance claims, there should be no barrier to developers basing their communications software on Windows 95. With the layered network architecture and MAPI, Windows 95 should provide a great platform for remote networking and applications that rely on electronic mail and other connectivity options. Windows 95 also addresses a few of the real practical problems of mobile computing: the synchronization of files, deferred printing, and (with Plug and Play) the dynamic adjustment of system configuration.

At one time I planned to discuss the capabilities of Windows 95 with respect to handwriting recognition and the use of handwriting recognition technology on the so called personal digital assistants (PDAs). The early Chicago presentations gave significant airtime to the handwriting technology planned for Windows 95, but the industry's love affair with pen-based systems has cooled off in recent months. Microsoft still plans to incorporate handwritten input recognition as a standard part of Windows 95, and the WinPad application is intended principally for use with a PDA. It doesn't seem likely that Windows 95 will usher PDAs into a new era of productive use—but we'll have the basis for some exciting applications when and if handwritten input becomes practical.

---

12. Naturally the other part of the home equation is what Windows 95 will offer game players and developers. Microsoft's announcement of the WinG graphics library and its recent efforts to court MS-DOS game software developers ought to help meet this particular need.

Although I've examined much of Windows 95 in a lot of detail, I've passed over some features, and other features are still changing as this book goes to the printer. In a concluding interview, I had a chance to ask Microsoft's Paul Maritz, Senior Vice President, Systems Software Division, and Brad Silverberg, Vice President, Personal Systems Group, about late-breaking news and Microsoft's goals and aspirations for the product during the latter part of 1994 and into 1995.

LEAVING CHICAGO

By the time this book went to press, the Beta-1 release of Windows 95 (née Chicago) had been distributed to about 15,000 developers and users around the world. Early reviews and product evaluations had appeared in industry magazines, and interest in the product had already swelled beyond the dull roar level. The early sightings of the product also raised a number of questions—about the positioning of Windows 95 vis-à-vis Windows NT, about the new user interface, and about the likely level of success for Windows 95.

Right before this book went to press, I talked with Paul Maritz, senior vice president of Microsoft's Systems Software Division, and Brad Silverberg, vice president of Microsoft's Personal Operating Systems Group—the group directly responsible for Windows 95. The interview took place in Paul's office at Microsoft on July 22, 1994. I asked Paul and Brad about their aspirations for Windows 95 and about some of the product features already receiving critical review. Their answers were candid and largely devoid of the marketing hype that Microsoft is so justly famous for. Brad in particular is an irrepressible Windows 95 enthusiast. Clearly, neither man had any illusions about the amount of work still left to do before Microsoft would be in a position to ship a great product, but their demeanor suggested that the light they saw at the end of the tunnel was not from an oncoming train. Here is the interview. It's been edited for syntax, and the sounds of lunch have been deleted, but the semantics remain untouched.

AK: Adrian King, Interviewer
PM: Paul Maritz, Senior Vice President, Microsoft Systems Software Division
BS: Brad Silverberg, Vice President, Personal Operating Systems, Microsoft

AK: *My first question relates to the potential for confusion when Chicago appears in the market. You'll have a Windows 3.1 product that's been very popular, Chicago, Windows NT, and Cairo coming up. As far as the evolution of the desktop is concerned, over what time frame do you see which operating system claiming the major share of the desktop market? And what should people be doing when they upgrade or when they really need to move to the more powerful product?*

PM: There are basically two ways you can approach that question. One is Chicago vs. Windows 3.1, and the other is Chicago vs. Windows NT. I'll let Brad address the 3.1 part of it.

BS: Chicago is simply the next major version of our high-volume desktop Windows operating system. So it's the successor to, replacement for, Windows 3.1 and Windows for Workgroups. Those products have been phenomenally successful. We're selling over 2 million units of those a month. We announced yesterday that we've shipped over 60 million copies of them. And Windows Chicago is just the next version. Anybody who will be buying a new version of Windows after Chicago comes out should be buying Chicago. Anybody who is running Windows should be running Chicago. Just as today I don't know anybody who is running Windows 3.0, I would expect in some period soon, maybe a year after Chicago ships, that if you talk to people who are running Windows—they'll be running Chicago. It's a replacement. And it's complementary with our version of Windows targeted for high-end workstations, mission-critical applications, technical workstations, and the most demanding corporate applications. That's Windows NT. Daytona is simply the next version of Windows NT, and Cairo is the next major version of that product line.

PM: I think there will come a day when we will shift more and more of our corporate customers toward the NT platform. But with Windows NT we deliberately bit off some very challenging things. Basically it's a tremendous investment in raw software technology—writing a code base that's truly portable across architectures, that's certifiably secure, that's suitable for distributed computing, that's highly extensible, etc. And all of those things come at a price. They require a lot of resources, which means that as of today Cairo is really targeted at the higher end of the line—to people for whom those features of security, extensibility, and scalability are very important, and who are willing to pay for the hardware resources necessary to allow them to have those features.

Over time, as the center of gravity in the hardware base shifts, particularly in the corporate environment, as people move toward Pentium-class machines, with 16 or more megabytes of memory, we'll be able to shift more of our corporate customers in the direction of the Windows NT code base. But we see forever having to maintain at least two implementations of Windows in order to be able to cover the broad spectrum of people who use PCs.

BS: The products represent two natural design centers, and that will continue. I mean the natural flow of technology is always—starts out at the high end, a couple of years later it becomes mainstream, a couple more years later it's obsolete. It's no different from what we see today.

PM: Today and in the future we see ourselves having a design center at the high end, where we're trying to push technology as fast as we can, realizing that we're probably using more resources than most people have in order to do that. On the other hand, we need to remain really focused on the broad market in two senses, making sure that we stay within the resource constraints that not only new machines but the installed base of machines has and that we stay very focused on producing software for ordinary people who don't want to understand anything complicated and just want to use their systems.

We see ourselves having to maintain these two design centers and two teams focused on doing that. That's been our strategy for the last three years, and I can see that as being our strategy in the future. What you're seeing is simply the output of those two focuses coming into the marketplace when we move from Windows 3.1 to Chicago, and there will be successors to Chicago. Some of those successors to Chicago might use a lot of the technology that you find only in Windows NT today, but they'll still be, from a design point of view and a philosophy point of view, targeted at a broad mass market. At the same time, we'll be using new technology at the high end—what you think of as the Windows NT line—where our focus is really on client-server computing, distributed computing, system administration, and a lot of other aspects. We hope we can increasingly share technologies between those two environments, but I think there's always going to be a difference between them.

It is a more complicated strategy, both to explain and to execute. It certainly does put some strains on us, but I think the result of it is that we'll be able to serve a broader class of customers in the future and not be forced to bifurcate the world and say that for corporate computing you use only Windows, and for home computing you have to go and buy some other random product that comes out of Nintendo-space or whatever.

BS: That's like with Intel when the 386 first came out. It was high end; you only ran the 386 for servers; and then it was on high-end desktops; and now it's pretty ubiquitous. And now, at least from an accounting standpoint at Microsoft, we've written off all our 386s. That's just a natural flow of technology. But there's still that high-end space. Intel is still producing very high end chips, and they are focused on the server first, and then they come down to the desktop. The hardware technology flows that way. You'll see the same thing in our operating systems.

PM: There are some things that flow the other way as well. Ease of use factors in particular. And that's what you see being pioneered in the Chicago area. Things like the new user interface and the Plug and Play framework, which are absolutely vital for the broad market but which you'd like to have in the business-oriented market and the high-end market as well. And those things will flow into our high-end product line and be used there. So Cairo has as one of its objectives to absorb some of the features that are being introduced with Chicago.

AK: *At least in the Windows NT product line, you've made a big investment in the portability of the code for adaptation to RISC processors, which is not a consideration for Chicago. Yet the RISC-based machines have had a minimal impact in the market so far. Do you see that changing? Or do you think Intel—Intel-compatible chips—is going to hold sway forever?*

PM: It's still hard to say. I mean, today, clearly Intel has been very successful in bringing new parts into the marketplace and increasing their price performance on a regular basis, which has meant that it's been tough sledding for anyone else to make enough of an impact to get some market share. But we still think we've done the right thing in terms of slowly but surely investing in technology that says, whenever, whatever happens down in the silicon, our customers are going to be insulated from it; that we can take advantage of innovation wherever it comes from; that it's not something that people need to be concerned about. I think Intel is very focused on the challenge posed to them by the Power PC chip. I think the huge investments that they're making in future processors, the kinds of deals they're announcing with companies like Hewlett-Packard, mean that they have every intention of not giving up their leadership.

AK: *For each of these products, and here I mean Chicago, Daytona, and Cairo, what's a good configuration for me to buy to run them?*

BS: What applications do you want to run?

AK: *Microsoft Office?*

BS: The goal with Chicago, and one we've worked super hard as a team to achieve, is that whatever you're running today, on Windows 3.1, if all you do is move from 3.1 to Chicago, you'll be at least as happy as you were before. So that the performance you saw before when you ran those applications you'll see with Chicago.

PM: And on higher-end machines you'll be even happier.

BS: The Chicago performance curve is that the more memory you add, the better we can really take advantage of it. And that is something a little different from 3.1. In Windows 3.1, we weren't able to take advantage of higher amounts of memory the same way, and the performance curve would flatten out. But with Chicago we have an integrated cache management system for the filesystem, the network, and virtual memory that allows us to dynamically balance the cache in real time to really take advantage of additional amounts of memory. But if you're running games or Microsoft Works or Microsoft Publisher, as with a lot of these home machines, and you go to a mass merchant like Costco, what you need and what they sell is a 4-MB machine. People take it home and they're happy. How many? Seven million home machines sold in the United States in 1994? People are buying 4-MB 486 systems for their homes.

PM: If you run some of the application benchmark suites that use normal features like cut and paste, printing, and things like that, with Chicago the knee of the performance curve is approximately 6 MB. For that user scenario you won't get a lot of performance increase by going

411

above 6 MB. And on Daytona *[Windows NT version 3.5—Ed.]* the knee is around 12 MB.

AK: *What is it going to be with Cairo?*

PM: You can't say at this point in time. Clearly the development team is going to work hard to make it as good as it can be. Both our teams, the Chicago team and the Windows NT team, have learned the religion of "you'd better stay on top of size and performance." It's very hard to put those things back into a product. You have to stay on top of them up front. The Cairo team—they're going to be working really hard trying to contain that. On the other hand, their goal is to be a very functional platform, so they have to set the trade-off dial in terms of resources vs. function. And it's set differently on that platform. And the kinds of customers who will buy Cairo are not nearly as concerned about whether it runs on a 4-MB machine.

BS: One of the missions of Chicago is to be able to upgrade the existing installed base. It's not just for new machines. That means. . .

PM: You've got to be religious about it.

BS: . . .you've got to be really hard core about making sure you run on what people have today and not have to have them buy more memory. And that means running well with whatever they're running today, and running in the same amount of memory. At the same time, I'm sure as people get into Chicago, as they want to start taking advantage of some of the new capabilities, sure they'll need more memory. As you take advantage of stuff you weren't using before, you might need additional resources.

PM: I think the other thing to say is that usage patterns of applications are changing as you go toward compound documents and things like that. You really have to have a lot more memory than many people do today. We're rapidly reaching the day when applications' usage of memory is getting to dominate the operating systems' use of memory. To really answer those "What configuration?" questions, you have to ask, "What kind of applications? How many? How complex are your interactions among them?"

AK: *My follow-up question would be, given that there's this big emphasis on OLE. . .*

PM: There's no question that if you want to get the full benefit out of OLE you've got to have more memory. If you really wanted to use one of the modern office suites, whether it be Microsoft Office or Lotus Smart Suite, to its fullest capability, you'd be looking at an 8-MB minimum machine.

BS: For that type of system. Some people are very content to run Works or Publisher or run their games. There are millions and millions of people like that.

PM: Or even within the suites, they may be using something but not using OLE. Perhaps just doing basic word processing, for example, so they don't need all that extra memory.

AK: *So if I walk into Computer City in a year's time to buy a new system. . .*

PM: You personally? Oh, 32 MB easy. . .

AK: *No. I'm buying it for my mother or somebody. Is Computer City going to have 8-MB machines as their standard boxes on the shelves?*

PM: In a year's time? I think so.

BS: Probably that will be typical for Computer City. Costco might still have quite a selection of 4-MB machines. Not as many as today. But Chicago won't be a factor in that.

PM: Brad and I were talking about that this morning. PCs, I mean really well-equipped PCs, 486-class machines, are almost down into the consumer appliance price band. And it's interesting to speculate about what happens when a decently equipped multimedia machine gets below $800. We might see a whole new segment of the market open up there. Which is another reason we have to remain very, very focused on assuring that we'll have software that continues to run on the 4-MB level for some time to come.

AK: *Talking about Chicago in particular, what I've noticed most as I've used it during all the testing periods is the amount of effort that has been applied to cleaning up everything in Windows that used to annoy you. I mean, every little detail has been gone into. There is no stone unturned. That plus the new features represents a huge amount of development and testing effort—in particular, compatibility testing. Given that you're now later than you would have liked to have been, in terms of releasing Chicago, do you regret any of that investment?*

BS: Oh no. No. That's Chicago's mission—first and foremost to make PCs really easy to use, delivering on the promise of PCs as an appliance. That's the number one thing we set out to do with Chicago.

There were really four things we set out to do in Chicago. One was to make PCs easy to use. That involves a new shell, Plug and Play, and this fit and finish polish you've just talked about. Number two is to have a modern 32-bit operating system underneath with threads and 32 bits and all that stuff. An aspect of that is to make Chicago a fully bootable, complete operating system so that it's not limited by DOS, not crippled by DOS, and has all the benefits of being a completely self-contained graphical operating system. The third element was connectivity— whether in a LAN or a WAN or a mobile dial-up environment. And the fourth is compatibility: being a no brainer upgrade.

Clearly number one was ease of use. And that was the thing that drove a lot of the things in category number two—the powerful operating system. For example, we added long filenames. When we set out to do Chicago, we didn't think we could figure out a way to do long filenames, in the FAT filesystem, in a compatible way. For years, I mean you know this, we've continued to look at this problem. The idea of long filenames is not a new one. Eight-dot-three names is not something that people have always said, "Wow, this is a really great thing. Let's stick with it." It's really painful. But every time we've looked at it and had good people look at it, they've failed to come back with solutions that were workable. But this time, when they came back and said, "We can't figure it out," we sent them back and said, "We don't have a product unless you fix that." I can't imagine coming out with the next major version of Windows, whose mission is ease of use, and we're still telling people they need to use eight-dot-three names. That's failure. So we went back, and the team came up with a very, very clever solution that allows us to have eight-dot-three names as well as long filenames in a compatible high-performance way. I think it shows the commitment to solving hard technical problems in the kernel that is one of the defining characteristics of Chicago. So I don't regret those efforts for a second. Chicago is going to last for a long time. The legacy of Chicago is going to be with us for years. And cutting corners to release the product a month or two earlier would have been a completely false economy.

AK: *Are there features you wish you hadn't included? For whatever reason? You don't like them. You don't think they're applicable in the current market. . .*

BS: I love the product. I'm so in love with this product. My history of using the product is that I have two identical machines in my office. Both 8-MB 386, 33-MHz systems. One runs Windows for Workgroups 3.11 and the other has been running Chicago since M5 time frame *[December 1993—Ed.]*. I wanted to be like a user and use the product like a user. So initially I spent most of my time, probably 80 percent of my time, on the WFW machine, and then I would just go over to Chicago and explore for a while and find some things I didn't like and send some mail to see if we could get this or that fixed. And as the product progressed, it got better and better and faster and easier and more robust—to the point now where 99 percent of my time is spent on the Chicago machine. When I have to go back to the Windows for Workgroups machine, it's like, "This is the old stuff. How did I ever use this? How did I ever like it?" And I think the shell team has done a phenomenal job of really delivering on the promise of ease of use—it becomes addictive, so much so that you just don't want to use the old stuff anymore. And Windows 3.1 really is, in comparison with Chicago, last generation. So, I can't really point out anything I wish we would have done differently. I wish, obviously we all wish, that the product was on the market today and we were working on version 2. But we're committed to making sure the product is right before we ship it.

AK: *Let's talk about the user interface some more. Already, in some of the reviews of the first beta release, there's been criticism that the shell is too different or simply a mix of lots of other things that have gone before. What's your response to that, and what do you think are the really original features of the shell?*

BS: I think the shell is tremendous. And the feedback I get from beta testers, the vast majority of beta testers—and I'm very active on the CompuServe beta test forum, I know these people, I've worked with them for years, and they don't hold back—what do they think? They love it. You know, the first day it feels like a new pair of shoes. It feels a little bit uncomfortable. You're just not used to how it feels. The second day it starts to get a little broken in. By the third day it feels like the most comfortable pair of shoes you've ever owned and how did you ever wear the old ones? Some of the people who are passing opinions haven't even used it! There are other people, who for whatever reasons, want to stick with the old user interface, for training or migration reasons, maybe. That's fine. We're glad. We'll supply that feature and we'll make it easy for people to use File Manager, Program Manager, and so on. And they can migrate to the new user interface at the pace they like.

I have heard some of the criticisms, that it's a collection of OS/2 and Motif features, and features from all these other things, and it just makes me laugh. We never even looked at Motif. I can't tell you what Motif looks like! I don't think Joe can either [*Joe Belfiore, the lead shell designer in the Chicago group—Ed.*].

PM: There were people who looked at Motif. We didn't put our heads in the sand and not look at what was going on around us. But what is certainly the case is that this thing was not designed from "Oh yes, let's take three features from there and three features from there." It was designed to solve problems that had been identified in the existing Windows 3.1 user interface.

BS: And problems in other graphical operating systems.

PM: We had guys go out and not only do the internal usability testing you traditionally do, where you get a bunch of guys in and videotape them as they try to do some tasks on a machine. We also went out and spent time with real users, just sitting in and watching. And we learned a lot of stuff there, like what nine-tenths of the world finds very difficult. It turns out that nine-tenths of the world can't find their windows, nine-tenths of the world finds overlapping windows confusing. Most people run with their windows maximized all the time. . .

BS: . . .or only run single applications. These are common problems people have that we went out to solve, and one of the things we learned as we worked on the Chicago user interface is that by having a really good design you solve a lot of problems you never anticipated you were setting out to solve. Good design really means that you have a small number of really good principles that work together, that combine freely and combine well. So that while we started out to make Chicago easy for novices, we found that having a small number of really useful, easy to combine principles means that we made the product a lot easier and a lot more powerful for power users too. That's the benefit of good design. I think we make quite a number of innovations and contributions in the Chicago user interface. I fully expect the developers of other operating systems to follow suit with some variation of what we're doing. Things like the taskbar. The taskbar is a breakthrough in how you manage multiple applications. On whatever graphical operating system, we've found that people can't do window management. They lose track of things. They don't run multiple applications because they just lose track of them. The taskbar makes it very easy for people to run multiple applications and not have to worry about window management. It's like Windows TV! You just click a button and you get the Excel channel or you get the Word channel or you get the Mail channel. It's a metaphor that people are very used to. It gives you an anchor point together with the Start button so that if you don't know how to get something done, you're led to that one place that's really the source of 90 percent of what the system can do.

The Start button. Having a uniform namespace so that all system objects are in a single namespace, so you don't have a Font Manager and a Program Manager and a File Manager and all these other managers. If you want to look at your printers, you go to the Printers folder. If you want to look at the attributes of your printer, you look at Properties on your Printers. You don't have to say, "I want to add a printer. Do I go to the Control Panel for Printers, do I want Setup or do I want something else. . ."

PM: Going back to your original question. People who say that this thing is like the Workplace shell, or Motif, or something else just really haven't used either product, or they wouldn't be able to say that.

BS: So having properties on all objects in the system—that's uniform. Anytime you see something, you know it has properties, and you can right-click and get to the properties. That eliminates the complexity bomb that would otherwise be there. If you want to add more and more capabilities to a system, unless you have this common framework that allows you to add things in a uniform way, you're just adding idiosyncratic feature after idiosyncratic feature. So the right-click for properties, the taskbar and the Start button, shortcuts or links—whatever we end up calling them—I think will all be important. They change the way you work. They absolutely change the way you use the system. You never have to remember crazy pathnames all over the network anymore. You just create a folder. Single-click to close. Stupid little things, but once you get used to it and then you go back to 3.1, you say, "This is really awkward. How did we ever live with this?"

AK: *So coming from that, name your three favorite Chicago features.*

BS: The shell itself. For sure, just the whole look and feel and gestalt of the shell. Second, I love shortcuts. I think shortcuts, particularly shortcuts to network resources, change the way I use the product. They make me more efficient on a day-to-day basis. The third feature I'd say is the integration of the network. How the network is seamlessly integrated into the system.

PM: I think a lot of the Plug and Play features are pretty nice. And not just at the "stick the boards in and pull them out" level. It's the whole way you can go in and reconfigure your desktop without rebooting your system and having to dink around like that.

BS: Plug in a CD ROM and not have to spend the weekend doing it.

PM: I think a lot of the mobile features are pretty nice. It's a real nice system to take on the road on your laptop. There was a bunch of stuff in M5 *[the release distributed at the December 1993 developer conference—Ed.]* that we got cleaned up in Beta-1, and more still needs to be done, but you can see that it's going to be a lot better for mobile users. The Briefcase and all those kinds of features that are really cool. Thirdly, there are elements in the user interface that you think, Boy, how did we live without these things? Like the Document list and the Start button. You notice how much easier it is than if you have to open up the File Manager, find the directory, scroll down the directory list, and find the document and then open it. It cuts four or five clicks out of every operation. You realize you're getting to stuff far more quickly than you were before.

AK: *Do you think Chicago is MS-DOS 7.0? Or is there going to be a different animal called MS-DOS 7.0?*

PM: I think that for all intents and purposes Chicago is MS-DOS 7.0, if by that you mean that MS-DOS 7.0 is the next version of the software that every PC comes equipped with. Will there be a nongraphical product that will have the familiar C:\ prompt as its fundamental interface? And as such is it MS-DOS 7.0? It's an interesting question. You have to ask yourself, "What is the market for the end product?" There would have to be somebody who for some reason has a complete aversion to graphical user interfaces and refuses to use one under any circumstances. On the other hand, we've always been surprised by the number of people who want to buy an upgrade to MS-DOS.

AK: *Have you identified the people who like the C:\ prompt, or are you just guessing that they're out there?*

PM: That's why we haven't made a decision one way or the other whether we want to do MS-DOS 7.0. It's hard for us to figure out how many of these things we'd sell. Logic would say you're not going to sell that many.

BS: Chicago would run the same MS-DOS apps that such a product would. We put a lot of effort into our support for MS-DOS applications so that we could run anything that's out there. It's not as if an MS-DOS 7.0 would run applications that Chicago wouldn't. It just wouldn't be able to run Windows applications. We just don't know yet if there's sufficient demand. If there's enough demand, we'll build it.

AK: *When do you see the release of a fully Chicago compatible version of Windows NT happening? By that I mean a release with the new shell, Plug and Play, and all the rest of it.*

PM: That's the next release after Daytona, called Cairo. Our goal is to get that out during 1995.

AK: *Do you worry that people will simply dismiss Windows NT when Chicago hits the streets with all the attendant publicity? That they'll just sort of forget about it and assume that Microsoft has aced itself again?*

PM: There's a very real reason they won't forget about NT. NT is our offering, quite apart from any other issues, for the server market. So we'll continue to sell NT very aggressively in the server market, where it offers tremendous advantages—where it can handle multiprocessors and offer security, reliability, and robustness—those sorts of things. Those features are not just "nice"—they're absolutely necessary.

And there are significant customers who have already selected Windows NT as their desktop operating system. They'll be buying Windows NT in fairly large numbers during 1995. These are customers like financial trading houses, who have long development and deployment cycles because they're planning to run some very critical applications. So there will be significant customers buying and deploying Windows NT during 1995. And our focus will be on servicing those customers. Windows NT is not an operating system that we have ever expected to sell through the corner store. It was built expressly in order to solve specific problems for people, and we'll concentrate our marketing efforts on servicing those customers. And then, when we get to Cairo, which does pick up the Chicago UI, that's when we'll expand our marketing of the NT product to an even broader segment of the corporate market.

AK: *Do you lose any sleep over the people who are trying to compete with you by attacking Windows? The WABI initiative, Taligent, OS/2, etc., etc.?*

PM: Do we take competitors seriously? Yes. We have to because of the very large sums of money that people are spending to compete with us. And these are not incompetent people, not stupid people. These are people who are very serious and have us steadily in their sights. We can't afford to grow lax or to ignore them. On the other hand, I think if we execute, if we deliver in a reasonable way, and above all, if we deliver quality, we'll be OK. My biggest concern with Chicago is that because it has to sell to so many people and be a successful upgrade for so many satisfied users today, it has to be a very high quality product. So if we execute well in a reasonably timely way and deliver a quality product, I think it's going to be a tough job for our competitors to try and match that.

AK: *Do you think it's technically feasible for somebody to run a Chicago-compatible system hosted on top of another operating system?*

BS: It's only software.

PM: It's a question of time. . .

AK: *Within our lifetime?*

PM: . . .and resources. You understand, we're not religious about this. We have licensed the Windows source code including the Chicago source code to people so that they can do precisely that—in the UNIX environment, for instance.

BS: If IBM wants to license Chicago, we're glad to license it to them. To us it's just a business decision. It's not a religious decision.

PM: Cloning these modern pieces of software is a tough challenge. I don't know the exact line count of Chicago, but it's millions of lines of code, and compatibility is just an incredible, incredible challenge. We have full access to all the Windows 3.1 source code and our test suites, and getting both Chicago and Windows NT to be compatible with Windows 3.1 and run all those applications has got to be the largest part, by far, of our expenditure of effort.

BS: All things said, I'd rather be playing our hand than their hand. We've got a tough challenge, and if we execute, we're in good shape. I'd rather be in our position than theirs.

AK: *You're re-emphasizing OLE with Chicago by including it as a standard component. How do you feel OLE is doing in terms of both the number of ISVs who are really adopting it and its position in competition with the other object architectures?*

PM: There's a tremendous amount of heat and light about "things object" at the moment—most of which has nothing to do with the average end user. This is truly an industry-induced storm here, where we're just talking to each other. But OLE is the only thing (a) that an ISV can concretely do something about and (b) that an end user can actually use to get some benefits from component-oriented software. We have done a lot of thinking about OLE, and a lot of design work has gone into it. A lot of what you hear bandied about, that OLE isn't good with a distributed environment, or isn't able to handle nonrectangular Windows, is all just nonsense. All that stuff has been thought about and provision made for it and, in fact, if you take the distributed case, designed very

421

elegantly for in the sense that all of the components that are written today will be able to play in a distributed environment with no change whatsoever. This is not true of models like DSOM, where you have to make source code changes to get your components to work in a distributed environment.

In terms of acceptance in the marketplace, the thing to do is to watch people's feet, not their mouths. There isn't any major software vendor who isn't making significant investments in OLE technology. OLE is a very broad thing. It's really an umbrella for a series of technologies—application automation, compound document support, etc. Not all ISVs are using all the options under that framework, but that's to be expected. It's like an operating system: not all ISVs use all the APIs in the operating system. There are many people making their applications OLE enabled. There isn't anybody of note at the moment who isn't.

AK: *The recent* Microsoft Developer Network News *listed "the magnificent seven" requirements for an ISV who wants to license the new Windows logo for display on the product box. One of these was that you've got to support OLE. That's a little bit aggressive, I would say. Why did you decide to do that?*

BS: I think to build a quality Chicago application requires developing Win32 OLE applications. That's part of what it means to build a great Chicago application.

PM: People should have certain expectations of their applications when they see that logo. What we're saying is that they should be able to see that this application, by virtue of carrying the logo, is going to be a first-class citizen in this environment. And, in our opinion, to be a first-class citizen this is what you need to do.

BS: Win32, OLE, long filenames. . .

PM: People don't have to use the logo. This is an issue of what you want the end user to be able to expect when he sees an application that has the Chicago logo on it.

AK: *One of the things I didn't understand looking through that requirements list was that a qualifying app must be able to run on Windows NT version 3.5. Given that you don't have all the Chicago facilities in that release, how does an ISV do that? On the one hand, you're insisting on adoption of the new look and feel, and on the other you're insisting on being able to run on Windows NT.*

PM: The answer is that we've made it very easy for people to produce a high-quality, first-class-citizen Chicago application and also have that application run on Windows NT 3.5. The controls that you'd use to get that new look and feel will be available on the Daytona platform, so we feel that that is actually a very modest requirement. And most ISVs plan to meet it.

AK: *So that will be a library that's going to ship with Daytona or a compiler or something?*

PM: Yes, with Daytona.

BS: The main thing that Daytona won't have will be integration with the shell. But that's OK because the key message for ISVs is that they just write to Windows. And there are two different implementations of Windows. There's the high-end NT implementation and there's the high-volume Chicago implementation. But it's just like when you write an Intel program: you don't write to a Pentium, you don't write to a 486, you just write to the Intel instruction set and depend on Intel to get the semantics of that instruction set uniform across the implementations. The same is true with Windows. We just want ISVs to write to Windows and leave it to Microsoft, with some testing by the ISVs, to make sure that it will run across the various implementations of Windows.

PM: And there are some rules you have to follow to do that, but by and large we feel that those are fairly commonsensical and that they won't be a big overhead.

AK: *Can you give some idea of the scope of the project? Number of programmers, testers, and those sorts of metrics.*

BS: I can't tell you exactly how many people. Chicago is done by my core team as well as by people both within Microsoft and outside Microsoft working on some external components. The OLE code, for instance, is done by a group in Daytona. Mail is done by a group in the Business Systems Division. And some components came from outside the company, like the file viewers, the terminal application, and the backup application. And I have no idea how many people are working on those components. If you eliminate those people, just within the

Chicago core group, it's approximately 350 people. That includes developers, program managers, testers, and marketing people. Of which, say 160 developers—I think there are 160 developers in the Chicago group. That's again just my team. That doesn't include Mail or OLE or some of the external components. And approximately the same number of testers.

AK: *Do you know the numbers of tests that have been done?*

BS: I know that to this point, we've done over 400,000 hours of stress tests. We've got about 20,000 beta sites. The product has been in a PDK (Programmers Development Kit) release for almost a year now. The first PDK was in August 1993. By the time we ship, it will be the most stress-tested, most beta-tested, most analyzed, most speculated-on piece of code ever delivered in the history of software. I think it's about 4 million lines of code altogether.

AK: *Do you think there are any features that you might yet drop?*

BS: Oh yes. I don't really want to discuss what they might be. But we have a list of features in the category "if we have a hard time with these, we'll find a way to get them done," and we've got another list of features in the category "if we have a hard time with these, they'll catch the next train." But as you can see from Beta-1, the product is awfully complete. In many ways, if we hadn't spent so much time talking about some of the features yet to come, it'd be a fine product—even if we didn't add anything that wasn't in Beta-1. We feel real good about the content that's in the beta. And stuff that's not yet in the beta? We hope to get most of it in, but if we don't, I'll still feel good.

AK: *And you're planning two more beta cycles before shipping?*

BS: Yes.

AK: *I think the first one went to about 20,000 people?*

BS: Beta-1 has gone out to about 15,000 now, and by the time we finish rolling it out it will be up to about 20,000.

AK: *Is that going to increase?*

BS: Oh yes, it'll only increase. And the last one will be truly massive. I mean, some of the numbers we're talking about are 100,000, 200,000. Because we want to make sure that the product really has those road miles underneath it so that when it comes out, people are really comfortable that it's solid production quality and they can roll it out broadly.

AK: *How many national languages are you going to ship in?*

BS: Simultaneously we will have seven languages. We'll go up to something like twenty-six languages altogether. And they will all be done within the first 180 days of shipment. The vast majority will come out within the first 30 to 60 days. The first seven languages are English, German, French, Italian, Swedish, Dutch, and Spanish.

Let me give you an example of just how broadly we're going to localize Chicago. We're doing a Thai version. We just approved, this week, a Slovenian version of Chicago. We're doing a Catalan version of Chicago. We're doing a Basque version. So there's really nowhere in the world you can go and not be able to get a localized version.

AK: *. . .and not run into Chicago. And one final detail question. The Pen extensions were heavily emphasized early on in some of the product presentations, and then discussion of them kind of disappeared. What happened there?*

BS: They're in the product. We're definitely planning to include the Pen extensions with Chicago. The level of visibility they get, I think, will be commensurate with the level of visibility that pen-based machines will have in the market. A couple of years ago, they were getting a lot more visibility than they are now. Some pen-based products came out, but they weren't particularly successful. We still think there's a place for them, particularly in vertical markets. We're just building the Pen extensions in as part of the product. It's not worth calling out that much attention to them, but if companies are building pen-based machines, they'll know that the pen support will be there.

AK: *Thanks for all the information. Good luck with getting the product out the door.*

And there it is—Chicago circa July 22, 1994. No doubt the long road from Redmond has a few twists and turns yet to be revealed. I'm sure we'll all be watching with a great deal of interest.

GLOSSARY

0:32 addressing   Memory addressing that uses the least significant 32 bits of the full address.

16:16 addressing   Memory addressing that uses a 16-bit selector and a 16-bit address.

access control list (ACL)   The data defining the access rights of network users to a particular network *resource*.

account   See *user account*.

address book   A database used by the *messaging* system to record usernames and electronic address information.

address space   See *virtual address space*.

AEP   See *asynchronous event packet*.

alias   At one time, a synonym for *shortcut*.

API   See *application programming interface*.

application programming interface (API)   The defined set of functions provided by the operating system for use by an application.

appy time (application time)   A Windows system condition in which it is safe for a *VxD* to make *filesystem* calls or request memory allocation services much as if it were an application program.

asynchronous event packet (AEP)   A data structure used in the *filesystem* software to notify the lower layers of the occurrence of an event such as the completion of a data transfer.

asynchronous event routine   A function that can be called by the operating system *kernel* upon the occurrence of a set of predefined events.

At Work   Microsoft's office product automation initiative, designed to allow common devices such as photocopiers, facsimile machines, and personal computers to exchange information in a common digital format.

authentication   Validation of a user's network logon information. See also *pass through authentication*.

automation   See *OLE automation*.

base system   The operating system components of Windows 95, comprising the memory management, *task* management, and *interrupt* management functions of the operating system.

Bézier curve   A mathematical technique for drawing a curved path given a set of discrete points. Frequently used in computer-based drawing systems.

BIOS (and Plug and Play BIOS)   The Basic Input Output System of the PC. The BIOS comprises the lowest-level interface to common devices such as the system clock, the hard disk, and the display. A *Plug and Play* BIOS supplements the BIOS functions with routines that support Plug and Play operations such as device enumeration.

bit blt   A bit block transfer, an operation that moves a collection of bits from one place to another. The most common example is the transfer of an in-memory image to a display device.

block devices   Devices addressed in terms of blocks of bytes, such as disks and tapes, as opposed to devices addressed in terms of single characters or *pixels,* such as printers or displays.

boot loader   The software responsible for starting the operating system—typically after power on. In Windows 95, the boot loader is a modified form of MS-DOS.

briefcase   A specialized shell folder that allows the synchronization of different versions of the same file.

browsing Looking around the network—locating files, programs, printers, and so on. See also *Explorer.*

bus A device that plays a role in the control of at least one other device. In the hardware context, adapter cards plug into a bus. In the *Plug and Play* context, any device that provides resources is a bus.

cache A transient storage area in main memory used for data that might be needed again in a very short time frame—for example, the directory information associated with a *filesystem.* Intel processors also implement a hardware cache to retain copies of frequently accessed memory locations. Windows 95 implements a shared cache (under control of the *VCACHE VxD*) used for file and network access and paging.

Cairo The codename for Microsoft's future release of the *Windows NT* operating system. See also *object filesystem.*

calldown chain An implementation technique (used in the *filesystem* architecture) that allows an arbitrary number of functions to be chained together for execution.

call gate See *gate.*

CDFS The Windows 95 *protected mode* implementation of an ISO 9660–compliant CD ROM filesystem.

CISC processor A complex instruction set computer processor. A CISC processor uses a large number of instructions containing multiple fields, addressing modes, and operands. Many CISC instructions take more than a single clock cycle to decode and execute.

client Usually a system attached to a network that accesses shared network *resources.*

client application A program that makes requests of a *server application* using a defined interface such as *named pipes, RPC,* or *NetBIOS.*

client-server networking A network architecture in which shared *resources* are concentrated on powerful *server* machines and the attached *desktop* systems fulfill the role of *clients,* making requests across the network for centralized information.

CMC   See *Common Messaging Calls.*

CMOS memory   Memory kept alive by the system battery. PCs use CMOS memory to store configuration information, and some *Plug and Play* systems use CMOS memory to store device information.

color profile   The definition of a device's color capabilities and current calibration. Used by the *image color matching system.* See also *image color matching.*

COM   See *Component Object Model.*

Common Messaging Calls (CMC)   The set of calls defined by the X.400 API Association for use in messaging applications. Similar in scope to *Simple MAPI.*

Component Object Model (COM)   The architecture from which *OLE* is derived. Microsoft is working to establish COM as an industrywide standard for object-oriented systems.

compound document   An *OLE* term that describes a single document containing multiple data types and operated on by multiple *OLE server applications.* See also *container.*

compound file   A file used by *OLE.* On Windows 95, a compound file is a single disk file that contains multiple independent data streams and indexing information.

configuration manager   The component of the *Plug and Play* system that's responsible for managing the software configuration associated with a system's current hardware configuration.

connection   A logical *link* between a local name and a network *resource.*

container   In *OLE,* an *object* that can hold other objects. See also *compound document.*

contention   A condition in which two or more active *threads* require access to a single *resource.* The operating system resolves the contention problem by providing a means for one *thread* to gain control of the resource and thereby block access to all other threads. See also *mutual exclusion service (mutex)* and *semaphore*.

context menu   See *popup menu*.

control   A fundamental *object* in Windows that defines the appearance and behavior of a particular visual element such as a menu or a scroll bar.

cooperative multitasking   An operating system scheduling technique that relies on running applications to *yield* control of the processor to the operating system at regular intervals. See also *preemptive multitasking*.

coordinate system   The Windows *GDI* definition of the drawing space available to an application. The coordinate system follows the simple geometric model you learned in grade school.

critical section   A sequence of instructions that must be guaranteed to execute without yielding control of the processor to another *thread*. A critical section is typically used to guarantee the integrity of a change to an in-memory data structure.

DC   See *device context*.

DCB   See *device control block*.

DDE   See *dynamic data exchange*.

demand paging   A technique that brings the memory pages of an application or operating system component into memory from disk only at the time the pages are needed. This technique is opposed to the one in which the entire memory image of an application is loaded when the application first starts. Demand paging requires support from the processor. Intel 386 and later processors provide this support. The earlier processors do not.

descriptor   On the Intel 386 series processors, an 8-byte area of memory used to fully describe a region of memory. Descriptors are grouped into either a local descriptor table (LDT) private to the process, or a global descriptor table (GDT) shareable among processes.

Every address generated on the 386 includes a selector that identifies which descriptor table to use and includes the index of the descriptor in the table. The descriptor tables themselves are held in memory with special purpose processor registers used to hold the starting addresses of the tables.

descriptor table   See *descriptor.*

desktop   What you see on your Windows screen. Also the logical container managed by the *shell.* See also *Z order.*

despooler   The system component responsible for taking the data in spool files and handing it to the software responsible for writing it to an output device.

device context (DC)   A *GDI* data structure that describes the current state of a device or drawing surface.

device control block (DCB)   A data structure used in the *IOS* to retain information about a particular hardware device.

device driver   A generic term used to refer to the lowest-level software in an operating system that deals directly with the hardware of a particular device.

device-independent bitmap (DIB)   An in-memory bitmap whose attributes are independent of any particular hardware device.

device node   The logical *object* in the *Plug and Play* subsystem's *hardware tree* that is used to describe a specific device. Also called a *Plug and Play object.*

device virtualization   A technique used in Windows to replicate the hardware characteristics of a device in a software interface. The virtualization technique allows more than one application to manipulate a single hardware device at the same time. The technique relies on hardware support from the Intel 386 processor. See also *VxD.*

dialog   A visual element of Windows that groups one or more controls. Usually employed to interact with the user.

DIB   See *device-independent bitmap.*

display driver   The Windows component responsible for manipulating the display hardware. See also *mini-driver.*

DLL   See *dynamic link library.*

DL VxD   See *dynaload VxD.*

DMA channel   A hardware interface that allows a device to transfer information to and from main memory without interrupting the processor.

document-centric design   A design technique that focuses the user on documents and the information therein rather than on the applications generating the data that combine to form the document.

domain   A collection of network *servers* and *resources* in a logical grouping.

DPMI   The DOS Protected Mode Interface. An older technique for allowing 32-bit *protected mode* programs to run under MS-DOS.

driver registration packet (DRP)   An *IOS* data structure used to initialize the logical connection between IOS and a particular device driver.

DRP   See *driver registration packet.*

dynaload VxD (DL VxD)   A dynamically loaded *VxD*—loaded as needed by the operating system.

dynamic data exchange (DDE)   An older form of data exchange between two or more cooperating application programs. Windows 95 aims to replace the use of DDE with *OLE* or *RPC.*

dynamic link library (DLL)   A library of shared functions that applications link to at runtime as opposed to compile time. A single in-memory copy of the DLL satisfies requests from all callers.

EGA   The Enhanced Graphics Adapter. Under Windows 95, no longer supported.

EISA The Extended Industry Standard Architecture. A *bus* design that allows 32-bit adapters and some automatic device recognition and configuration. EISA hasn't achieved the success expected for it. See also *ISA*.

embedding An *OLE* term for the inclusion of an *object* within a *container*. The data associated with the *object* actually resides in the *container*. See also *link*.

enumerate To list a set of related *objects*—for instance, all of a *server*'s resources.

event The occurrence of a condition that's of interest to one or more software components. The term is typically used to describe the internal manifestation of an action such as a mouse click.

event-driven program A programming technique in which the application is driven by events rather than by data. The event-driven model dominates modern personal computer operating systems.

exception An event that results from an error such as division by zero. See also *structured exception handling*.

Explorer The *shell* function that provides the user with the ability to *browse* files, *folders,* and other *resources.*

export table The definition of callable functions included in a *DLL.* The linkage between an application and a DLL is formed by means of the entries in the export table.

Extended MAPI The complete set of Microsoft's *MAPI* functions. Extended MAPI enhances *Simple MAPI* by adding features such as *address book* manipulation and *message store* querying. See also *MAPI* and *Simple MAPI*.

FAT The File Access Table. The default MS-DOS *filesystem* organization.

filesystem A logical structure of files and associated indexing information, typically stored on a disk.

filesystem driver (FSD)   The component of *IOS* that implements the interface to a particular type of *filesystem*. Windows 95 supports multiple concurrent FSDs.

folder   A logical container implemented by the *shell* that allows the user to group any collection of items—a set of documents, for instance. Folders are most usefully thought of as directories.

frame buffer   The region of memory directly associated with a display. Changes to the data in the frame buffer result in changes on the visible screen.

FSD   See *filesystem driver.*

gate   A specialized *descriptor table* entry that allows control transfers between *protection rings* on the Intel 386 processor.

GDI   Graphics Device Interface. The component of Windows responsible for implementing the graphical functions such as line drawing and color management. GDI is a *DLL* that includes all of the graphical *APIs* in Windows.

GDT   See *descriptor.*

geometry (of a device)   The organization of a device, such as the number of sectors per track and bytes per sector of a disk drive device.

global descriptor table (GDT)   See *descriptor.*

grabber   See *screen grabber.*

granularity (of allocation)   The amount of the smallest storage increment that can be used to satisfy any request for additional storage.

handle   A program data *object* that provides access to an allocated Windows *resource*. Almost every item manipulated by a Windows application is addressed by means of a handle. Individual windows, memory regions, files, timers, and other *objects* have handles.

hardware tree   The logical representation of a system's current hardware configuration built and managed by the *Plug and Play* subsystem.

heap   A region of in-memory storage that can contain data items of different sizes, types, and attributes.

ICM   See *image color matching*.

IFS   See *installable filesystem*.

IFS manager   See *installable filesystem manager*.

image color matching (ICM)   A new Windows 95 subsystem responsible for the manipulation of color information in a way that is device-independent.

import library   A compile time library used to satisfy references to external functions that will ultimately be resolved at runtime by a *DLL*.

in-place activation   In *OLE*, a technique whereby a user can make use of functions of a *server application* on a data *object* in situ within a document. In-place activation supersedes the more common current technique, in which the user sees the screen display change focus to another application.

in-place editing   See *in-place activation*.

installable filesystem (IFS)   A technique used by Windows 95 and *Windows NT* in which more than one active *filesystem* type is supported by the operating system. Windows 95 allows an IFS to be dynamically loaded. See also *installable filesystem manager*.

installable filesystem manager (IFS manager)   The component that provides the interface between application requests and the specific *filesystem* addressed by an application function. The IFS manager routes *filesystem* requests to the appropriate *filesystem driver (FSD)*.

interrupt   A hardware signal that causes the processor to begin execution at a different address upon completion of the current instruction. A hardware device uses an interrupt to gain the attention of the operating system. See also *interrupt service routine*.

interrupt service routine (ISR) A sequence of instructions executed as a result of a hardware *interrupt*.

I/O packet (IOP) An *IOS* data structure that describes a single data transfer operation.

I/O port An addressable location on the Intel 386 processor to and from which hardware control information is read and written.

IOS See *I/O supervisor.*

I/O supervisor (IOS) The Windows 95 subsystem responsible for control of the attached *block devices*.

IPX/SPX Novell's lower-level network *protocol*.

IRQ The *interrupt* request level. Each hardware device raises an *interrupt* on a predetermined IRQ (numbered 0 through 15). The processor associates specific interrupts with different *interrupt service routines*.

ISA The Industry Standard Architecture. An acronym used to describe PCs compatible with IBM's original IBM PC AT design. See also *EISA*.

ISR See *interrupt service routine.*

kernel The core component of an operating system. The kernel is usually considered to include the lowest level of memory, *interrupt,* and process management functions.

Kernel The Windows memory management, process management, and file management functions.

LDT See *descriptor.*

least recently used (LRU) technique A memory management technique used to ensure that a page reclaimed for use is the "oldest" (least recently accessed) page in memory.

legacy Older hardware and software still in use. In the *Plug and Play* context, the installed base of device cards that don't conform to the *Plug and Play* standard.

linear addressing A memory addressing scheme that organizes memory so that incrementing an address pointer guarantees a valid pointer to the next byte in memory. See also *segmented addressing*.

link An *OLE* term for a reference within a *container* to an *object* whose data is maintained by another application. Also used in earlier versions of the *shell* for *shortcut*.

local descriptor table (LDT) See *descriptor*.

locale A Windows term that refers to the system's current international configuration, including the national language and other items such as date and time formats.

locality of reference A program pattern of behavior that results in heavy access to closely grouped memory locations.

look and feel The appearance of a system and the response of the system to user input.

LRU See *least recently used technique*.

MAC driver See *media access control driver*.

MAPI The messaging *API* defined by Microsoft to allow applications to use a consistent interface to message-related subsystems such as those handling electronic mail messages, voice mail, and facsimile data. MAPI comes in two forms: simple and extended. See also *Extended MAPI* and *Simple MAPI*.

mapped file A file whose contents are directly addressable as part of an application's address space.

MDI The multiple document interface. A user interface technique that allows an application to support several active documents whose windows are clipped to the application's parent window. Microsoft is advising developers to discontinue use of MDI. See also *SDI*.

media access control driver (MAC driver) A device driver responsible for the lowest level of network device control. A MAC driver deals directly with the network adapter.

memory mapped device A device, such as a display, that can be addressed directly as part of the system's address space.

message In Windows, a message is a unit of data the operating system hands to an application to inform it of an event. The word *message* is also used as a generic term to describe the data manipulated by *MAPI*-based applications.

message loop The common Windows application program structure in which a control loop repeatedly receives and processes *messages*.

message store The structured storage associated with *messages* handled by *MAPI*-based applications.

messaging The generic term applied to applications that manipulate communicated information such as that found in electronic mail or voice mail messages, or facsimile documents.

metafile A file format that describes a series of graphical operations in a high-level, device-independent data format.

Micro Channel IBM's PS/2 series hardware *bus*.

mini-driver The hardware-dependent component of a device driver in which the driver is structured as a collection of shared functions and a smaller hardware-dependent driver module. Mini-drivers emerged first for printers and in Windows 95 are available for displays, modems, disks, and pointing devices. See also *universal driver*.

miniport driver In the Windows 95 filesystem architecture, a driver specific to a particular *SCSI* device.

monitor A low-level device driver responsible for interfacing to a printer, either directly or via the network. The monitor is specialized in that it can receive input from a (usually) output only device and, as a result, return status and error information to higher layers of the operating system.

MPR See *multiple provider router*.

multiple provider router (MPR) The routing component for Windows 95 network operations. The MPR, a 32-bit *protected mode DLL*, implements network operations common to all network types. See also *print request router.*

multitasking   An operating system feature that allows several independent programs to run concurrently.

mutex   See *mutual exclusion service.*

mutual exclusion service (mutex)   A software technique designed to ensure that only one *thread* can execute a certain sequence of instructions or gain the ability to manipulate a particular data structure, at one time. See also *critical section* and *semaphore.*

named pipe   A high-level data exchange *protocol* used by *client-server* applications on Microsoft networks.

native mode   The 32-bit mode of the 80386 processor.

NDIS   See *Network Driver Interface Specification.*

NetBEUI transport   The NetBIOS Extended User Interface. A *network transport* commonly used on Microsoft networks.

NetBIOS   A high-level network interface that provides reliable, error-free transmission of data between two cooperating applications on a local area network.

Network Driver Interface Specification (NDIS)   A software specification that defines the interaction between a *network transport* and the underlying *device driver.* The NDIS is vendor independent.

network filesystem driver   A 32-bit protected mode *VxD* responsible for implementing the semantics of a particular remote *filesystem.*

network provider (NP)   An implementation of the network service provider interface. Called by the *multiple provider router (MPR)* only, never directly by an application, the NP encompasses operations such as making and breaking network connections and returning network status information.

network transport   The lowest layer of the network subsystem, responsible for transmitting and receiving data packets via the underlying network device driver.

not-present interrupt   A fault condition generated by the Intel 386 to signify that a memory page is not currently present in main memory. See also *demand paging*.

NP   See *network provider*.

object   In formal terms, an encapsulation of both data and access methods, some or all of which may be usable by another application. Object-oriented techniques allow an object's developer to expose well-defined interfaces to the object's behavior and to hide the details of the object's implementation, which ought to allow the use of the object by many unrelated applications. Although the term is heavily used throughout Windows 95, in many cases it is simply a more attractive way of saying "data" or "thing." *Object* is also the current favorite for most overused term in the software industry.

object filesystem   A *filesystem* designed by means of object-oriented methods and suitable for use by object-oriented applications. *Cairo* is reputed to have such a filesystem. *OLE compound files* are a prototype for an object filesystem.

ODBC   Open Database Connectivity. Microsoft's standard for allowing applications to access different database systems by means of a common *API*.

OLE   Microsoft's implementation of its *Component Object Model (COM)* architecture on Windows systems.

OLE automation   A technique that enables a *client application* to control an *OLE server* without direct input from the user. The automation capability relies on an application's providing defined interfaces to its functions for use by the *client application*.

Open Datalink Interface (ODI)   Novell's network device driver interface standard.

page On the Intel 386, a contiguous physical memory region of 4K.

paging See *demand paging*.

paragraph Originally a region of 16 bytes of memory on an Intel processor. It's becoming an obsolete term now that 32-bit linear addressing is here.

pass through authentication An *authentication* technique that relies on another system or software subsystem to perform validation. The caller-supplied information is passed to the validating system, and the results are passed back to the caller.

path In *GDI,* a description of a series of points that GDI can connect (the stroke) with a particular type of pen or brush. The characteristics of the pen determine the pattern and color (fill) of the connecting stroke. A path (or pathname) to a file or directory is a name that describes the logical location of the file or directory.

pathname See *path.*

PCI bus A *bus* definition whose design was led by Intel. The design is intended to support high-speed 32-bit data paths between devices, memory, and the processor. *Plug and Play* fully supports the PCI bus.

PCMCIA A *bus* definition that defines a hardware interface suitable for peripherals with a very small (credit card size) form factor. Such peripherals are typically used on portable machines, for which weight, size, and power consumption are important considerations.

peer-to-peer networking A network architecture in which each connected system can act as both *client* and *server.*

persistent connection A network connection that has a lifetime beyond a single session or working day. The Windows 95 *shell* will return persistent connections to their prior states when the user logs in to the network.

physical address A memory address whose physical location matches its address. See also *virtual address.*

pixel The smallest element of a display that can be modified under software control. Pixels typically have color attributes individually associated with them.

Plug and Play The specification for a hardware and software architecture that allows automatic device identification and configuration. In Windows 95, the *Plug and Play* subsystem is responsible for these functions on behalf of the operating system.

popup menu A menu that appears disconnected from other visual elements (unlike the drop-down menus associated with most application menu bars). Windows 95 frequently displays popup menus when the user clicks the right (secondary) mouse button. Popup menus are sometimes called shortcut menus or context menus.

port driver A component in the Windows 95 *filesystem* architecture that controls a specific adapter. A port driver manages adapter initialization and device *interrupts*.

POSIX A definition of a standardized UNIX. The POSIX standard is not supported by Windows 95.

PPP The point to point *protocol*. An industry standard protocol intended for use over lower-speed, potentially unreliable connections such as telephone lines.

preemptive multitasking An operating system scheduling technique that allows the operating system to take control of the processor at any instant regardless of the state of the currently running application. Preemption guarantees better response to the user and higher data throughput. See also *scheduler*.

print request router (PRR) The routing component for Windows 95 print requests. The application calls are directed to the appropriate print subsystem via the PRR.

process A common term, used also by Windows 95, to describe the running state of a program.

property An attribute of an *object*. The term is used widely throughout Windows 95 to describe settings such as the color of a title bar or the connected state of a modem. The guidelines for Windows 95 applications suggest that an *object*'s properties should always be available as the result of a right mouse click. See also *property sheet*.

property sheet   A new Windows 95 dialog box intended to allow the convenient grouping of an *object*'s *properties* in a single place.

protected mode   A mode of the Intel 386 processor in which the hardware carries out numerous validation checks on memory references, function calls, *I/O port* accesses, and other items. A protection failure allows the operating system to gain control and deal with the condition. An application must run in *protected mode* if it is to make use of the full address space and *virtual memory* capabilities of the 386.

protected mode mapper   In the Windows 95 *filesystem* architecture, a module that disguises *real mode* drivers so that new *protected mode filesystem* modules don't have to take account of the different interface for existing MS-DOS drivers.

protection ring   One component of the Intel 386 processor's *protected mode* validation capabilities. Windows 95 uses protection ring three for application-level software and ring zero for operating system components. Software executing at ring three can be prevented from executing privileged instructions or accessing defined memory regions. Software executing at ring zero has no such restrictions placed on it.

protocol   The definition of an interaction between two software components that ensures reliable, error-free communication between the components. Typically used to refer to network-based exchanges.

protocol stack   The collection of software modules that implement a particular network *protocol*.

PRR   See *print request router*.

RAS   See *remote access services*.

rasterizer   The software component that turns a description of a font into a physical rendition of the characters suitable for use on a display or a printer device.

raw input queue   The data structure maintained by the operating system into which all input *events,* such as mouse clicks and keystrokes, are placed before they are distributed to the *message* queues associated with individual applications.

real mode   The Intel 8086–compatible mode of the Intel 386 processor. Real mode allows no access to the 386's large *virtual address space* or *demand paging* capabilities. Real mode does not enable the processor's protection system.

real mode driver   An existing MS-DOS device driver that Windows 95 will run in *virtual 8086 mode.*

redirector   The *client*-side software that accepts file access requests and transforms them into network requests.

registry   A database maintained by Windows 95 for storing hardware and software configuration information. The registry is used heavily by the *Plug and Play* subsystem.

remote access services (RAS)   A Windows 95 subsystem that implements remote dial-in and *connection* functions. See also *remote network access.*

remote network access (RNA)   In Windows 95, the subsystem that allows a remote user to log in to a network much as if he or she were logging in locally. By means of RNA, network *resources* become accessible to the remote user.

remote procedure call (RPC)   A software technique that allows an application to execute a function call in which the callee is executing on another machine on a network.

resource   A network *object* such as a printer, or a collection of files grouped in a directory, that is available for shared access.

resource arbitrator   A component of the *Plug and Play* system that understands the specific hardware *resource* requirements of a particular device and can resolve conflicts between devices that request the same *resource.* The arbitrator allocates the resources that will satisfy the device's requirements.

rich text Textual information that includes formatting information such as font, layout, and other *properties.*

ring See *protection ring.*

RISC processor A reduced instruction set computer processor. A RISC processor uses a small number of simple instructions. The technique allows the processor chip to be smaller (it has fewer transistors) and thus faster (the paths between individual gates are shorter), and cooler (so that it can run at higher clock speeds). Typically, every instruction on a RISC chip executes in a single clock cycle. See also *CISC processor.*

RNA See *remote network access.*

RPC See *remote procedure call.*

safe driver In Windows 95, a *real mode* driver whose functionality can be offered by an equivalent *protected mode* driver. The protected mode driver can thus take control of the real mode driver and safely bypass it while the system is running in protected mode.

scheduler The operating system component responsible for allocating processor time to a *thread* for execution.

screen grabber The component of a Windows display driver that saves and restores the screen state on behalf of an MS-DOS *virtual machine.*

SCSI The Small Computer System Interface. An industry standard hardware *bus.* SCSI devices respond to a defined set of commands and can be addressed by means of a unit number.

SCSI manager The Windows 95 *filesystem* component that provides the translation between a *Windows NT miniport driver* and Windows 95.

SDI The single document interface. SDI (in comparison to *MDI*) uses one window per document. Users switch between full screen windows (and thus documents) rather than switching between child windows within an application's parent window.

segment   On the Intel 386, a region of *virtual memory* specified by a single *descriptor.*

segmented addressing   An Intel processor memory addressing scheme in which the address is specified as the combination of a segment and an offset within a segment. This addressing technique (finally) goes the way of the dodo in use of the Win32 *API* on Windows 95. See also *linear addressing.*

semaphore   A software mechanism used to implement *resource* or *critical section* management. A semaphore differs from a *mutex* in that it has a finite value that is usually greater than 1 initially. The controlling entity can thus allocate a predetermined number of copies of a particular *resource.*

server   The system on a network that owns the *resources* available to *clients.* Server resources can be files, printers, or *server applications* (such as a multiuser database).

server application   The software that controls access to a *resource* via a programmatic interface. *Client* software typically connects to a server application using one of the supported high-level *protocols* such as *named pipes* or *RPC.*

service provider   A component of *WOSA* that provides the lower-level interface to a specific service, such as a messaging system, a database system, or a mainframe communications system. The Service Provider Interface (SPI) is defined for each service but never called directly by an application.

service table   The definition of functions supported by a *VxD* and available to other VxDs.

shared memory   A technique that allows a memory region to appear in the *virtual address space* of more than one *process.* Windows 95 supports a variety of shared memory features.

share-level security   A network security method that relies on the administrator to associate access privileges with each network *resource.* See also *access control list.*

share name   The name given to a *share point*.

share point   A file *resource* that a remote user can connect to. All of the directories and files in the share point's subtree become part of the connected network resource.

shell   A program that provides the user with a means of control over the system. In Windows 95, the shell controls the *desktop* and much of the interaction with the system's *resources*.

shell VxD   The *VxD* responsible for loading the ring three components of the system. The shell VxD also implements services that allow *messages* to be sent between applications and VxDs.

shortcut   A *shell* technique that allows the use of an alternative name to refer to an object. Many shortcuts can be defined for a single object. Shortcuts were at one time or another in the development of Windows 95 called *links* or aliases.

Simple MAPI   The basic message addressing, transmission, and reception features of Microsoft's messaging *API* subsystem. See also *MAPI* and *Extended MAPI*.

SMB protocol   The Server Message Block network *protocol*. The default protocol for Microsoft networks.

sockets   The application interface to a *TCP/IP protocol* stack.

SPI   See *service provider*.

spooler   The component that takes application generated output intended for a printer and stores it temporarily on disk.

Start menu   The name for the *shell*'s most obvious access point to the functions of Windows 95. The *popup menu* associated with the Start button on the *taskbar*.

static VxD   A *VxD* loaded during the system boot process and never unloaded.

structured exception handling   A software technique that enables controlled recovery from unexpected error conditions.

swap file The disk file used by Windows 95 to hold the active system and application memory pages that are not currently present in main memory.

system tray The early name for the Windows 95 *taskbar.*

system VM The *virtual machine* context in which all Windows applications execute.

TAPI The Telephony *API.* Microsoft's API definition for the *WOSA* telephony functions.

task Synonymous with *process.*

taskbar The final (?) name for the Windows 95 *shell* visual element that gives the user access to the *Start menu* and to currently running programs.

TCP/IP The Transmission Control Protocol/Internet Protocol. The default wide area network *protocol* used by both Windows 95 and *Windows NT.*

thread A single path of execution within a *process.* A single process can initiate multiple threads. The threads in a process share the code and global data of the parent.

thumbnail In *OLE,* the reduced image of a document stored within an *OLE compound file.* The *shell* can display OLE thumbnails to help the user during file *browsing* operations.

thunk An implementation technique that, for example, allows 16-bit code to call 32-bit code and vice versa. Originally defined simply as a piece of code that gets you from one place to another.

timeslice The amount of processor time the *scheduler* allocates among *threads* before its next evaluation of thread priorities.

transfer model The conceptual process of moving data from one application location to another. Implemented under Windows 95 using the Cut, Copy, and Paste operations.

transport See *network transport.*

TSD   See *type specific driver.*

type specific driver (TSD)   A component of *IOS* that manages all devices of a particular type.

UAE   Unrecoverable Application Error. An error that would compromise the integrity of the system if it were to be ignored. In reality, it's a bug in the application program.

UNC   See *Universal Naming Convention.*

Unicode   A standard that defines an international character set encoding scheme.

Unimodem   The Windows 95 name for the universal modem driver. In reality, a driver-level component that uses modem description files to control its interaction with the communications driver *VCOMM.*

universal driver   A shared set of hardware-independent functions called on by the *mini-drivers.* Originally used by printer drivers, in Windows 95 used by modem, display, disk, and pointing device drivers.

Universal Naming Convention (UNC)   A file naming convention that uses a \\NAME prefix to specify a network-unique path for a file or directory.

UNIX   An operating system with many features similar to those of *Windows NT,* including *multitasking* and multithreading. Available on many different hardware architectures, with versions from Sun Microsystems, Novell, IBM, and others.

User   The Windows 95 component that implements the window, *dialog,* and *control* manipulation capabilities of the system.

user account   A database of information, accessed by means of the user's network logon name, that defines the user's access rights to network *resources.*

user level security   A network security method that associates *resource* access privileges with a particular network login name.

VCACHE   The *VxD* that implements a common disk caching capability used by all the *filesystem* drivers.

VCOMM   The *VxD* that implements the common communications *port driver* functions.

vendor supplied driver (VSD)   A layer in *IOS* that allows a particular vendor to extend *IOS* functionality.

VFAT   The *protected mode* implementation of the *FAT* filesystem.

VFLATD   The universal display driver *VxD*.

VGA   Video Graphics Adapter. The default display type for Windows 95.

virtual 8086 mode   The Intel 386 processor mode that allows an operating system to run software in an Intel 8086–compatible fashion while retaining a degree of protection.

virtual address   An address in a thread's virtual address space. The physical memory corresponding to a particular virtual address may or may not be present in main memory. See also *demand paging, physical address,* and *virtual address space.*

virtual address space   The collection of addresses that make up the total *virtual memory* allocated to a particular *thread.*

virtual machine (VM)   The Windows context for execution of an application. The context includes a *virtual address space,* processor registers, and privileges.

virtual machine manager (VMM)   The component of the Windows 95 base system that controls the initialization, *resource* allocation, and termination of individual *virtual machines.*

virtual memory   Memory allocated to the address space of a *thread* but not necessarily present in main memory, or indeed not necessarily backed up by physical memory.

visual cue   A technique used by the Windows 95 *shell* to suggest the purpose behind a particular visual element, or an association between different elements.

VM   See *virtual machine*.

VMM   See *virtual machine manager*.

volume tracking driver (VTD)   The component of *IOS* responsible for managing removable devices.

VTD   See *volume tracking driver*.

VxD   Literally, virtual anything driver. A low-level software component that manages a single *resource*, such as a display screen or a serial port, on behalf of possibly many concurrent *threads*. This enables, for example, applications running in separate MS-DOS *VMs* to use a single screen. A VxD is always 32-bit *protected mode* code and is frequently written in assembly language.

widening   The expansion of a bit quantity to a larger number of bits. Typically used to transform 16-bit integers into 32-bit integers of the same value.

Win16   The 16-bit subsystem of Windows 95.

Win16Lock   The old name for *Win16Mutex*.

Win16Mutex   The software *semaphore* that controls entry to the non-reentrant components of the 16-bit *kernel*. Called *Win16Lock* early on in the Windows 95 project.

Win32   The 32-bit subsystem of Windows 95.

Win32s   The subset of the Win32 *API* implemented for Windows 3.1.

window menu   What used to be called the system menu.

window procedure   The function in a Windows application that is associated with a specific window.

Windows NT   Microsoft's high-end 32-bit operating system.

Windows Open Services Architecture (WOSA)   Microsoft's umbrella term for its definition of application-specific services, such as *MAPI* and *ODBC*, available under Windows.

Windows Sockets   The Windows implementation of the *TCP/IP socket* interface.

working set   The collection of memory *pages* belonging to a particular *thread* that must be present in main memory for the thread to execute.

WOSA   See *Windows Open Services Architecture*.

yielding   An application's handing control back to the operating system. See also *cooperative multitasking*.

Z order   The order in which windows appear on the *desktop*.

INDEX

X–Z

Adrian King is a native of London and graduated in 1976 from the University of Liverpool with a master's degree in computer science. That same year he joined the European consulting firm Logica, working in its system software division on real time control and communications projects. While at Logica, he founded the Software Products Group, which became Microsoft's European XENIX partner in 1981. Adrian moved to the U.S. in 1984 to become Microsoft's XENIX product manager.

At Microsoft, Adrian worked for Steve Ballmer as XENIX product manager and later became director of operating systems products, assuming responsibilities for MS-DOS and Microsoft OS/2. He later managed the group that developed Windows/386, the product that pioneered the use of software virtual machine technology in Microsoft operating systems.

In the late 1980s Adrian took over product responsibility for the SQL Server and Communications Server products and later Microsoft LAN Manager. In July 1991 he left Microsoft to become vice president of engineering at Artisoft. While he was in charge of development at Artisoft, LANtastic—Artisoft's local area network product—won *PC Magazine*'s Editors Choice award.

In 1992 Adrian founded Gravity Communications, a consulting firm specializing in the preparation of technical literature. He has written the book *Running LANtastic* (Bantam, 1991) and articles for *Microsoft Systems Journal* and other computer magazines.

Adrian is an active general aviation pilot and participates enthusiastically in soccer, skiing, golf, and other sports.